"中国法治论坛"编辑委员会

主　任：陈　甦
副主任：莫纪宏　周汉华
委　员（以姓氏拼音为序）：
　　　　陈　洁　邓子滨　管育鹰　胡水君　李洪雷
　　　　李明德　李　忠　刘洪岩　刘仁文　吕艳滨
　　　　孙宪忠　田　禾　席月民　谢海定　谢鸿飞
　　　　谢增毅　熊秋红　徐　卉　薛宁兰　姚　佳
　　　　张　生　邹海林

学术秘书：张锦贵

中国法治论坛
CHINA FORUM ON THE RULE OF LAW

中国法治论坛
CHINA FORUM ON THE RULE OF LAW

法制改革与法治发展
中国与芬兰的比较

Legal Reform and the Development of Rule of Law:
A Comparison between China and Finland

主 编 / 〔中国〕陈 甦
〔芬兰〕尤拉·柳库恩

社会科学文献出版社
SOCIAL SCIENCES ACADEMIC PRESS (CHINA)

总　序

改革开放迎来40年，引发了许多的回忆与思考。其中，有关法治建设与法学发展的回顾、梳理、总结以及在此基础上的期待与展望，成为认真致力于法治进步与法学繁荣的人应为之事、共为之举，并由此引发了许多学术话题，举办了许多学术活动，形成了许多学术成果。确实，回顾也是一种创新，因为每一个携带思考的回顾都不仅仅是一个往日重现的过程，其间必定含有叠加或更新的阐释与评价，赋予学术因素的回顾尤其如此。

有规划地激发或促进法治建设与法学发展的回顾及展望，曾是"中国法治论坛"系列出版的最初动因。那是在2003年，中国社会科学院法学研究所决定将20世纪70年代末以来（也就是改革开放以来）组织出版的具有重要文献价值的学术文集再行出版，以强化法学研究的连续性和反思性。在当时具有很大学术影响力和社会引导力的法学专题讨论，诸如，改革开放初期逐次兴起的人治与法治问题、法律面前人人平等问题、1982年宪法起草问题，以至法律的阶级性问题，20世纪90年代以来的人权问题、社会主义市场经济法律体系问题、依法治国问题、司法改革问题、加入

WTO与中国法治发展问题等，都是在中国特色社会主义建设的关键节点上关涉改革与法治的重大问题。法学所在组织这些法治理论研讨中，充分发挥了论题倡导与成果集萃作用，相关文集的出版以及其后的重新出版，也都发挥了应有的学术传播与评价作用。

顺便说一句，"中国法治论坛"系列创设的2003年并不是一个特别的年份，只因是法学所成立45周年而被法学所人特别提起。"中国法治论坛"系列的出版规划当时得以实施，多少有一些纪念的意思在里面。但是，"中国法治论坛"确实是一个好名称，其作为法学科研成果发表的平台载体别有昭示价值，因此被保留至今，用于法学所组织的研究项目或学术会议的论文集系列上。

"中国法治论坛"系列创设以来，承蒙学界同行支持，至今已陆续出版了30多部论文集，规模相当可观，成为国内持续时间较长、学术质量较高、学术影响较大的系列丛书。十几年来，"中国法治论坛"系列已经形成了如下特征。一是现实性。突出当代依法治国的重大理论和实践问题，紧扣时代主题，紧随我国经济社会发展和法治进程，出版了改革司法、科学发展观与法治建设、人身权与法治、依法治国与廉政建设、依法治国与司法改革等专题文集。二是前沿性。立足法治进步与法学发展潮头，把握法治实践与法学理论动向，进行前瞻性研究，集中讨论了诸如国际人道主义法及其实施、全球化与多元法律文化、社团的法律问题、妇女权利、少数人的权利等专题。三是国际性。"中国法治论坛"系列结集出版的很多就是国际合作项目或国际会议的学术论文，其中许多是国外法学研究者在中国首发的学术成果，有的文集则是法学所和国外法学专家共同编辑而成。这也是本论坛的突出特点。

2018年是改革开放40周年，也是法学研究所建所60周年。"中国法治论坛"系列能够与改革开放同行，能够彰显法学所为中国法学繁荣和法治进步作出的贡献，作为"中国法治论坛"系列的组织者和编辑者，为此感到特别欣慰。与此同时，也为"中国法治论坛"系列在依法治国新时代如何发挥更大作用而倍感压力。毋庸讳言，在法学核心期刊对学术论文稿源的巨大吸纳力下，"中国法治论坛"系列如何集萃优质成果以保持应有的学术水准，是办好"中国法治论坛"系列的关键问题。仔细分析一下，可以发现"中国法治论坛"系列仍有与核心期刊争彩的优势。其一，"中国法治论坛"系列具有专题优势，其上发表的论文选题集中，不须兼顾学科平衡而致选题分散。在其上刊载文章，不仅能够从特定文章上知晓特定作者的理论观点，也能从全部文章上掌握论题的研讨状态，如专题之下的论题分布、观点异同及学术对垒。其二，"中国法治论坛"系列具有时效优势，可以将作者对法治理论与实践的最新观察及思考及时予以发表，使其在学术创新竞争中居于争先地位。由此作者不必因过于精雕细琢而失去及早展示真知灼见的机会，也不必因核心期刊发表之路的排队拥挤而嗟叹相同观点被别人抢先发表。其三，"中国法治论坛"系列具有国际交流优势，中国学者可以在其上与国外同行对等开展学术对话，由此可以近距离地衡量其在国际交流中的专业能力与学术水平。在当下，国外法学研究者少有在我国的核心期刊发表学术论文的，而"中国法治论坛"系列正可弥补国内学术载体的这一内容缺陷。正因如此，"中国法治论坛"系列有信心在以法学核心期刊为主导构筑的学术载体阵营中，占有并占住一席之地。

无论法学研究的任务多么艰巨，无论学术竞争的态势多么严峻，我们将牢记宗旨、保持特色、发挥优势，继续办好"中国法治论坛"系列。特别是在策划选题、精选论文、传播推广等方面，我们将集思广益，进一步采取创新优化措施，把"中国法治论坛"系列办成有吸引力和影响力的学术平台。

在依法治国新时代，法学研究面临从未有的广阔视野与发展前景，法学研究者肩负继往开来的学术使命与学者责任。让我们共同努力，锐意进取，为中国的法治进步与法学繁荣提供优质的理论支撑和智识支持。

陈 甦

2018 年 12 月 30 日

目 录

第一部分　法制改革

走向新时代中国法理学之回眸与前瞻 …………… 李　林　齐延平 / 3
宪法审查在北欧国家的发展 …………………… 皮亚·莱托 - 瓦纳莫 / 31
行政体制改革与法治政府建设四十年（1978 - 2018） ………… 李洪雷 / 42
欧洲和芬兰有关公共采购的法律和经验
　　…………………………………………… 克里斯蒂安·西卡维尔塔 / 52

第二部分　可持续与环境法治

芬兰的环境宪法权利：成就、问题与前景 ……………… 朱卡·维尔雅宁 / 67
促进商业领域的可持续性选择：排放信息的作用
　　………… 艾米莉·伊利赫里欧　艾伦·艾弗斯托尔 - 威尔海姆森 / 79
促进芬兰环境权利发展的国际人权义务
　　………………………………………… 赫塔 - 艾琳娜·海斯卡宁 / 101
北欧价值链可持续性最新发展趋势 …………………… 雅克科·萨尔米宁 / 111

第三部分　互联网、人工智能与法律应对

作为工具的人工智能对法律和立法的挑战
　　………………………………………… 哈丽特·隆卡　蒂莫·鸿克拉 / 131
互联网平台用工劳动关系认定 ………………………… 谢增毅 / 147
论人工智能的法律主体地位 ……………………… 赵　磊　赵　宇 / 178
技术、平台与信息：网络空间中私权力的崛起 ………… 周　辉 / 196

第四部分　民法典编纂

没有民法典的民法：对北欧法独特性的反思 ……… 迪特列夫·塔姆 / 227
民法典编纂：民事部门法典的统一再法典化 …………… 朱广新 / 235
芬兰合同法：普遍原则是否仍有广泛空间？
　　………………………………………………… 佩特拉·松德·诺尔戈德 / 260

CONTENT

Part I Legal Reform

Towards the Chinese Jurisprudence in a New Era:
   Retrospect and Prospect   *Li Lin and Qi Yanping* / 3
Constitutional Review: Developments in the Nordic Countries
                                                Pia Letto-Vanamo / 31
Forty Years of Reform of the Administrative System and Construction
   of a Law-based Government (1978 – 2018)   *Li Honglei* / 42
European and Finnish Public Procurement Law and Experience
                                               Kristian Siikavirta / 52

Part II Sustainability and Environment Law

The Environmental Constitutional Right in Finland:
   Achievements, Problems and Prospects   *Jukka Viljanen* / 67
Promoting Sustainable Choices in Business: the Role of
   Emission Information   *Emilie Yliheljo and Ellen Eftestøl-Wilhelmsson* / 79
International Human Rights Obligations Contributing to
   Finnish Environmental Rights   *Heta-Elena Heiskanen* / 101
Recent Nordic Trends in Developing Value Chain Sustainability
                                               Jaakko Salminen / 111

Part Ⅲ Internet, Artificial Intelligence and Law

Artificial Intelligence as a Tool for Legal and Legislative Challenges
　　　　　　　　　　　　　　Harriet Lonka and Timo Honkela / 131
Determination of Labor Relations in Internet Platform Employment
　　　　　　　　　　　　　　　　　　　　　　　Xie Zengyi / 147
The Legal Subject Status of AI　　　　*Zhao Lei and Zhao Yu* / 178
Technology, Platform & Information: The Rise of Private Power
　　in Cyberspace　　　　　　　　　　　　　　　　*Zhou Hui* / 196

Part Ⅳ Codification of the Civil Law

Civil Law without Civil Codes: Reflections on a Peculiarity of
　　Nordic law　　　　　　　　　　　　　　　　*Ditlev Tamm* / 227
Codification of the Civil Law: The Unified Re-codification of
　　Civil Branch Codes　　　　　　　　　　　*Zhu Guangxin* / 235
Contract Law in Finland: Plenty of Room for General Principles?
　　　　　　　　　　　　　　　　　　　Petra Sund-Norrgård / 260

第一部分

法制改革

走向新时代中国法理学之回眸与前瞻

李　林[*]　齐延平[**]

【摘要】经过40年勠力求索，中国法理学已提升到了可以与国际同行共时对话的水平，已在学术思想界占有了独立的地位。在坚持中国化马克思主义指导和正确方向的前提下，法理学术共同体包容各派学说，综合各研究方法之长，立基于中国文化传统和国情，顺应中国特色社会主义建设大势，锚定中国法治建设实践，推动中国法理学乃至整个法学回归常识、回归学术，为中国法学理论体系完善和法治实践体系的优化提供了理论支撑和思想支援。而欲实现新时代法理学的创新性，需更进一步体察人类文明颠覆性巨变的深刻性，需紧盯国际学术前沿和当下人类面临的共同问题与挑战。

【关键词】法理　法治　法学　学术包容　方法开放　实践创新

改革开放40年是中国经济、政治、文化、社会、精神形态与内外关系深刻巨变的40年；40年的励精图治，中华文明迎来了新的历史运势，开启了中国特色社会主义新时代。目光向历史深处稍作回溯，这也是晚清忠臣李鸿章所察中华文明体系"三千年未有之大变局"历经百余年演化后新的历史起点。历史的进步与发展，可以经济体量、军事实力度量，但更为恒久的度量应是制度的文明性、思想的震撼力和文化的影响力。改革开放40年，是中国法治改革创新的40年，更是中国法学凤凰涅槃的40年。中国法治发展是各种社会因素综合作用的结果。其中，中国法学的理论和学术贡献，是不可或缺的关键一环。法理学作为中国法学的有机组成部分，作为

---

[*] 中国社会科学院学部委员、研究员。
[**] 北京理工大学法学院教授。

在"哲理—实务"轴上偏哲理一端的一门学问,更是发挥了不可忽视的重要作用。

每到逢十或具有重要意义的年份,法理学界同仁均会对过往中国法理学的概况、成就与不足进行系统的学术梳理①,这些高屋建瓴的梳理已经为学界同仁描述了中国法理学不同时期的样貌,为推进法理学的进深研究提供了重要的参照基准和问题线索。因此,本文不再狗尾续貂,而是基于这些成果,就行进至当下的中国法理学之独立性、包容性、开放性、创新性等特征略陈管见,以求教于同仁。

一 中国法理学的学科独立性

40年来,法理学在中国是不是一门独立学问之问,常常会在某些重要时间节点浮上学界同仁的心头,成为争论商榷的焦点。一方面"法理学向何处去"的追问、争鸣与研讨此起彼伏,另一方面"中国法学向何处去"的主要指向也是中国法理学向何处去,而在法理学似乎仍然没有找到去处之时,又有学者宣告了中国法理学的死亡。② 在中国,要回答法理学是否已经是一门独立的学问之问,首先需要对什么是法理学有所交代。无问西东,

---

① 这方面的梳理性文章有:张文显、马新福、郑成良:《新时期中国法理学的发展与反思》,《中国社会科学》1991年第6期;孙国华、张恒山、韩旭:《法理学研究的回顾与展望》,《法学家》1994年第1期;刘瀚、李林:《开创跨世纪法理学研究的新局面——近年来中国法理学研究的回顾与前瞻》,《法律科学(西北政法学院学报)》1998年第2期;徐显明、齐延平:《走出幼稚——十一届三中全会以来法理学的新进展》,《山东大学学报》(哲学社会科学版)1998年第4期;张文显、姚建宗、黄文艺、周永胜:《中国法理学二十年》,《法制与社会发展》1998年第5期;孙国华:《十一届三中全会以来的中国法理学》,《法学家》1999年第Z1期;李龙、汪习根:《二十世纪中国法理学回眸》,《法学评论》1999年第4期;汪太贤:《20年中国法理学的嬗变及其时代课题》,《现代法学》1999年第5期;张文显:《世纪之交法理学研究的五年回顾与展望》,《法制与社会发展》2001年第1期;陈金钊:《"思想法治"的呼唤——对中国法理学研究三十年的反思》,《东岳论丛》2008年第2期;刘雪斌、李拥军、丰霏:《改革开放三十年的中国法理学:1978-2008》,《法制与社会发展》2008年第5期;胡水君:《〈法学研究〉三十年:法理学》,《法学研究》2008年第6期;刘东升:《近三十年法理学研究进路:1978-2008》,《社会科学战线》2008年第8期;石伟:《论中国法理学的实践转向——三十余年法理学学术史考察》,《现代法学》2012年第4期;季卫东、舒国滢、徐爱国、桑本谦、陈景辉、聂鑫、马剑银:《中国需要什么样的法理学》,《中国法律评论》2016年第3期;《清华法学》学术访谈:《中国法理学:从何处来?到何处去?》,《清华法学》2017年第3期;等等。在本文列举某一问题上的代表性作品时,考虑到学者出版的专著中最核心的观点一般会先期以论文的形式发表,所以仅梳理、列举代表性论文,对著作一般不再列举。

② 徐爱国:《论中国法理学的"死亡"》,《中国法律评论》2016年第2期。

学术界对法理学下定义的欲望从来没有停止，也似乎从未取得实质性进展；现有定义不下千百种，但仍没有一个能够得到大家公认的版本。或许，这本就是法理学的魅力和存在的必要性之所在？

也许，首先讨论"法理学不是什么"更有利于我们对法理学的理解。法理学不一定是各种各样的法理学专著和教科书对应的对象。无论奥斯汀、魏德士、博登海默的法理学，还是国内张文显、徐显明等主编的法理学，其中专著类的往往不过是著者基于自身特定自然法哲学、实证主义法哲学或社会法哲学观对法理学的主观阐释，而其中作为教材类的法理学——特别是中国法学教育界使用的法理学教材——因为要承担基础知识传授、理论学说普及、法学方法初训等主要侧重实践指向而非理论研究指向的功能，则是一个兼顾知识、理论、法律职业伦理的教育拼盘，其更非一般意义上的法理学。法理学的范围也不一定是当今各大学法学院法理学教师所研究的对象范围。基于教学与科研组织机构划分而被赋予法理学教师身份者，其研究、教学的兴趣与重点并不一定是一般法理学，而既可能聚焦偏实务的法律技术和法律政策研究，也可能远超出了法学的范围，主要学术脉络是哲学的、社会学的或政治学的。与此相反，被赋予部门法教师身份者——比如陈兴良等——在很多时候也经常会从部门法问题入手追问一般法理学的问题。法理学的范围更不一定是类似国际法哲学—法社会学协会（IVR）、中国法学会法理学研究会等学术组织及其所组织的各类研讨会所对应的对象范围，类似机构关注点的变化和会议选题的选定，在很多时候并不会受哲学、法学、政治学、社会学等学科边界范围的严格限制。当然，一般法理学更不是当今大多数中国法科学生心目中为申请学位和通过国家法律职业考试所不得不研习的法理学。[①]

那么，法理学是什么？不可否认，法理学的内涵深度和外延宽度在不同法理学家的理解中会有差异，坚守不同哲学立场的学者研究法理学之结论也必然会大相径庭。但是，在何为法理学之中心这一问题上，学者们是有相当的共识的。葛洪义极为中肯地给出了这一共识："法理学是一个运用哲学方法研究法律基本问题的学科门类。与法律哲学或法哲学含义相同，都是探讨法律的一般性问题的学科。"[②] 陈景辉也认为，"法理学、法理论

[①] 除了少数天性喜欢思辨、具有理论兴趣的学生，法理学课程对大多数学生而言不仅是无用的，甚至是令人厌烦的、可恨的。

[②] 葛洪义：《法理学的定义与意义》，《法律科学（西北政法学院学报）》2001年第3期。

（Legal Theory）与法哲学（Legal Philosophy）这三个语词的含义差不多"，在学术活动中是可以不加区别运用的。但他也精致分析了三个语词的差异，认为法理学与部门法学的重叠部分具有属于法理学的范围且有部门法学所不可替代的独特意义；更为重要的是法理学还存在一个独特的"二阶理论"领域，一阶理论是关注实践的，二阶理论是关于一阶理论的"元（后设）理论"，也就是法理学独占的"法哲学"（即分析法哲学）。① 当然，我们也会发现陈景辉之论是建立于"分析哲学"立场之上的。

综上可以看出，从学术功能主义的角度划分，法理学由两部分组成：一是与哲学重叠部分的法哲学，二是与部门法学重叠部分的法理学；前者进一步趋向形而上学则为哲学，后者进一步趋向法律技术则为部门法学。法理学一端勾连着哲学，一端勾连着法律实践，形成了"运用哲学方法研究法律一般问题"的哲学和部门法学均不可替代的独有研究领域。必须注意的是，法理学独有的研究领域并不为所谓的"法理学者"所独占，而是向两端开放的。一般来说，民法学、刑法学等部门法学是为各自的研究主体独占的，一位非长期研习这些领域法律规范的学者一般很难成其为本领域的专家；哲学一般也为哲学家群体所独占，一位非专门致力于哲学领域研究、对哲学学术脉络烂熟于胸的学者，一般也很难被认同为哲学家。但哲学家中以法律一般问题为对象开展哲学研究者和部门法学者中因长于对部门法问题进行一般法理追问被认同为法理学家的，却大有人在，这就是法理学开放性特质的最佳证明。

基于上面的理解，我们认为徐爱国"需要死亡的，首当中国法理学"②之命题是对象错误的。③ 中国法理学40年是伴随中国改革开放逐步成熟的40年，其在中国已经成为一门独立的学问——即使尚未达到徐爱国期冀的"一门学科称得上是一门值得研究的科学，至少应包括统一的观念主题、连贯的逻辑体系、独到的研究方法等最基本的条件"。④ 由改革开放之初的一元教条理论独尊走到今天研究主题驳杂、研究方法多样、学术观点纷呈，中国法理学研究实现了初步的（仅仅是初步的）精神自由并为实现完全的

---

① 陈景辉：《法理论为什么是重要的——法学的知识框架及法理学在其中的位置》，《法学》2014年第3期。
② 徐爱国：《论中国法理学的"死亡"》，《中国法律评论》2016年第2期。
③ 至于说中国当下大同小异的《法理学》教科书体系是否应当死亡、应当重构，则是可以探讨的。
④ 徐爱国：《论中国法理学的"死亡"》，《中国法律评论》2016年第2期。

精神自由提供了基本条件，这也正符合我们深以为然的——同时也是徐爱国的主张——"法律研究的客观性并不存在于法理学之中，法理学是一门主观性显著的学说"。①

改革开放40年的中国法理学突破了单一客观性公理桎梏，走向了复数主观性思考。如果说中国法理学在"立"的向度上尚处于起步阶段的话，那么在"破"的向度上可以说已经为中国法理学的繁荣与发展奠定了必要基础。法学界往往自比经济学界而感望尘莫及，殊不知经济学界的40年之功也主要体现在"破"的向度上，在"立"的向度上中国经济学界可以载入世界经济思想史的学说与思想也基本是没有的。法理学界又往往自比部门法学界而感自惭形秽，试问部门法学界在"立"的向度上可以载入世界法律思想史的学说与思想又有哪些呢？无论理工医农还是经济学、法学，改革开放的40年都是中国见贤思齐、勤力前行、努力追赶的40年，也是学术组织与队伍日益壮大、学术研究正常化的40年。虽然其中不乏波折，而且未来也不可能没有波折，但历史的发展不是从来如此吗？1978年真理标准大讨论和党的十一届三中全会的召开揭开了中国历史的新篇章，基于苏联的、所谓的马克思主义教条枷锁被打破，中国化的马克思主义思想解放开启，僵化的国家与法之客观性公理神话被解构，中国法理学界坚持马克思主义的历史唯物主义和唯物辩证法，迅速融入了世界法理学的研究主流之中。法律平等观，法的概念与本质，法的起源与发展，法的价值与作用，法定权利与义务，法律关系，法律体系，法律责任，法律意识，法律方法，民主与法治（法制），人治与法治，法律与政策，法律文化与法律信仰，法与经济、社会、政治、道德之关系等法学基本范畴和法理学领域经久不衰的命题，均被中国法理学界同仁纳入了自己的研究视野中，全方位开启了与国际同行沟通对话的进程。可以说，改革开放40年是中国法理学"融入法学"、"回归法理"、"重返法治"的40年。

改革开放40年，中国政治、经济从非正常状态回归常态并取得突飞猛进的发展，与思想界回归理性、回归学术、回归常识密不可分，二者互为因果。法理学与生俱来连接着哲学，但其形而上的思考又为实践所锚定，中国法理学深切关怀着中国40年的激荡变革。姑且不论学者们自发组织的难以统计的成百成千次的各类专题研讨会——比如围绕法社会学、法学基本范畴、法律与社会发展、市场经济与现代法的精神、依法治国与建设社

---

① 徐爱国：《论中国法理学的"死亡"》，《中国法律评论》2016年第2期。

会主义法治国家、依法治国与精神文明建设、法制现代化与中国经济发展、法律文化、法律全球化、后现代法学、法律思维与法律方法、民间法、人工智能与未来法治等主题举办的研讨会——均体现了深刻的现实实践意识；单是从中国法理学研究会历年年会主题来看，这一特点也体现得十分明显。法理学首届年会（1985年，庐山）主题是"法学的概念和法学改革"，1986年年会（重庆）主题是"社会主义民主的制度化和法律化"，1992年年会（武汉）主题是"人权与法治"，1993年年会（杭州）主题是"社会主义市场经济与法制建设"，1995年年会（昆明）主题是"走向21世纪的中国法理学"，1997年年会（北京）主题是"依法治国的理论与实践"，2005年年会（广州）主题是"和谐社会与法制建设"，2007年年会（武汉）主题是"以人为本与法律发展"，2010年年会（哈尔滨）主题是"法治与中国的社会转型"，2011年年会（重庆）主题是"法治发展与社会管理创新"，2013年年会（大连）主题是"法律权威与法治体系"，2014年年会（南京）主题是"推进法治中国建设的理论与实践"，2015年年会（昆明）主题是"中国法治发展道路"，2016年年会（北京）主题是"全球化背景下的国家治理与制度建构"，2017年年会（厦门）主题是"信息时代的法律与法治"。在有的学者看来，上述主题大多可能难以逃脱简单照搬政治口号的质疑；但是又不能否认，这些主题是中国政治、经济、社会、法治发展至关重要的时间节点上难以回避的，是需要各学科共同进深研究的。法理学界同仁发表的大量文章，虽然不乏口号式的非学术化的篇目，但同时也有大量基于学术理性与实践理性的严肃篇章，这些篇章在特定时空条件局限下所贡献的思想与智慧，融入了中国法治发展与完善进程中，推动了中国制度文明乃至物质文明、精神文明的进步。法理学界关注中国改革开放重要时间节点上关键命题的研究，是因为这些命题必然是当下法理学研究的出发点和安身立命之所系。

　　锚定现实并趋向哲学思考，然后回馈、影响现实，在此之间往来穿梭，构成了法理学存在的独特性。在时空提供的可能性之中，中国法理学历经40年励精图治，学术视野日趋包容，研究方法日趋多样，创新意识日趋显露，具备了与国际同行对话的能力，更具备了从多维度多视角对现实法治进程作出分析的能力，因而已成为一门独立的学问。不能否认的是，关于中国法理学的幼稚论、无用论、死亡论诸说，也同样构成了中国法理学历史进程中的必要组成部分，也在助推着中国法理学的独立性、包容性、开放性、创新性的提升。

二 中国法理学的学术包容性

海纳百川，兼容并蓄，乃学术事业发展之根本。包容性是一门学问是否成熟——或者更准确说是能否走向成熟——的首要条件。中国学术自汉初罢黜百家、独尊儒术始就进入了一元化封闭通道，魏晋玄学、宋明理学、明清考据学陈陈相因，思想之大一统发挥了文明维系功能的同时，也封闭了学术创新的可能性。改革开放前相当长的时期内，由于受到苏联僵化教条主义的思想钳制，整个中国学术界可谓学术停滞、思想凋敝。及至改革开放，中国学术"数千年未有之大变局"方得发生，学术意义上的新中国法理学研究真正开启，其标志就是，凡上下数千年之学说、凡东西南北之学派均被纳入了中国法理学者的研究视野中。可以说，40年中国法理学涉及了法理学最大可能范围内的主题、命题与论题，凸显了学术应有的包容性。

中国法理学界40年研究的问题林林总总，发生的争鸣与争论此起彼伏。有的研究主题和争鸣在今天看来可能显得过于粗疏和表面化，亦不见得有公认的学术深度，更难以被载入世界法律思想史中，但对各种学术观点——特别是对中国法理学观点——的评价应当建立在历史维度之上。在具体的时空背景中，一种学术观点——在纯学术意义上可能不是创新性观点——被倡导、被传播和被接受，可能是与学术创新同样重要的，推动社会向一种新的生产生活方式、新的治理方式、新的文明形态根本转型的思想谋划与思想行动，是一种实践向度上的学术创新。法的概念与本质、法理学的对象与范围、权利本位与人权、依法治国、法律方法论等主题的讨论就是中国法理学40年中可圈可点的重大理论事件和实践思想创新（相对国际学术界已有理论而言，如果不算纯学术创新的话），这些理论事件和实践思想创新影响了并将继续影响中国的法治进程和中国人的生活样态。

（一）"法的概念与本质"之争鸣开启中国法理学独立历程

法是什么？这是一个常思常新的问题，可以说一切属于法本体论问题——比如法的定义、法的渊源、法的效力、法的作用——的研究均是从此问题出发而最后又归结于此问题本身的，此问题可谓是法理学的元问题。对此问题的不同回答体现了不同的哲学立场和理论进路，还决定着对一系列法理学基本问题的回答，甚至还决定着对法治方案与道路的选择。

40年中关于法的概念与本质的争论有三次高峰：第一次是改革开放初期围绕法的阶级性和社会性展开的争论，这次争论重创了源自苏联的、基于"以阶级斗争为纲"路线的法概念体系；第二次是伴随20世纪90年代中国开启市场经济建设进程而展开的，这次争论开启了中国法理学与世界法理学界主流知识与学术体系的对接；第三次是进入 21 世纪延续至今的争论，这次争论的发生是伴随海量域外文献的引入、伴随新生代法理学者走向学术前台而发生的，是内含于中国法理学向何处去、政治法理与学术法理、国家法与民间法、社科法学与法教义学等类似的理论争鸣之中的，因为这些争鸣本质上是由对法的不同认知而发生的。

上述围绕法的本质的争论事实上均没有超出"是"和"应当"哲学关系范畴之论域，也就是说没有超出哲学上实证论与价值论的永恒对垒问题。在此问题上，也有学者主张要解构"法律本质论"，主张从法的"本质"转向法的日常生活。但建构知识原点和思想基石，却是法理学天生的基因本能诉求。在科学建构学派看来，一切科学结论均不过是人为设定实验条件、人为建构的结果。库恩就认为一切常规科学研究本质上都不过是某一种科学"范式"规制下的解谜活动罢了，"各种承诺——概念的、理论的、工具的和方法论的——所形成的牢固网络的存在，是把常规科学与解谜联系起来的隐喻的主要源泉"。[①] 而在法学这一兼具人文与社科属性的领域，更可能受制于语言建构之规制，人们对法的概念与本质的不同设定，一定会生成不同的法学理论体系，进而生成不同的法律生活样态设计版本。当下，人类文明正进入大变革、大调整时期，传统工业乃至信息技术时代正在被"云大物移智"时代所取代。人们基于工业文明时代的生产、生活方式对法的概念和本质的认知面临重大危机与挑战，在近几年已有学者开始探讨"云大物移智"时代法的本质与法的概念重构问题。[②] 可见，法的概念与法的本质问题，归根到底是受马克思主义学说中物质生活条件决定或影响的。当然对法的概念与本质的不同理解和不同设定偏好，既受制于物质生活条件的变化，还受制于人们的理性（或者也包括主观感性？）取舍。无论我们

[①] 〔美〕托马斯·库恩：《科学革命的结构》（第四版），金吾伦、胡新和译，北京大学出版社，2012，第 35 页。

[②] 2017 年被称为人工智能元年，法学界开始更加关注云计算、大数据、物联网、移动支付、人工智能技术发展对传统法律体系和法学理论的挑战。发表的论文如郑戈：《人工智能与法律的未来》，《探索与争鸣》2017 年第 10 期；胡凌：《人工智能的法律想象》，《文化纵横》2017 年第 2 期；吴汉东：《人工智能时代的制度安排与法律规制》，《法律科学（西北政法大学学报）》2017 年第 5 期；李晟：《略论人工智能语境下的法律转型》，《法学评论》2018 年第 1 期；高奇琦：《论人工智能对未来法律的多方位挑战》，《华中科技大学学报》（社会科学版）2018 年第 1 期；季卫东：《人工智能时代的司法权之变》，《东方法学》2018 年第 1 期；朱体正：《人工智能时代的法律因应》，《大连理工大学学报》（社会科学版）2018 年第 2 期；等等。

多么信奉与崇尚非意志论法学观,但吊诡的是,我们的"信奉与崇尚"本身仍然是基于我们的意志的,这是人类的宿命,更是法理学的宿命,真正的非意志性法律也许只会在强人工智能时代或曰人工智能预言家们所谓的后人类时代方有可能发生。中国法理学界时兴时衰的对法的概念与本质的争鸣与思考之意义,并不在于给出一个法的定义或者本质性答案,其反映的是思考者对自身深陷其中的整个法学理论体系、法律生活结构及其背后的整个社会生活结构、国家运行机制乃至整体的人类文明运转体系的焦虑,因而其真正的意义不在于常规性的一般法理进步上,而在于对常规性法理的"范式革命"上。当法理学群体像库恩所言均沉浸于常规范式并受益于常规范式之中时,法的概念与本质的零星思考者就一定是另类的,也必然是孤独的,被排斥也是一种自然的学术现象。

法的概念与本质的争鸣与法的起源、法的渊源、法的效力等问题的争论在中国法理学界是同时发生的,可以说上述诸争论论题的实质是大同小异的,又或者说上述诸问题是需要交叉证立、循环支撑的。法源自道德?源自人类理性?源自社会契约?法的渊源仅仅是国家制定法?法的效力和发挥作用的依据是什么?人们为什么遵守法律?过去40年法理学界对此类种种形而上的法理问题的探讨与思考,构成了中国法理学蹒跚前行、摸索爬升的层层阶梯。

(二)"法理学范畴"之研究拓展了中国法理学的广度、深度

任何一法理学派之所以成其为学派,必有其视为"轴心"的概念或范畴,其思考的起始、思想的生发、结论的生成、体系的构建必围绕此轴心、趋向此轴心、回归此轴心。不同的范畴选择体现着不同的法哲学观,基于不同法理范畴选择而成的理论体系又会发挥不同的理论功效。

改革开放之前的中国法理学乃至整个法学的核心范畴是具有独尊地位的"阶级性"。"自从苏联法学引进中国之后,中国法学一直把阶级性作为法学的基调或者说作为基石,阶级性几乎成为人们观察、认识、评价法律现象的唯一视角和超稳定的定势。"① 这种基于僵化教条主义的法学思潮在中国改革开放甫一启航便根基动摇了,但其彻底走下独尊神坛却是伴随改革开放缓慢发生的。②

中国法理学界关注法学范畴的转换问题始自20世纪80年代。1988年

---

① 张文显:《改革开放新时期的中国法理学》,《法商研究(中南政法学院学报)》2001年第1期。
② 需要注意的是,中国法理学界否定的是僵化教条的阶级论法学的定于一尊之地位,而并不是否定阶级分析方法本身的方法论价值。

在吉林大学召开了首次全国性的法学基本范畴研讨会，学者们在以权利和义务为基本范畴重构中国法学理论体系上，达成了广泛共识，并迅速波及、扩散至整个中国法学各界。① 这次学术高峰是中国改革开放十年、中国思想理论界解放思想十年的结果。从法律体系、法律关系的一般理论看，法学理论（特别是部门法学）以权利与义务、权力与责任为核心研究范畴可谓是常识，但此次学术高峰的历史意义恰恰在于回归常识，在僵化教条已冰冻三尺、已不知常识为何物的当时中国，回归常识是需要卓越的理论勇气与智慧的。

在权利与义务关系的讨论中，进一步衍生出了何者为本位的问题。部分学者从价值论角度严密论证了权利本位[②]，少数学者从法律技术角度坚持义务本位[③]。权利本位与义务本位并非非此即彼的关系，只是立论视角不同罢了。权利本位论之价值不仅在于技术层面，更深刻的时代意义在于对国家价值观、法律价值观、法律文化和法律精神的革命。权利与义务关系理论与权利本位论的提出，彻底改变了法理学的研究范式，并很快波及、影响了诸部门法学的知识体系改造。

与权利义务关系理论和权利本位论并行兴起的还有有关人权和公民权利问题的研究，毋庸讳言，人权和公民权利研究与20世纪90年代伊始官方在人权政策上的重大转向密切相关。这一重大转向是国家哲学、政治理据、法治价值的根本转向，正如胡水君所言："大体上，人权和公民权利作为现

---

① 仅是《当代法学》就推出了多篇文章，比如：1987年第3期发表了张光博的《法定权利义务是法学研究的重大课题》一文；1988年第3期发表了4篇，分别是张文显的《关于权利和义务的思考》，沈国明的《关于"权利"的几点思考》，张宗厚的《"权利本位"对于宪法学研究的意义》，葛洪义的《论法律权利的本质》。

② 此方面的代表性论文主要有张文显：《从"义务本位"到"权利本位"是法的发展规律》，《社会科学战线》1990年第3期；张文显：《"权利本位"之语义和意义分析——兼论社会主义法是新型的权利本位法》，《中国法学》1990年第4期；郑成良：《权利本位说》，《政治与法律》1989年第4期；郑成良：《权利本位论——兼与封日贤同志商榷》，《中国法学》1991年第1期；葛洪义：《论法律权利的概念》，《法律科学（西北政法学院学报）》1989年第1期；葛洪义：《法律·权利·权利本位——新时期法学视角的转换及其意义》，《社会科学》1991年第3期；文正邦：《有关权利问题的法哲学思考》，《中国法学》1991年第2期；孙笑侠：《"权利本位说"的基点、方法与理念——兼评"法本位"论战三方观点与方法》，《中国法学》1991年第4期；孙笑侠：《"权利本位说"的基本方法与理念》，《中国法学》1993年第3期；郭宇昭：《析"权利本位"说》，《中国法学》1991年第3期；林喆：《权利本位——市场经济发展的必然要求》，《法学研究》1992年第6期；等等。

③ 坚持义务本位说的学者以张恒山为代表，其主要论文是：《论法以义务为重心——兼评"权利本位说"》，《中国法学》1990年第5期；《"义务重心"与"权利本位"辨析》，《中外法学》1992年第3期。专著有《义务先定论》，山东人民出版社，1999。

代之道,构成了现代法律实践以及现代法学的主要价值取向。"① 在理论界,人权和公民权利的研究出现了四波高峰:第一波出现在改革开放伊始阶段,与思想瞬间喷薄解放并行,出现了大量探讨人性、人道主义、人权的文章;第二波出现在 1991 年中国政府发布首份《中国的人权状况》白皮书之后,与官方人权政策调整并行,理论界翻译引介了西方众多人权文献,开启了人权理论的系统化研究工作②;第三波出现在 2004 年人权入宪之后,人权入宪意味着国家价值观的制度化,这一时期的研究也主要由法理、宪法学界的学者围绕这一主题展开③;第四波出现在 2009 年中国政府发布首份国

---

① 胡水君:《〈法学研究〉三十年:法理学》,《法学研究》2008 年第 6 期。
② 这一时期代表性的人权原理方面的论文如李步云:《论人权的三种存在形态》,《法学研究》1991 年第 4 期;李步云:《社会主义人权的基本理论与实践》,《法学研究》1992 年第 4 期;李步云:《人权的两个理论问题》,《中国法学》1994 年第 3 期;徐显明:《人权主体之争引出的几个理论问题》,《中国法学》1992 年第 5 期;徐显明:《生存权论》,《中国社会科学》1992 年第 5 期;徐显明:《论人权的界限》,《文史哲》1992 年第 6 期;张文显:《论人权的主体与主体的人权》,《中国法学》1991 年第 5 期;张文显:《人权·权利·集体人权——答陆德山同志》,《中国法学》1992 年第 1 期;刘瀚、李林:《马克思主义人权观初论》,《中国法学》1991 年第 4 期;李林:《国际人权与国家主权》,《中国法学》1993 年第 1 期;沈宗灵:《人权是什么意义上的权利》,《中国法学》1991 年第 5 期;沈宗灵:《二战后西方人权学说的演变》,《中国社会科学》1992 年第 5 期;郭道晖:《论人权的阶级性与普遍性》,《中外法学》1991 年第 5 期;郭道晖:《对人权的法哲学沉思》,《中国社会科学》1994 年第 4 期;孙笑侠:《论法律程序中的人权》,《中国法学》1992 年第 1 期;童之伟:《人权理论若干基本问题的再探讨》,《法学评论》1993 年第 1 期;等等。
③ 有关的论文包括徐显明:《世界人权的发展与中国人权的进步——关于人权法律史的理论思考》,《中共中央党校学报》2008 年第 2 期;李林:《人权的普遍性与相对性:一种国际的视角》,《学习与探索》2006 年第 1 期;秦前红、陈俊敏:《"人权"入宪的理性思考》,《法学论坛》2004 年第 3 期;焦洪昌:《"国家尊重和保障人权"的宪法分析》,《中国法学》2004 年第 3 期;郭道晖:《人权观念与人权入宪》,《法学》2004 年第 4 期;韩大元:《宪法文本中"人权条款"的规范分析》,《法学家》2004 年第 4 期;韩大元:《国家人权保护义务与国家人权机构的功能》,《法学论坛》2005 年第 6 期;林来梵、季彦敏:《人权保障:作为原则的意义》,《法商研究》2005 年第 4 期;郭道晖:《宪法的社会性与人权的至高性》,《法制与社会发展》2005 年第 1 期;齐延平:《国家的人权保障责任与国家人权机构的建立》,《法制与社会发展》2005 年第 3 期;齐延平:《论中国人权精神的建设》,《文史哲》2005 年第 3 期;齐延平:《人权精神的危机与拯救》,《法律科学(西北政法学院学报)》2006 年第 6 期;齐延平:《和谐人权:中国精神与人权文化的互济》,《法学家》2007 年第 2 期;叶必丰:《人权、参政权与国家主权》,《法学》2005 年第 3 期;何志鹏:《人权的来源与基础探究》,《法制与社会发展》2006 年第 3 期;曲相霏:《人·公民·世界公民:人权主体的流变与人权的制度保障》,《政法论坛》2008 年第 4 期;曲相霏:《论人权的普遍性与人权主体观》,《文史哲》2009 年第 4 期;等等。

家人权行动计划之后，这一时期的研究开始从原理面向转向制度与实践面向。①

40 年人权与公民权利研究的主要理论使命在于调整中国的价值观和正义观，虽然近些年此领域的研究逐渐转向了人权与公民权的国内法保护、国际法保护等规范法学面向，但人权之起源与根基、人权文化与中国文化传统、人权的普遍性和中国特色发展道路、个人人权与集体安全和福利等问题仍然悬而未决——或者说这些问题永远会是没有终局答案的问题，随着时势的变迁，这些问题仍然会被不断提及、不断重述②，发挥其不可或缺的反思与批判功能。

在近几年关于法理学走向的讨论中，出现了以"正义"、"法理"为法理学基石范畴或中心主题的主张。钱继磊认为正义是古今中外法理学或法哲学讨论的具有终极意义的永恒话题，正义不仅应作为法理学的最核心命题而且也应是各部门法学要追求和实现的永恒的最高目标，作为法理学基石范畴的正义是包括法理学在内的整个法学与人文社科各学科的桥梁与纽

---

① 代表性文章有郭道晖：《人权的国家保障义务》，《河北法学》2009 年第 8 期；贺鉴：《论中国宪法与国际人权法对三代人权的保护》，《法律科学（西北政法大学学报）》2010 年第 2 期；郭三转：《国家人权机构的设立与作用》，《环球法律评论》2010 年第 3 期；朱力宇、熊侃：《过渡司法：联合国和国际社会对系统性或大规模侵犯人权的回应》，《浙江大学学报》（人文社会科学版）2010 年第 4 期；杨成铭：《国家人权机构对国家司法机关的关系研究》，《政法论坛》2010 年第 5 期；杨成铭：《国家人权机构对国家行政机关关系研究》，《政法论坛》2011 年第 6 期；夏泽祥：《我国宪法人权条款之实施——从美国宪法"保留权利条款"生效方式说起》，《法学》2010 年第 12 期；罗豪才、宋功德：《人权法的失衡与平衡》，《中国社会科学》2011 年第 3 期；常健：《新时期中国人权发展的挑战与战略选择》，《人权》2010 年第 4 期；常健：《价值内涵与实现方式：人权研究的两个视角》，《人权》2011 年第 1 期；等等。

② 比如陈佑武、李步云：《中国特色社会主义人权理论体系论纲》，《政治与法律》2012 年第 5 期；黄金荣：《人权的中国特色及其普遍性之途——评安靖如的〈人权与中国思想：一种跨文化的探索〉》，《清华法学》2014 年第 6 期；邱本、康宇杰：《类、人类与人权的起源和基础》，《中国社会科学院研究生院学报》2014 年第 3 期；李步云：《中国特色社会主义人权理论体系论纲》，《法学研究》2015 年第 2 期；王凌皞：《公共利益对个人权利的双维度限制——从公共利益的平等主义构想切入》，《华东政法大学学报》2016 年第 3 期；孙萌：《中国履行国际人权义务的路径与特色》，《东岳论丛》2017 年第 6 期；齐延平：《论中国人权文化的正当性根基》，《法制与社会发展》2018 年第 2 期；黄爱教：《中国传统文化促进世界人权发展的机遇、障碍与基因》，《内蒙古社会科学》（汉文版）2017 年第 4 期；单纯：《论儒家的人权伦理》，《中国政法大学学报》2018 年第 1 期；等等。

带，是社会正义或社会问题能否引入法学研究领域的联结点。① 张文显主张在法理学研究中应当把"法理"作为中心主题，使之成为法治中国的精神内涵，系统论述了法治实践和政治与公共生活中的"法理"图谱。他认为："随着'法理'成为法理学的中心主题和中国法学的共同关注，成为法治中国的精神内涵，中国法学必将迎来法理时代，'法治中国'必将呈现'法理'中国的鲜明品质。"② 锚定法理、求索正义，可谓是法理学的天然使命。这些主张极为有力地回应了中国法理学死亡论和各种悲观情绪，肯定了中国法理学不仅会存在而且会是一种充满勃勃生机的存在。肯定论者大多带有浓厚的价值论底色或中国法治实践导向，但问题的关键也许在于是谁之正义？何种法理？因为基于不同哲学观和法学流派，一定会有不同的正义观和法理叙述。

（三）"人治与法治"之争鸣开拓中国法理学的现实意义

前面诸问题的研究热度是忽冷忽热的、研究强度是忽弱忽强的，但人治与法治问题在40年的中国法理行程中却一直是一个从未低迷、从未趋冷、从未中断的热点。法理学界乃至整个法学界对此问题的共识度也达到了惊人的程度，基本没有形成具有理论价值的批判性意见（法治本身——特别是具体的法治模式与道路——也需要严肃的批判），这或许与中国法治历程之曲折不无关系。当规则下的生活仍然没有成为常态的情况下，当法治在一个社会中仍然没有作为常识确立的时候，"坚持不懈的追问"就具有了特别的理论与实践价值，哪怕此类研究有时并不被承认为是经典的法理命题，特别是不属于实证主义法学限定的范围。

法治问题的研究作为一个政治领域、法律领域共享的问题，③ 其潮起潮落必然与中国社会政治、经济、法治形态的摸索变迁与曲折进取相呼应。改革开放之初的"人治与法治"大讨论揭开了中国真正意义上的法治理论研究的序幕。非常具有标志意义的是1979年《人民日报》发表了署名文章《人治与法治》，《光明日报》刊载了《论以法治国》，随即各个科研院所开始主办有关人治与法治问题的专题讨论会，就法治的概念、内涵、功能及

---

① 钱继磊：《迈向法理时代的中国法学——兼与徐爱国教授商榷》，《法学评论》2018年第1期。
② 张文显：《法理：法理学的中心主题和法学的共同关注》，《清华法学》2017年第4期。
③ 张文显在其《法理：法理学的中心主题和法学的共同关注》（《清华法学》2017年第4期）一文中使用的"法治实践和政治与公共生活中的'法理'"这一标题提示我们："法理"问题的研究隔绝于政治、社会只能是缘木求鱼，虽然我们秉持法理自身的独立立场。

其与人治的本质不同进行研讨，摒弃人治、厉行法治被明确提出。1997年党的十五大明确提出要"依法治国，建设社会主义法治国家"，这就意味着法治成为我国社会主义建设的治国方略，法治的内涵与构成、法治的标准与要件、如何实现人治向法治的转变等问题就成为法理学界的用力重点。[①] 2001年中央提出依法治国与以德治国相结合，2006年中央提出建设社会主义和谐社会，2007年党的十七大系统阐述了科学发展观，党的这些重大理论创新和实践创新也反映到了法理学界，围绕上述党的重大理论成果对法治可能产生的影响以及法治如何回应时代的要求，法理学界进行了集中讨论。[②]

党的十八届四中全会通过了《中共中央关于全面推进依法治国若干重大问题的决定》，这是中国共产党历史上首次就法治国家建设作出全面系统的专门战略部署，强调要坚持党的领导、人民当家作主、依法治国的有机统一，坚定不移走中国特色社会主义法治道路；坚持依法治国、依法执政、依法行政共同推进；坚持法治国家、法治政府、法治社会一体建设。党的

[①] 代表性的文章包括王家福：《论依法治国》，《法学研究》1996年第3期；徐显明：《论"法治"构成要件——兼及法治的某些原则及观念》，《法学研究》1996年第3期；刘海年：《依法治国：中国社会主义法制建设新的里程碑》，《法学研究》1996年第3期；吴德星：《法治的理论形态与实现过程》，《法学研究》1996年第5期；刘升平：《实行法治是历史发展的必然》，《法学》1996年第10期；李林：《法治的理论、制度和运作》，《法律科学（西北政法学院学报）》1996年第4期；郭道晖：《实现法治的"四要"》，《法律科学（西北政法学院学报）》1996年第3期；陈金钊：《法治之路的技术选择》，《法律科学（西北政法学院学报）》1996年第3期；马长山：《公民意识：中国法治进程的内驱力》，《法学研究》1996年第6期；孙笑侠：《法治、合理性及其代价》，《法制与社会发展》1997年第1期；齐延平：《论法治的基础》，《山东大学学报》1997年第4期；蒋立山：《中国法治道路问题讨论》，《中外法学》1998年第3、4期；苏力：《二十世纪中国的现代化与法治》，《法学研究》1998年第1期；孙笑侠：《法治国家及其政治构造》，《法学研究》1998年第1期；张春生、阿喜：《准确把握"法治"的含义》，《中国法学》1998年第5期。

[②] 比如郝铁川：《法治及其与德治关系论》，《求是》2001年第6期；孙莉：《德治与法治正当性分析——兼及中国与东亚法文化传统之检省》，《中国社会科学》2002年第6期；温晓莉：《实践哲学视野中的"法治"与"德治"》，《法学》2003年第3期；王晨光：《和谐社会中的法律调节机制》，《法学杂志》2005年第4期；张文显：《构建社会主义和谐社会的法律机制》，《中国法学》2006年第1期；胡金光、刘飞宇：《法治与和谐社会论纲》，《法学家》2006年第6期；朱景文、叶传星：《和谐社会构建过程中的法制发展》，《法学家》2007年第1期；石泰峰：《依法治国与科学发展观》，《法学研究》2007年第4期；王家福：《进一步推进依法治国基本方略实施》，《法学研究》2007年第4期；罗豪才、宋功德：《科学发展的公法回应——通过公法均衡化推动中国社会发展科学化》，《中国法学》2007年第6期；徐祥民：《从科学发展与社会和谐的内在统一看法制建设的任务》，《法学论坛》2007年第6期。

十九大确立了习近平新时代中国特色社会主义思想，在法治建设方面进一步明确、深化了上述法治国家建设战略。法理学界就新时代法治规范体系、法治实施体系、法治监督体系、法治保障体系、党内法规体系的建设与完善，产出了一大批兼具理论价值与实践指导意义的成果。[①] 这些研究成果比

---

① 仅仅是发表在"三大刊"上的代表性学术论文就有徐显明：《坚定不移走中国特色社会主义法治道路》，《法学研究》2014年第6期；张文显：《建设中国特色社会主义法治体系》，《法学研究》2014年第6期；信春鹰：《中国特色社会主义法律体系及其重大意义》，《法学研究》2014年第6期；江必新、王红霞：《法治社会建设纲》，《中国社会科学》2014年第1期；江必新：《以公正司法提升司法公信力》，《法学研究》2014年第6期；姜伟：《全面深化改革与全面推进依法治国关系论纲》，《中国法学》2014年第6期；应松年：《加快法治建设促进国家治理体系和治理能力现代化》，《中国法学》2014年第6期；李林：《全面推进依法治国的时代意义》，《法学研究》2014年第6期；周汉华：《构筑多元动力机制 加快建设法治政府》，《法学研究》2014年第6期；陈甦：《构建法治引领和规范改革的新常态》，《法学研究》2014年第6期；莫纪宏：《坚持党的领导与依法治国》，《法学研究》2014年第6期；付子堂、胡夏枫：《立法与改革：以法律修改为重心的考察》，《法学研究》2014年第6期；陈光中、魏晓娜：《论我国司法体制的现代化改革》，《中国法学》2015年第1期；沈德咏、曹士兵、施新州：《国家治理视野下的中国司法权构建》，《中国社会科学》2015年第3期；李龙：《中国特色社会主义法治体系的理论基础、指导思想和基本构成》，《中国法学》2015年第5期；公丕祥：《中国特色社会主义法治道路的时代进程》，《中国法学》2015年第5期；关保英：《法治体系形成指标的法理研究》，《中国法学》2015年第5期；雷磊：《适于法治的法律体系模式》，《法学研究》2015年第5期；龙宗智：《庭审实质化的路径和方法》，《法学研究》2015年第5期；钱弘道、王朝霞：《论中国法治评估的转型》，《中国社会科学》2015年第5期；曾令良：《国际法治与中国法治建设》，《中国社会科学》2015年第10期；王旭：《"法治中国"命题的理论逻辑及其展开》，《中国法学》2016年第1期；李林：《习近平全面依法治国思想的理论逻辑与创新发展》，《法学研究》2016年第2期；顾培东：《当代中国司法生态及其改善》，《法学研究》2016年第2期；陶凯元：《法治中国背景下国家责任论纲》，《中国法学》2016年第6期；侯猛：《当代中国政法体制的形成及意义》，《法学研究》2016年第6期；王若磊：《依规治党与依法治国的关系》，《法学研究》2016年第6期；周尚君：《党管政法：党与政法关系的演进》，《法学研究》2017年第1期；顾培东：《当代中国法治共识的形成及法治再启蒙》，《法学研究》2017年第1期；马长山：《从国家构建到共建共享的法治转向——基于社会组织与法治建设之间关系的考察》，《法学研究》2017年第3期；陈光中、邵俊：《我国监察体制改革若干问题思考》，《中国法学》2017年第4期；陈柏峰：《党政体制如何塑造基层执法》，《法学研究》2017年第4期；张文显：《治国理政的法治理念和法治思维》，《中国社会科学》2017年第4期；陈卫东：《中国司法体制改革的经验——习近平司法体制改革思想研究》，《法学研究》2017年第5期；王敬波：《我国法治政府建设地区差异的定量分析》，《法学研究》2017年第5期；张文显：《新时代全面依法治国的思想、方略和实践》，《中国法学》2017年第6期；张文显：《新思想引领法治新征程——习近平新时代中国特色社会主义思想对依法治国和法治建设的指导意义》，《法学研究》2017年第6期；杜宴林：《司法公正与同理心正义》，《中国社会科学》2017年第6期；魏晓娜：《依法治国语境下检察机关的性质与职权》，《中国法学》2018年第1期。

较鲜明的特征是既坚持法治核心理念与一般原则,又注重从中国国情实际出发,力图就当下中国法治建设过程中出现的带有中国独特性的问题作出理论解释,提供解决方案。

中国法理学界 40 年涉及领域之宽广、涉及主题之众多是前所未有的,试图在一篇综述文章中予以全面梳理是不可能的。我们仅选取法的概念与本质、法理基本范畴、法治三个代表性问题作为切入点,观察中国法理学 40 年的历程,以证明本部分开篇所提出的中国法理学的包容性。而学术的包容性又是以研究方法上的开放性为条件的。

三 中国法理学的方法开放性

改革开放 40 年中国法理学的进取本质上是方法上的进取,取得的成绩在某种意义上也可以概括为方法上的全面开放。法学研究如果定改革开放前僵化教条范式与方法于一尊,中国法理学绝不可能有今天的局面。范式多样并存,方法多元开放,为中国法理学可能的创新提供了必要条件。

坚持以马克思主义为指导,是当代中国哲学社会科学区别于其他哲学社会科学的根本标志,必须旗帜鲜明地加以坚持。中国法理学 40 年发展是在坚持马克思主义立场上的发展,是坚持历史唯物主义和唯物辩证法基础上的发展,是马克思主义法学中国化的坚持和发展。支撑中国法理学 40 年的老中青学者均接受过系统的马克思主义教育和训练,这是中国法理学乃至整个法学界最鲜明的特征,也是不容否认与回避的史实与事实。改革开放后大量青年才俊出国学习,搭建起了中国法理学与世界法理学沟通的桥梁,他们拥有良好的国际视野和国际学术交流能力,他们系统、全面译介了国际学术界方方面面的成果与思想,可以说世界各国法律思想史上和当今法理学界有影响的代表人物、代表作品、代表性学说均被引入了中国法理学界,构成了中国法理学界思考与前行的重要资源。但我们注意到,即使对西方学术传统有着精深研究的学者,无论是以沈宗灵、孙国华、吴大英、刘瀚等为代表的老一代学者,还是以张文显、徐显明、朱景文、季卫东、苏力、许章润、张骐等为代表的中生代学者,还是人数更为众多的 70、80 后的青年学者,在自己的学术研究中均有着深刻的中国国情意识,从中国现实出发、回答中国法治实践中提出的法理问题,构成了中国法理学群体的共同使命。而在回答这些问题时,法理学群体总体上又是自觉地立基于马克思主义立场之上的,因为马克思主义构成了中国法理学同仁共同的学术世界观和价值观底色。在马克思主义立场之上,种种法学研究方法被纳入了中国法理学的版图之中。

如果说近代以来西方法理学行进的路线有着从"侧重应然与理性的自然法学派"到"侧重实然法的实证主义法学"再到"侧重外部视角的以社会法学派为代表的反思与批判法学派"这一较为清晰的历时特征的话，中国法理学乃至整个法学却是三者叠加共时的。此特点的形成与中国法治与法学乃后起者、法治任务与法学命题共时叠加、世界范围内法治进程与法学思想大调整等因素是密切相关的。

在当今纷繁多样的中国法理学研究方法中，我们会发现非实证主义的方法是占据主流的。如果我们仔细思量，又可以说改革开放之前的中国法理学是可以被划入实证主义法学的，因为当时坚奉国家意志与命令是法的唯一合法性来源，而这是区分实证主义与非实证主义的终极标识，虽然我们不愿意称之为"学"，更愿意较为贬义地称之为政治附庸之术。

改革开放伊始，刚刚走出学术独尊阴霾的中国法理学界，是以摒弃、批判概念法学开启新航程的。自然法学派、哲理法学派、社会法学派、自由法学派、利益法学派、现实主义法学派、实用主义法学派、综合法学派等纷纷登场，或许还应当加上独具中国特色的政治法学派（可以归于实用主义法学派之中）。不容否认的一个事实是，上述诸学派的观点在中国法理学研究场域中仅仅是作为支援性的思想资源而存在的，并不是作为鲜明的学派而存在的。在撰写学术史时人们有一种主观偏好——或者说是不得已而为之的倾向——那就是有选择性地进行非黑即白式的谱写。从格老秀斯、霍布斯、孟德斯鸠、洛克、卢梭到康德、费希特、萨维尼，再到边沁、奥斯丁、密尔，最后到拉德布鲁赫、霍姆斯、庞德、狄冀、卢埃林、凯尔森、富勒、罗尔斯、哈特、拉兹等法哲学巨擘，毫无疑问是近代以来法律思想史上熠熠生辉的明星，他们的思想影响了世界并将继续影响着我们当下法律思想与法律生活的建构，在一些重要的历史节点上，我们甚至可以说他们提出的学说影响了历史的进程。但如果我们跳出法学，从人类文明进程更为宏阔的角度观察，我们也可以说他们的影响是非常有限的。思想史撰写者有选择地记录了他们的思想与功绩，而他们在其生活的时代不过是众多思想家之一罢了，我们不能理所当然地认为他们是唯一的存在，尤其不能认为他们是没有对立面的唯一正确的存在。根据这样的"思想史假象"诊断当下中国的法理学，结论往往是否定的；根据这样的"思想史假象"评价当下中国的法理学，它一定是没有价值观立场、没有方法论坚守、没有逻辑自洽理论体系的。而事实上，根据这样的"思想史假象"，西方思想学术界也已经得出了西方思想已经死亡的结论，西方形形色色的意识形态终结论、历史终结论以及与之反叛的人权终结论①、自由主义终结论②此起彼伏，就反映了西方学术界的焦虑、不安和失望。当下的中国法理学面对的中国自身的独特问题与国际法理学界面对的共同问题相叠加，更使得期盼在方法论上有一个最大公约数的共识这一愿望是不可能是实现的。不仅整个中国法理学界不可能形成一个主流的方法论与研究范式，甚至就某一个法理学者而言，要求其有一个一以贯之的方法论贯穿其学术生命的始终，也是勉为其难的，因为虽然还是有大量学者做到了这一点，但更多的中国法理学者采取的是为我所用的综合性进路，这或许是学术后发群体必然的选择，在一定程度上也可以说是一种优势。当然，对中国法理学研究方法混杂、变动不居、难成学派等现象予以不断批判又是必要和富有价值的。

另外，较长一段时间内，中国法理学整体上与关注实证法、持内部视角的分析实证主义法学不同，其更多采取的是法的外部观察视角。这与中国法律体系、法治体系尚不完善、尚处于大破大立阶段是密切关联的。从法的外部视角出发，以道德哲学、政治哲学、社会哲学等学科知识为工具研究法的一般理论问题，也就是徐爱国仰慕的"在天上"③的研究将是法理学永恒的追求，其对命运多舛的中国良法善治秩序的形成更具有不可替代的特定历史意义。但是在中国特色社会主义法律体系初步形成后，特别是较为令人满意的良法善治秩序稳定之后，分析实证主义法学在中国法理学界的占比与影响力自然会提升。

我们前面提到法理学一端天然连着形而上学，另一端则锚定在法律生活上；一只眼睛关注着道德与价值，另一只眼睛则关注着实在法。如果抛弃了前者，过度趋向后者，法理学就会演化为一般法律技术与技艺；而如果抛弃了后者，过度趋向前者，法理学就会演化为纯粹的哲学或政治哲学、社会哲学，同样也会丧失其学问的独立性。在学术界，主张"是"的问题与"应当"的问题完全切割，以实在法为客观研究对象，也就是较为趋向实在法的研究方法，常被统称为实证主义法学派。我们发现，实证主义法学派其实也是一个学派林立的大筐，注释法学派、历史法学派、功利主义法学派、分析法学派、纯粹法学派、社会法学派、自由法学派、利益法学

---

① 可参考〔美〕科斯塔斯·杜兹纳《人权的终结》，郭春发译，江苏人民出版社，2005。
② 可参考〔美〕伊曼努尔·华勒斯坦等《自由主义的终结》，郝名玮、张凡译，社会科学文献出版社，2002。
③ 徐爱国：《论中国法理学的"死亡"》，《中国法律评论》2016年第2期。

派、现实主义法学派、经济分析法学派都可以归于其名下，而事实上许多子学派与自然法学派、价值论法学派都或多或少存在知识的共享。

如果说偏好自然法学派、哲理法学派的学者更多关注的是法的内容的形成，其更多热衷于列举、论证、研究法应当具有哪些实质性的原则与规则的话，实证主义法学派则首先以追求一种形式上的客观性为圭臬。在法的诸环节上，前者关注的主要是立法环节（包括法官适用法律时的解释），后者关注的主要是法律适用环节（包括对立法者的意图、目的等问题的探讨）。在立法上，自然法学派、哲理法学派更关注法的原则与规则构成之正义理据，实证主义法学认为法律是价值无涉的，更侧重从技术性和工具性层面思考法的效力等问题。在司法上，二者的价值冲突并不体现在普通案件中，而是体现在疑难案件中，前者主张恶法非法倾向强一些，而后者主张恶法亦法倾向强一些。每每遇到重大社会变迁或出现前所未有的法律难题，上述争论就会凸显。

上述论争也构成了中国法理学40年争鸣的底色。这些在西方法学界呈历时性代代相因、上下承接、前后递进的方法论，在中国却呈现出迭代共时性特征，这与中国法治任务、法学研究任务迭代共时、后发的综合特征是密切相关的。在短短的40年中，中国经济上要实现从计划到市场的转轨，在政治上要实现从人治向法治的历史性跨越，在法治上要初步构建起中国特色社会主义法律体系和法治体系，要完成这样一种并非自生自发、自然演进而是后生后发的、理性建构的政治、经济、社会、法制现代化任务，任何一种单一的方法论都是无法胜任的。所以，在学术上看似属于常识的方法论之争，由于背后关联着中国的国情、中国的法治走向，也就具有了极为重要的意义。40年中，法的阶级性和社会性、人治与法治、法治与法制、人权与公民权、党的领导权与人民主权、权利本位与义务本位、良性违宪的是与非等争鸣的背后，都关联着特定的方法论偏好，在根本上都属于法学方法论之争，在不太严格的意义上都可以归于非实证主义与实证主义法学之争，或者也可以归于价值论法学与规范法学之争，在取向截然对立的方法论之上出现观点的对立与冲突既是正常的也是必然的。

法教义学与社科法学之争是近几年出现的一大热点。这场论争主要是在法理学、宪法学内部展开的，将之定性为"法理学这次向部门法学发起了进攻"[1]是定性错误。主张民法、刑法等部门法学首先是法教义学是没有

---

[1] 徐爱国：《论中国法理学的"死亡"》，《中国法律评论》2016年第2期。

错的，但法理学界关注法教义学，就意味着"法理学把自己降低到法律教义学的层次，玷污了我们内心神圣而向往的法理学。法理学走下神坛，与庸俗的、市侩的、粗俗的市井之技为伍了"[①] 吗？首先需要说明的是，法教义学层次的法学（各部门法学）不是庸俗的、粗俗的市井之技，更为重要的是法理学关注法教义学并不是要去从事部门法学者、实务者所从事的法律规范之解释与体系化工作，法理学者也无能力从事这项工作；法理学者关注法教义学，仍然是徐爱国期冀的"在天上"的关注，关注的是一般的法教义学思想与思潮，而非一国具体的某一法律部门的教义学。在研究对象上，社科法学将法视为社会现象之一种，而法教义学则将法视为一种有效力的规范；法教义学是以对现行法秩序合理性的确信为工作前提的，而社科法学不仅不一定非要以之为工作前提，甚至可以是以质疑、批判现行法秩序为出发点的；法教义学主张要与种种道德学说和实践理性保持中立，而社科法学在这一点上却恰恰相反。不同的对象设定会推导出不同的法理体系，不同的工作前提与学术意旨会形成截然不同的法治理念，法律规范在何种意义与程度上容纳道德与实践理性，会导致案件处理上南辕北辙的结果，法理学应如何应对？这才是法理学讨论法教义学与社科法学各自优长短缺之本意。这场争论归根到底还是关涉着中国法治与法理的自我定位、未来走向等根本性问题。需要特别提及的是，在这场争论中多数参加者是法理、宪法两个学科（如果这种划分是科学的话）的两栖学人，法教义学在刑法学、民法学领域根本不成其为问题，为什么在宪法学领域的关注度如此之高？为什么近乎所有有代表性的宪法学者均参与了规范宪法学与政治宪法学、法教义学与社科法学之争？[②] 联系早些年林来梵主张规范宪法学

[①] 徐爱国：《论中国法理学的"死亡"》，《中国法律评论》2016 年第 2 期。
[②] 此领域较有代表性的论文有白斌：《论法教义学：源流、特征及其功能》，《环球法律评论》2010 年第 3 期；郑贤君：《宪法"人格尊严"条款的规范地位之辨》，《中国法学》2012 年第 2 期；张翔：《形式法治与法教义学》，《法学研究》2012 年第 6 期；林来梵：《宪法规定的所有权需要制度性保障》，《法学研究》2013 年第 4 期；许德风：《法教义学的应用》，《中外法学》2013 年第 5 期；张翔：《宪法教义学初阶》，《中外法学》2013 年第 5 期；李忠夏：《宪法教义学反思：一个社会系统理论的视角》，《法学研究》2015 年第 6 期；古斯塔夫·拉德布鲁赫、白斌：《法教义学的逻辑》，《清华法学》2016 年第 4 期；侯猛：《社科法学的传统与挑战》，《法商研究》2014 年第 5 期；陈柏峰：《社科法学及其功用》，《法商研究》2014 年第 5 期；李晟：《实践视角下的社科法学：以法教义学为对照》，《法商研究》2014 年第 5 期；谢海定：《法学研究进路的分化与合作——基于社科法学（转下页注）

倡议之起因和继之而起的规范宪法学与政治宪法学之争中各派的冲突立场，我们当明白规范宪法学与政治宪法学、法教义学与社科法学之争背后还关联着中国宪法如何实施、中国法治如何实现等重大法理关切。如此看来，法教义学与社科法学在很多时候不过是一种方法论技术，但技术主张的意义却不在技术（所以无须担心形而上的法理会下降到技术层次），技术主张背后隐藏的仍然是一般法理中那些亘古不易的命题及其如何回应当下现实的问题。

如果说一般法理意义上的法教义学是一种主张从法律内部出发的"法学研究方法的世界观"的话，法律解释、法律推理、法律论证、法律思维等法律方法研究就是此种"法学研究方法的世界观"的技术落实。法律解释、法律推理、法律论证、法律思维之研究在中国法理学界可谓已成蔚为大观之势，此领域的研究也是中国法理学界少有的可以与国际同行并驾齐驱的领域之一，众多学者潜心于此或许与本领域的问题大多纯属法律技术而无意识形态撕裂之虞有关。陈兴良、张志铭、葛洪义、舒国滢、张骐、陈金钊、张继成、张保生、焦宝乾、陈景辉、雷磊等学者是这一领域的持续关注者。[①]当然法理学界研究法律解释、法律推理、法律论证与法律思维

（接上页注②）与法教义学的考察》，《法商研究》2014年第5期；熊秉元：《论社科法学与教义法学之争》，《华东政法大学学报》2014年第6期；孙海波：《法教义学与社科法学之争的方法论反省——以法学与司法的互动关系为重点》，《东方法学》2015年第4期；宋旭光：《面对社科法学挑战的法教义学——西方经验与中国问题》，《环球法律评论》2015年第6期；刘涛：《法教义学危机？——系统理论的解读》，《法学家》2016年第5期；谷川：《法律实践需求下的法教义学与社科法学：对照及反思》，《河北法学》2016年第8期；蔡琳：《略论社科法学与教义法学的理论分歧——以对中国法律实践的认知为视角》，《江苏社会科学》2016年第6期；陈柏峰：《事理、法理与社科法学》，《武汉大学学报》（哲学社会科学版）2017年第1期；侯猛：《社科法学的研究格局：从分立走向整合》，《法学》2017年第2期。

① 较有代表性的论文包括陈兴良：《刑法教义学的逻辑方法：形式逻辑与实体逻辑》，《政法论坛》2017年第5期；张志铭：《司法判例制度建构的法理基础》，《清华法学》2013年第6期；葛洪义：《作为方法论的"地方法制"》，《中国法学》2016年第4期；舒国滢：《波伦亚注释法学派：方法与风格》，《法律科学（西北政法大学学报）》2013年第3期；舒国滢：《欧洲人文主义法学的方法论与知识谱系》，《清华法学》2014年第1期；舒国滢：《逻辑何以解法律论证之困？》，《中国政法大学学报》2018年第2期；张骐：《论类似案件的判断》，《中外法学》2014年第2期；张骐：《再论类似案件的判断与指导性案例的使用——以当代中国法官对指导性案例的使用经验为契口》，《法制与社会发展》2015年第5期；陈金钊：《法治与法学研究中的"方法"问题》，《法学论坛》2016年第5期；陈金钊：《多元规范的思维统合——对法律至上原则的恪守》，《清华法学》2016年第5期；陈金钊：《体系思维的姿态及体系解释方法的运用》，《山东大学学报》（哲学社会科学版）2018年第2期；张继成：（转下页注）

并不同于各部门法为解决具体案件对法律规范所作的融贯性解释与体系化工作，法理学者关注的仍然是法律解释、法律推理、法律论证与法律思维的一般原理，而且在这种"一般原理"的深处与基础层又关联着各法律流派的思想资源与知识。而且，我们还观察到从事法律方法领域的研究者往往会将自己的研究与中国司法改革、公正司法、引发争议的重大疑难案件处理等更为宏阔的一般法理问题和法治实践问题相结合而进行。

民间法研究热潮自20世纪90年代涌现至今不衰。之所以将其归到法学研究方法部分，是因为在我们看来伴随着民间法研究的展开，人类学、诠释学等西方时新的，而对于中国法理学界而言尚付之阙如的诸方法尚未得以运用。苏力、高其才、谢晖、田成有等学者是这一领域的代表。[①]这一方向上的研究在早期对于摆脱"国家与法"教条之思想桎梏具有"破"之功，在后来的研究中，对于拓展法律的概念、重构法律渊源理论、认知基层日常秩序之运行规律又发挥了"立"之功效。

（接上页①）《论命题与经验证据和科学证据符合》，《法学研究》2005年第6期；张继成：《命题获得证据地位的内在逻辑》，《中国法学》2011年第4期；张保生：《法律推理中的法律理由和正当理由》，《法学研究》2006年第6期；张保生：《推定是证明过程的中断》，《法学研究》2009年第5期；焦宝乾：《逻辑与修辞：一对法学研究范式的中西考察》，《中国法学》2014年第6期；焦宝乾：《逻辑与修辞：一对法学范式的区分与关联》，《法制与社会发展》2015年第2期；焦宝乾：《我国司法方法论：学理研究、实践应用及展望》，《法制与社会发展》2018年第2期；雷磊：《为涵摄模式辩护》，《中外法学》2016年第5期；雷磊：《法律规范冲突的逻辑性质》，《法律科学（西北政法大学学报）》2016年第6期；雷磊：《法律逻辑研究什么？》，《清华法学》2017年第4期；雷磊：《法律概念是重要的吗》，《法学研究》2017年第4期；陈景辉：《法律与社会科学研究的方法论批判》，《政法论坛》2013年第1期；《法理论的性质：一元论还是二元论？——德沃金方法论的批判性重构》，《清华法学》2015年第6期；等等。

① 代表性的论文有苏力：《公民权利论的迷思：历史中国的国人、村民和分配正义》，《环球法律评论》2017年第5期；高其才：《乡土法杰与习惯法的当代传承——以广西金秀六巷下古陈盘振武为对象的考察》，《清华法学》2015年第3期；高其才：《尊重生活、承续传统：民法典编纂与民事习惯》，《法学杂志》2016年第4期；高其才：《习惯法的当代传承与弘扬——来自广西金秀的田野考察报告》，《法商研究》2017年第5期；高其才：《延续法统：村规民约对固有习惯法的传承——以贵州省锦屏县平秋镇魁胆村为考察对象》，《法学杂志》2017年第9期；谢晖：《论民间法结构于正式秩序的方式》，《政法论坛》2016年第1期；谢晖：《论民间法对法律合法性缺陷的外部救济》，《东方法学》2017年第4期；田成有、李懿雄：《乡土社会民间法与基层法官解决纠纷的策略》，《现代法学》2002年第1期；田成有：《国家与社会：国家法与民间法的分化与调适》，《江海学刊》2004年第2期；田成有：《民俗习惯在司法实践中的价值与运用》，《山东大学学报》（哲学社会科学版）2008年第1期；陈柏峰、董磊明：《治理论还是法治论——当代中国乡村司法的理论建构》，《法学研究》2010年第5期。

从法外到法内，从自然哲理到分析实证，从法教义学到社科法学，从立法导向到司法导向，从国家法视角到民间法视角，构成了中国法理学40年五彩斑斓的方法论图景。方法上的开放性，是后发的中国法理学能够独立成学、能够达致学术包容、能够向国际学术界看齐的必要条件，同时也是能够基于中国立场、面向中国问题实现创新的必要前提。

四 中国法理学的实践创新性

任何一个国家法理学界形而上学的思考一定是受特定文化传统、经济形态、政制架构、法治样态、社会惯习等种种因素制约的，虽然法理学者往往以追求超越国别特色的一般法理为学术志趣。中国法理学界走过的40年是沿着从破除僵化范式到全方位学习补课再到自立创新这一逻辑链环行进的。始终坚持马克思主义的立场与方法，又以开放的心态包容各种学说与法学研究方法，自觉扎根于中国文化、国情与法治现实问题，将一般法理与中国法治实践相结合，在中国特色社会主义法治理论与法学理论领域取得了一系列独具中国特色的创新性成果，推动了中国的法治进步，提升了中国法理在国际上的显示度和影响力。

德治与法治关系上的创新。法治作为现代社会治理的主控模式，在中外学术界和实践界是取得了普遍共识的。但是，这并不意味着法治可以独自前行，一个良好的法治社会的运转，需要多种社会要素特别是伦理道德系统的支持与支援。西方法治国家大多是从教会国家脱胎而来的，当教阶教会制度作为社会管控系统被法治系统取代、退出历史舞台后，浸润社会数千年的宗教伦理仍然被保留了下来，构成了西方诸国社会发展和法治进步的信仰源泉和伦理支撑系统。而中国总体上自始就是一个世俗性的国家，社会发展和法治进步不可能求助于宗教。但注重礼仪教化、德主刑辅、情理法融贯的历史传统，却可以为中国法治提供必要的道德伦理资源支撑。"德润人心，法安天下"这一政治宣示也正是基于此。从实证主义法学、纯粹法学立场出发，法律与道德应当分离，但我们需要注意的是这一立场是西方社会环环相扣的社会发展和法治进步的结果，其背后作为法治运行不可或缺的、已成为社会常识的观念与人们日常无意识的行为模式因为已经完全内化进了人们的观念之中、内嵌进了社会结构之中而不再被人提及、被人关注，并且还要注意上述立场首要的导向是司法导向的，而中国学界主张德治与法治并行是在立法、执法、司法、法治监督诸环节统合层面上而言的，继续向外推演，甚至学术上是在政治法哲学意义上、实践上是在实现中国社会整体法治现代化意义上而言的，而不是说主张在司法裁判中可以以道德情理突破法律原则与规则。从学者们的争论中就可以发现这一鲜明的特点。① 即使在实践层面，比如坚守法教义学立场的学者也已经放弃了纯粹法学的纯粹主张，也为伦理道德预留了必要空间，"因此，法教义学必然为'价值衡量'留下空间。也正是在这个意义上，法教义学的中立性是指决不能固定性地主张某一种道德伦理、坚持一种特定的理论立场，而应当在具体的实践'情境'中对各种实践理性和道德哲学理论进行权衡，再作出选择。"② 当然，目前法理学界关于道德与法律、德治与法治的关系的讨论仍然是宏观层面的，至于真正精致化的学说——特别是在法治诸环节中二者关系如何具体实现的技术性程序方面——还有待于法理学界的进深研究。

法制现代化与现代法精神上的思考。以公丕祥领衔的学术团队为代表的学者群体长期以来致力于法制现代化问题的研究。③ 此问题的研究起因是

---

① 参见杨长泉《法治与德治互动结合发展研究——以对欧美法学家论法律与道德关系的评析为视角》，《法学杂志》2008 年第 2 期；孙莉《德治与法治正当性分析——兼及中国与东亚法文化传统之检省》，《中国社会科学》2002 年第 6 期；孙莉《德治及其传统之于中国法治进境》，《中国法学》2009 年第 1 期；郭广银《德治：政治文明的伦理维度》，《苏州大学学报》（哲学社会科学版）2009 年第 6 期；郭道晖《为政以德与良心入宪》，《求是学刊》2011 年第 1 期；潘西华《在法治与德治的双向互动中推进依法治国》，《江西社会科学》2015 年第 1 期；肖琴《法治环境下"德治"文化的地位、作用及其培育》，《湖南社会科学》2016 年第 2 期；周永坤《"德法并举"析评——基于概念史的知识社会学视角》，《法学》2017 年第 9 期；吴俊明《论现代中国治理模式的选择——以法治与德治并举为分析视角》，《法学杂志》2017 年第 5 期；张晋藩《论中国古代的德法共治》，《中国法学》2018 年第 2 期；等等。

② 白斌：《论法教义学：源流、特征及其功能》，《环球法律评论》2010 年第 3 期。

③ 公丕祥、夏锦文：《历史与现实：中国法制现代化及其意义》，《法学家》1997 年第 4 期；公丕祥、夏锦文：《法制现代化进程中的东西方关系》，《法学》1997 年第 7 期；公丕祥：《全球化与中国法制现代化》，《法学研究》2000 年第 6 期；公丕祥：《法制现代化的分析工具》，《中国法学》2002 年第 5 期；公丕祥：《全球化时代的中国法制现代化议题》，《法学》2009 年第 5 期；公丕祥：《全球化、中国崛起与法制现代化——一种概要性的分析》，《中国法学》2009 年第 5 期；夏锦文：《论法制现代化的多样化模式》，《法学研究》1997 年第 6 期；夏锦文：《法律职业化与司法现代化关系的若干理论问题》，《法学论坛》2005 年第 2 期；夏锦文：《中国法制现代化的方法论立场》，《政法论坛》2006 年第 5 期；刘作翔：《法制现代化进程中的中国法律教育》，《中外法学》1994 年第 5 期；刘作翔：《概念与目标：中国法制现代化的意义分析》，《法制现代化研究》1999 年第 5 卷；刘作翔：《现代法律观念的培植是实现法治国家的观念基础》，《法学研究》2007 年第 4 期；郝铁川：《中国法制现代化与移植西方法律》，《法学》1993 年第 9 期；苏晓宏、郝铁川：《中国法制现代化历程的特点》，《法学》1994 年第 5 期；郝铁川、傅鼎生：《中国法制（转下页注）

着眼于中国的法制现代化，但此问题又是世界各国共同面临的问题。西方近代以来的法治至今已300年，在其渐趋成熟的同时，也暴露出了一系列问题，司法民粹思潮、司法专制主义在不断冲击着既存司法体制，同性恋、安乐死、大规模移民、环境污染、恐怖主义、能源与资源的短缺、国际机构与跨国公司宪治化、贸易信息物流人流全球化下的主权与人权、基因技术、克隆技术、转基因工程、"云大物移智"技术突飞猛进发展等问题在当下纷纷涌现，前所未有地形成了对传统法学理论、法治体系与法治机制的冲击，人类已有的法治原则、法治体系、法治机制如何应对，应是法制现代化研究中全新的课题。现代法的精神建设是法制现代化的有机组成部分，而法的精神一定是时代精神的反映。过去40年，中国法理学界孜孜以求于现代法的精神的研究，结合一般法理和中国特色社会主义建设理论与实践，提出了一系列现代法的精神学说。① 在当下中国言法制现代化和法的现代精神建设，至少应包括两个方面：一是公认的法治原则与规则如何与中国实际相结合，实现国家治理能力与治理体系的法治化、现代化；二是积极回应当下人类共同面临的法治困境与挑战，提出中国方案，引领世界法治迈向新时代。

（接上页注③）现代化的难点和重点》，《法学》1995年第7期；梁迎修：《辛亥革命以来的中国法制现代化——历史演变及其实践逻辑》，《河北法学》2011年第9期；朱新林：《法律移植之外的第二条道路——中国法制现代化路径之反思》，《河北法学》2011年第12期；魏治勋：《论法律移植的理念逻辑——建构全球化时代中国法制现代化的行动方略》，《东方法学》2012年第1期；李贵连：《民主法治：法制现代化的诉求》，《政法论坛》2012年第3期；姜小川：《清末司法改革对中国法制现代化的影响与启示》，《法学杂志》2012年第7期；钱锋：《清末立宪运动：近代中国法制现代化的开端》，《复旦学报》（社会科学版）2014年第3期；王立民：《中国租界的法学教育与中国法制现代化——以上海租界的东吴、震旦大学法学教育为例》，《法学杂志》2016年第7期；何勤华、陈梅：《法制现代化研究与当代中国法学（1986—2016）——一个学说史的考察》，《法治现代化研究》2017年第1期；等等。

① 张文显：《市场经济与现代法的精神论略》，《中国法学》1994年第6期；孙潮：《论现代法精神的实现》，《法学》1994年第12期；陈弘毅：《西方人文思想与现代法的精神》，《中国法学》1995年第6期；子谦、文娟：《论现代法的精神》，《法学家》1996年第6期；马梦启：《"现代法的精神"质疑》，《当代法学》1996年第6期；杜力夫：《公民与公民权利再探讨——兼评"现代法的精神"》，《当代法学》1997年第3期；刘武俊：《市民社会与现代法的精神》，《法学》1995年第8期；李步云：《现代法的精神论纲》，《法学》1997年第6期；杜宴林：《人文主义：现代法精神的革命性变革》，《吉林师范大学学报》（人文社会科学版）2004年第1期；李少伟：《现代文化与现代法的精神》，《贵州大学学报》（社会科学版）2005年第4期；等等。

人类命运共同体理念将成为中国法理走向世界的思想源泉。现有的法理和整个法学体系是建立在近代以来的工业文明和主权国家基础之上的。而伴随着方兴未艾的全球化进程，特别是"云大物移智"技术的发展，人类的生产、生活方式将发生颠覆性巨变，人类已来到了文明更新换代的门槛处。正是基于对人类文明大变革、大调整态势的深刻体察，习近平主席提出了构建人类命运共同体的倡议。在世界各国深陷各类困境和挑战之时，这一理念甫一提出就得到了联合国各层面、越来越多的国家和众多有识之士的积极回应。在各类传统和非传统的困境与挑战面前，各自为政不仅是行不通的，甚至将制造出更多的国际冲突、生态环境和科学技术灾难。源自中国"天下"观念和"和合"文化的人类命运共同体理念，为世界各国走出困境，实现人类文明的脱胎换骨、代际更替提供了新的哲学视野。这一理念必将深刻改变现有的国际经济、政治、外交、贸易、金融、科技、教育、环境等体系，也必将影响到包括法理学在内的整个法学理论体系乃至政治理论体系、国际关系理论体系的变革。中国法理学界在过去几年围绕人类命运共同体与法治、法学的关系展开了有针对性的研究。[1] 已有的研究明显借鉴了多种资源，既有中国文化传统中的思想资源，也有哲学、政治学、国际关系学的资源。法理上对这一问题的回应，不仅会影响到国内法理与法学理论体系的重塑，也会影响到国际法基础理论的再造。

五　结语

通过上述梳理，可以发现中国法理学的 40 年是全面学习、深耕、消化各家各派学说的 40 年，是融入主流、回归学术、重返常识的 40 年，也是扎根中国特色法学实践的 40 年。40 年上下求索，为中国特色社会主义法理学的锻打成型提供了不可或缺的熔炼历程。中国法理学界已具备了与国际学术同行沟通对话的学术能力和学术自信；也具备了对生动丰富的法治变革与发展予以理论提炼和批判的能力。过去 40 年中，中国法理学界同仁积极参与了改革开放过程中和国家政治、经济、社会、文化、制度历史性转型过程中重大理论问题和实践问题的研讨，尚显粗糙稚嫩但也多姿多彩的中

---

[1] 比如张文显：《推进全球治理变革，构建世界新秩序——习近平治国理政的全球思维》，《环球法律评论》2017 年第 4 期；黄进：《习近平全球治理与国际法治思想研究》，《中国法学》2017 年第 5 期；谢海霞：《人类命运共同体的构建与国际法的发展》，《法学论坛》2018 年第 1 期；陈金钊：《"人类命运共同体"的法理诠释》，《法学论坛》2018 年第 1 期；等等。

国法理正在成为世界法理拼图的有机组成部分。

四十而立的中国法理学已经成年,"成年"的意思是心智已经成熟到足以就理论与实践的各种可能性持包容开放的态度,或者说已经具备了独立思考的强烈意识,并不见得说已经有了独立完备的、逻辑严密的理论体系,或者说有了可以载入人类思想史的法理思想。在历史大变革、大调整时期,人们对美好法律生活的向往和理想法治的规划已经不可逆转地开放,这远比是否已经有一种罗尔斯定义的宗教性的、形而上学的、道德意义上的"完备性学说"要重要得多。包容万家,方能成自家之言;方法开放多元,方能成创新之功。

当今世界变动不居,如果说工业文明时代的法理呈现的模式是"西方主导—他者学习回应"型的,那么作为经济、政治、法治现代化后发国家的法理学术群体,就历史性地享有了学术创新的机缘与机会,经济的领先和部分技术应用领域的领先为包括法理学者在内的中国学者提供了难得的学术研究优势,积极回应新时代的问题与挑战,提出融汇东西方文化的法理学说,为应对人类面临的共同问题与挑战提供具有前瞻性的思想、智慧与方案,是包括中国法理学者在内的所有法理学者的历史使命。当然,如何能够在严格的"法理"意义上实现新时代的理论突破和理论建构,一定不是一蹴而就的。

Towards the Chinese Jurisprudence in a New Era: Retrospect and Prospect

Li Lin and Qi Yanping

【Abstract】After 40 years of exploration, China has raised its jurisprudence to such a level that it new occupies a unique position in the international academic circle and Chinese jurisprudents are able to carry out synchronic dialogues with their international colleagues. Under the precondition of adhering to the guidance of Chinized Marxism and correct political direction, the jurisprudential community in China has embraced various schools of legal thoughts, learnt widely from the strong points of different research methodologies, based itself on the Chinese cultural tradition and national conditions, followed the general trend of development of socialism with Chinese characteristics, focused on the Chinese practice of construction of the rule of law, and promoted the return of jurisprudence, even the law science as a whole, back to common sense and scholarship, thereby providing theoretical and ideological supports for the perfection of the system of legal theory and the optimization of legal practice. To innovate the Chinese jurisprudence in a new era, it is necessary to further observe and experience the profoundness of the subversive changes in human civilization and pay close attention to international academic frontiers and the common problems and challenges faced by mankind.

【Key words】 jurisprudence; the rule of law; law science; academic inclusiveness; methodological openness; practical innovation

Constitutional Review: Developments in the Nordic Countries

Pia Letto-Vanamo [*]

〔Abstract〕 The Nordic Countries belong to the very few in Europe not having a constitutional court. However, a tradition of constitutional review exists. Constitutionality is safeguarded first and foremost by mechanisms for review by the ordinary courts of the constitutionality of legislation. There are different constitutional arrangements as to how constitutional review is organised. In the following, the Norwegian, Swedish and Finnish models are discussed. Nevertheless, all Nordic countries share a spirit of constitutionalism and rule of law with general respect for the rules of the constitution and for the hierarchy of legal rules. This spirit is reflective of a parliamentary system with respect for the will of the legislator—in line with the ideology of separation of powers and consensual democracy.

1. Nordic Constitutional Landscape

Two legal phenomena regularly surprise foreign exchange students participating in my comparative law course on "Nordic Law in the European Context": They learn that the Nordic countries are countries without a civil code, and that they do not have constitutional courts. Since Ditlev Tamm writes in this volume about the Nordic civil law systems, I will only discuss issues of Nordic constitutional review in the following.

As noted, no Nordic constitutional courts exist. Thus, these countries belong to

---

[*] Professor of Law, Faculty of Law, University of Helsinki.

the very few in Europe not organizing constitutional review through a special court. Globally, too, this phenomenon is quite uncommon. Nevertheless, a tradition of constitutional/judicial review exists. Actually, one can speak of several models of constitutional review in the Nordic Countries. Differences between the models have historical reasons, but the basic idea is the same. The parliament is the most important legal actor; it is the parliament—not the judiciary—that has the last word on the law.

Thus, Nordic judicial systems hold great respect for their national parliaments as democratically chosen legislators. Furthermore, none of the Nordic supreme courts plays such a political role as do constitutional courts. At the same time, none of the supreme courts or other controlling organs possess the competence to formally nullify parliamentary acts.

The non-existence of constitutional courts does not mean that Nordic legal systems do not share some features of the continental European legal tradition.[①] For instance, legal systems are based on the idea of a division between private and public law. Key constitutional documents are written or codified even though they are supplemented by other formal acts, amendments, constitutional conventions or customary praxis. Nordic systems also favour the idea of constitutional acts with the status of *lex superior*, where constitutional acts are located at the top of the hierarchy of national legal sources.

Constitutionality is safeguarded first and foremost by mechanisms for review by ordinary courts of the constitutionality of legislation. However, constitutional arrangements differ as to how judicial review is organised. Denmark does not have an explicit constitutional provision concerning judicial review. None the less, it hesitantly recognises judicial review. Finland and Sweden have written constitutional provisions concerning judicial review, although in practice these provisions are applied cautiously. Norway added judicial review to the Constitution by an amendment in 2014. The Norwegian, Swedish and Finnish

---

[①] For a brief comparative overview see Jaakko Husa, Nordic Constitutional Mentality, in Pia Letto-Vanamo et al., *Nordic Law in European Context* (Springer Nature Switzerland 2019), pp. 41 – 60; See also Husa, *Nordic Reflections on Constitutional Law: A Comparative Nordic Perspective* (Frankfurt am Main, Peter Lang 2002).

systems are described in more detail below, in Section 4. ①

Furthermore, a difference exists between the degree of "judicial activism". Sweden, Finland, Denmark and Iceland all are less active, whereas in Norway the Supreme Court plays an active role in judicial review. At the same time, its case law occupies a crucial position among Norwegian national legal sources. Nevertheless, all Nordic countries share a spirit of constitutionalism and rule of law with general respect for the rules of the constitution and for the hierarchy of legal rules. This spirit is reflective of a parliamentary system with respect for the will of the legislator—and avoidance of conflicts between the parliament and the supreme courts—in line with the ideology of separation of powers and consensual democracy.

Nordic parliamentarism also protects fundamental rights. Hence, three types of legal sources are applied: domestic constitutions, European conventions, and global conventions. Constitutional protection varies from country to country, but in general the European Convention on Human Rights (ECHR) is the most important human rights instrument. All the Nordic countries have incorporated the ECHR into their domestic legal systems.

2. Supreme Court as Guardian of the Constitution in Norway

The Norwegian Constitution Act ② was adopted in 1814, and is the second oldest written constitutional document in the world still in force. At the same time, the role of customary constitutional law is greater than in the other Nordic systems. Furthermore, the constitution enjoys a stronger political and cultural position in Norway than in the other Nordic countries. To Norwegians, their constitution symbolizes freedom, independence and democracy.

The constitutional system in Norway consists, as in Sweden and Denmark, of a constitutional monarchy with a parliamentary democratic system of governance. In contrast to Denmark, Finland and Sweden, Norway is not a European Union (EU) member. According to the Constitution Act, public power is distributed among three institutions: the parliament, holding legislative power; the government,

---

① For the Danish constitutional system see Helle Krunke, "Constitutional Identity seen through a Danish lens", Retfaered. *Nordisk Juridisk Tidsskrift* 2014, pp. 24 – 40.
② *Kongeriket Norges grunnlov* 1814 no 17.

holding executive power; and independent courts, holding judicial power. The monarch wields very little actual political power, but holds a symbolic function as the head of state and official representative of the country.

Norway's exceptional role in the Nordic constitutional landscape is linked to the fact that *ex post* control of the constitutionality of legislation is actively exercised. The central actor is the Supreme Court (*Høyesterett*). As noted, the constitution is highly respected. The same concerns the Supreme Court, which is seen as the final guardian of the constitution. Furthermore, of all the Nordic countries Norway maintains the strongest tradition of judicial review of legislation. The Supreme Court reviews whether a statute is in conflict with the constitution.[①]

As in the USA, in Norway, too, this competence was originally not included in the written Constitution Act before 2015. Nevertheless, a tradition of constitutional / judicial review emerged as early as the 19th century. In the reform of 2015 a novel provision was added to the Constitution Act. This provides that "[i]n cases brought before the courts, the courts have the power and obligation to review whether Acts and other decisions by the state authorities are contrary to the Constitution".

In more general terms, the Norwegian system is seen as a combination of the strong US-style judicial review and the Nordic parliamentary-friendly approach. Thus, the Supreme Court does not declare an act null and void but sets aside the provision in question. Moreover, there is very little similarity with the European constitutional court approach, because the *Høyesterett* eliminates the legal-normative power of a provision only in the actual concrete case before the Court. Nevertheless, the decision means that the provision loses its *de facto* authority in other cases too.

3. Power of "the People" in Sweden

Sweden has five constitutional documents. These are the Instrument of Government (1974)[②], the Act of Succession (1810), the Freedom of the Press

---

[①] Rune Slagstad, The Breakthrough of Judicial Review in the Norwegian System, in R. Slagstad, E. Smith (eds.), *Constitutional Justice under Old Constitutions* (The Hague, Kluwer 1995), pp. 81 – 111.

[②] *Kungörelse* (1974: 152) *om beslutad ny regeringsform. Successionsordning* (1810: 0926). *Tryckfrihetsförordning* (1949: 105). *Yttrandefrihetsgrundlag* (1991: 1469), *Riksdagsordning* (2014: 801).

Act (1949), the Fundamental Law on Freedom of Expression (1991), and the Parliament Act (1974). As noted, Sweden is a constitutional monarchy with a parliamentary system. Like Finland, Sweden has been an EU member since 1995.[1]

The Instrument of Government contains the basic principles of the form of government, dealing with government functions, fundamental freedoms and rights and elections to the parliament (in Swedish *Riksdag*). In 1979, the Instrument of Government was reformed and a cautious form of judicial review was introduced as part of the written constitution. The rule concerned stated that a court could declare a provision of a parliamentary act or a government decree to be in violation of the constitution and thus inapplicable, but only if the error was of an "evident" nature. However, this rule—which was worded similarly to Finland—had very little practical effect on the behaviour of the courts.

Since 2011 an act no longer needs to be in evident conflict with a constitutional rule in order to be set aside by a court or other public body. Thus, "(I) f a court finds that a provision conflicts with a rule of fundamental law or other superior statute, the provision shall not be applied…." However, the reform did not mean a dramatic change in the role of the Swedish parliament because the provision in question also contains a second part which states that: "In the case of review of an act of law under paragraph one, particular attention must be paid to the fact that the Parliament (the *riksdag*) is the foremost representative of the people and that fundamental law takes precedence over other law."

In other words, even while giving in to pressure for stronger judicial review, the Swedish system in fact sought to fuse together the traditional parliament-centred thinking and the more recent idea of separation of powers with a stronger judicial review approach. Actually, Swedish constitutional-political culture involving a strong role for the parliament also characterises Swedish doctrine on sources of law. Preparatory works (*travaux préparatoires*) to legislation are actively used by Swedish lawyers to obtain more information about the law—about the will and the *ratio* (reasoning) of the legislator for the rules concerned.

---

[1] For a general overview see Joakim Nergelius, *Constitutional Law in Sweden* (Alphen van den Rijn, Kluwer 2011).

4. Unique Role of Constitutional Law Committee in Finland

The Finnish Constitution is written in a single act,[1] which entered into force in 2000.[2] Before that there were four separate constitutional acts. The Constitution Act contains provisions about the principles for the exercise of public power, the organisation of the government and the relationships between the highest state organs. Additionally, the Act contains a catalogue of fundamental and human rights, which has had a great impact both in legal practice and in Finnish constitutional law scholarship.

In 2012 the Constitution Act was amended to clarify the division of powers between the President of the Republic and the government. Generally speaking, Finland is a parliamentary democracy with semi-presidential elements: It has a president as head of state and with the competences listed in the Constitution Act. Hence, legislative power is exercised by the parliament, whereas the President of the Republic plays a minor role. According to the Constitution, the top level of governance is the Council of State (the government), which is headed by a prime minister and a requisite number of other ministers. Following the principle of parliamentary systems, the government and its individual members must enjoy the confidence of the parliamentary majority. Again, judicial power is vested in independent courts—at the highest level in the Supreme Court and the Supreme Administrative Court.

In comparative analysis the most distinctive feature of the Finnish system is the way the constitutionality of legislation is safeguarded. Even in a global context this is a unique system. As noted, Finland has no constitutional court. However, courts are allowed to perform judicial review to a certain extent. Since the new Constitution Act of 2000, courts can perform judicial review of legislation. Moreover, it is stated that the courts and other public authorities are obliged to "interpret legislation in such a manner that adheres to the Constitution, and to respect fundamental and human rights".

---

[1] Suomen perustuslaki / Finlands grundlag 731/1999.

[2] See in more detail Jaakko Husa, *The Constitution of Finland—A Contextual Analysis* (Oxford, Hart 2011).

Hence, according to the Constitution Act (Article 106), the courts must give preference to the Constitution when they decide a case, if applying a parliamentary act would be in "evident conflict" with the Constitution Act. In a handful of cases, starting from 2004, the courts have applied Article 106, but in the overall picture judicial review by the courts plays a minor role in terms of safeguarding the constitutionality of legislation.[1] However, certain signs are indicative of the gradually growing constitutional role of the judiciary.[2]

In practice, the constitutionality of laws is examined in advance, before an act enters into force. The key actor in this process is the Constitutional Law Committee of the Finnish parliament. The function of such control is to prevent bills (draft laws) that conflict with the Constitution being enacted through the parliamentary legislative procedure. From the constitutional point of view, the Committee's key role is to issue opinions / reports on bills sent to it for consideration and on the constitutionality of other legislative matters as well as their bearing on human rights.

Although its members are ordinary members of the parliament, the Committee operates on a non-party-political basis (there is no party-political discipline) in reporting to the parliament on constitutionality. Further, the Committee calls academic experts (on the basis of constitutional convention) to hearings, to advise the Committee in its discussions on the constitutionality of the bill concerned. Statements/reports by the Committee are official statements. They are also respected by the parliament as well as the government, which seeks to redraft the provisions of a bill that the Committee has found to be unconstitutional before the bill is passed into law. If unconstitutionality is significant, this means in practice that the bill is withdrawn and the government has to think of another way to proceed. Statements/reports by the Constitutional Law Committee are published, and they hold a special status as legal sources. Additionally, the Committee follows its own "precedents".

All this results in a unique system of controlling the constitutionality of

---

[1] See J. Husa (2011), pp. 186 – 187.
[2] Tuomas Ojanen, "From Constitutional Periphery toward the Center-Transformations of Judicial Review in Finland", *Nordic Journal of Human Rights* (2009), pp. 194 – 207.

legislation, which combines an abstract *ex ante* and concrete case-bound *ex post* review. Here, the role of the Constitutional Law Committee is significant, as indeed is the role of the academic experts guiding the Committee's views. Professors and other leading constitutional law scholars are regularly invited to Committee hearings: It is not uncommon for a professor from the University of Helsinki to write (and then orally present) 40 −60 opinions/a year, which thus has a great impact on the interpretation and application of the Constitution and fundamental rights in the country.

Interestingly, during the last two to three years the special status of the Constitutional Law Committee as well as the power of constitutional scholarship have provoked some tension between legal (constitutional) and political approaches. Not only have statements by the Constitutional Law Committee been criticized—more often, the views of constitutional law scholars are seen as "blocking" political reforms or complicating the drafting of new legislation. This has concerned, for example, government proposals for changes to (privatisation of) the social security and health care system.

In this context, even reforms towards constitutional review by a constitutional court have been mooted. That, however, would mean a farewell to the Nordic constitutional family, as well as a fundamental change to Finnish legal and political culture. In fact, these ideas are not merely about creation of a new court. In the following, this will be examined in more detail.

5. A Non-Nordic Model: Constitutional Review by Special Courts

The structural difference between the two main models of constitutional review—between the US model and the European model of the constitutional courts—is well known. Each model has its own history. The history of the first model is largely linked to the US Supreme Court case *Marbury vs. Madison* of 1803. The characteristics of the latter have their origin in the Austrian Constitutional Court (*Verfassungsgerichtshof*) of 1920, but the majority of constitutional courts emerged during the second half of the 20th century. Nevertheless, constitutional courts are not a part of the ordinary judiciary but are special constitutional organs, with power to review the constitutionality of legislative acts. Typically, this involves an abstract review.

The European constitutional courts[①] cannot be separated from fundamental political changes in the countries concerned. There are three generations of courts-all born from a so-called system change. The first generation of constitutional courts—the German and Italian courts—were founded in the early 1950s after the fall of the Nazi/Fascist regimes. The second generation—the Spanish and Portuguese constitutional courts—followed the collapse of the authoritarian regimes of Franco and Salazar in the 1970s. The third generation—the constitutional courts of the new (post-communist) democracies of Central and Eastern Europe—were founded in the 1990s. The courts of all generations were founded as symbols of a new democratic system. [②]

None of the three waves of democratization, however, had its origin among the people. In Germany and Italy, a democratic system was established under the tutelage of the victors (mainly the USA). The other changes were mostly based on negotiations between the political elites, not democratically legitimized. At the same time, the new constitutional courts were founded out of a mistrust of the former majoritarian institutions, which had been misused and corrupted by the Nazi/Fascist or Communist regimes. Thus, the constitutional courts were seen as representing the essence of democratic change. In that way they also enjoyed "revolutionary legitimacy". The image was supported especially by the abstract competence of the courts, the competence to declare an unconstitutional law to be null and void—the competence of a "negative legislator", as defined by Hans Kelsen, the founding father of the Austrian Constitutional Court.

In fact, the judges of the European constitutional courts are not "ordinary" judges. In spite of the political role of the courts, many of their judges are university professors of law elected or nominated for a fixed term. At least during the early years of a new constitutional court, it has been important to guarantee and create an image that the judges do not sympathize with the ideas and opinions of the former regime. At the same time, decisions and opinions of the constitutional

---

① As a brief overview see Giuliano Amato, *Corte costitutiozionale e Corti europee. Fra diversita nazionali e vision commune* (Bologna I Mulino 2015).

② László Sólyom, "The Role of Constitutional Courts in the Transition Democracy. With Special Refrence to Hungary", *Internation Sociology* 18/1 (2003) pp. 3 – 31.

courts are often long and theoretical, and based on comparative analysis.

Since the establishment of the German Constitutional Court in 1951,[1] constitutional courts have been founded not only in Europe but also in other continents. For instance, there is a strong "German style" constitutional court in Seoul, in South Korea, and another in Bogota, in Columbia. For their part, the constitutional courts are witnessing a strong global trend of constitutionalization of the law. In addition to Kelsenian abstract competence, protection of individual fundamental rights (on the basis of constitutional complaints) today belongs to the competence of the German constitutional court—and many others besides constitutional courts.

6. Conclusion

The general trend of constitutionalization,[2] as well as the strong European human rights approach, have also had an impact in the Nordic Countries, both in legal practice and in legal scholarship.[3] Especially clear have been the impacts in Finland, where application and interpretation of the rules and principles of the new Constitution of 2000 have been under active discussion. Still, the idea of a constitutional court as guardian of the constitution and its institutions is strange in the Nordic context. Until now, the democratic systems in the North have been based on a certain degree of social stability and on ideas of continuity and consensus. Transferring a "foreign" legal institution to the Nordic environment could have unexpected and unwished consequences not only for Nordic constitutional practice but also in the Nordic constitutional mind.

---

[1] Michael Solleis (ed.), *Herzkammern der Republik, Die deutschen und das Bundesverfassungsgericht* (Munich, Beck 2015).
[2] See e. g. Kaarlo Tuori, European Consitutionalism (Cambridge University Press 2015).
[3] See e. g. Helle Krunke, Björg Thorarensen (eds.), The Nordic Constitutions. A Comparative and Contextual Study (Oxford, Hart 2018).

宪法审查在北欧国家的发展

皮亚·莱托-瓦纳莫

【摘要】 北欧国家属于极少数没有宪法法院的欧洲国家，但是它们却有着宪法审查的传统。这些国家主要是通过普通法院对立法的审查机制来保障合宪性的。至于如何组织宪法审查，不同国家有着不同的宪法安排。本文讨论了挪威、瑞典和芬兰三个国家的模式。尽管如此，所有北欧国家都具有宪制和法治精神，以及对宪法规则和法律规则等级制度的普遍尊重。这一精神体现在尊重立法者意愿、符合三权分立和共识型民主意识形态的议会制度之中。

行政体制改革与法治政府建设四十年
（1978－2018）

李洪雷[*]

【摘要】 改革开放四十年来，我国行政体制改革与法治政府建设经过了四个发展阶段，行政管理体制和行政组织法制日趋完善，初步实现了行政管理的规范化、程序化与法治化，有效加强了对公民权利的保护和对行政活动的监督。但是，我国行政体制改革和法治政府建设也存在很多缺陷，与推进国家治理现代化和建设法治中国的要求相比还存在很大差距。在新时代，需要大力推进行政体制改革，加快建设法治政府。

【关键词】 行政体制　法治政府　行政组织　行政行为　监督　救济

改革开放以来，我国持续进行行政体制改革，大力推进法治政府建设。经过四十年的努力，我国行政机关的职能配置不断走向规范合理，初步实现了行政管理的规范化、程序化与法治化，大力加强了对公民权利的保护和对行政组织及其活动的监督，为经济社会的发展提供了重要支撑和保障。在新时代，需要大力推进行政体制改革，做到权责一致、分工合理、决策科学、执行顺畅、监督有力，建设职能科学、权责法定、执法严明、公开公正、廉洁高效、守法诚信的法治政府。

一　行政体制改革与法治政府建设的主要阶段

（一）恢复发展期（1978－1989）

1978年12月召开了中共十一届三中全会。会议提出，为了保障人民民

---

[*] 中国社会科学院法学研究所研究员、宪法行政法研究室主任，博士生导师，法学博士，主要从事行政法学和立法研究。

主,必须加强社会主义法制,使民主制度化、法律化,做到有法可依、有法必依、执法必严、违法必究。这为行政体制的改革和行政法制的发展指明了方向。1980年8月邓小平在中央政治局扩大会议上作了题为《党和国家领导制度的改革》的讲话,成为20世纪80年代进行政治体制改革的指导性文件。1982年12月4日八二宪法的颁布,为行政体制改革和行政法制建设提供了宪法保障。

1982年国务院进行了改革开放以后的第一轮机构改革,这次改革最主要的成绩是精简了各级领导班子。1987年10月十三大对政治体制改革进行了系统部署。1988年启动了第二轮机构改革。这次改革首次提出了"转变政府职能是机构改革的关键",强调政府的经济管理部门要从直接管理为主转变为间接管理为主,强化宏观管理职能,淡化微观管理职能。

在行政法制建设方面,这一时期的主导观念是"行政管理法制化",强调按照稳定性的法律规则来对公共事务进行管理,重点放在依法治事、依法管理老百姓上。对于保障公民权利、规范政府权力,尽管已经有所认识和落实,但还没有成为主导。

(二) 加速发展期(1989-1997)

1989年4月《行政诉讼法》颁布,这部法律对保障公民、法人和其他组织的合法权益,促进和监督行政机关依法行使行政职权,具有极为重要的意义,标志着我国行政体制改革和行政法制建设进入了一个新的阶段。另外,在这一时期,社会主义市场经济体制被确立为经济改革方向,这为行政体制改革和行政法制建设提出了新的更高要求。

1992年10月,党的十四大明确提出经济体制改革的目标,即要建立社会主义市场经济体制。十四大报告指出,要按照政企分开和精简、统一、效能的原则,对现行行政管理体制和党政机构进行改革。1993年3月八届全国人大一次会议审议通过《国务院机构改革方案》,启动了第三轮机构改革。在这次会议上通过的政府工作报告中,首次正式提出了依法行政的原则。

这一时期,除了《行政诉讼法》以外,还颁布了《国家赔偿法》、《行政复议条例》、《行政监察条例》和《行政监察法》、《审计法》、《行政处罚法》、《国家公务员暂行条例》等重要的行政法律、法规。这些法律、法规一方面强化了对公民权利的救济和对行政权的监督,另一方面强化了对行政权行使过程和程序的规范与控制。这一时期的行政法制建设,在强调行政管理法制化的同时,更加关注对公民权利的保障和对行政权行使的规范制约。

(三) 全面发展期 (1997–2012)

1997年中共十五大报告提出要按照社会主义市场经济的要求推进机构改革。1998年3月九届全国人大一次会议审议通过了《关于国务院机构改革方案的决定》，启动了第四轮机构改革。改革的目标是：建立办事高效、运转协调、行为规范的政府行政管理体系，完善国家公务员制度，建设高素质的专业化行政管理队伍，逐步建立适应社会主义市场经济体制的有中国特色的政府行政管理体制。这次机构改革取得了很大的成绩。

2002年中共十六大报告提出了深化行政管理体制改革的任务。2003年3月10日，十届全国人大一次会议通过了《关于国务院机构改革方案的决定》，启动了第五轮机构改革。这次改革的重点是，深化国有资产管理体制改革，完善宏观调控体系，健全金融监管体制，继续推进流通体制改革，加强食品安全和安全生产监管体制建设。这次改革适应了我国加入WTO的形势变化，抓住当时社会经济发展阶段的突出问题，进一步转变了政府职能。

2007年中共十七大报告要求加快行政管理体制改革、建设服务型政府。2008年2月，中共第十七届中央委员会提出了《中共中央关于深化行政管理体制改革的意见》。意见明确，深化行政管理体制改革的总体目标是，到2020年建立起比较完善的中国特色社会主义行政管理体制。2008年3月，十一届全国人大一次会议通过了关于国务院机构改革方案的决定，启动了第六轮机构改革。这次改革突出了三项重点内容：一是加强和改善宏观调控，促进科学发展；二是着眼于保障和改善民生，加强社会管理和公共服务；三是按照探索职能有机统一的大部门体制要求，对一些职能相近的部门进行整合，实行综合设置，理顺部门职责关系。

1997年中共十五大报告中提出了"依法治国，建设社会主义法治国家"的治国方略，这是我国法治建设中的一项标志性事件，具有划时代的重要意义。1999年九届全国人大二次会议将"依法治国，建设社会主义法治国家"载入了宪法，使依法治国基本方略得到国家根本大法的保障。依法行政是依法治国的关键环节，为贯彻依法治国方略，1999年国务院颁布《关于全面推进依法行政的决定》，这是我国历史上第一份关于推进依法行政的中央政府文件。2004年3月，国务院在《政府工作报告》中第一次明确提出了建设"法治政府"的目标，随后国务院颁布《全面推进依法行政实施纲要》作为指导各级政府依法行政、建设法治政府的纲领性文件。2008年颁布了《国务院关于加强市县政府依法行政的决定》,就加强市县政府依法行政提出了具体要求和举措。2010年颁布《国务院关于加强法治政府建设的意见》,强调以增强领导干部依法行政的意识和能力、提高制度建设质量、规范行政权力运行、保证法律法规严格执行为着力点,全面推进依法行政。

这一时期,行政领域立法工作步伐加快,质量不断提高,同时行政执法体系逐步健全,执法力度加大,各级行政机关工作人员特别是领导干部依法行政意识增强,依法行政能力有了很大提升。

(四) 深化发展期 (2012—2018)

2012年中共十八大报告强调,要深化行政体制改革。要求按照建立中国特色社会主义行政体制目标,深入推进政企分开、政资分开、政事分开、政社分开,建设职能科学、结构优化、廉洁高效、人民满意的服务型政府。2013年3月14日第十二届全国人大第一次会议通过了《关于国务院机构改革和职能转变方案的决定》,启动了第七次国务院机构改革,重点围绕转变职能和理顺职责关系,稳步推进大部门制改革,实行铁路政企分开,整合加强卫生和计划生育、食品药品、新闻出版和广播电影电视、海洋、能源管理机构。

2017年十九大报告提出,要深化机构和行政体制改革。2018年2月党的十九届三中全会通过了《中共中央关于深化党和国家机构改革的决定》,对深化党和国家机构改革作出了统一部署和顶层设计。2018年3月17日第十三届全国人民代表大会第一次会议通过了国务院机构改革方案。这是改革开放以来力度最大的一次机构改革。这次改革适应新时代我国社会主要矛盾变化,按照优化协同高效的原则,优化了国务院机构设置和职能配置,理顺了职责关系。

2012年中共十八大以来,党中央进一步强调依法治国是坚持和发展中国特色社会主义的本质要求和重要保障,是实现国家治理现代化的必然要求,事关党和国家长治久安。与此相应,我国依法行政和法治政府建设也进入了一个全新的阶段。十八大报告明确提出法治是治国理政的基本方式,强调加快建设社会主义法治国家,全面推进依法行政,并给出了具体的时间表,也即"到2020年,依法治国基本方略全面落实,法治政府基本建成,司法公信力不断提高,人权得到切实尊重和保障"。2013年中共十八届三中全会作出了《中共中央关于全面深化改革若干重大问题的决定》,把全面深化改革与法治建设紧密结合,提出建设法治中国,必须坚持依法治国、执法执政、依法行政共同推进，坚持法治国家、法治政府、法治社会一体建设，努力推进国家治理体系和治理能力现代化。2014年中共十八届四中全会作出了《中共中央关于全面推进依法治国若干重大问题的决定》，对全面推进依法治国作出了总体部署和系统谋划，阐明了全面推进依法治国的指导思想、基本原则、总目标、总抓手和基本任务以及法治工作的基本格局。这是中国共产党历史上第一次就法治建设专门作出决议，具有重要的里程碑意义。十八届四中全会《决定》用了较大的篇幅对"深入推进依法行政，加快建设法治政府"进行论述。为实现十八大提出的2020年法治政府基本建成的战略目标，并落实《决定》对依法行政、法治政府建设提出的具体要求，2015年中共中央、国务院印发了《法治政府建设实施纲要（2015－2020年）》，这是第一次以中共中央、国务院文件的形式，对法治政府建设作出重大部署。其中明确了法治政府建设的总体目标，也即到2020年基本建成职能科学、权责法定、执法严明、公开公正、廉洁高效、守法诚信的法治政府，确立了法治政府建设的衡量标准，即政府职能依法全面履行，依法行政制度体系完备，行政决策科学民主合法，宪法法律严格公正实施，行政权力规范透明运行，人民权益切实有效保障，依法行政能力普遍提高，并部署了相关的主要任务和具体措施。十九大报告提出，到2035年基本建成法治国家、法治政府、法治社会。

这一阶段的行政领域立法工作覆盖面更广，为促进经济、社会、文化和生态文明等各领域建设，提供了重要法制保障；"放管服"改革持续推进，清单管理全面实行，政府法律顾问制度普遍建立，行政决策科学化、民主化、法治化水平进一步提高，"双随机、一公开"全面推行，事中事后监管不断加强，行政执法体制改革深入推进，严格规范公正文明执法水平明显提升，法治政府建设考核评价制度正在建立，督促检查力度显著加强。推进依法行政进入"快车道"，法治政府建设展现出前所未有的"加速度"。[①] 在这一阶段，我国法治政府建设的一大特点，在于党中央、国务院加强了对依法行政、法治政府建设的顶层设计，对依法行政和法治政府建设的总体目标、基本要求、衡量标准、推进机制等进行了统筹规划，将依法行政、法治政府建设纳入国家治理体系和治理能力现代化的大局中进行考量和推进；更加强调重大改革要于法有据，必须在法治的轨道上进行改革；更加强调放管服相结合，充分激发市场和社会活力。

---

① 袁曙宏：《党的十八大以来全面依法治国的重大成就和基本经验》，《求是》2017年第11期。

二 我国行政体制改革与法治政府建设的经验

经过四十年来的努力，我国的行政体制不断优化，法治政府建设取得了长足进展，表现在：依法行政制度体系更加完备，行政决策的科学化、民主化和法治化程度日益提高，行政执法体制向着权责统一、权威高效的方向持续迈进，对行政权运行的监督制约机制更加有效，各级行政机关及其工作人员的依法行政水平和观念有了很大提高。这些重大成就的取得，可以归纳为如下几个方面的经验。

其一，坚持中国共产党的领导。中国特色社会主义最本质的特征是党的领导，最大的优势也是党的领导。党在整个国家治理中处于总揽全局、协调各方的领导核心地位。中国共产党决定了我国行政体制改革和法治政府建设的总体方向与重大举措。党的领导是行政体制改革和法治政府建设顺利进行最重要的政治保障。

其二，坚持服务于国家的改革开放事业大局。政府职能的转变，行政权力的规范运行，对公民、组织合法权益的保障，这些是行政体制改革和法治政府建设的核心要义，其实也是我国经济体制改革和政治体制改革的重要内容，是随着改革开放和社会主义现代化建设的发展而持续推进和不断深化的。

其三，坚持以人民为中心。为人民服务是我国各级政府的根本宗旨。我国行政体制的改革和法治政府的建设，之所以能取得成绩、持续推进，极为关键的原因在于自始至终将保护人民、造福人民、保障人民根本权益作为根本目标，从而能取得人民群众的拥护、各方面力量的支持。

其四，坚持从中国实际出发。四十年来，我们一方面以开放的心胸"学习外来"、借鉴域外行政管理和行政法治建设有益经验，同时又坚持不照搬外国管理和法治的理念与模式，坚持从我国的基本国情出发，坚持与经济、社会、文化和生态文明等领域改革的不断推进相适应，坚持不断总结我们自己的经验教训，使得我国的行政体制改革和法治政府建设能够真正符合自己的实际、回应自己的问题、达到自己的目标。

其五，坚持多元力量推动。中国行政体制改革和法治政府建设的一大特点是中央政府的自我革命、自我规制、自我推动。中央政府通过一系列决策部署，以及行政系统内部的考核、评价和监督机制，对行政体制改革和依法行政发挥着关键的推动作用。另外，为克服政府自我规制的局限性，我们也注重健全党内监督、人大监督、政务公开、行政诉讼、民主监督等制度，完善社会监督和舆论监督机制，强化对行政权运行的外部监督制约机制。特别是行政诉讼制度，对我国的依法行政发挥了重要的倒逼作用。

其六，坚持将中央的顶层设计和地方的改革创新相结合。四十年来，我们一方面不断加强对行政体制和法治政府建设的顶层设计，促进国家的法制统一、政令统一、市场统一；另一方面注重发挥地方的积极性和主动性，鼓励地方进行制度创新和实践创新，将中央的决策部署与本地区的实际创造性地结合，同时为中央层面的制度发展提供有益经验和借鉴。

三　我国行政体制改革与法治政府建设的发展展望

尽管我国行政体制改革和法治政府建设的成绩辉煌、成就巨大，但我们也应清醒地认识到，我国的行政体制和法治政府建设还存在不少问题。其一，行政组织法律制度尚不完善，行政职能、机构、权限等未能实现法定化；中央与地方关系尚不协调，各级政府事权划分不合理、事权和财权不匹配，政府与企业、市场、社会的基本关系尚未理顺，履行政府职能不够全面，职能越位、错位、缺位的情况同时存在；党政关系尚待理顺。其二，行政立法质量不高，在民主性与科学性上有欠缺，解决焦点和关键问题的能力不足，一些立法存在部门保护和地方保护倾向；行政决策机制和程序尚不健全，违法决策、专断决策、不当决策等仍较为常见，对违法决策缺乏问责和制约。其三，行政执法体制不够协调统一，执法程序不够规范，程序空转现象较为突出，执法的权威性和公正性不足。其四，对行政权运行的制约和监督机制尚不健全，监督机制未能完全发挥实效，尤其是对行政行为司法审查的权威性、独立性、公正性尚有很大不足。其五，一些行政机关工作人员的法治观念还比较淡薄，存在人治思想和长官意识，认为依法行政条条框框多、束缚手脚，依法行政的思维、能力和水平有待提高。

在新时代，为实现全面推进依法治国、实现国家治理体系和治理能力现代化的目标，在行政体制改革和法治政府建设上要着力做好如下几个方面的工作。

其一，加快政府职能转变。要结合新时代社会主要矛盾的变化，从统筹推进"五位一体"总体布局出发，切实转变政府职能。完善行政组织法律制度，推进机构、职能、权限和责任法定化。进一步推行权力清单和责任清单。要将简政放权置于政府全面正确履行职责的大背景中，坚持简政放权、放管结合、优化服务"三管齐下"，既要解决"越权、越位"的问题，又要解决"缺位、不到位"的问题,坚持有效监管,优化公共服务。建立权责统一、权威高效的行政执法体制,纵向上,应考虑调整行政区划、减少行政层级、明细各级政府职能,合理配置执法力量,推进执法重心向市县两级政府下移,加强重点领域的基层执法力量,注意处理好垂直管理和地方政府负总责之间的关系。横向上,整合执法主体,精简执法机构,推进综合执法,实现行政执法和刑事司法的有效衔接。理顺城市管理执法体制。

其二,优化行政立法和决策。行政立法要坚持解放和发展生产力、维护社会公平正义、规范行政权力运行的价值取向,防止立法中的部门保护主义和地方保护主义。坚持开门立法,保障公众对行政立法的有效参与,建立和完善政府立法分析、评价、评估机制,提高立法质量和实施效果。加强对行政规范性文件的审查和监督。抓紧出台《重大行政决策程序暂行条例》,健全科学民主决策机制,完善重大事项公众参与、专家论证、风险评估、合法性审查、集体讨论决定、决策后评估和责任追究等制度。

其三,坚持严格规范公正文明执法。行政执法是法律实施的关键环节,是建设法治政府的重中之重。要加强对执法活动的监督,排除对执法活动的非法干预,防止和克服地方保护主义和部门保护主义,做到有权必有责、用权受监督、违法必追究。创新执法方法和技术,提高执法效能,全面推行"双随机、一公开"和"互联网+监管",加快推进部门政府信息联通共用,打破"信息孤岛"。全面推广行政执法公示、执法全过程记录、重大执法决定法制审核"三项制度"。综合运用"威慑式"和"合作式"执法模式,实现政府、企业和社会的良性互动。合理配置执法资源,大力加强关系群众切身利益的重点领域执法力度,统筹用好"集中式"与"常态化"执法机制。

其四,强化对行政权的监督和对公民权利的救济。贯彻《监督法》,把事关改革发展稳定大局的重大问题和人民群众普遍关注的突出问题,作为监督工作的重点,坚决纠正人大监督工作中的"粗、宽、松、软"等问题,使人大监督更有力度、更有权威。贯彻《监察法》和《审计法》,深化监察审计体制机制改革,加强国家监察和审计监督。完善纠错问责机制,规范问责程序,推进问责法治化。高度重视舆论和网络监督,支持新闻媒体对违法不当行政行为进行曝光。完善《行政复议法》,改革行政复议机制,充分发挥行政复议在解决行政争议中的作用。完善行政审判体制机制,切实保证行政审判的独立性、公正性和权威性。完善国家赔偿补偿制度,增强救济实效。

其五,改进法治政府建设的领导和推进机制。切实加强各级党委对法治政府建设的领导，把法治政府建设真正摆在全局工作的突出位置，压实党政主要负责人作为推进法治建设第一责任人的责任，抓住领导干部这个"关键少数"。[①] 用好督查考核这一法治政府建设的有力指挥棒和重要抓手，将主观指标和客观指标、内部评审和外部评审有机结合，完善法治政府考核指标体系，健全法治政府考核机制。

学术界也亟待提高理论研究水准，更加有效地回应行政体制改革和法治政府建设中的重大理论问题。例如，党的领导权与政府的行政权之间存在何种差异和联系，在实行党政一体的部门中，如何贯彻法治的要求；如何在统筹考虑政治、经济、行政、社会、文化、历史、地理、民族等多因素的基础上，优化我国的行政区划设置；在行政执法中，如何体现行政执法与司法相比的独特性质；在从人治向法治过渡或转型过程中的转型期法治有何特点；[②]"依法治国，首先是依宪治国；依法执政，关键是依宪执政"，[③] 在强化合宪性审查机制的背景下，作为动态宪法的行政法如何为宪法的实施作出自己的贡献；[④] 如何处理违法行为大量存在和执法资源有限性之间的矛盾；以及在立法落后于改革需要的情况下行政机关应当如何执法，等等。

Forty Years of Reform of the Administrative System and Construction of a Law-based Government (1978 – 2018)

Li Honglei

【Abstract】 In the forty years since the reform and opening-up to the outside world, the reform of the administrative system and the construction of a law-based government in China have undergone four stages of development at which the government has gradually perfected the administrative management system and the

---

① 马怀德主编《行政法前沿问题研究》，中国政法大学出版社，2018，第 26 页以下。
② 张树义：《变革与重构——改革背景下的中国行政法理念》，中国政法大学出版社，2002，第 3 页。
③ 习近平：《在首都各界纪念现行宪法公布施行 30 周年大会上的讲话》，《人民日报》2012 年 12 月 5 日，第 2 版。
④ 李洪雷：《我国法治政府建设面临的课题与挑战》，《法学研究》2013 年第 2 期。

administrative organic law system, standardized, routinized, and brought under the rule of law the administrative management system, and effectively strengthened the protection of civil rights and the supervision over administrative activities. Nevertheless, there are still many problems in the reform of the administrative system and the construction of law-based government, which are still far from meeting the demands of the modernization of the state governance and construction of the rule of law in China. In a new era, China needs to vigorously advance the reform of the administrative system and speed up the construction of a law-based government.

【Key words】 administrative system; law-based government; administrative organization; administrative activities; supervision; relief

European and Finnish Public Procurement Law and Experience[*]

Kristian Siikavirta[**]

【Abstract】 The paper describes the legal principles and the structure of the European public procurement system. The aim of common European Procurement Directives is to give firms located in different Member states fair and open chance to take part in public procurement across Europe. Member states have their own procurement laws based on European directives. The performance of the national procurement law and practice is evaluated by the European Commission. Evaluation in general is an important part of modern European and national legislation. This paper analyses the evaluation results. The analysis explains some features of the Procurement Law in member states where law may cause additional costs to public authorities and to firms. This paper concerns European Union and Finnish laws but the real life phenomenon of public procurement is global.

I will first describe in this paper the legal structure of European public procurement. The system is rather clear but it is evident that the diversity of different goods and constructions works auctioned has created additional complexity and legal risk for public authorities.

After that, I will show how the Commission monitors the performance of member states on public procurement. Member state performance does not really

---

[*] The paper was first presented in the Sino-Finnish Bilateral Seminar on Comparative Law on 28th of August 2017 in Helsinki, Session III Public Procurement. The Author is pleased with valuable comments from commentator Professor Tian He, Institute of Law, CASS and the audience but the views are own.

[**] Doctor of Law's, Senior Lecturer, University of Vaasa.

tell us if the public procurement law and procurement procedure are reaching the goals. However, measurement shows how the procedure is working in general. If there are problems in some area, there is a chance for improvement.

I will shed some light to Finnish experience on public procurement from lawyer's perspective. Observations may be cautiously generalized concerning other member states because the legal framework is similar inside European Union. I will try to illuminate why public procurement legislation is seen cumbersome although it has goals that are understandable.

This paper concerns European Union and Finnish law but the real life phenomenon of public procurement is global. All over the world, there is a need for public authorities to buy different goods from private markets using public funds. There are different legal solutions to this task and in this paper I will explain the European approach.

View on Procurement Legislation in EU

European public procurement legislation is harmonized by Procurement Directive in 2014. [1] Purchases over certain threshold value must be auctioned in an open procedure. In general, public authorities must arrange open competitive bidding when they are purchasing goods, services or construction works from markets outside their own organization. The aim is to get better value for public money, to give equal opportunities for cross border sellers and to improve economic growth. European commission supervises compliance and European court has the ultimate power to interpret the procurement directive in detail. National courts have jurisdiction on national procurement law. In Finland, that is Procurement Act on 2016 (1397/2016).

The goals of European procurement directives since 1990 have been to achieve transparent, fair and competitive public procurement across the EU's Single Market thus generating business opportunities, driving economic growth and creating jobs. EU directives are by nature minimum regulation which refers to that member states

---

[1] The latest directive is Directive 2014/24/EU of the European Parliament and of the Council of 26th February 2014 on public procurement and repealing Directive 2004/18/EC Text with EEA relevance, OJ L 94, 28.3.2014, pp. 65–242.

have an opportunity to enact more strict rules.

The directive regulates only the auction procedure so the law does not tell what should be bought. Instead, it orders one to buy with the certain open procedure. That principle is weakened a little by the latest reform trying to make public procurement a stronger policy instrument.

The effects of the legislation are not always as expected so there is lively academic discussion on the real effects of the procurement law. ① Also best practices are eagerly looked after. ② Over the years the European legislator has made changes to the procurement directives in order to develop the law and to respond to the main concerns. These are the complexity of the rules, high administrative costs, the fear of clustered markets, and modest share of cross border procurement deals.

The procurement performance of the member states is well documented by the commission but real economic effects on costs or on markets is not explicit though they are considered positive. Discussion in member states can be skeptical against the effectiveness and costs of public auctions.

Legal Principles in Procurement Law

Public procurement law in Europe is about the formal process by which public authorities, such as government departments or the local authorities, purchase goods, services or constructions works from private companies.

General legal principles guiding decision making under procurement law can be found in the Procurement Directive (paragraph 1) and they are used in Union Court decisions as a guiding rule. Member states may have their own additional principles but they may not contradict EU-principles. Key Principles in the EU can be expressed in many ways but in general they are as follows.

Equal treatment and Non-discrimination mean that discrimination against bidders from other Member States or on some other grounds is not allowed. Furthermore, discrimination against bidders from another area inside a member state is not allowed. Court of Justice of the European Union (CJEU) has stated that "the equal

---

① See for example Journal of Public Procurement. Emerald Publishing Limited.
② Communication from the Commission to the Institutions: Making Public Procurement Work in and for Europe, COM (2017) 572 final, Strasbourg, 3. 10. 2017, page 5.

treatment principle requires that comparable situations are not treated differently and that different situations are not treated similarly unless such a difference or similarity in treatment can be justified objectively". [1]Furthermore, the contracting party is not allowed to plan auctions in a way that only certain firms are able to make offers.

On an individual tender level, it is still possible to try to shape the selection criteria favoring some predetermined firms. If this is suspected and demonstrated before a national court, the tender has failed. Selected technical criteria may also bring up equality problems although public authors are free to decide what to buy. [2]

However, in general the low volume of cross border deals is not a consequence of discrimination but normal market conditions, meaning higher costs. [3]

The principle of transparency means in practice that information on coming tenders must be available to all potential bidders in Europe in a transparent form and language. [4] Directive sets out step-by-step procedures related to the notice and advertisement of tenders, leaving little choice as to when, where, and how to advertise procurement events. The general idea includes also that impartiality of the contracting authorities' decision can be reviewed.

The Procurement Directive (for example articles, 2, 42) requires that all performance and/or functional requirements should be sufficiently precise as to allow the tenderer to determine the subject matter of the contract. Reasonably well informed and normally diligent tenderer must be able to interpret the notice in the same way. [5]

Special standards (for example environmental standards or labels) in contract notices may be used but there must be an option available to tenderers to show that required equivalent standards are met. This may be cumbersome for small firms. Highly technical tender documents create misunderstandings and legal disputes.

Member State public procurement policies must comply with *the principle of proportionality*. The CJEU has consistently defined the principle of proportionality as

---

[1] Case C-21/03 and C-34/03, Fabricom v Belgium [2005] ECR I-1559.
[2] Case C-448/01, EVN AG and Wienstrom GmbH v Austria [2003] ECR I-4527 at paragraph 69.
[3] See closer for example Public procurement in Europe-Cost and effectiveness. A study on procurement regulation. Prepared for the European Commission, March 2011, pages 95-102.
[4] https://ted.europa.eu/TED/main/HomePage.do.
[5] Case C-19/00 SIAC Construction v County Council of Mayo [2001] ECR I-7725, paragraph 42.

one of the general principles of EU law, which requires that measures implemented through EU provisions should be appropriate for attaining the objective pursued and must not go beyond what is necessary to achieve it. [1]

All above threshold tenders must be carried out through the open procurement process even if this would not create any economic benefits. Open tender may in some cases cost more than is gained by the lower price.

Procurement Process

The purchasing process is ordered by the European Union directive, which means that member states must implement the rules into their own national laws. The basic feature of the directive is an open invitation to take part in the public tender process. All European firms have an equal right to make offers. The winner is chosen according to predetermined, open and nonrestrictive criteria. The simple idea is that with this procedure the public purchaser finds the best deal and the best provider.

In general, the rules are meant to achieve the efficient use of public resources and enhance competition in European Union thus generating economic growth. From that perspective it is perhaps surprising that some public authors in member states and member states themselves have found it sometimes uncomfortable to play along the public procurement directives and rules. [2]

Slight unwillingness to comply is the most significant in local administrative levels in the member states. This is seen for example in Finland where local level officials sometimes try to find ways not to comply with procurement laws. These attempts are however stopped by rival tenderers complaining to the Finnish Market Court. Firms are eager to take unlawful practices to the court. Both the European and Finnish legislators have seen these compliance problems and the new procurement legislation tries to make the procurement process easier and more flexible.

---

[1] Case No. C-491/01, The Queen v Secretary of State for Health, ex parte British American Tobacco (Investments) Ltd. and Imperial Tobacco Ltd. [2002] ECR ("British American Tobacco") at paragraph 122; see also cases cited therein.

[2] Christopher Bovis (2005). *Public Procurement in the European Union*. Palgrave MacMillan, GB, page 1.

System Description, Procurement Market

There are over 250 000 individual public authorities in the EU to spend around 14% of GDP on the purchase of services, works and supplies. Total annual value is nearly 2000 billion euro. In Finland, the total value of public tenders is about 35 billion euro per year. Purchasing volume under the directives is lower, about 400 billion euro per year and about 3.6 percent of the EU's GDP because of the threshold values. [1]

The volume of award notices is high in Europe reaching over 140 000 notices in 2010. In Finland, there are over 17 000 award notices per year. The number of notices is not rising rapidly as it did during the last decade.

The procurement market in Europe is vast in monetary terms, in terms of number and variety of different parties like public authorities and private firms, and in terms of variety of different goods, services or construction works.

This immediately creates a problem for the legislator and for procurement authorities. The same law must be applied to all tenders with some exceptions. In order to solve the problem, the legislator has made the law quite complex. The public author must in turn try to find the most advantageous solution when arranging a separate tender. The law itself does not say what option would be the best.

The large monetary value of procurement induces politicians and legislator to use public procurement as a strategic tool for different policies. Currently the rules emphasize policies aimed at creating a more innovative, green and socially inclusive economy, as well as those boosting jobs, growth and investment. However, the real effect of procurement on public policies depends heavily on the actual design of awards, competence of public authorities, market share of public authorities, and bidders desire to take part in tenders including strategic elements. Changing policy recommendations may create uncertainty within public authors and firms.

---

[1] http://www.eipa.eu/files/topics/public_procurement/cost_effectiveness_en.pdf.

Performance Analysis[①]

In European Union there is a Commission driven initiative to assess the effectiveness of the public procurement system in all member states.[②] One major task is to evaluate how different EU countries are performing on the public procurement process. That does not however describe directly how efficient the system is ensuring the best value for money in individual procurement awards or how procurement can be used as a policy instrument.

The success of the public procurement system is evaluated with nine indicators. The information assessing indicators comes from notices published in the Tenders Electronic Daily (TED) where all above threshold auctions are published. Performance indicators are expressed below. Commission experts have made the qualitative policy judgement on what is good or bad practice. The bold indicators picture the competitiveness of the procurement system. Indicators 7 to 9 indicate transparency. Indicators 4 to 6 indicate mainly the expertise of public authors in procurement.

Indicator	Good performance	Bad performance	
1. One Bidder Auction	≤10 %	> 20 %	competitiveness
2. No Calls for Bids	≤5 %	≥10 %	competitiveness
3. Publication Rate	> 5 %	< 2.5 %	competitiveness
4. Cooperative Procurement	≥10 %	< 10 %	expertise
5. Award Criteria in auctions, lowest price	< 80 %	≥80 %	expertise
6. Decision Speed	≤120 days	> 120 days	expertise
7. *Missing Values (Bad info)*	≤3 %	> 3 %	transparency
8. *Missing Calls for Bids (Bad info)*	≤3 %	> 3 %	transparency
9. *Missing Registration Numbers (Bad info)*	≤3 %	> 3 %	transparency

---

① http://ec.europa.eu/internal_market/scoreboard/performance_per_policy_area/public_procurement/index_en.htm.

② See more analysis on Anthony Flynn, (2018) "Measuring procurement performance in Europe", *Journal of Public Procurement*, Vol. 18, Issue: 1, pp. 2 – 13.

Explanation[①]:

One bidder auction (No. 1) means that there is only one offer delivered to the auction. This indicates that lively competition does not exist and best value for money is perhaps not achieved. The more bidders are participating the better results are expected.

No calls for bids (No. 2) means that procurement is done without prior notification. Only private negotiation between a public purchaser and a firm is carried out. In this case, there is no competition between bids or bidders and the best value for money is not guaranteed by competition.

The publication rate (No. 3) illustrates the monetary value of published auctions compared with Gross Domestic Product (GDP) where GDP is the denominator. The larger value means a larger share of published auctions in domestic economy, which is considered advantageous.

The cooperative procurement indicator (No. 4) tells how often public authors cooperate with each other when they engage in procurement. Cooperation may involve purchasing on behalf of other public author or joint procurement, or even using central purchasing body. Cooperation gives public authors the stronger market position and is thought to lead to lower prices and better value for money. Cooperation also gives an opportunity to exchange expertise for good procurement practices and for different markets.

Award criteria indicator (No. 5) tells how public buyers choose the companies they award the contract to. This indicator measures whether decision is based on the price alone, or if also the quality is taken into account. The over-reliance in price suggests better criteria could have been used.

Decision speed (No. 6) measures the mean length of the decision-making period. This is the time between the deadline for receiving offers and the award of the contract. Lengthy procedures are considered expensive and causing unnecessary uncertainty for both the public buyers and private companies.

Missing values (No. 7) illustrates transparency and tells that public buyers provide insufficient information on their procurement. The indicator measures the

---

[①] European Commission, DG GROW G4. TED CSV open data. Advanced notes on methodology. http://data.europa.eu/euodp/repository/ec/dg-grow/mapps/TED_advanced_notes.pdf.

proportion of contracts awarded without full information about the expected value. A lower "Missing Values" indicator score is better, as it means companies can make better bidding decisions and citizens know how their money is spent.

Missing calls for bids (No. 8) tells that public buyers provide insufficient information about their procurement. The indicator measures the proportion of contract awards for which a call for bids took place, but it is not evident what the name of the call was or what the conditions were. A lower "Missing Calls for Bids" indicator score is better, because it means businesses and citizens can understand how contractors have been selected.

Missing registration number (No. 9) tells that public buyers provide insufficient information about their procurement. The indicator measures the proportion of procedures where the business registration number was not included meaning that it is not easy to identify the buyer or the seller.

Procurement Risk—Material and Legal Risk

There is always a risk in public procurement. Risk can be separated at least into internal, commercial, and legal risks. Internal risk refers to the public author's ability to buy right commodities in right time. Commercial risk means the probability that the winner does not deliver the goods as promised. Legal risk means a threat that the procedure goes wrong and public author's procurement decision is overruled by the court. There may be even economic penalties on unlawful conduct. Legal risk in public procurement is perhaps more severe than in private procurement.

Law on public procurement is procedural in nature. It is not possible or reasonable to dictate what should be bought. Of course, the procedural nature of the law creates an administrative burden to the buyer and to the seller.[1] Another consequence is increased legal risk. The bidder treated in an illegal manner is entitled to compensation if there is a reason to believe that the bidder would have won the auction.

Legal risk has unfortunate effects on procurement practices. The public author

---

[1] See for example European Commission. Evaluation Report. Impact and Effectiveness of EU Public Procurement Legislation. SEC (2011) 853 final, Brussels, 27.11.2011, page 148.

may want to avoid risk. This is done for example by relying on conventional technology and on large established providers, or by arranging larger auctions. Risk may be avoided by cooperating with other public institutions. This may lead to market concentration on buyers' side but also on sellers' side.

Procurement law has changed a few times in Europe and in member states. The general aim of these changes has been a more flexible and simpler procurement procedure. Judicial safeguards for sellers are made stronger and strategic procurement is encouraged.

An open and straight forward bidding procedure is not ideal for buying complex services. It is considered for example troublesome to use auctions for buying services that include long and personal care relations in social and health care sectors. In addition, demanding building projects are not easy for procurement authorities. Problems emerge usually in the difficulty of drafting reasonably clear procurement documents.

Failed procurement process opens an opportunity for competitors to take the public author to the national court. Opportunity is usually open to firms that have participated in the auction and are treated unequally. Legal risks are additional risks above normal commercial risks.

In Finland, the procurement procedure fails most often in the phases of preparing procurement documents and selecting the winner. An invitation for a bid must be so exact that firms can make comparable offers. If the invitation is not exact, bids will not be comparable and the best offer is not found. Then the firms have an interest to take the decision to the court if they have lost the auction. If the court annuls the decision, a new auction has to be organized.

The most advantageous offer has to be chosen according to predetermined rules. When final bids are delivered, the public author cannot change the rules any more. In cases where the winner is chosen not only by the lowest price but also by the best quality, there is a high probability to make mistakes. In Finland, unclear selection criteria are a common ground to take the decision to the court.

For the competitors court proceedings give a possibility to get the deal or harm competitors. If the procurement decision goes to the court, it means delay and an additional cost. Public authors of course avoid court cases for example by using cautious procurement strategies that are however thought to have negative consequences to innovation.

Although the possibility to take procurement decision to court may cause additional costs to auctions, it is considered highly necessary both at EU and at the national level.

Summary

There is a lot of information on how procurement process works in Europe and in Member States. However, there is not a sound picture on what are the effects of procurement law compared with a state without mandatory legislation. So, one cannot without question be convinced that the law has only beneficial effects. The administrative cost and legal risk are identified and they are taken into account in legal reforms.

When one considers experience by now, it may be pointed out that procurement costs do not always allow cross border procurement where competitiveness is weaker anyhow. Furthermore, market reactions are not perhaps what expected since concentration has been noticed and prices can go up or down. In some fields of operations, procurement may hurt customers. Legal risk increases costs and has other negative effects in public procurement.

Country performance is analyzed by the Commission according to the success of the procedure. It does not tell how markets and prices are behaving neither what are the administrative costs. Assumption is that the more competitive and transparent procurement process is the better is the price and quality. Real changes in prices are harder to find out.

It is not easy to say if the awarded contract really is the best there is. The reason is imperfect information. One cannot for example compare the results of competitive bidding with the results of private negotiations. There is lack of imaginative surveys measuring the impact of procurement rules on economy in general and on specific markets. However, general understanding is that competitive bidding gives economic benefits.

欧洲和芬兰有关公共采购的法律和经验

克里斯蒂安·西卡维尔塔

【摘要】 本文介绍了欧洲公共采购系统的主要法律原则和结构。《欧洲采购指令》制定的目的是向位于欧盟不同成员国的公司提供参与整个欧洲公共采购的公平和公开的机会。欧盟成员国在《欧洲采购指令》的基础上制定了自己的公共采购法。欧洲委员会对各国在其国内公共采购法律和实践方面的表现进行评估。一般而言，评估是现代欧盟和国内立法的一个重要部分。本文对评估结果进行了分析。这一分析解释了欧盟一些成员国中的公共采购法的特征。在这些国家中，法律可能会给公共机构和公司带来额外的成本。本文主要讨论相关的欧盟和芬兰法律，但是在真实世界中，公共采购是一个全球性的现象。

第二部分
可持续与环境法治

The Environmental Constitutional Right in Finland: Achievements, Problems and Prospects

Jukka Viljanen[*]

[Abstract] Section 20 of the Finnish Constitution provides the provision of protecting environmental constitutional right, which entered into force in 1995. Despite of early references as a declaratory right the importance of the environmental constitutional provision is significant. The change in the constitutional interpretation is related to putting more weight on environmental issues and less on the question of right to property. In the legislative processes the constitutional environmental right has been providing a stimulus to improve environmental legislation. This positive trend is also apparent in the case-law of the Finnish courts with the famous case of Vuotos providing a turning point by the Finnish Supreme Administrative Court. Environmental rights considerations were taken into account in the major water energy building project. However, more is yet to be expected from the Finnish courts in relation to applying international human rights sources and especially the case-law of the European Court of Human Rights, which is related to environmental protection. There are many elements under the environmental rights which are not yet consistently applied in the domestic courts' reasoning.

1. Introduction

There has been an obvious need to have a comprehensive research for effects of

---

[*] Professor of Public Law, Faculty of Management and Business, Tampere University.

the Finnish constitutional environmental right during the period of over 20 years since the fundamental rights reform entered into force. This means that there was a need to evaluate how the new type of constitutional rights was implemented in practice and how it has influenced the legislative processes in environmental matters. The Ministry of Environment financed Environmental Constitutional Right project that was done by the University of Tampere Public Law Research Group. The project provided results in the form of both an academic article and a report for the Ministry. Heta Heiskanen and Siina Raskulla co-wrote the report with me[1]. In addition, we have published an article in the Finnish Environmental Law Review[2].

I will discuss in this article how constitutional environmental right has been developed in Finland, what are the major achievements, what have been the most serious problems and what kind of prospects we can see in the future.

As a part of the Finnish fundamental rights reform in 1995 (969/1995, entered into force 1.8.1995), the right to healthy environment (14a §) was introduced and it was later incorporated into the new Constitution (Act 731/1999) which entered into force 1 March 2000. The Section 20 was named as responsibility for the environment.[3]

Section 20 − Responsibility for the environment
Nature and its biodiversity, the environment and the national heritage are the responsibility of everyone.

---

[1] Jukka Viljanen, Heta Heiskanen, Siina Raskulla, Timo Koivurova & Leena Heinämäki: Miten ympäristöperusoikeus toteutuu? Ministry of Environment, 2014.

[2] Jukka Viljanen, Heta Heiskanen and Siina Raskulla: Ihmisoikeuksien yleiset opit ja suomalainen ympäristöoikeudellinen argumentaatio. Ympäristöjuridiikka (2016), 86 – 109.

[3] See more on environmental constitutional right in Finland e. g. Pekka *Vihervuori*: Oikeus ympäristöön (PL 20 §). In Pekka *Hallberg*, *Heikki Karapuu*, *Tuomas Ojanen*, *Martin Scheinin*, *Kaarlo Tuori* and *Veli-Pekka Viljanen* (eds.): Perusoikeudet. Helsinki 2011, 753 – 782; Tapio *Määttä*: Ympäristö eurooppalaisena ihmis-ja perusoikeutena: kohti ekososiaalista oikeusvaltiota. In Liisa *Nieminen* (ed.): Perusoikeudet EU: ssa. Helsinki 2001, ss. 263 – 326; Elina *Pirjatanniemi*: Vihertyvä rikosoikeus. Oikeus (2005): 34, 316 – 318; Veli-Pekka *Viljanen*: Perusoikeusjärjestelmä ja ympäristö. In *Veli-Matti Thuren* (ed.): Oikeus ja oikeudenmukaisuus: Oikeustieteen päivät 3.´– 4. 6. 1999 Joensuussa. Joensuu 1999, 91 – 101; Leena *Heinämäki*: Ihmisoikeudet ympäristönsuojelussa. In *Elina Pirjatanniemi*—*Timo Koivurova* (eds.): Ihmisoikeuksien käsikirja. Tallinna 2014, 528 – 554.

The public authorities shall endeavour to guarantee for everyone the right to a healthy environment and for everyone the possibility to influence the decisions that concern their own living environment.

The first paragraph includes a general responsibility clause towards nature and biodiversity. Primary dealing of environmental issues as administrative in their nature illustrates the strong role of the state as a both duty-bearer but also as a supervisor of environmental interests.

However, the responsibility for environment is placed not just on authorities but on everyone. This means that corporations and individuals are duty-holders in ensuring the environmental protection. This requires that necessary environmental legislation and criminal law have been enacted in such way that the responsibility is shared by those who produce environmental harm.

The specific duty of public authorities to protect the healthy environment concerns both direct and indirect actions of the state and local authorities. When the threshold of duration and severity of the environmental harm is attained, obligations may include duties to regulate, supervise and enforce acts of private actors. The Finnish fundamental rights reform was strongly influenced by the European case-law and other international treaty obligations, which will be discussed in other articles.

The second paragraph of the Section 20 should be understood as including constitutional commission to develop legislation that would expand people's possibility to influence decision-making concerning their living environment (Constitutional Law Committee Opinion PeVL 38/1998 vp, p. 2). Participatory rights in the Finnish environmental system include not just public hearings but also an obligation to distribute necessary information especially in relation to environmental permits, city planning and construction. The transparency of the environmental decision-making is also important in order to guarantee sufficient access to information.

The good practices in the field of participatory rights have been constructed on a premise that when individuals are capable of following the environmental decision-making process from the early stage by receiving information, and thus their rights related to participation are better ensured. These practices also increase the possibility to take an environmentally relevant action at the right time of the process rather than having the irretrievable harm to be taken place. Often the timing of the participatory action is crucial in achieving the sought outcome.

In the Finnish legal system there is no constitutional court which would have the highest authority to interpret the content of the constitutional provision and ensure that the legislation is in compliance with the constitutional provision. Every court is empowered to provide rulings relating to the interpretation of the constitutional provision and when the application of an Act would be in evident conflict with the Constitution, a court would give primacy to the provision of the Constitution (Section 106 of the Constitution). In Finland application of human rights in environmental litigation has concentrated mostly on the administrative courts and more specifically on certain fields of environmental issues such as environmental permits or environmental impact assessment.

The constitutional interpretation is guided by the prior scrutiny by the Constitutional Law Committee of the Finnish Parliament (perustuslakivaliokunta). The Committee supervises that the legislative proposals and other matters brought for its consideration are in compliance with the Constitution and international human rights obligations and gives the authoritative interpretation of the constitutional provisions (Section 74 of the Constitution). The Committee is comprised of members of the Parliament, but its reasoning is juridical rather than political. This is due to the fact that the Committee's opinions are heavily influenced by expert statements made by the constitutional scholars and other experts. The Committee's opinions and especially interpretation on the which legislative order should be applied are considered to be binding on other parliamentary committees. They have to make necessary modifications in order to avoid procedure for the constitutional enactment that requires higher majority (Section 73 of the Constitution).

Next this article illustrates how the constitutional environmental right has supported the development of the environmental legislation. After that the environmental right is discussed in light of the interpretation of the Constitutional Law Committee and the Finnish courts.

2. Comparative Research Describing Positive Effects of Constitutionalizing the Right to a Healthy Environment

Finland is not the only country that has introduced some kind of constitutionalizing of the right to a healthy environment. According to David R. Boyd there are 147 countries in which constitution provides environmental rights or/and responsibilities. [1] In his book "the Environmental Rights Revolution" David R. Boyd has strongly supported the side effects of the constitutionalizing the right to a healthy environment. His comparative research on the environmental rights revolution is listing several benefits of the constitutional right. [2] These include:

① provide a stimulus for stronger environmental legislation

② enhance implementation and enforcement of environmental laws and policies

③ create a level playing field with competing economic, social and cultural rights

④ offer a safety net, filling gaps in environmental legislation

⑤ compel progress in alleviating the unjust distribution of environmental harms

⑥ play educational role, need for environmental protection

⑦ increase accountability

⑧ protect laws from future rollbacks

⑨ encourage greater citizen participation in decisions and actions to protect environment

From the perspective of the Finnish constitutional law the recognition of content of the right to environment in the legislative work has been one of the clearest benefits that can be identified back to the constitutionalizing environmental right. This development has provided a counter force to strong reliance on the right to property, which was typical in the previous constitutional argumentation. In the Finnish legal discourse this is transparent in the change of limitation test applied in the context of the right to property (Section 15 of the Constitution). A similar limitation doctrine is applicable for every right. This test includes doctrines that are

---

[1] David R. Boyd, *The Environmental Rights Revolution, A Global Study of Constitutions, Human Rights, and the Environment* (UBC Press Vancouver-Toronto) 2012, pp. 51–52, 122.

[2] David R. Boyd, p. 122.

consistent with the European Court of Human Rights limitation clauses.

Most of other benefits in the Finnish legal system relate to the relationship between the legislation and the Constitution. The constitutional right provides a stimulus for stronger environmental legislation. The Environmental Protection Act (EPA) was reformed and new Act entered into force in 1 September 2014. The participatory rights are provided under EPA or the general provisions of the Administrative Procedure Act (APA, 6.6.2003/434). The Administrative Procedure Act includes both obligation for authorities to make clarifications and also the obligation to organize hearings. Especially Section 41 of APA refers to the obligation that possibility to influence has to be reserved in those issues where decision has a significant impact on a living environment, work or other circumstances. Also the Environmental Protection Act includes provisions both distributing information to the public and organizing public hearings.

The Constitutional provision is also protecting environmental laws from rollbacks under future governments. In addition, while in the early decisions the Constitutional Law Committee described the right as declaratory and focused on its divergence compared to other constitutional rights, the Committee's cumulative practice gives a more comprehensive picture of the provision and its influence on the legislation.

I want to highlight that there is a consensus that Section 20 is not only declaratory in nature, but it can be used as an interpretive guide both at the legislative process and by courts while they apply laws in practice.

The constitutionalizing the environmental right has placed an added weight on environmental issues in the balancing of different competing rights, especially with right to property. The Committee has reiterated that because the right to property and right to healthy environment are part of the same fundamental rights catalogue, both of these rights can have influence on each other's interpretation in situations where the new legislation is intended e.g. to achieve sustainable balance between individuals and nature (Constitutional Law Committee Opinion PeVL 20/2010 vp).

The Constitutional Law Committee has found that Section 20 is applicable and relevant e.g. in assessing restrictions on fishing (PeVL 14/2010 vp), restrictions on certain type fishing methods (PeVL 20/2010 vp), safeguarding architectural heritage (PeVL 6/2010 vp), mining industry (PeVL 32/2010 vp), control of drinking water (PeVL 44/2010 vp), export and import of cultural property (PeVL 47/1998 vp), extraction of soil (PeVL 2/1997 vp) and private forestry (PeVL 22/1996 vp).

One of the concrete examples of the constitutional provision's influence is related to the protection of endangered species (PeVL 20/2010 vp). The Constitutional Law Committee criticized the high threshold for using restrictions. The ban of certain catching methods cannot be introduced even if this is required in order to preserve the endangered species in the particular region. The initial wording implied that restrictions could be enacted just in the stage that the relevant species is almost extinct.

This environmentally rights-oriented opinion of the Constitutional Law Committee was taken into account by the Parliament and the initial provision was reformulated in order to lower the threshold for protective measures. The prohibition of certain types of traps could be instigated also when the measures were necessary in order to preserve the species. This modification was significant especially in order to provide necessary protection for Saimaa ringed seal, which was endangered due to certain types of fishing traps.

3. The Role of the Constitutional Environmental Right in the Finnish Jurisprudence

The sporadic appearance of environmental constitutional right in the case-law is typical to the environmental case-law. The Supreme Administrative Court has taken a very cautious approach in order to apply the right. The constitutional argumentation is normally applied in cases where there is a some kind of a lacuna on the law or it is a hard case that needs more argumentation than in uncomplicated cases.

One of the first transparent environmental rights cases was the landmark Vuotos judgment (KHO 2002: 86). The environmental permit was sought to include a huge artificial water area that would extend to 242 square kilometers and would include a water power plant. Thus, the case concerned nationally important energy project with major environmental impacts in the northern part of Finland. The Supreme Administrative Court confirmed the rejection of environmental permit for building the Vuotos reservoir and interpreted the legislation in a human rights friendly way.

The rejection of the permit to build the Vuotos reservoir illustrates the transformation of interpretation of the Water Act. Even though the interpretation according to the water legislation included balancing of interests but it used to be dominated by the interests of the energy industry whereas the environmental values were subsidiary to those of building water energy. During the process the power company Kemijoki made a strong argument based on previous case-law trying to diminish the interpretative value of the constitutional right to environment. However, they failed to convince the Supreme Administrative Court. The Court clearly distinguished the Vuotos case from its previous approach to Water Act cases. The Court confirmed that the right to environment provides a statement on the value of the nature and guides application and interpretation of the law.

It could be analysed that one of the key premises to allow a departure from earlier continuum of water building was that Section 20 of the Constitution was enacted in 1995 (entered into force 1.8.1995, 14 a §, incorporated to the Finnish Constitution 1.3.2000, 20 §) and it should be taken into account while interpreting Water Act provisions.

Overall, the rejection of the Vuotos reservoir was a major turning point in the Water Act interpretation and in the Finnish environmental law in general. While traditionally the environment used to provide justification for restricting the property rights only in very limited circumstances, the Vuotos case illustrates that the balancing is made in a similar way as is done with other conflicting fundamental rights.

The right to effective remedy has been one of the issues where the Finnish courts have relied on the right to environment. In the Hunting Act case (KHO 2004: 76) the Supreme Administrative Court relied heavily on the Section 20.2 as a critical part of its argumentation. The problem has been that conservation of birds was considered under the Hunting Act rather than a legislation that would follow the logic of environmental legislation.

The Supreme Administrative Court reiterated that in the first instance the Constitution is fulfilled by enacting legislation, but the provision of the Constitution can also have influence on the interpretation of flexible legal norms. The right to appeal in the context of hunting legislation was therefore widened to include also the similar type of associations that had the right to appeal in accordance of the Nature Conservation Act. Thus, the local ornithological association was granted a right to appeal.

An analogous judgment of applying right to environment in order to promote the right to appeal can be found in the case allowing hunting of wolves (KHO 2007: 74). The Supreme Administrative Court founded its widened interpretation on the right to appeal to the Section 20.2 of the Constitution together with references to the logic of the Nature Conservation Act. Therefore the Supreme Administrative Court considered that two regional nature conservation associations had a right to appeal on the decision of hunting authorities providing an exception to the preservation of wolves.

4. International Human Rights Obligations Concerning Environmental Protection in the Finnish Law

The relationship between international human rights obligations and how they are contributing to Finnish environmental rights will be dealt in an article by Heta Heiskanen[①]. I want to shortly point out that it is clearly stated in the preparatory work and subsequent practice that Section 20 should be considered in light of other constitutional rights and environmentally relevant international human rights obligations. Thus, the connection to international human rights system is inherent to the environmental constitutional right.

On the right-holder side even the future generations are mentioned as one of the right-holders/subjects in the preparatory texts of the Constitution. It is also mentioned that there are such specific values that are not only considered to be rights for individuals. It is inherent to the concept of environmental protection that certain values come out of the intrinsic value of nature.

Thus, The Finnish environmental constitutional right is incorporating similar concepts that can be found in the principle 3 of the Rio Declaration on Environment and Development (1992) in relation to inclusion of future generations into the scope of protection (Government proposal, HE 309/1993

---

① See Article "International Human Rights Obligations Contributing to Finnish Environmental Rights" by Heiskanen in this book.

vp, p. 66).

The Finnish practice confirms findings emphasizing the importance of dialogue between different legal orders on environmental issues. The trend to make fairly few references to the international case-law could be related to the fact that there have not been any clear environmentally relevant judgments among the Finnish cases before the Strasbourg Court.

It would be relatively easy to introduce more references to the European Court of Human Rights in the future. This requires of course also that the applicants acknowledge in their submissions the relevant case-law and requires that the courts also take these judgments seriously.

5. Concluding Remarks

The development of the Finnish legal culture cannot be described as Boyd's "environmental rights revolution". However, both the case-law and constitutional practice are however implying that in the Finnish legal culture environmental protection has established a prominent position both at the legislative and judicial proceedings. It is reasonable to state that the list of benefits presented by David R. Boyd is also relevant in evaluating the impacts of the process of constitutionalizing environmental right in Finland. The high quality of the Finnish environmental legislation does not make the constitutional provision as redundant.

Instead, the constitutional environmental provision and high-quality substantive environmental legislation could be seen as complementing each other. The constitutional provision gives weight to the environmental argumentation both at the drafting of new environmental legislation and applying legislation in force in accordance with human rights friendly interpretation.

The role of the Section 20 has been significant especially, during the legislative process, introducing new measures and mechanisms to environmental protection system. Like David R. Boyd has identified there are positive effects as the constitutionalizing the right to a healthy environment can provide a stimulus for stronger environmental legislation. In the Finnish context the right to environment has removed the imbalance building into the Finnish constitutional rights system.

However, there are absorbing potentials in Section 20 which are not yet fully utilized. There is a manifest failure to incorporate relevant international case-law to national jurisprudence in environmental cases.

Section 20 itself has been used relatively rarely in environmental cases, even though some cases can be identified especially from the recent years. The Supreme Administrative Court is cautious on using the human rights argumentation, if the ordinary environmental legislation provides a sufficient basis for its legal reasoning. The courts have taken cautiously positive approach to the role of environmental NGOs in the environmental litigation.

Finally, the protection of participatory rights can be enhanced with new technical devices and applications that collect data from internet. Some cities have also promoted public participation with introducing regional working groups. These good practices allow individuals access to information in early phases of the decision-making process in matters related to environment.①

芬兰的环境宪法权利：成就、问题和前景

朱卡·维尔雅宁

【摘要】1995 年生效的芬兰宪法第 20 条规定了环境宪法权利。尽管在早期被认为是一项宣告性权利，有关环境宪法权利的规定仍然具有非常重要的意义。在宪法解释方面的主要变化就是更强调环境问题，而弱化非财产权的重要性。在立法过程中，环境宪法权利促进了环境立法的改善。这一积极的发展趋势明显地反映在芬兰法院的判例法中：芬兰最高行政法院

---

① See the Finnish good practices mentioned in the report of the UN Independent Expert John H. Knox. Report of the Independent Expert on the issue of human rights obligations relating to the enjoyment of a safe, clean, healthy and sustainable environment, 3 February 2015, A/HRC/28/61, para 45. "In 2009, the Government of Finland implemented the Action Programme on eServices and eDemocracy, which was designed to develop new tools for citizen participation in land-use planning. One aspect of the programme is Harava, an interactive map-based application used by local governments to collect feedback from citizens, including by marking on an online map where they believe a new protected area should be located. Another programme, called Alvari, has been adopted at the subnational level in Finland by the city of Tampere. It created public advisory groups that have participated in more than 350 planning-related decisions since 2007."

在沃托斯（Vuotos）案中的判决是这方面的一个转折点。在重大水力发电建设项目的规划过程中必须考虑环境权利，但是芬兰法院在适用有关环境保护的国际人权法律渊源，特别是欧洲人权法院的案例法方面还需进一步努力。环境权利的许多要素尚未在国内法院的推理中得到一致的适用。

Promoting Sustainable Choices in Business: the Role of Emission Information[*]

Emilie Yliheljo[**] and Ellen Eftestøl-Wilhelmsson[***]

【Abstract】 Transport is one of the worst polluters of the modern world. What is more, the global trade in goods is expected to double in volume (measured in value) between 2013 and 2030. Transport is responsible for 23 percent of the greenhouse gas (GHG) emissions in the European Union (EU), making it the second biggest emissions sector after the energy sector, industry being the third. Moreover, despite different EU transport policies and action plans on greening transport, the transport sector has failed to show the same decline in emissions as other sectors. In fact, whereas transport accounted for 15 percent of emissions in 1990, by 2016 that figure had risen to 27 percent. This paper discusses how emissions from transport can be mitigated by utilizing the information on emissions from transport in different ways.

1. Introduction

Transport is one of the worst polluters of the modern world. Moreover, a two-fold increase in the volume of global trade in goods (measured in value) is

---

[*] The article is based on ongoing research by the INTERTRAN research group, which is part of Helsinki Institute of Sustainable Science, HELSUS, as well as on the authors' individual contributions in the forthcoming Ellen Eftestøl-Wilhelmsson, Suvi Sankari and Anu Bask, eds., *Sustainable and Efficient Transport: Incentives for Promoting a Green Transport Market* (Cheltenham, UK: Edward Elgar Publishing, 2019).

[**] Doctoral Candidate, LLM, University of Helsinki.

[***] Professor Dr. Juris, Universities of Helsinki and Oslo.

expected between 2013 and 2030.① Transport currently accounts for 23 percent of greenhouse gas (GHG) emissions in the European Union (EU), making it second biggest emissions sector after the energy sector, placing it ahead of industry.② Moreover, different EU transport policies and action plans on greening transport have failed to trigger the same decline in emissions as other sectors. Indeed, whereas transport accounted for 15 percent of emissions in 1990, by 2016 that figure had risen to 27 percent.③ This paper discusses the role of information in different policy instruments and how emissions from transport can be mitigated by utilizing the information on emissions from transport in new ways. The paper's aim is to explore how the EU currently uses information in its climate policies regarding transport and to analyse the further potential for using information as a steering mechanism in contractual business to business (B2B) relationships.

The paper begins by outlining the role of transport in the EU's (climate) policies and the potential for information to act as a steering mechanism for achieving GHG emission reductions and behavioural change. Next the paper discusses various EU strategies for mitigating transport emissions, such as the EU Emission Trading Scheme (ETS), currently applicable to aviation, EU policies to reduce GHG emissions from shipping and policy instruments adopted pursuant to Effort Sharing between member states regarding road transport.④ Common to many of the strategies adopted for the sector is their reliance on information as a key

---

① For example, estimated in Pricewaterhouse Coopers' *Global Economy Watch*, October 2014 <c> (Accessed 14.1.2019).

② Communication from the Commission to the European Parliament, the Council, the European Economic and Social Committee and the Committee of the Regions "A European Strategy for Low-Emission Mobility", COM (2016) 501 final, ANNEX I: Historical developments in transport activity, energy use and emissions, at 89–90.

③ https://www.eea.europa.eu/data-and-maps/indicators/transport-emissions-of-greenhouse-gases/transport-emissions-of-greenhouse-gases-11 (Accessed 11.1.2019).

④ Regulation (EU) 2018/842 of the European Parliament and of the Council of 30 May 2018 on binding annual greenhouse gas emission reductions by Member States from 2021 to 2030 contributing to climate action to meet commitments under the Paris Agreement and amending Regulation (EU) No. 525/2013.

factor for emission reduction, as green technology and digital solutions alone are insufficient to achieve reductions. Thus, the ability of transport-emissions information to trigger behavioural change in the industry, and the way this change can be achieved, are discussed in relation to the theory of nudging.

The EU already relies on information as an instrument to promote sustainable behaviour in the transport sector. By measuring the emissions from transport, those emissions are capped, traded or used for marketing purposes. Although measuring (emissions) as such will positively influence environmental behaviour in the transport industry, we argue that the potential for emissions information to act as a driver for behavioural change in the sector through its utilization in the B2B context remains unexploited. Ideas for how this can be achieved are provided before conclusions beingdrawn.

2. EU Climate and Transport Policy

In November 2018, the Commission of the European Union published its ambitious *A European Strategic Long-Term Vision for a Prosperous, Modern, Competitive and Climate Neutral Economy*. [1] Also known as the 2050 Long-Term Strategy, it increases the 2050 emission reduction targets adopted in 2009 in the *Road-map for moving to a competitive low carbon economy in 2050*. [2] The new strategic vision of the European Union is to achieve a net-zero GHG economy by 2050. [3] The long-term targets are to be implemented through packages of legislation with intermediate emission reductions targets, measures and instruments to achieve these intermediate targets. Thus, the 2020 Energy and Climate Package adopted in 2009 sets out measures and targets to be met by 2020, and the 2030 Climate and Energy Framework contains targets for 2030, which are currently being worked into

---

[1] Commission, "A Clean Planet for All: A European Strategic Long-Term Vision for a Prosperous, Modern, Competitive and Climate Neutral Economy" (Communication) COM (2018) 773 final.

[2] Commission, "A Road-map for Moving to a Competitive Low Carbon Economy in 2050" (Communication) COM (2011) 112 Final. The target adopted in 2050 was to achieve an 80 percent emission reduction compared to 1990 – levels, see the aforesaid Road-map, p. 3.

[3] COM (2018) 773 Final, p. 3.

binding legislation following the same model as the 2020 Package.① The 2020 Climate and Energy Package and the 2030 Climate and Energy Framework are based on three overarching but distinctive targets to be met by the Union and/or individual member states: (i) a GHG emission reduction target, (ii) a renewable energy target and (iii) an energy efficiency target.②

The emission reduction target is a combination of two targets: The first is a union-wide emission-reduction target for the European Emissions Trading Scheme (EU ETS), which covers energy production, energy intensive industry and civil aviation within the EU.③ The second target is a combination of different national emission-reduction targets for sectors within the scope of Effort Sharing.④ The Effort Sharing Decision covers all emission sources falling outside the scope of the EU ETS, including industrial processes, agriculture and the waste sector.⑤ The transport sector (with the exception of aviation) is hence within the scope of the Effort Sharing Decision, and emissions from transport are calculated towards the member states' emission-reduction target.

In addition to forming part of the Union's economy-wide emission-reduction target, the transport sector has a distinctive union-wide target of its own. The 2011 White Paper on a Roadmap to a Single European Transport Area sets a 60 percent

---

① At the date of writing this paper, the revisions to the Emissions Trading Directive and the new Effort Sharing Regulation, which are more discussed in detail below, have been adopted. Moreover, a political agreement on the Energy Efficiency and Renewable Energy Directive has been reached, but the adoption of binding acts is still pending.

② The emission reduction target is transposed into the Emissions Trading Directive and Effort Sharing Decision, the renewable energy target into the Renewable Energy Directive and the energy efficiency into the Energy Efficiency Directive.

③ Directive 2003/87/EC of the European Parliament and of the Council of 13 October 2003 establishing a scheme for greenhouse gas emission allowance trading within the Community and amending Council Directive 96/61/EC OJ L 275/2003, consolidated version (the *Emissions Trading Directive*), annex 1.

④ Decision No. 406/2009/EC of the European Parliament and of the Council of 23 April 2009 on the effort of Member States to reduce their greenhouse gas emissions to meet the Community's greenhouse gas emission reduction commitments up to 2020 OJL 140/136.

⑤ In other words, the Effort Sharing Decision covers energy from fuel combustion and fugitive emissions from fuels, which are outside the scope of the EU ETS.

emission-reduction target for transport and a 40 percent target for shipping (compared to 1990 levels) by 2050. [1]

To reach these emission-reduction targets, both the EU and its member states have implemented a variety of policy instruments. For transport, the aim of these policies and measures is to reduce the carbon intensity of transport fuels, improve the energy efficiency of vehicles and influence the way individuals and companies use transport. [2] Nevertheless, the results have remained unsatisfactory despite the efforts undertaken. GHG emissions from transport are not decreasing; on the contrary, emissions from road transport, for instance, have increased in recent years. [3] Additional measures are thus called for, and the EU has been actively pushing for new policy instruments for the transport sector, calling for a system-based approach to decarbonising the transport sector. [4]

3. Information as a Steering Mechanism and the Theory of Nudging

Information as a Steering Mechanism

Reducing GHG emissions from all sectors of society requires policy action on multiple political and societal levels. Moreover, it raises questions of the optimal choice of policy instruments to achieve emission-reduction targets. [5] This choice involves selecting the most appropriate tools from a toolkit. From a theoretical

---

[1] Commission, "Roadmap to a Single European Transport Area—Towards a Competitive and Resource Efficient Transport System" (White Paper) COM (2011) 144 final, paras. 6 and 29.

[2] Ian Skinner, "The Mitigation of Transport's CO_2 Emissions in the EU: Policy Successes and Challenges" in Van Calster, G et al., eds., *Research Handbook on Climate Mitigation Law* (Cheltenham, UK: Edward Elgar, 2014), p. 104.

[3] European Environmental Agency, "Analysis of Key Trends and Drivers in Greenhouse Gas Emissions in the EU Between 1990 and 2015" (EEA Report No. 8/2017) < https://www.eea.europa.eu/publications/analysis-of-key-trends-ghg > accessed 7 December 2018, pp. 13 and 20.

[4] COM (2018) 773 final, p. 10.

[5] See e.g. David Benson and Andrew Jordan, "Climate Policy Instrument Choices" in Daniel A. Farber and Maarjan Peeters, eds., *Climate Change Law* (Elgar Encyclopedia of Environmental Law, Cheltenham, UK: Edward Elgar, 2016), p. 57.

perspective, information has long been recognized as a steering instrument.[1] Informational regulation is generally among the least interventionist, either prohibiting the provision of false or misleading information or requiring disclosure of specific information to, for instance, the public or specific government officials.[2] Production and disclosure of information can lead to better decision-making, increase transparency and accountability as well as trigger social, political and market responses that eventually produce better environmental outcomes.[3] The information allows market participants, such as consumers, investors or officials, to make informed decisions about the acceptability of a product or services in terms of, for example, their carbon footprint.[4] Information on emissions has an undeniable impact on the choices of market actors. For example, studies show that companies which measure and report their carbon footprints can reduce their emissions by 10% −15%.[5] Information asymmetries between market actors alone are thought to be one of the main market barriers to improvements in energy

---

[1] The classification and typology of policy instruments varies to some extent between scholars. For instance, according to Kokko, one way of classifying the steering instruments of environmental regulation is to divide them into three main categories: (1) informational steering (such as certificates), (2) economic steering (such as taxes or emissions trading), and (3) legal steering and other steering (such as environmental permits or prohibitions). See Kai Kokko, *Ympäristöoikeuden perusteet: Yleiset opit, sääntely ja ratkaisun teoria* (Helsinki, Finland: Edita Publishing, 2017), pp. 256 – 262. Baldwin et al. divide the regulatory strategies or techniques available to (governmental) regulators into categories based on (1) command-and-control, (2) incentive based regimes (such as taxes), (3) market harnessing controls (including emissions trading), (4) disclosure regulation (supply of information) and finally (5) direction action and design solutions undertaken by the state. See Robert Baldwin, Martin Cave and Martin Lodge, *Understanding Regulation: Theory, Strategy, and Practice* (2nd ed. Oxford, New York: Oxford University Press, 2012), pp. 105 – 136.

[2] Baldwin et al., 2012, p. 119.

[3] Bradley C. Karkkainen, "Information as Environmental Regulation", in Leroy Paddock, Robert Glicksman and Nicholas Bryner, eds., *Decision making in environmental law* (Elgar Encyclopedia of Environmental Law Vol. II, Chelthenham, UK: Edward Elgar 2016), p. 199.

[4] Baldwin et al., 2012, p. 119.

[5] SWD (016) 244 final. Commission Staff working document accompanying the white paper: A European Strategy for Low-Emission Mobility COM (2016) 501 final at p. 125. The study referred to in the working document was performed by Dutch "Lean & Green".

efficiency.① For instance, in the shipping industry, where the potential for cost-efficient energy-efficiency improvements has been identified, the realization of this potential would require not only additional incentives and prevention of market failures, such as the lack of financing for technological improvements, but also information on such factors as vessels' fuel consumption (and thus indirectly on GHG emissions).② Indeed, studies demonstrate that the lack of reliable information on GHG emissions per vessel has prevented the integration of energy efficiency concerns into transactions involving vessels between owners and vessel users (ship operators, charters etc.), and consequently ship owners have lacked incentives to invest in energy efficiency improvements.③

While regulatory strategies based on information and disclosure have the potential to generate cost-effective GHG emission reductions, especially when combined with more stringent and coercive command-and-control measures, there are limits to what these strategies can achieve, and the information must meet certain requirements. According to Baldwin et al., one such limitation, due to various factors, is the potentially high cost of producing information.④ This is a problem, for instance, in the road transport sector, which consists of a large number of vehicles, i.e. small emission sources. Accurate monitoring of emissions at a vehicle level has thus been expensive and administratively burdensome to manage and verify, thereby preventing the inclusion of the sector in the emissions trading scheme.⑤ Informational policy instruments are also prone to the risk of false or misleading information being provided to the market, and some level of policing of information is therefore required. Moreover, in some cases, the risk or damage

---

① Alex Bowen and Sam Fankhauser, "Good practice in low-carbon policy", in Alina Averchenkova, Samuel Fankhauser and Michal Nachmany, eds., *Trends in Climate Change Legislation* (Cheltenham, UK Edward Elgar, 2017), p. 131.

② Commission, "Integrating Maritime Transport Emissions in the EU's Greenhouse Gas Reduction Policies" (Communication) COM (2013) 479 final, section 1.

③ Maddox Consulting, "Analysis of market barriers to cost effective GHG emission reductions in the maritime sector" (Brussels, Belgium: European Commission, 2012), p. 65.

④ Baldwin et al., 2012, p. 120.

⑤ Commission, Accompanying document to the Proposal for a Directive of the European Parliament and of the Council amending Directive 2003/87/EC so as to improve and extend the EU greenhouse gas emission allowance trading system—Impact Assessment (Commission Staff Working Document) SEC (2007) final 52, section 3.3.

caused by a product or activity might simply be so severe that informational steering alone is insufficient and more coercive regulation is therefore required to complement it. [1]

From the perspective of the efficacy of regulation, of central importance is the way information is received by and impacts market participants. Disclosure might require, for instance, some standard setting by regulators to promote disclosure in a format that is informative and supports decision-making. Challenges might also exist in relation to the characteristics of the users or recipients of information and to mistakes made by the aforementioned in their use of the information or failures in understanding its implications. There is also a risk that users will not respond to the information as anticipated by the regulator, for example by continuing to choose products based solely on their price rather than their environmental impact. In such cases, attending to informational asymmetries in relation to the availability of information is insufficient. [2] The next section therefore explores how behavioural insights can be applied to mitigate some of these risks and increase the effect of informational steering.

The Theory of Nudging

The use of behavioural insights to tackle environmental problems has interested academic scholars, [3] international organisations and decision-makers alike for some time. The EU, the Nordic Council of Ministers (Nordic Council) and the Organisation for Economic Co-operation and Development (OECD) have recently published reports on the use of behavioural science to promote environmental change. Why international organisations and decision-makers are interested in this is reflected in the title of the 2017 OECD report *Tackling Environmental Problems with the*

---

[1] Baldwin et al., 2012, p. 120.

[2] Baldwin et al., 2012, p. 120. For a more in-depth discussion on consumer response to information see e.g. Suvi Sankari, "Product Information on Freight Emissions For Consumers—Changing the Market Towards Sustainability", in the forthcoming Ellen Eftestøl-Wilhelmsson, Suvi Sankari and Anu Bask, eds., *Sustainable and Efficient Transport: Incentives for Promoting a Green Transport Market* (Cheltenham, UK: Edward Elgar Publishing, 2019).

[3] An overview is provided by Matthias Lehner, Oksana Mont and Eva Heiskanen, "Nudging—A promising tool for sustainable consumption behaviour?" (2016) 134 Journal of Cleaner Production 166 in their literature review on research on nudging as a tool for sustainable consumption behaviour.

Help of Behavioural Insights. [1] With the growing challenges of climate change, all available tools for reaching the common goals on emission reduction must be considered. The OECD addresses a variety of questions related to how behavioural insights can help overcome environmental problems. The idea of so-called *homo economicus*, who is fully informed makes rational choices, is challenged by an understanding of the fact that people are not always rational. Individual decision-making is often based on framing and reference points, altruism and heuristic methods. [2] In fact, individuals often fail to make deliberate choices at all, relying instead on shortcuts and habits. [3] In the economic literature, this is characterised as deviations from rational decision-making, and hence labelled *behavioural biases* or *limitations*. These insights often termed *behavioural insights*, are based on a multitude of studies on human behaviour from different disciplines, including psychology, economics, sociology and neuroscience. [4]

One such behavioural insight is that people can be *nudged* towards certain behaviour without depriving them of free choice. In other words, it is possible to influence the way people behave without forcing them to behave in certain way. It was in this context that the behavioural economist Richard Thaler and legal scholar Cass Sunstein coined the term "nudging" in their 2008 book *Nudge. Improving decisions about health, wealth and happiness.* [5] Thaler and Sunstein define nudges as any aspect of the decision environment "that alters people's behaviour in a predictable way without forbidding any options or significantly changing their economic incentives". [6] In other words, the idea is that by implementing various small changes, people's decisions can be affected and redirected in the right way. The interesting part is that a behavioural change is made while freedom of choice is

---

[1] Elisabetta Cornago, Alexandros Dimitropoulos, Walid Ouselati and Shardul Agrawala, *Tackling Environmental Problems with the Help of Behavioural Insights* (OECD Publishing 2017, Paris).
[2] Ibid. at p. 23.
[3] Lehner et al., 2016, at p. 1.
[4] Joana Sousa Lourenco, Emanuele Ciriolo, Sara Rafael Rodrigues Vieira de Almeida, Xavier Troussard: *Behavioural Insights Applied to Policy*—European Report 2016. (Publications Office of the European Union, 2016) p. 9.
[5] Richard H. Thaler and Cass R. Sunstein, *Nudge, Improving decisions about health, wealth and happiness* (Yale University Press 2009).
[6] Ibid. at p. 8.

retained by the person taking the decision. According to Thaler and Sunstein, there are several ways to present a choice to the decision-maker, and in many cases the final decision depends on how that choice is presented.[1] From this perspective, policy makers are seen as *choice-architects* who facilitate the way people make choices. As a policy-tool, Nudging is hence also described as "choice architecture". Another way of describing the phenomena is to use the less attractive term manipulating. However, as a form of libertarian paternalism, where people are steered in directions that will promote their own welfare and common good, nudging is considered both possible and legitimate means for private and public institutions to affect behaviour while also respecting freedom of choice.[2]

Nudges are particularly interesting in relation to the EU's policy on sustainable transport, as it rests on the notion of freedom of choice. So when, on one hand, a behavioural change is desired, but on the other hand, freedom of choice should be protected[3]—and business as usual is not considered an option[4]—the EU must be creative and seek new means of reaching its stated policy goals. In our case, these are radical goals on major reductions of emissions from transport. In this context, nudging is a fascinating policy tool that should be recognised and integrated in the legislative process to a larger degree than has so far been the case. Indeed, nudges have mainly been studied in relation to so-called business-to-consumer, or B2C, relationships.[5] However, firms also can be subject to nudges.[6] Firms are not

---

[1] Eric J. Johnson, Suzanne B. Shu, Benedict G. C. Dellaert, Craig Fox, Daniel G. Goldstein, Gerald Häubl, Richard P. Larrick, John W. Payne, Ellen Peters, David Schkade, Brian Wansink, Elke U. Weber, "Beyond nudges: Tools of choice architecture" (2012) Marketing Letters, Volume 23 Issue, 2012, pp. 487 – 504.

[2] Lehner et al., 2016, pp. 174 – 175.

[3] COM (2011) 144 final at 48 (p. 13).

[4] Ibid. at 13 (p. 4).

[5] See e.g. Hans-W. Micklitz, Lucia A Reisch and Kornelia Hagen, "An Introduction to the Special Issue on 'Behavioural Economics, Consumer Policy, and Consumer Law'" (2011) 34 (3) J Consum Policy 271.

[6] Armstrong, Mark and Huck, Steffen, "Behavioral Economics as Applied to Firms: A Primer" (2010) No. 2937 CESifo Working Paper Series.

theoretical entities or "black boxes".[1] Rather, human beings, individual managers, boards or employees make corporate decisions. Hence, decision-making in firms can also be biased. In other words, decisions in firms are not strictly rational. [2] Accordingly, corporate decision-making can also be nudged with the right incentives. Despite sometimes failing—due to the "human factor"—to guarantee the desired behaviour, information clearly has an impact on people's behaviour, as discussed in Section 3.1. In other words, information is a powerful tool in the struggle for a behavioural shift in the transport industry and is hence an essential part of the nudging "package". [3] When presented in an optimal manner, *information* is considered as a "promising tool to increase pro-environmental choices". [4] However, information will only have a strong effect when presented in an accessible manner. It is hence essential to consider both the *kind of information* required and the way this information is presented to market actors. [5]

Neither information production or collection nor information disclosure requirements exist exclusively for the purposes of information steering. Other steering instruments, such as pollution permits or emissions trading, also rely on information. [6] In the case of the European Emissions Trading Scheme, the policy instrument is generally categorised as a market-based steering mechanism which contains elements of an administrative steering mechanism; [7] however, as will be further discussed in Section 4 below, the environmental integrity of the instrument relies on accurate data on GHG emission from various sources. This information, collected for compliance purposes, has affected decision-making by market actors. A carbon price, generated, for instance, by emissions trading, provides information on

---

[1] Andreas Heinmann, "Behavioral Antitrust A 'More Realistic Approach' to Competition Law", in Klaus Mathis (ed.), *European Perspectives on Behavioural Law and Economics* (Economic analysis of law in European legal scholarship Vol. 2. Springer International Publishing 2015) p. 214.
[2] Ibid. at p. 212.
[3] Folke Ölander and John Thøgersen, "Informing Versus Nudging in Environmental Policy" (2014) 37 (3) J Consum Policy 341, p. 354.
[4] Anne S. E. Nielsen, Henrik Sand and Pernille Sørensen, "Nudging and pro-environmental behaviour" (TemaNord, Nordic Council of Ministers, 2017).
[5] Ölander and Thøgersen, 2014, p. 354.
[6] Karkkainen, 2016, p. 200.
[7] Kokko, 2017, pp. 259–260.

the negative impacts of activities and is thought to incentivise behavioural change in relation to investments, production and consumption patterns and to promote technological development.[1] Conversely, case studies in the financial sector have shown that carbon pricing has a de-incentivizing effect on financial support for high-emitting industries and projects already based on the information provided on emissions. For example, emissions trading thus affects the non-economic aspects of decision-making through the perceived reputational risks of being associated with high-emitting clients.[2] One of our central questions therefore concerns the collection methods and type of information acquired under these other policy instruments and the way that information can be optimally used to promote the desired behavioural change.

4. Current Use of Emission Information in the EU's Transport Policies

The EU Emission Trading Scheme—Information on GHG Emissions from Civil Aviation within the EU

As noted in Section 2, intra-EU civil aviation falls within the scope of the EU Emissions Trading Scheme (EU ETS). In the EU ETS, emissions from the trading sectors are capped at set emission reduction levels, and a corresponding number of pollution rights (referred to as emission allowances in the EU ETS) are created and allocated to the market. By creating transferable pollution rights, optimal allocation of those rights is expected to occur through the market, meaning that they are acquired by those individuals who value them the most and that abatement occurs where the marginal costs are lowest. Consequently, the right to pollute is priced and becomes a production factor, like fuel or raw material, and the negative externalities of pollution, such as climate change caused by GHG

---

[1] High-Level Commission on Carbon Prices, "Report of the High-level Commission on Carbon Prices" (Washington, D. C., World Bank, 2017) < https://static1.squarespace.com/static/54ff9c5ce4b0 a53deccfb4c/t/59b7f2409f8dce5316811916/1505227332748/CarbonPricing _ FullReport. pdf > accessed 21 April 2018, Section 3.3.

[2] Megan Bowman, *Banking on Climate Change: How Finance Actors and Transnational Regulatory Regimes are Responding* (International Banking and Finance Law Series, Kluwer Law International, 2015), p. 187.

emissions, are internalised in the production costs. [1] The purpose of the EU ETS is *to promote reductions of greenhouse gases in a cost-effective and economically efficient manner.* [2] The use of markets for allocation of the pollution rights distinguishes the mechanism from traditional command-and-control environmental licenses; [3] however, the scheme also contains elements and features of traditional administrative command-and-control regulation, as, for example, the creation and (partly) the allocation of allowances are based on administrative acts by national authorities and the Commission. GHG emissions information and its collection nevertheless play a fundamental role in emissions trading. [4] Once a year, entities regulated under the Emissions Trading Directive are required to surrender the number of emission allowances corresponding to their emissions from the previous year. [5] The environmental integrity and effectiveness of the system and the functioning of the market are thus dependent on accurate information on emissions from GHG sources. [6] Consequently, regulated entities are obliged to perform accurate monitoring, verification and reporting of GHG emissions on an annual basis in accordance with a pre-approved plan. [7] The information on annual emissions is publicly available in the Union Registry, the electronic register that functions as the infrastructure of the emissions trading scheme. For aviation, the point of regulation under the Emissions Trading Directive is the aircraft operators. [8] Consequently, annual verified information is publicly available on emissions from aircraft operators for their intra-EU flights.

---

[1] See e. g. R. H Coase, R. H., *The firm, the market and the law* (Chicago: University of Chicago Press, 1990), pp. 12 and 155. H. Dales, *Pollution, Property & Prices: An Essay in Policy-making and Economics*, 2nd ed. (Canada: University of Toronto Press, 1968) and T. H. Tietenberg, *Emissions Trading-Principles and Practice*, 2nd ed. (Washington, D. C.: Resources for the Future, 2006).

[2] Emissions Trading Directive, art 1.

[3] Charlotte Streck and Moritz von Unger, "Creating, Regulating and Allocating Rights to Offset and Pollute: Carbon Rights in Practice" (2016) CCLR 178, p. 179.

[4] SEC (2007) final 52, Section 3.3.

[5] Emissions Trading Directive, art.

[6] SEC (2007) final 52, Section 3.3.

[7] Emissions Trading Directive, art. 3g, 14, 15 and 15a.

[8] Emissions Trading Directive, annex 1.

Shipping MRV Regulation—Information on GHG Emissions from Shipping

The impact of a framework for the monitoring, reporting and verification of GHG emissions is well recognised by the Commission and has been utilised to achieve emission reductions in the shipping sector. The EU's preference has been for an international agreement, as shipping is an international sector. [1] Unlike aviation, however, shipping remains outside the EU's emission reduction targets. In April 2018, a breakthrough occurred when states in the International Maritime Organisation (IMO) Marine Environmental Protection Committee adopted an initial strategy for reducing GHG emissions from international shipping by at least 50 percent by 2050 compared to 2008 levels, including a list of proposed measures pursuant to a roadmap adopted in 2016. [2]

Prior to this progress, the EU had adopted a strategy for the inclusion of maritime transport in the EU's climate policies, setting out the legislative steps required to achieve a global market-based mechanism. [3] The first step involved the establishment of a framework for the monitoring, reporting and verification (MRV) of GHG emissions from shipping. In response to the continuing absence of a global framework, union-wide rules for MRV were adopted in 2015. [4] As of January 2018, GHG emissions from intra-EU voyages, incoming voyages from a non-Union port to a port within the Union, as well as outgoing voyages from a Union port to a non-Union port are monitored, verified and reported, irrespective of the flag under which the ships sail. [5] Ships become subject to these monitoring, verification and reporting obligations upon entrance to a port in the jurisdiction of a member state. The point of regulation is the "shipowner or any other organisation

---

[1] SEC (2007) final 52 (n 60), Section 3.6.2.

[2] IMO Marine Environment Protection Committee Resolution MEPC. 304 (72): "Initial IMO Strategy on reduction of GHG emissions from ships", April 2018.

[3] Commission, "Integrating maritime transport emissions in the EU's greenhouse gas reduction policies" (Communication) COM (2013) 479 final, Section 1.

[4] Regulation (EU) 2015/757 of the European Parliament and of the Council of 29 April 2015 on the monitoring, reporting and verification of carbon dioxide emissions from maritime transport, and amending Directive 2009/16/EC OJL 123/55 as amended by Commission Delegated Regulation (EU) 2016/2071 of 22 September 2016 amending Regulation (EU) 2015/757 of the European Parliament and of the Council as regards the methods for monitoring carbon dioxide emissions and the rules for monitoring other relevant information [2015] OJ L320/1 (MRV Shipping Regulation).

[5] Subject to a threshold for small emitters and an exemption for certain fishing vessels.

or person... which has assumed the responsibility for the operation of the ship from the shipowner". ①

The MRV Framework was perceived as the first step towards carbon pricing (preferably through a global mechanism) at a later stage, but the implementation of the requirements for the collection and publication of data are already believed to have removed some of the market barriers to energy efficiency improvements. ② The MRV requirements for international shipping have faced less political resistance than the more comprehensive inclusion of aviation in the EU ETS. ③ One of the purposes of the MRV framework was to act as a model for a global mechanism, ④ and it did speed up the international negotiations. Prior to the breakthrough in 2018, the IMO had adopted mandatory data-collection provisions for the fuel consumption of ships in 2016, ⑤ with which the MRV Shipping Regulation is now harmonised. ⑥

As 2018 is the first compliance year under the new Shipping MRV Framework, the impact of the information and its public availability has yet to be confirmed. What is certain, however, is that information on annual GHG emissions from vessels will be made publicly available during 2019. Of special interest is the fact that the information is not limited to GHG emissions but also includes information on the

---

① MRV Shipping Regulation, arts 3 and 4.
② MRV Shipping Regulation, recitals 9 – 13.
③ The inclusion was rejected politically by e.g. the US House of Representatives and the Chinese government and was ultimately brought to the European Court of Justice in the Case C – 366/10 *Air Transport Association of America, American Airlines Inc., Continental Airlines Inc., United Airlines Inc. v Secretary of State for Energy and Climate Change* (ATA). For a discussion on the inclusion of aviation in the EU ETS and the reasoning of the CJEU, see Sanja Bogojević, "Legalising Environmental Leadership: A Comment on the CJEU'S Ruling in C – 366/10 on the Inclusion of Aviation in the EU Emissions Trading Scheme" (2012) 24 (2) Journal of Environmental Law 345.
④ MRV Shipping Regulation, recital 34.
⑤ IMO Marine Environment Protection Committee Resolution MEPC. 278 (70): Amendments to the Annex of the Protocol of 1997 to Amend the International Convention for the Prevention of Pollution from Ships, 1973, as Modified by the Protocol of 1978 Relating Thereto Amendments to MARPOL Annex VI (Data collection system for fuel oil consumption of ships), October 2016.
⑥ Commission Delegated Regulation (EU) 2016/2071 of 22 September 2016 amending Regulation (EU) 2015/757 of the European Parliament and of the Council as regards the methods for monitoring carbon dioxide emissions and the rules for monitoring other relevant information [2016] OJ L320/1.

cargo carried during the voyage. Moreover, the information to be made publicly available each year by the Commission will include information on *the annual average fuel consumption and CO_2 emissions per distance travelled and cargo carried on voyages*. [1]

The Effort Sharing Regulation—Information on GHG Emissions from Road Transport

While the regulation of greenhouse gas emissions from aviation and shipping has been centralised at a Union level through the Emissions Trading Scheme and the Shipping MRV Regulation respectively, the approach is different for road transport. The road transport sector falls within the scope of Effort Sharing between the member states. The Effort Sharing Decision (ESD)[2] and the Effort Sharing Regulation (ESR),[3] which will replace the ESD as of 2021, have a so-called framework character. [4] The ESD and the ESR set out binding national emission-reduction targets for 2020 and 2030 respectively. The choice of suitable policy instruments is nevertheless left to the member states. Consequently, member states have adopted various policy instruments to reduce GHG emissions from the transport sector. [5] The array of policy instruments adopted by member states varies, but they can include economic instruments, like the CO_2 taxes on transport adopted throughout the Nordic countries, or one-off taxes on the registration of vehicles that are linked to fuel efficiency or emissions standard. The policy mix also contains pure information steering instruments, such as the eco-driving training offered to coach and bus drivers in Finland or the labelling of passenger cars in Sweden.

---

[1] MRV Shipping Regulation, arts. 9 and 21.

[2] Decision No. 406/2009/EC of the European Parliament and of the Council of 23 April 2009 on the effort of Member States to reduce their greenhouse gas emissions to meet the Community's greenhouse gas emission reduction commitments up to 2020 OJ L 140, 5.6.2009, pp. 136 – 148.

[3] Regulation (EU) 2018/842 of the European Parliament and of the Council of 30 May 2018 on binding annual greenhouse gas emission reductions by Member States from 2021 to 2030 contributing to climate action to meet commitments under the Paris Agreement and amending Regulation (EU) No. 525/2013.

[4] Marjan Peeters, "Governing towards Renewable Energy in the EU: Competences, Instruments, and Procedures" (2014) 21 (1) Maastricht Journal of European and Comparative Law 39, at p. 51.

[5] For an overview of the policy instrument adopted in the Nordic Countries see Hrafnhildur Bragadóttir, Roland Magnusson, Sampo Seppänen, David Sundén, Emilie Yliheljo, *Sectoral Expansion of the EU ETS—A Nordic Perspective on Barriers and Solutions to Include New Sectors in the EU ETS with Special Focus on Road Transport* (Copenhagen: Nordic Council of Ministers, 2016).

In addition to these national policies and measures, the Union has adopted measures to promote low-emission mobility. These measures can be roughly divided into three categories, as discussed in Section 2: (1) instruments aimed at reducing the carbon intensity of transport fuels by, for example, promoting the use of renewable energy in transport; (2) instruments aimed at improving the energy efficiency of vehicles; and (3) measures aimed at influencing the way individuals and companies use the transport sector.[①] The second category includes emission standards, which have been central steering instruments in the road sector for cars and vans, with current CO_2 standards in force until 2020. Post-2020 standards until 2030 are currently being negotiated for cars and heavy duty vehicles.[②] Informational steering has been used to complement emissions standards in the form of car labels intended to inform consumers on fuel consumption and CO_2 emission of new cars.[③] The standards have included reporting obligations on vehicles for member states, and, in conjunction with the new standards for post-2020, the Commission is seeking to strengthen the impact of standards.[④] A regulation for the monitoring and reporting of GHG emissions from heavy-duty vehicles has already been adopted, obliging member states and manufacturers to monitor emissions from

---

① Skinnar 2014, p. 104.

② The current CO_2 standards for light-duty vehicles are in force until 2020 under Regulation (EC) No. 443/2009 of the European Parliament and of the Council of 23 April 2009 setting emission performance standards for new passenger cars as part of the Community's integrated approach to reduce CO_2 emissions from light-duty vehicles. Currently negotiations are on-going for the adoption of new post-2020 CO_2-standards for cars and also for heavy-duty vehicles, see Commission, Proposal for a Regulation of The European Parliament and of The Council setting emission performance standards for new passenger cars and for new light commercial vehicles as part of the Union's integrated approach to reduce CO_2 emissions from light-duty vehicles and amending Regulation (EC) No. 715/2007 (recast) COM (2017) 0676 final and Commission, Proposal for a Regulation of the European Parliament and of the Council setting CO_2 emission performance standards for new heavy-duty vehicles COM (2018) 284 final.

③ Directive 1999/94/EC of the European Parliament and of the Council of 13 December 1999 relating to the availability of consumer information on fuel economy and CO_2 emissions in respect of the marketing of new passenger cars OJ L 12/16.

④ Proposal for a Regulation of The European Parliament And of The Council setting emission performance standards for new passenger cars and for new light commercial vehicles as part of the Union's integrated approach to reduce CO_2 emissions from light-duty vehicles and amending Regulation (EC) No. 715/2007 (recast) COM (2017) 0676 final.

heavy-duty vehicles registered in the Union. Monitoring is to be performed by manufacturers using the standardised Vehicle Energy Consumption Calculation Tool (VECTO). The information will be published annually in the form of the performance of the Union's fleet and the average fuel consumption and GHG emissions of member states and manufacturers.[①]

5. Future Use of Emissions Information in the EU (and Beyond)

The emissions in the examples above are reported either to the relevant authorities or to the market as general product information. However, based on the theory of nudging, more could be done to promote behavioural change towards sustainable decision-making in the transport sector while preserving freedom of choice for stakeholders by, for example, providing emissions information to the parties to a contract of carriage in a B2B relationship.

The legal persons involved in a contract of carriage of goods are shippers and carriers. When it comes to organising freight, however, the central figure is the freight forwarder. Freight forwarders are intermediaries or agents who organise the freight and bring the parties together without (normally) being part of the contract of carriage themselves. The distinction between a freight forwarder and a carrier is important from a contractual perspective because carriers are subject to mandatory international liability conventions[②] whereas freight forwarders are normally not.[③]

[①] Regulation (EU) 2018/956 of the European Parliament and of the Council of 28 June 2018 on the monitoring and reporting of CO_2 emissions from and fuel consumption of new heavy-duty vehicles, [2018] OJ L 173/1.

[②] Whether this holds true under multimodal contracts of carriage varies in different jurisdictions. This problem is not discussed here, however. For an in depth discussion of the problem, see Marian Hoeks, *The Law Applicable to the Multimodal Contract for the Carriage of Goods* (Kluwer 2010). For an overview of relevant articles, see Ellen Eftestöl-Wilhelmsson, Anu Bask and Mervi Rajahonka, "Intermodal Transport Research: A Law and Logistics Literature Review with EU Focus" (2014) European Transport Law Vol. XLIX. No. 6, pp. 609 – 674.

[③] The mandatory international conventions on contracts of carriage govern (largely) the carrier's liability for non-performance and do not concern the business factors affecting the agreement. For an analytical outline of the different legal conceptualisations of a freight forwarder, see: Frank Smeele, "Legal Conceptualisations of the Freight Forwarder: Some Comparative Reflections on the Disunified Law of Forwarding" (2015) 21 JIML 445 – 459.

In terms of sharing emission information, however, the freight forwarder plays an important role. The freight forwarder is the entity who knows the different freight alternatives and how shippers can obtain carriage for their cargo to the desired destination. According, for example, to the General Conditions of the Nordic Association of Freight Forwarders (NSAB art 5), "[t] he freight forwarder undertakes to perform services, to pick up, take care of or procure the handling of the goods in accordance with the contract terms and in a suitable way for the customer with generally used means and routes of transport". ① Usually, these "generally used means and routes of transport" are chosen on the bases of *reliability, transport quality and price*, leaving environmental issues aside. In this respect, there has been little development in the industry,② despite growing concerns over environmental issues and calls for sustainable solutions. Few behavioural changes have occurred and, unfortunately, environmental impact seems to be one of the least important factors in the choice of transport. ③

A 2003 study conducted on behalf of the EU Commission, "The Freight Integrator Study",④ suggests that freight forwarders fail to take environmental protection into consideration because they *lack the relevant information and knowledge* on how to utilise environmentally friendly modes of transport, such as railways. ⑤ Furthermore, the study identified *mentality and attitude* as major obstacles to "environmental awareness". According to the study, people in the industry where nonetheless conscious of environmental issues, but this failed to influence their behaviour. ⑥ One problem was the lack of incentives for changing their attitude: "Companies... not engaging in the field of intermodal transportation often [saw]

---

① General Conditions of the Nordic Association of Freight Forwarders NSAB 2015.
② Ralf Elbert and Lowis Seikowsky, "The influences of behavioral biases, barriers and facilitators on the willingness of forwarders' decision-makers to modal shift from unimodal road freight transport to intermodal road-rail freight transport" (2017) 87 (8) J Bus Econ 1083 – 1123 at p. 1104 with further references.
③ Catrin Lammgård and Dan Andersson, "Environmental considerations and trade-offs in purchasing of transportation services" (2014) *Research in Transportation Business & Management*, Volume 10, pp. 45 – 52.
④ European transport policy for 2010: time to decide. COM (2001) 370.
⑤ Ibid. at 7 and 6.3.7.
⑥ Ibid. at 6.3.7.

no reason why they should do so", [1] while shippers at large were indifferent to how their goods were transported. [2] According to *Lammgård and Andersson*, the low priority given to the environmental impact of transport has implications for the marketing of environmentally preferable transport. As the freight transport market as a whole might not be ready for this type of marketing, the authors claim that a further segmentation of the industry based on environmental priorities is needed. [3] The challenge thus seems to be how to strengthen environmental consciousness in the transport sector. Here, insights into human behaviour can work as tools to help politicians and stakeholders design the right strategies. Emission information is part of the solution, but how that information is utilised is nevertheless crucial: it must be orchestrated to nudge the desired solution.

As explained in Section 4 above, information on emissions related to carriage is already measured and reported to the relevant authorities. The challenge is to integrate that information into the contractual process that occurs between the shipper and carrier. One possibility is to utilise the newly established EU electronic system for information sharing. The proposed regulation on electronic freight transport information will establish a legal framework for the electronic communication of regulatory information related to transport. [4] Thus far, the regulation is restricted to information flows between transport businesses and authorities (B2A). [5] However, it is expected that once the authorities within the Union accept the exchange of electronic information, the industry will move towards full digitalization and will include business-to-business (B2B) information exchanges. [6] In other words, it will be possible to both measuring and reporting emissions from carriage in real time.

This will provide an excellent opportunity to provide the market with emissions information as a competitive factor. Businesses that apply, for example, the Triple

---

[1] European transport policy for 2010: time to decide. COM (2001) 370, at 6.3.8.
[2] Ibid. at 6.1.
[3] Lammgård and Andersson (2014) p. 47.
[4] Proposal for a regulation of the European Parliament and of the Council on electronic freight transport information COM (2018) 279 final Art 1.1.
[5] Ibid. art 1.1 (a).
[6] Ibid. at p. 6.

Bottom Line (TBL) accounting system, where social and environmental considerations are added to the traditional economic bottom line perspective, could receive a competitive advantage. The TBL-reporting system measures a company's degree of social responsibility, its economic value and its environmental impact. When this information is available to the market, it might potentially lead to the desired behavioural change. ① Moreover, when emissions information from different transport alternatives is available to transport logistic service providers or freight forwarders, it seems but a small step to introduce the information to the market and use it as a trigger for more environmental friendly behaviour in the industry. Shippers will then have a choice of different transport alternatives, where emissions, in addition to time and costs, are a decisive factor. New technology will provide the necessary practical means for measuring emissions and delivering the results in real time.

We argue that emissions information should be integrated into the legal framework applicable to the transport industry. Both existing and new conventions for the international carriage of goods should include rules on measuring and reporting emissions related to individual consignments. In addition to weight and numbers, emissions from the carriage—measured in relation to the cargo—should be included in the (electronic) transport document. The information and the technical solutions for its provision are available and already in use in passenger traffic. ②

6. Conclusions

Information has long been recognised as a policy instrument and utilised by policy makers on multiple levels. Moreover, other policy instruments, such as environmental permits and emissions trading, rely on the collection of information on GHG emissions. The purpose of this paper was to explore the use of information by EU policy makers in the context of transport and to investigate the

---

① Matthias Klumpp, (2018) "How to Achieve Supply Chain Sustainability Efficiently? Taming the Triple Bottom Line Split Business Cycle." *Sustainability* 10, 397.

② See the example from France on an easy CO_2 calculator. https://www.sncf.com/sncv1/en/services/train-CO_2-emissions (Accessed 3.10.2010).

possibilities for furthering increasing the impact of such information to achieve GHG emission reductions. Information on GHG emissions is collected and published annually by the EU and members states for aircraft operators under the EU Emissions Trading Scheme and for vessels entering or leaving a port in the EU under the Shipping MRV Regulation. In addition, the monitoring and reporting of emissions from road transport is also being further developed in the EU and the member states under road transport policies for the post-2020 period. Extensive use of information already occurs in the business to authority context in the EU. Nonetheless, further research is required on how this information can be more effectively utilised by applying behavioural science approaches, such as the theory of nudging. This will be the focus of our future work.

促进商业领域的可持续性选择：排放信息的作用

艾米莉·伊利赫里欧　艾伦·艾弗斯托尔－威尔海姆森

【摘要】运输业是现代社会最严重的污染源。全球货物贸易总额（按价值计算）预计将于2013年~2030年增加一倍。运输业所排放的温室气体占欧盟温室气体总排放量的23%，在各经济部门中名列第二，名列第一的是能源部门，而工业部门则名列第三。另外，尽管欧盟采取了各种运输政策和绿色运输行动计划，运输行业仍没有能够像其他经济部门一样减少排放量。事实上，运输行业的排放量占各经济部门总排放量的比例从1990年的15%上升到了2016年的27%。本文主要讨论如何通过各种方式利用排放信息缓解运输业排放问题。

International Human Rights Obligations Contributing to Finnish Environmental Rights[*]

Heta-Elena Heiskanen[**]

【Abstract】 Development of environmental rights has taken place both in international and national level. The aim of the paper is to identify and analyze the role of international human rights obligations in the development and interpretation of Finnish environmental rights protection. The paper will first discuss the relevant human rights law instruments related to environmental rights. In the latter part of the paper the relevance of the international human rights law instruments to the Finnish environmental rights protection is discussed. References are made in particular to two different contexts, namely the rights of indigenous peoples, Sami people and climate change.

Introduction

Relationship between human rights and the environment, is strongly interrelated.[①] Extreme weather conditions, environmental pollution, extreme heats, erosion and many other environmental problems endanger also the human health or even life. Thus the human rights approach to the environment is a highly relevant topic in

---

[*] The research was funded by the Strategic Research Council at the Academy of Finland, project ALL-YOUTH with decision no. 312689.

[**] Doc. Admin. Sc., Post-Doc, ALL-YOUTH STN, Faculty of Management and Business Tampere University.

[①] H. Heiskanen, *Towards Greener Human Rights Protection. Rewriting the Environmental Case Law of the European Court of Human Rights*, Tampere University Press, 2018, pp. 15 – 18, H. Heiskanen, R. Knuutila, L. Heinämäki (2017). *Ympäristöllinen haavoittuvuus Euroopan ihmisoikeustuomioistuimen tapausten valossa*. Oikeus 2017 (1), 35 – 55.

the contemporary societies that are facing various environmental problems. [1]

The Finnish environmental legislation is heavily influenced by the international environmental law and policy instruments. Relevant frameworks that the Finnish Government is involved include the United Nations, the European Union and the Council of Europe. Not all of these international environmental instruments include explicit human rights dimensions. However, there also are a significant amount of international environmental law instruments combining human rights, that inspire, guide and bind the Government of Finland. [2]

Wide Range of Human Rights Agreements are Relevant to Environmental Rights

At international level, the human rights approach to the environment has been continuous. It has taken place in different frameworks from the 1960s. There is review of relevant instruments from Finnish and European perspective on the below. There are other relevant regional developments, but they are not mentioned here, as they do not bind European states. In addition, due to the large amount of the case law of the European Court of Human Rights, only some of the landmark decisions are mentioned as an example of the continuance development. [3]

Timeline

1966: The International Covenant on Economic, Social and Cultural Rights, Article 12, entered into force in 1976

1972: Stockholm Declaration

1977: Protocol I to the Geneva Convention, Article 54 (2), Article 55

1979: The UN Convention on the Elimination of All Forms of

---

[1] H. Heiskanen, R. Knuutila, L. Heinämäki (2017). *Ympäristöllinen haavoittuvuus Euroopan ihmisoikeustuomioistuimen tapausten valossa.* Oikeus 2017 (1), 35–55.

[2] J. Viljanen, H. Heiskanen, S. Raskulla (2016). *Ihmisoikeuksien yleiset opit ja suomalainen ympäristöoikeudellinen argumentaatio.* Ympäristöjuridiikka 36 (1), 86–109.

[3] For more research on the environmental case law of the European Court of Human Rights, see: H. Heiskanen, *Towards Greener Human Rights Protection. Rewriting the Environmental Case Law of the European Court of Human Rights*, Tampere University Press, 2018.

Discrimination against Women, Article 14 (2) (5)

1985: The Commission: UK, 11185/84, Dec. March 11, 1985

1989: The Declaration of the Hague on the Environment, the Convention on the Rights of the Child, Article 25 (1) (c), the International Labour Organization Convention Concerning Indigenous and Tribal Peoples in Independent Countries (ILO No. 169), Article 4, 6, 7 (4), 8

1990: UN General Assembly declared a right to live in an environment that ensures health and welfare.[①] Human Rights Committee of the United Nations: Bernard Ominayak, Chief of the Lubicon Lake Band v. Canada, 26 March 1990, Communication No. 167/1984

1991: European Court of Human Rights: *Fredin v. Sweden* (no. 1), 18 February 1991, Series A no. 192

1992: Rio Declaration on Environment and Development, Principle 10

1994: The Draft Declaration of Principles on Human Rights and the Environment. Special Rapporteur published her final report on the relationship between human rights and the environment[②]

1995: The Beijing Declaration and its Platform for Action was adopted by the Fourth World Conference on Women in Beijing on September 15, 1995, Section K

1995: The European Court of Human Rights: Lopez Ostra, 9 Dec 1994, Serie A 303 – C

1998: The Aarhus Convention, entered into force in 2001[③]

2006: The UN Convention on the Rights of Persons with Disabilities, Articles 11, 29a, 30. Entered into force in 2008. The Committee of the European Social Charter, *Marangopoulos Foundation for Human Rights* (*MFHR*) *v. Greece*, Decision of 6 December 2006

2007: Declaration on the Rights of Indigenous Peoples, Article 29

2008: The European Court of Human Rights *Budayeva and Others v.*

[①] UN GA Resolution, 45/94, 14 December 1990.

[②] Final Report of the Special Rapporteur, Human Rights and the Environment, UN Doc. E/CN. 4/ Sub. 2/1994/9, 6 July 1994.

[③] Aarhus Convention on Access to Information, Public Participation in Decision-Making and Access to Justice in Environmental Matters (Aarhus Convention) 38 I. L. M. 517, 25 June 1998.

Russia, 20 March 2008

2009: The European Court of Human Rights: Tǎtar v. Romania, 27 January 2009

2012: UN Resolution 19/10 called for the Independent Expert on human rights and the environment

2014: The European Court of Human Rights: Brincat and Others v. Malta, 24 July 2014

As can be concluded on the basis of this time line, there are different types of relevant legal instruments. These instruments include binding agreements, that Finland have ratified and should take into account, when it prepares its national legislation. In addition, authorities have an obligation to comply with the obligations. Furthermore, the domestic courts and ombudspersons have a duty to supervise the execution of the international human rights obligations.

The European Court of Human Rights Has Well-established Case Law on Environmental Rights

Case law from the European Court of Human Rights has been dealing with environmental matters, even though the Convention or the Additional Protocols do not specifically mention the environment. The European Court of Human Rights provides an additional judicial safeguards for the victims of environmental problems, as they can take their case before the court after exhaustion of domestic remedies. It should be noted, that this legal avenue is effective, as the judgments of the European Court of Human Rights have a direct impact on Finland, when they have a binding force. The impact for the victim can be monetary compensation, but there can also be wider societal impacts, if the compliance with the Convention requires introduction of new legislation, authorities or other measures. Also, it should be noted the case law which does not directly concern Finland, but which forms a European minimum standard, will guide Finland in its legislative work. The national courts can also make references to the case law.

The role of non-binding instruments and soft law is milder: these instruments have guiding role and political impact, but the rules cannot be enforced through effective judicial means. Soft law instruments can also provide inspiration. The content of the instruments vary from general declatory statements, such as in Stockholm Declaration 1972 to recognized rights, such as in Aarhus Convention, which includes environmental procedural rights such as the right to access to information on environmental matters, right to participation and the right to access to court. Some of the instruments guarantee rights for everyone and some instruments concerns certain limited groups of peoples, such as children, women, disabled or indigenous peoples.

For example, the environmental case law of the European Court of Human Rights has developed detailed set of obligations for the State Parties, requiring preventive measures, protection of procedural rights and effective remedies. [1] However, the European Court of Human Rights has focused currently mainly on establishing the responsibility of a single state to its citizens instead of shared liability or extraterritorial liability. However, the future is to show, how the European Court of Human Rights responses to such global environmental problems as climate change. [2] Couple of Portuguese children are planning to take a climate change case before the European Court of Human Rights due to the severe and widespread forest fires in Portugal. The aim is to establish shared liability for several State Parties to the Council of Europe. [3]

International Human Rights Law Has Strong Relevance to the Finnish Environmental Rights

The role of the international human rights obligations in developing the Finnish

---

[1] H. Heiskanen, *Towards Greener Human Rights Protection. Rewriting the Environmental Case Law of the European Court of Human Rights*, Tampere University Press, 2018, p. 18.

[2] H. Heiskanen & J. Viljanen (2014). *Reforming the Strasbourg Doctrine on Extraterritorial Jurisdiction in the Context of Environmental Protection*. European Law Reporter 2014 (11), 285 – 295. H. Heiskanen (2018). *Climate Change and the European Court of Human Rights: Future Potentials*. Duyck Sébastien, Jodoin Sébastien, Johl Alyssa (eds.) in The Routledge Handbook of Human Rights and Climate Governance. Oxon: Routledge, 319 – 324.

[3] H. Heiskanen (2018). Voiko Suomi olla oikeudellisesti vastuussa Portugalin metsäpaloista? Vaikuttaja-blog (https://vaikuttaja.uta.fi/voiko-suomi-olla-oikeudellisesti-vastuussa-portugalin-metsapaloista/). H. Heiskanen (2018). *Pysäyttäkää ilmastonmuutos-nuoret ilmastokanteiden tekijöinä*. ALL YOUTH-blog (http://www.allyouthstn.fi/pysayttakaa-ilmastonmuutos-nuoret-ilmastokanteiden-tekijoina/). Heiskanen, Heta, Kun ilmastopolitiikka ei riitä, soita lakimiehelle. Alusta 2018: https://alusta.uta.fi/2018/09/21/kun-ilmastopolitiikka-ei-riita-soita-lakimiehelle/.

environmental rights take place in legislative stage, in judicial review stage and in introducing new practical tools. I will first discuss the role in the legislative stage and then in the practice of the courts and ombudspersons and the last but not least the role of human rights in creating good practices.

The international human rights law development explains in some extent establishment of the national Finnish environmental constitutional right, when the constitution was renewed.[①] The international human rights law standards have continued since that to guide the legislative development of Finland.

After ratification of the human rights instruments, the Government aims to comply with the obligations in preparing the legislation and in executing the decisions. To do so, during the preparation of the legislation, typically there is some sort of assessment on the implications of the bill to the Finnish human rights obligations. Recently, the Government has started to develop the human rights impact assessment of the bills, which is relevant also in the context of the preparation of environmental legislation.

In comparing to the use in legislative stage, the current usage of the international human rights obligations before the national courts, such as administrative courts and the Supreme Administrative Court, have not been vivid. There are only a few cases, in which the court has utilized international human rights law argumentation in its rulings. In these cases, the references have been made to procedural rights, such as right to access the court and right to access of environmental information, protected in Aarhus Convention, European Union law and the European Court of Human Rights. Most often the courts make references to EU legislation, which forms in the contemporary Finnish environmental legislation a significant part.[②]

However, even though the situation is as the current, this does not mean, that Finland would not comply with the standards of international human rights law, but that the tradition of the domestic courts is not to use constitutional or

---

① See for constitutional right, Section 20: H. Heiskanen (2014). *Ympäristöperusoikeus-mitä jokaisen tulisi tietää?* Ympäristökasvatus 2014 (4), J. Viljanen, H. Heiskanen, S. Raskulla, T. Koivurova, L. Heinämäki (2014). *Miten ympäristöperusoikeus toteutuu?* Tampere: Ympäristöministeriö, Tampereen yliopisto, Pohjoisen ympäristö- ja vähemmistöoikeuden instituutti.

② J. Viljanen, H. Heiskanen, S. Raskulla (2016). *Ihmisoikeuksien yleiset opit ja suomalainen ympäristöoikeudellinen argumentaatio.* Ympäristöjuridiikka 36 (1), 86 – 109.

international human rights law argumentation, if there is regular law available. The Finnish legal culture on fundamental rights and human rights is relatively young, which explains this in its major parts. The judges themselves have told in the interviews, that they do think and take into account human rights in their decisions, but they do not necessary spell them out. In the context of the environmental matters, it can be said, that the development on using human rights argumentation is even lower, than in some other areas of law. To increase the transparency of the argumentation and to develop the quality of the argumentation of the judges, it would be recommendable for the Finnish courts to mention the relevant international agreements to the case that support its findings. ①

In addition to the courts, the ombudspersons, namely the Chancellor of Justice and the Parliamentary Ombudspersons have a mandate to supervise the legality of the actions of public authorities. ② There are environmentally related decisions that have adopted human rights approach for example in relation to the indoor air conditions at public spaces.

International Human Rights Law Provides Additional Legal Safeguards

If Finland has failed to take into account sufficiently the human rights in environmentally related legislative processes, the human rights organs of the United Nations have capacity to intervene. This has happened in the past few years as the Special Rapporteur of human rights and the environment, John H. Knox from the United Nations, the Special Rapporteur on indigenous peoples and the Office of the High Commissioner of Human Rights have given statements. In particularly, the involvement of the United Nations was significant in the process concerning the amending of the Finnish act on Metsähallitus, the authority which governs the public forests. The amendment process took long and one purpose of it was to

---

① J. Viljanen & H. Heiskanen, S. Raskulla (2016). *Ihmisoikeuksien yleiset opit ja suomalainen ympäristöoikeudellinen argumentaatio.* Ympäristöjuridiikka 36 (1), 86 – 109.

② J. Viljanen & H. Heiskanen (2018). *Suomalaisen ihmisoikeusarkkitehtuurin ja ihmisoikeuskulttuurin nykytila ja tulevaisuus.* Teoksessa Karppi Ilari et al. (toim.) Governance III: Hallintaa ja yhteistyötä. Tampere: Tampereen yliopisto, johtamiskorkeakoulu, 33 – 47.

improve and clarify the land rights of Finnish indigenous peoples, namely the Sami people. The previous government had included specific provision on Sami rights, which would have strengthened their position, but the current government took them off, without negotiating with the Sami Parliament. In addition, the government failed to facilitate adequate right to participation in the process for environmental NGOs. The Special Rapporteurs of the United Nations on human rights and the environment and indigenous peoples, communicated to the Finnish Government about its failures to protect the rights effectively. As the Finnish Government did not response to this critique by the United Nations, the United Nations gave twice public statements on the issues. ①

International Human Rights Provides Inspiration to Develop Good National Policies

Furthermore, in certain specific areas, the international human rights law has provided inspiration to develop environmental policies further. One area is indigenous rights and their environmental rights. The Convention of Biodiversity, Article 8 (j) has inspired the Finnish authorities to create so-called Ak we Kon: groups, which is a model, where the local Sami people can consult and give their comments to the relevant authorities in relation to environmental decision making, that takes place in the Homeland of Sami, in Northern Finland, Lapland. The model is a good practice that has been reported also internationally. ②

---

① H. Heiskanen, Consultation on law of Metsähallitus 12.11.2015. Office of the High Commisioner of Human Rights, United Nations, Heiskanen, Heta, Expert opinion on law proposal on Metsähallitus, environmental rights and indigenous rights 11.03.2016. Office of the UN High Commissioner for Human Rights, Metsähallituslain hallituksen esityksen arviointi saamelaisten oikeuksien näkökulmasta 16.02.2016. Ympäristövaliokunta, Parliament of Finland, H. Heiskanen & L. Heinämäki (2015). *Saamelaiset on huomioitava metsähallituslaissa. Helsingin sanomat* 21.10.2015, H. Heiskanen & J. Lavapuro (2015). *Metsähallituslaissa tulee säätää saamelaisten oikeuksista.* perustuslakiblogi.wordpress.com. (https://perustuslakiblogi.wordpress.com/2015/11/22/heta-heiskanen-juha-lavapuro-metsahallituslaissa-tulee-saataa-saamelaisten-oikeuksista/), J. Viljanen Jukka, H. Heiskanen (2015). *Ihmisoikeudet unohtuivat metsähallituslain valmistelussa.* Suomen Kuvalehti 2015 (43), 59.

② L. Olsén, A. Harkoma, L. Heinämäki, H. Heiskanen (2017). *Saamelaisten perinnetiedon huomioiminen ympäristöpäätöksenteossa.* Rovaniemi: Lapin yliopisto. (Juridica Lapponica 41).

I would like to remind that the interaction between the international human rights law instrument is not only one way. Finnish environmental rights developments have also contributed to the work of the United Nations. With my colleague Jukka Viljanen, we have for example reported Finnish good practices for the Special Rapporteur on human rights and the environment, John H. Knox, who has prepared a compilation of good practices of the field. Some of the Finnish good practices were even mentioned in the session of the United Nations in Geneva. In this way, the Finnish developments have provided inspiration for the United Nations and its member states.

Conclusions

Currently the role of the different human rights instruments relating to the environment have been important in developing the Finnish legislation. Finland has incorporated the main principles from the international human rights law into its domestic legislation and tries to ensure the compliance of the domestic legislation with the international human rights law standards.

In relation to the level of protection in Finland, the international human rights standards form a minimum standard for the protection of the human rights, including environmentally related rights. However, it is important to remind that the international and regional human rights standards are often not the highest standards, but minimum standards in relation to national Finnish constitutional rights. Thus the Finnish development of environmental rights has not been limited to the international human rights law development and should not be in the future: but, Finland should aim at even higher standards, when there is necessity to guarantee the effective protection of the environment and the well-being of humans.

There are also future areas of development such as climate change, which is global and shared environmental concern as well as a major threat to the realization of human rights. In Finland there is yet no such climate change litigation or climate change related judgments that would contribute to the international development. However the international and regional human rights protection relating climate change is developing continuously and quickly. It is only a matter of time, when Finnish authorities such as Parliamentary Ombudsperson or courts will also consider climate change related matters. It is very important that on that time Finnish courts and other authorities are aware of the international developments.

促进芬兰环境权利发展的国际人权义务

赫塔-艾琳娜·海斯卡宁

【摘要】 环境权利在国际和国内两个层面上得到了发展。本文的目的在于确定和分析国际人权义务在芬兰环境权利保护的发展和解释方面所起到的作用。它首先讨论了与环境权利相关的人权法文书，然后讨论了国际人权法文书与芬兰环境权利保护的相关性。本文特别提到了两个不同的语境：土著居民萨米人的权利和气候变化。

Recent Nordic Trends in Developing Value Chain Sustainability

Jaakko Salminen[*]

【Abstract】 Over the last few decades, global value chains have become the dominant form of economic production. Law has been slow to respond to this change. We have only recently begun to comprehend and regulate global value chains organized as corporate groups and the recent move towards contractually organized value chains pushes law even further away from its comfort zone. In particular, the current state-of-the-art of value chain regulation cannot effectively tackle issues of sustainability in contractually organized value chains. At the same time, several global trends related to private governance, private law litigation and public regulation are driving the development of sustainable value chain governance and developing law's responses to contractually organized production. In this paper, I look at recent Nordic versions of these global development trends under private governance, private law litigation and public regulation and set them in the global context that they aim to regulate. While on the outset it seems that the Nordic approach tries to go beyond the global state-of-the-art, a key challenge remains in how the local economic interests that are an important driver of Nordic approaches to sustainability are balanced with a more global perspective on sustainability.

1. Introduction—Law and the New Realities of Global Production

Over the last two hundred years, two major shifts have changed the way goods

---

[*] (LL. D., LL. M., M. A.) Postdoctoral Researcher, University of Turku Faculty of Law.

are produced.① First, during the 19th century technological innovations such as steam ships and railroads made possible the distribution of goods over vast distances, allowing production to be physically separated from consumption. This, coupled with a drive towards increased returns on investment via bureaucratic efficiency led to the rise of centralized mass production and fragmented distribution chains. Second, during the 20th century, advances in communication technology enabled the efficient control of production over long distances. Thus it was no longer necessary for bureaucratic efficiency that all aspects of production would be bundled together into one centralized mass production complex. Organizational focus shifted towards so-called "core competences": companies focused on higher value producing aspects of production, such as intellectual property rights, design, marketing, and research and development, while outsourcing less value producing aspects of production, such as manufacturing and various administration functions.②

The end result of these technological and management developments are centrally governed but globally dispersed production networks that can be referred to as global value chains.③ The United Nations Conference on Trade and Development (UNCTAD) estimated in 2013 that 80% of international trade takes place in global value chains that are organized and governed by so-called "lead firms" under contractual and corporate principles.④ But while global value chains enable

---

① Richard Baldwin, "Trade and Industrialization after Globalization's 2nd Unbundling: How Building and Joining a Supply Chain Are Different and Why It Matters" (2011) *National Bureau of Economic Research Working Paper* 17716.

② Coimbatore Krishnarao Prahalad and Gary Hamel, "The Core Competence of the Corporation" (1990) 68 *Harvard Business Review* 79.

③ Gary Gereffi, "Global value chains in a post-Washington Consensus world" (2014) 21 *Review of International Political Economy* 9. In many ways, the value chain can be seen as synonymous to other concepts such as supply chain or commodity chain, even if the different terms relate to distinct research traditions. I opt to use the term value chain because of its conceptual openness and the governance model developed under it. See Jennifer Bair, "Global Commodity Chains: Genealogy and Review", in Jennifer Bair (eds.), *Frontiers of Commodity Chain Research* (Standford University Press 2009).

④ UNCTAD, *World Investment Report* 2013 (2013). For governance, see Gary Gereffi, John Humphrey and Timothy Sturgeon, "The governance of global value chains" (2005) 12 *Review of International Political Economy* 78. For different types of lead firms, see Gary Gereffi, "Shifting Governance Structures in Global Commodity Chains, With Special Reference to the Internet" (2001) 44 *American Behavioral Scientist* 1616.

efficiency on an unprecedented scale, they have also become emblematic of the many problems of global trade and production, ranging from appalling labour conditions to environmental degradation and tax evasion. ① If lead firms outsource production to subsidiaries and suppliers located in other jurisdictions, they may, for example, simultaneously outsource resource extraction and greenhouse gas emissions to jurisdictions that are less well able to cope with them.

At the same time, global value chains are dependent on legal infrastructure. ② In particular, the basic building blocks of private law, contract and corporation, have provided lead firms with the possibility of externalising liabilities, first in the form of multinational corporate groups and more recently in the form of contractually organized global value chains. Current approaches to regulating global value chains, from private governance to private litigation and public regulation, have barely begun to comprehend multinational groups of companies as unified entities, to say nothing of contractually organized value chains. ③

At the same time, it is clear that a hundred years ago law did develop effective responses to the liability deficits inherent in the first shift in global production practices, the move towards centralized mass production and fragmented distribution chains. For example, *product liability* was developed to overcome the lack of a direct relationship between manufacturers and users of goods in a contractually organized distribution chains, provide claimants with more beneficial burdens of proof in relation to allocating liability for damage caused by defective products in complex production complexes, and provide manufacturers with select defences designed to encourage them to keep up with technological advances related to product safety. ④

Current approaches to lead firm liability for damage caused by the inadequate

---

① IGLP Law and Global Production Working Group, "The role of law in global value chains: a research manifesto" (2016) 4 *London Review of International Law* 57.

② IGLP Law and Global Production Working Group, "The role of law in global value chains: a research manifesto" (2016) 4 *London Review of International Law* 57.

③ Jaakko Salminen, "Sustainability and the Move from Corporate Governance to Governance Through Contract", in Beate Sjåfjell and Christopher Brunner (eds.), *Cambridge Handbook of Corporate Law, Corporate Governance and Sustainability* (forthcoming Cambridge University Press 2019).

④ Generally, see Jane Stapleton, *Product Liability* (Butterworths 1994) and Simon Whittaker (eds.), *The Development of Product Liability* (Cambridge University Press 2010).

governance of their global value chains to third parties, such as labour and environmental interests, seem to be in a state of development comparable to early phases of product liability law a hundred or so years ago.① These approaches, fuelled by societal debate, play out on at least three levels: private governance, private law litigation, and public regulation. In this paper, I will briefly tackle recent Nordic trends coupled to these topics based on recent examples of how Nordic law has begun to respond to the liability deficits posed by the inadequate governance of global value chains.

2. Private Governance and the *Bangladesh Accord*

Private governance lies at the heart of global value chains. Richard Baldwin's hypothesis that the development of advanced communication technology is a prerequisite for the fragmentation of production entails, that the *possibility* of effective control of fragmented production is a condition precedent for fragmentation.② In many cases, effective control is a derivative of regulation: within a jurisdiction a lead firm knows that law generally requires similar product safety, labour and environmental standards from most if not all actors. This may also apply in transnational situations, for example where lead firms operating in one jurisdiction wish to comply with the requirements of the target market in relation to product safety or emission standards.③

However, in both cases public regulation may not always be able to effectively regulate all relevant actors. Outsourcing production within a jurisdiction may allow lead firms to escape regulations that target specific actors, for example by using labour-hire firms to avoid sector specific labour regulations or collective agreements.④

---

① Jaakko Salminen and Vibe Ulfbeck, "Developing Supply Chain Liability: A Necessary Marriage of Contract and Tort?" in Vibe Ulfbeck, Alexandra Andhov and Katerina Mitkidis (eds.) Law and Responsible Supply Chain Management: Contract and Tort Interplay and Overlap (Routledge 2019).

② Richard Baldwin, "Trade and Industrialization after Globalization's 2nd Unbundling: How Building and Joining a Supply Chain Are Different and Why It Matters" (2011) *National Bureau of Economic Research Working Paper* 17716.

③ Dan Danielsen, "Local Rules and a Global Economy: An Economic Policy Perspective" (2010) 1 *Transnational Legal Theory* 49.

④ David Weil, *The Fissured Workplace: Why Work Became So Bad for So Many and What Can Be Done to Improve It* (Harvard University Press 2014).

In transnational contexts regulation and enforcement frameworks may differ radically among jurisdictions, and thus for example a lead firm outsourcing production to another country may be confronted with a very different level of building code enforcement or environmental standards than in its home jurisdiction. ① In many cases, effective control thus requires lead firms to be proactive, either on their own or in cooperation with other private and public actors. These situations can range from compliance with target market standards, for example in relation to product quality, maintaining cost-effectiveness and research and development throughout the lead firm's value chain, or for ethical reasons, such as ensuring labour and environmental compliance throughout the value chain. ②

Various private governance mechanisms can be used to extend control in a chain of contracts. ③ Standards and monitoring provide one starting point, with lead firms requiring compliance with specific standards throughout the value chain and then monitoring compliance for example via audits. In many cases, however, merely requiring suppliers to comply with set standards is not enough as suppliers may not have the financial, technical, social or other capabilities to implement standards. Instead, in order to ensure compliance lead firms may have to put in place capability building mechanisms to help suppliers develop compliance. Even capability building may fall short and more intensive cooperation, for example in the form of partnering between lead firms and suppliers, has been proposed.

---

① Thus for example in Bangladesh transnational private initiatives seem necessary to ensure the enforcement of public building codes. Beryl ter Haar and Maarten Keune, "One Step Forward or More Window-Dressing? A Legal Analysis of Recent CSR Initiatives in the Garment Industry in Bangladesh" (2014) 30 *International Journal of Comparative Labour Law & Industrial Relations* 5.

② For some examples, see Peter Kajüter and Harri I. Kulmala, "Open-book accounting in networks: Potential achievements and reasons for failures" (2005) 16 *Management Accounting Research* 179; Ronald J Gilson, Charles F. Sabel and Robert E. Scott, "Contracting for Innovation: Vertical Disintegration and Interfirm Collaboration" (2009) 109 *Columbia Law Review* 431; Richard M. Locke, *The Promise and Limits of Private Power: Promoting Labor Standards in a Global Economy* (Cambridge University Press 2013).

③ For one typology, see Jaakko Salminen, "From Product Liability to Production Liability: Modelling a Response to the Liability Deficit of Global Value Chains on Historical Transformations of Production", forthcoming in *Competition and Change* (2019).

All forms of private governance, however, share one fundamental deficit: ultimately they rely on lead firm benevolence. ① Private governance related to the so-called externalities of production, such as labour, environmental and social interests, has often been developed only *after* a crisis. ② The use of forced labour, mismanagement of toxic waste, a factory burning down or collapsing or climate change may all turn into global media events that force the hand of lead firms in developing more adequate forms of private governance. Furthermore, it is unclear to what extent private responses to such catastrophes are intended as efficient remedies or merely stop-gap efforts to influence customers, financiers, regulators and other relevant actors. ③

At the same time, it is clear that if a lead firm sees private governance as crucial to its bottom-line, the creativity and effect of such mechanisms knows no bounds. For example in relation to value-chain-wide cost-management and research and development, lead firms are known to have created mechanisms that easily transgress contractual and corporate boundaries, that precisely map complex value chains and that provide mechanisms for intervention in the form of cooperative capability building, the costs and profits of which are mutually shared on a case-by-case basis. ④ Such mechanisms, however, are typically closely guarded business secrets and there is comparatively little publicly available information on how lead firms can and do govern their value chains. ⑤ Divulging private governance mechanisms may open up liabilities and is typically only done in any detail when there are clearly beneficial

---

① Robert B. Reich, *Supercapitalism: The Transformation of Business, Democracy, and Everyday Life* (Knopf 2007).

② For the proverbial example of labour conditions at Nike's foreign suppliers in the early 1990s, see Richard M. Locke, *The Promise and Limits of Private Power: Promoting Labor Standards in a Global Economy* (Cambridge University Press 2013).

③ Jaakko Salminen, "The Accord on Fire and Building Safety in Bangladesh—A New Paradigm for Limiting Buyers' Liability in Global Supply Chains?" (2018) 66 *American Journal of Comparative Law* 411.

④ E. g. Peter Kajüter and Harri I. Kulmala, "Open-book accounting in networks: Potential achievements and reasons for failures" (2005) 16 *Management Accounting Research* 179, pp. 186 – 190.

⑤ In addition to Kajüter and Kulmala, see, for example, Gary Gereffi, John Humphrey and Timothy Sturgeon, "The governance of global value chains" (2005) 12 *Review of International Political Economy* 78; Richard M. Locke, *The Promise and Limits of Private Power: Promoting Labor Standards in a Global Economy* (Cambridge University Press 2013).

reasons to do so, for example to turn a tide of negative media attention. ①

The possibilities and problems of private governance can be exemplified by what seems to be the current *publicly available* state-of-the-art of private governance: the Accord on Fire and Building Safety in Bangladesh ("Bangladesh Accord"). The Bangladesh Accord (both the five year term of the original 2013 version and its second iteration from 2018) is a governance contract arising out of the ashes of the 2013 Rana Plaza disaster where unenforced building codes contributed to the collapse of a building in Savar, Bangladesh. While the building had been partially evacuated due to clear signs of structural weakness, managers ordered workers to return to work in factories housed in the upper stories of the building, soon after which the building collapsed causing the deaths of over a thousand workers. This caused a global media backlash that resulted in two novel governance mechanisms: the Bangladesh Accord, which can be seen as the more advanced alternative, and the Alliance for Worker Safety in Bangladesh (Bangladesh Alliance), which can be seen as less advanced. ② While the less advanced Bangladesh Alliance was primarily championed by North American firms, the more advanced Bangladesh Accord has to a considerable degree been championed by European and Nordic companies, in particular the Swedish firm Hennes & Mauritz. ③

In a nutshell, the Bangladesh Accord connects two ends of a value chain, lead firms representing global brands and the global and local representatives of supplier

---

① Salminen, "The Accord on Fire and Building Safety in Bangladesh—A New Paradigm for Limiting Buyers' Liability in Global Supply Chains?" (2018) 66 *American Journal of Comparative Law* 411.

② E. g. Beryl ter Haar and Maarten Keune, "One Step Forward or More Window-Dressing? A Legal Analysis of Recent CSR Initiatives in the Garment Industry in Bangladesh" (2014) 30 *International Journal of Comparative Labour Law & Industrial Relations* 5; Mark Anner, Jennifer Bair and Jeremy Blasi, "Toward Joint Liability in Global Supply Chains: Addressing the Root Causes of Labor Violations in International Subcontracting Networks" (2013) 35 *Comparative Labor Law & Policy Journal* 1.

③ Beryl ter Haar and Maarten Keune, "One Step Forward or More Window-Dressing? A Legal Analysis of Recent CSR Initiatives in the Garment Industry in Bangladesh" (2014) 30 *International Journal of Comparative Labour Law & Industrial Relations* 5; Mark Anner, Jennifer Bair and Jeremy Blasi, "Toward Joint Liability in Global Supply Chains: Addressing the Root Causes of Labor Violations in International Subcontracting Networks" (2013) 35 *Comparative Labor Law & Policy Journal* 1; Salminen, "The Accord on Fire and Building Safety in Bangladesh—A New Paradigm for Limiting Buyers' Liability in Global Supply Chains?" (2018) 66 *American Journal of Comparative Law* 411.

employees in Bangladesh, with a governance contract.① The aim of the agreement is to increase the capabilities of suppliers in a way that accounts for the interests of the whole value chain—the focus of the contract is thus not limited to the parties to the agreement themselves, but provides a mechanism for the parties to extend governance in a mutually beneficial way to all involved value chain actors. Towards this, apart from putting in place a complex governance mechanism the agreement also grants specific benefits to supplier employees and places on lead firms obligations to collectively help fund and organize factory inspections and repairs. In many ways the agreement resembles what appears to be the state-of-the-art of private governance in more established (and more secretive) fields such as value chain wide cost-management and research and development, and from a transnational labour sustainability perspective the result has been hailed as ground-breaking.

There is, however, a dark side to the Bangladesh Accord. First, it operates in the shadow of the law: it is the *private* result of the failure of publicly regulating global value chains. Because of this, while being ground-breaking and apparently efficient, it is limited to a very specific set of problems in a specific sector of production in a single jurisdiction. Second, it externalizes control to a contractual mechanism that can be used not only to develop governance but also specifically to limit liabilities arising out of inadequate governance. In both ways the end result depends on lead firm benevolence: first, it is up to lead firms whether they wish to engage in effective governance mechanism in a specific context, and second, it is up to lead firms to decide on the contents of the mechanism and to what extent it can be used to not only expand governance but to limit any liabilities arising out of it.② Neither is the result easily standardized. Having all global value chains governed solely by such private agreements would probably lead to considerable confusion in understanding the differences and individual benefits of each separate initiative.

At the same time, the Bangladesh Accord does provide an important and public example of what companies can do together with interest groups to govern global

---

① Salminen, "The Accord on Fire and Building Safety in Bangladesh—A New Paradigm for Limiting Buyers' Liability in Global Supply Chains?" (2018) 66 *American Journal of Comparative Law* 411.

② Salminen, "The Accord on Fire and Building Safety in Bangladesh—A New Paradigm for Limiting Buyers' Liability in Global Supply Chains?" (2018) 66 *American Journal of Comparative Law* 411.

value chain sustainability. This example can no doubt be transplanted into other than labour contexts, such as in relation to environmental interests and, in particular, the governance of greenhouse gas emissions in global value chains. ① Thus, instead of seeing such mechanisms as examples of how *good* lead firms act, they should perhaps be seen as examples of how *all* lead firms *could* act. The best practices portrayed by governance mechanisms such as the Bangladesh Accord could be used as a general standard of care in private law and public regulation in relation to governing value chain externalities, thus guaranteeing their general application. A similar approach is already in place for example under product liability law. ②

3. Value Chain Litigation and *Arica Victims KB* v *Boliden Mineral AB*

In several cases claimants have tried to impose liability on lead firms for inadequate value chain governance under private law doctrines such as contract and tort. Scenarios range from substandard and even dangerous working conditions, such as in the Californian *Doe* v *WalMart* and Canadian *Das* v George Weston cases,③ to environmental degradation, such as in the English *Trafigura* and Dutch *Shell* cases,④ to climate change. ⑤ Claims have been based on contract, tort and other causes of action, set in both domestic and transnational contexts and have focused on lead firm governance in both parent-subsidiary and buyer-supplier relationships. While many cases have not been successful, others have resulted in

---

① Jaakko Salminen, "Sustainability in Contractually Organized Supply Chains: Coordinating Transport", in Ellen Eftestøl-Wilhelmsson, Suvi Sankari and Anu Bask (eds.), *Sustainable and Efficient Transport: Incentives for Promoting a Green Transport Market* (forthcoming, Edward Elgar 2019).

② For the standard of care under product liability law, see Jane Stapleton, *Product Liability* (Butterworths 1994) and Simon Whittaker (eds.), *The Development of Product Liability* (Cambridge University Press 2010), e. g. at Chapter 10.

③ *Doe v Walmart*, United States Court of Appeals, 9th Circuit, 08 – 55706, July 10, 2009 and Das v George Weston Ltd. , ONSC 4129, Ontario Superior Court of Justice, July 5, 2017 (under appeal).

④ For *Trafigura and Dutch Shell*, see e. g. Liesbeth Enneking, *Foreign Direct Liability and Beyond* (Eleven International Publishing 2012) 102 – 107.

⑤ Generally Geetanjali Ganguly, Joana Setzer and Veerle Heyvaert, "If at First You Don't Succeed: Suing Corporations for Climate Change" (2018) 38 *Oxford Journal of Legal Studies* 841.

important precedent, such as the *Chandler* v *Cape* ruling,[1] or large settlements, such as in *Trafigura*.

It is difficult to adequately summarize the current status of global value chain litigation related to inadequate lead firm governance.[2] However, it can be noted that due to the practicalities of current cases and reigning ideas of private international law, most current cases seem to focus on the common law.[3] These cases, in turn, have focused on transposing the precedent set in *Chandler* v *Cape*, which centred around a domestic parent-subsidiary relationship, into a transnational buyer—supplier context. Examples include cases such as *Das* v *George Weston*, currently under appeal in Canada, and *Jabir* v *KiK*, which was in January 2019 dismissed by a trial in Germany due to a Pakistani statute of limitations but which may yet be appealed.[4]

Focus on the common law and the *Chandler* precedent causes a number of challenges for litigation at present. In particular, under *Chandler* it is required *both* that a lead firm controls its subsidiaries or suppliers, *and* that this control was negligent. Thus if a lead firm does not govern its suppliers, there seems to be little chance of liability. This deficit may to some extent be offset by lead firms potentially being liable also in cases where they knowingly outsourced production to incompetent actors, such as in the *Trafigura* scenario. This possible exception to the *Chandler* rule, however, seems for now limited and uncertain. For example, in *Das* v *George Weston* a Canadian trial court found that requiring suppliers to follow standards set by and monitored by a lead firm was not enough to ground liability. This would imply that *Chandler* is applicable only in select cases where lead firms specifically interfere with or extend governance to specific value chain actors,

---

[1] *Chandler v Cape*, [2012] EWCA 525. See Martin Petrin, "Assumption of Responsibility in Corporate Groups: Chandler v Cape plc" (2013) 76 *Modern Law Review* 603.

[2] For one approach, see Salminen, "From Product Liability to Production Liability: Modelling a Response to the Liability Deficit of Global Value Chains on Historical Transformations of Production", forthcoming in *Competition and Change* (2019).

[3] Jaakko Salminen and Vibe Ulfbeck, "Developing supply chain liability: A necessary marriage of contract and tort?" in Vibe Ulfbeck, Alexandra Andhov and Katerina Mitkidis (eds.), *Law and Responsible Supply Chain Management* (forthcoming, Routledge 2019).

[4] *Jabir v KiK Textilien und Non-Food GmbH*, LG Dortmund, 7 O 95/15, January 10, 2019 (Germany).

for example through advanced private governance mechanisms such as those related to capability building or partnering referred to in Section 2. Furthermore, showing such control is not easy for claimants when governance is generally a closely guarded business secret.

It has been argued that claims would be easier in civil law contexts. ① The recent Swedish case of *Arica Victims KB* v *Boliden Mineral AB* (under appeal) might corroborate this. ② In *Arica* v *Boliden*, claimants allege that the Swedish mining and smelting company Boliden outsourced the treatment of toxic sludge to a Chilean company that was incapable of properly taking care of the sludge which was stored outdoors so that desert winds spread toxic substances into nearby settlements, poisoning several hundred inhabitants.

While it is impossible to generalize solely on the basis of the current district court decision in *Arica*, in particular as the appeal is still being heard, it is nonetheless interesting that the court comparatively easily seemed to find Boliden was negligent in selling sludge to the Chilean company for processing. Unlike in *Chandler*, there was little need to show that Boliden had extensive control over the Chilean supplier or even tried to govern it. Instead, the Swedish court focused primarily on the fact that some Boliden personnel had been aware that the sludge would be stored uncovered in the open so that prevailing desert winds could carry toxic substances to nearby settlements. This awareness of conditions at the supplier's facilities was enough to ground negligence. Ultimately, though, despite negligence on Boliden's part the court did not rule for the claimants because questions of causation and damage were left unclear. In particular, the court was uncertain of whether the elevated arsenic content in the claimants' blood could found a claim for damages or not.

Furthermore, it is up for debate whether *Arica* v *Boliden* should in its current form be seen more generally to corroborate a less rigorous standard of lead firm

---

① Cees van Dam, "Tort Law and Human Rights: Brothers in Arms On the Role of Tort Law in the Area of Business and Human Rights" (2011) 2 *Journal of European Tort Law* 221, 243 - 244.

② *Arica Victims KB v Boliden Minerals AB*, Skellefteå tingsrätt, T 1021 - 13, March 8, 2018 (Sweden, under appeal). For discussion prior to the district court ruling, see Rasmus Kløcker Larsen, "Foreign Direct Liability Claims in Sweden: Learning from Arica Victims KB v. Boliden Mineral AB?" (2014) 83 *Nordic Journal of International Law* 404.

control than *Chandler* or merely be seen to represent the line of cases similar to *Trafigura that seem to provide an exception to Chandler's* requirements of control. Hopefully this uncertainty will be clarified in the upcoming appeal court's ruling.

Nonetheless, it seems very much possible that in cases where civil law approaches to negligence are applied, such as in Jurisdictions like France, Germany, the Netherlands, and the Nordic countries, lead firms could more easily be found liable for the inadequate governance of their value chains than under the common law. For one, our developing understanding of how lead firms can and do use private governance mechanisms to control third party externalities, as discussed in Section 2 above, contributes to notions of what lead firms can be held liable for under law. For another, civil law cases could be on the rise due to increased focus on *mandatory rules of private international law* in public regulation focusing on standards of global value chain governance, as discussed next in Section 4.

4. Public Regulation of Global Value Chains and the Finnish Campaign for a Corporate Responsibility Law

Until recently, the regulation of production has generally not extended beyond national borders except in specific cases, such as the 1977 US Foreign Corrupt Practices Act focusing on corruption in global value chains. [1] This does not mean that local regulations, focusing for example on import restrictions or local emission standards, do not have transnational effects. [2] It does, however, mean that nation states have been very reluctant to directly regulate those parts of global value chains that are situated in other jurisdictions. Instead, transnational regulation has been seen to be the domain of international public law, private governance, or a combination of both. [3] While several public international law instruments have been enacted, such as the UN Guiding Principles and the OECD Guidelines for

---

[1] David Kennedy and Dan Danielsen, *Busting Bribery: Sustaining the Global Momentum of the Foreign Corrupt Practices Act* (Open Society Foundations 2011).

[2] Dan Danielsen, "Local Rules and a Global Economy: An Economic Policy Perspective" (2010) 1 *Transnational Legal Theory* 49.

[3] Kenneth W. Abbott and Duncan Snidal, "Strengthening International Regulation through Transnational New Governance: Overcoming the Orchestration Deficit" (2009) 42 *Vanderbilt Journal of Transnational Law* 501.

Multinational Enterprises, these are ultimately non-binding soft law. And while there is increasing momentum for a hard business and human rights treaty,[1] any such treaty faces an uphill battle at least as hard as that of the climate change related Paris Accord.

The problems associated with private governance, public international regulation, and private litigation have all driven states to focus on local hard laws that aim to require or motivate lead firms in their territory to aim governance measures at those parts of their global value chains that lie in other jurisdictions. Over the last ten years, several such regulations have sprouted up, in particular in the United States, Australia and Europe. These regulations are in many ways experimental in nature and face several challenges that cannot be discussed in detail here, but a brief overview of the main challenges can be provided.[2]

First, in many cases the regulations tend to focus on corporate governance instead of contractually organized value chains. This highlights the general problems of conceptualizing governance in contractually organized value chains, which is a comparatively new topic from both a legal and non-legal perspective, as opposed to the already well-established legal and non-legal literature on corporate governance.[3] Thus in some cases, such as in relation to a proposed Swiss law on corporate social responsibility, there is a clear legal division between corporate governance and governance through contract.[4] Under the current Swiss proposal

---

[1] See e. g. "Legally Binding Instrument to Regulate, in International Human Rights Law, the Activities of Transnational Corporations and Other Business Enterprises", *Zero Draft* 16. 7. 2018. Available at (accessed December 3, 2018): www. ohchr. org/Documents/HRBodies/HRCouncil/ WGTransCorp/Session3/DraftLBI. pdf. For discussion, see e. g. Olivier De Schutter, "Towards a New Treaty on Business and Human Rights" (2016) 1 *Business and Human Rights Journal* 41.

[2] For some examples and discussion, see Salminen, "Sustainability and the Move from Corporate Governance to Governance Through Contract", in Beate Sjåfjell and Christopher Brunner (eds.), *Cambridge Handbook of Corporate Law, Corporate Governance and Sustainability* (forthcoming Cambridge University Press 2019).

[3] Salminen, "Sustainability and the Move from Corporate Governance to Governance through Contract", in Beate Sjåfjell and Christopher Brunner (eds.), *Cambridge Handbook of Corporate Law, Corporate Governance and Sustainability* (forthcoming Cambridge University Press 2019).

[4] See Nationalrat (Schweiz), "Zusatzbericht der Kommission für Rechtsfragen vom 18. Mai 2018 zu den Anträgen der Kommission für einen indirekten Gegenentwurf zur Volksinitiative 《Für verantwortungsvolle Unternehmen-zum Schutz von Mensch und Umwelt》 im Rahmen der Revision des Akt" (2018).

for a corporate sustainability law, lead firms are on the one hand required to extend due diligence throughout their value chains notwithstanding whether these are structured contractually or as a corporate group. On the other hand, under the proposed Swiss law lead firms can be held liable only for the inadequate governance of their subsidiaries, not for contractual suppliers. Naturally, such an approach would leave a great deal of a lead firm's value chain outside the scope of liability. Thus there is a clear need to develop a general duty of care that applies to both corporate groups and contractually organized value chains.

Second, instruments may differ greatly in relation to their personal and material scope. Many of the earlier sustainability laws focused on narrow topics, such as modern slavery under the UK Modern Slavery Act's Transparency in Supply Chains provisions or conflict minerals under the US Federal Section 1502 of the Dodd Frank Act, and restricted their applicability primarily to large actors, based for example on turnover or employee count.[1] Some more recent approaches, such as the new French law on a corporate duty of care,[2] the EU Non-Financial Reporting Directive,[3] and the proposed Swiss corporate sustainability law,[4] have adopted material scopes that more broadly cover human and environmental rights. Even these statutes, however, are still restricted in personal scope to larger lead firms or those operating in sectors that are particularly prone to abuse.

Third, many of the instruments focus on requiring lead firms to undertake human rights due diligence and to publicly present reports of their due diligence measures. However, there is considerable variation in reporting standards, ranging from the comparatively strict and detailed, as under the French law on a corporate

---

[1] For examples of both, see the United Kingdom Modern Slavery Act 2015, c. 30 and Section 1502 of the US Federal Dodd-Frank Wall Street Reform and Consumer Protection Act, H. R. 4173.

[2] Loi n° 2017 - 399 du 27 mars 2017 relative au devoir de vigilance des sociétés mères et des entreprises donneuses d'ordre, JORF n°0074, 28. 3. 2017.

[3] Directive 2014/95/EU of the European Parliament and of the Council of 22 October 2014 amending Directive 2013/34/EU as regards disclosure of non-financial and diversity information by certain large undertakings and groups.

[4] See Nationalrat (Schweiz), "Zusatzbericht der Kommission für Rechtsfragen vom 18. Mai 2018 zu den Anträgen der Kommission für einen indirekten Gegenentwurf zur Volksinitiative 《Für verantwortungsvolle Unternehmen-zum Schutz von Mensch und Umwelt》 im Rahmen der Revision des Akt" (2018).

duty of care, to potentially extremely lax, as under the UK Modern slavery Act's Transparency in Supply Chains provisions, under which lead firms may simply report that they do not report on human rights due diligence. And even where comparatively strict reporting requirements are in place, there may nonetheless be considerable variation in how and what lead firms report. ① There is a major need for developing unified and functional standards in order for reporting and transparpency to work.

Fourth and finally, the relationship of the different regulations to liability under private law is in many cases unclear. Some regulations merely acknowledge that they do not rule out any liability that might arise on grounds of the general principles of e. g. tort law, as under the French law on a corporate duty of care. Other regulations put in place specific sanctions, such as criminal penalties under the UK Modern Bribery Act and the penalties related to filing reports in bad faith under Section 1502 of the US Federal Dodd Frank Act. In this regard the proposed Swiss law is highly interesting as it clearly places on lead firms liability for inadequate governance, even if only in relation to subsidiaries, not suppliers. ② The Swiss proposal would also include a defence against liability in case lead firms have adequately governed value chain externalities.

More interestingly, the Swiss proposal also accounts for questions of private international law. If no effective remedies would be found under a foreign law applicable to a dispute under the rules of private international law, then the mandatory overriding rules included in the Swiss proposal might make Swiss law applicable instead if it would provide better access to remedies. ③ Such an approach could make litigation much easier from a procedural perspective as claimants could

---

① Galit A. Sarfaty, "Shining Light on Global Supply Chains" (2015) 56 *Harvard International Law Journal* 419.

② See Nationalrat (Schweiz), "Zusatzbericht der Kommission für Rechtsfragen vom 18. Mai 2018 zu den Anträgen der Kommission für einen indirekten Gegenentwurf zur Volksinitiative 《 Für verantwortungsvolle Unternehmen-zum Schutz von Mensch und Umwelt》 im Rahmen der Revision des Akt" (2018).

③ See Nationalrat (Schweiz), "Zusatzbericht der Kommission für Rechtsfragen vom 18. Mai 2018 zu den Anträgen der Kommission für einen indirekten Gegenentwurf zur Volksinitiative 《 Für verantwortungsvolle Unternehmen-zum Schutz von Mensch und Umwelt》 im Rahmen der Revision des Akt" (2018).

rely on the law governing the lead firm instead of the law of the place where the damage occurred, as the latter would typically be the law of a supplier's or subsidiary's domicile instead of the law of the lead firm responsible for governing its value chain.

Generally, the legal conceptualization of contractually organized value chains is perhaps the biggest legal-technical problem faced by the growing wave of regulation. The other challenges are related to political issues, such as extending the material and personal scope of the laws to cover all lead firms instead of just larger ones, to the technicalities of regulation, such as developing reporting standards, and legal-procedural challenges, such as developing the procedural parameters of litigation under private international law. Additional challenges might be related to shifting burdens of proof more in favour to claimants, as happened historically in relation to product liability law, and questions of whether select defences could exempt lead firms from liability if they put in place adequately stringent governance measures, as also happened under product liability law. [1] In particular, narrow but nonetheless applicable defences might motivate lead firms to continuously develop governance in light of best available techniques. [2]

Currently there is no single approach that would provide an overarching regulatory approach accounting for all these challenges. Current Finnish debate on a corporate sustainability law *proposes* to do so by basing the regulation on best practices gathered through a comparison of existing regulations. [3] Of course, while there is currently considerable and growing public and political support for such a law in Finland, the end result, if any, will probably depend on political compromise. Thus, instead of looking in detail at the ways in which a possible Finnish law might overcome the challenges listed above, it might be more fruitful at pointing out the possible *political justifications* supporting such an extensive

---

[1] Jane Stapleton, *Product Liability* (Butterworths 1994) and Simon Whittaker (eds.), *The Development of Product Liability* (Cambridge University Press 2010).

[2] For all these issues, see Salminen, "From Product Liability to Production Liability: Modelling a Response to the Liability Deficit of Global Value Chains on Historical Transformations of Production", forthcoming in *Competition and Change* (2019).

[3] See www. ykkösketjuun. fi and Finnwatch, "Laki yritysten ihmisoikeusvastuusta: Vertaileva katsaus eri maiden lakihankkeisiin ja parhaisiin käytäntöihin" (2018).

regulatory approach. A key factor here is that legislative development is supported by several actors in Finland: industry, labour, and consumers. [1]

Of these, consumer interest is probably the most obvious as consumers wish to have a good conscience when buying foreign goods: they do not want to buy products that contribute to forced labour or environmental degradation. Industry and labour interests, however, may be seen as more sinister: in effect, both are interested in maintaining a competitive advantage against foreign actors. Requiring strict compliance in e. g. labour and environmental standards would no doubt help secure labour, environmental and other interests globally. However, doing so in relation to foreign lead firms entering local markets will also raise the bar in relation to whether foreign actors can enter local markets in the first place. This entails a delicate balancing of global labour and environmental standards, local interests related to market access, and the ebbs and flows of globally intertwined production and free trade.

5. Conclusion: The New Trends of Nordic Law and Their Relation to Global Interests

From a Nordic perspective, it would seem that there is interest in considerably raising the bar from current standards in relation to the governance required from lead firms over their global value chains. This is visible in the development of novel private governance mechanisms, new approaches to private litigation, and new local public regulations, all focusing on the governance of global value chains and placing on lead firms a concrete measure of liability over the inadequate governance of labour, environmental and other contingencies related to their value chains. Such an approach is no doubt necessary to ensure that the world remains within the planetary boundaries required for a sustainable future.

However, this positive trend does not come without a dark side. Together, the *local* developments described above are global in nature. They directly touch global flows of trade and production in today's world of global value chains. They are a reaction to the problems of unhinged global production and can be seen as

---

[1] See www. ykkösketjuun. fi.

necessary developments for the global governance of labour, environmental and other interests. At the same time, they in turn raise delicate questions related to market access and protectionism against global competition. These questions need to be balanced from a global and not just a Nordic perspective to ensure a sustainable future for all.

北欧价值链可持续性最新发展趋势

雅克科·萨尔米宁

【摘要】在过去几十年中，根据合同约定组织的"全球价值链"已经成为主要的生产形式。但是法律却对这一变化反应迟钝。公私领域的规制机构直到最近才开始理解和规制公司集团，而最近对根据合同约定组织的价值链所采取的行动使法律进一步远离了其舒适区。特别是目前最新的价值链规制体系仍然不能有效处理根据合同约定组织的价值链的可持续性问题。与此同时，一些与私人治理、私法诉讼和公共规制有关的全球性趋势正在推动可持续价值链治理的发展，以及法律对根据合同约定组织的生产的回应。本文考察最近北欧版的这些有关私人治理、私法诉讼和公共规制的全球发展趋势，并将其置于其所要规制的全球语境中加以分析。虽然这一北欧路径乍看似乎超越了全球最新的规制体系，但是它仍面临着一项关键性的挑战，那就是如何平衡作为推动北欧可持续性路径的一项重要动力的本地经济利益与可持续性的全球视角。

第三部分
互联网、人工智能与法律应对

Artificial Intelligence as a Tool for Legal and Legislative Challenges

Harriet Lonka[*] *and Timo Honkela*[**]

[Abstract] The Artificial Intelligence (AI) is expected to reshape our society vastly in the becoming years. It has become obvious that it is about not only technology solutions, but AI demands attention also from the Social Sciences. The urge to better understand the ways in which AI reforms our future society has challenged the Finnish Law Schools to turn their focus more to the AI driven tools and solutions. The demand for new knowledge and new approaches from the legal scientists is at least twofold. The use of AI in different parts of the society urges for new regulatory innovations and at the same time the legal discipline and legal practices need to be able to apply AI technologies in delivering their services. One aspect yet raising less awareness is the ways in which AI can help us to better understand the background data used in shaping legislation and regulatory system in general. This is the focus of our interest in the common project between the University of Eastern Finland and the University of Helsinki. This paper gives an overall view on central development of AI in the field of Social Sciences in general. To deepen the view it presents some cases and foreseen future developments in the Legal Tech arena connected to legislative studies.

---

[*] University Researcher at the Law School, University of Eastern Finland.
[**] Professor at the Department of Digital Humanities, University of Helsinki.

1. AI and Social Sciences

Artificial Intelligence is not a novelty. Its recent developments are part of the continuum, which started already early 1900's. A well-known pioneer who studied the crucial questions of the characteristics of human intelligence as compared to the machine was Alan Turing (1912 – 1954). Turing influenced in an important manner the development of theoretical computer science. His key invention was formalization of the concepts of algorithm and computation with the Turing machine, which is considered as a model of a general-purpose computer. Turing is widely seen as the father of theoretical computer science and artificial intelligence. He addressed the problem of artificial intelligence, and proposed an experiment, the Turing test, an attempt to define a standard for a machine to be called "intelligent". The idea was that a computer could be said to "think" if a human interrogator could not tell it apart, through conversation, from a human being.

Since the early days the characteristic feature of the modern AI work has been that large proportion of it focuses on numerical data. Linguistic data is transferred into numerical (vector-spaced) representations through considering contextual information. [1]

The tradition in AI has for decades been struggling with the dilemmas of representation and reasoning. The key questions are: how to represent our knowledge and on the other hand, how to reason over knowledge? We had GOFAI solution[2] where symbolic logic was the underlying basis. GOFAI failed in the 1980s not only for quantitative reasons but also for qualitative reasons. Currently popular methods include multilayer perceptions (neural networks; convolutional neural networks for pattern recognition) and reinforcement learning for numerical data and Latent Dirichlet Allocation[3] for text data analogical to

---

[1] Honkela 2018.

[2] John Haugeland gave the name GOFAI ("Good Old-Fashioned Artificial Intelligence") to symbolic AI in his 1985 book *Artificial Intelligence: The Very Idea*, which explored the philosophical implications of artificial intelligence research.

[3] In natural language processing (NLP), latent Dirichlet allocation (LDA) is a generative statistical model that allows sets of observations to be explained by unobserved groups that explain why some parts of the data are similar.

WordICA.[1] Data is increasingly "natural", not formalised to be easily dealt with traditional programmed systems with fixed formal framework (explicit or implicit; cf. e. g. relational databases and SQL).[2]

The statistical machine learning can be categorized in three classes: supervised learning, unsupervised learning and reinforcement learning. In supervised learning, the system is given both the input and the desired output, and it learns to construct a mapping between them[3]. The main shortcoming of the supervised learning is that it carries with it potential for violence through strict categorizations. It tends to support keeping the old concepts[4]. In unsupervised learning, a model is fitted to observations, and there is no a priori output. Thus, unsupervised learning may give rise to novel model constructions autonomously emerging from the data.[5] The outcomes of unsupervised learning depend on data selection and parameterization. Reinforcement learning is able to build systems with goals and values and is the most developed version of machine learning.

The key issue for how machine learning would work for social sciences is how it can serve intentions. A commonly recognized problem is that machine learning results are based on data given to the algorithm. This often leads into a poor quality model if the data is not representative and/or to a model that does not match the intentions or goals. The development must be enhanced to reach computational creativity, which enables machine learning to find novel solutions. In our reach for becoming years is also next steps like deep learning of data that indicates what are the nature and characteristics of good intentions and successful means to reach positive results. Like a system can learn a different game, it can learn to build means to reach positive goals in new domains and different levels of abstraction.[6]

---

[1] Honkela et al. 2010.

[2] SQL is Structured Query Language, a domain-specific language used in programming and designed for managing data held in a relational database management system (RDBMS), or for stream processing in a relational data stream management system (RDSMS). It is particularly useful in handling structured data with relations between different entities/variables of the data.

[3] Janasik et al. 2009.

[4] Timo Honkela 2018: My AI in Peace Machine. My Data Conference, Aug 29, 2018, Helsinki University.

[5] Janasik et al. 2009.

[6] Honkela 2018.

As a field of study, Social Science adds immense value to AI development both in its high applicability to the task at hand and as a counterpart to the technical focus of the science, technology, engineering and mathematics (STEM) fields. AI systems have a reputation for being impartial. While it is technically true that numbers don't lie, the blind trust in automated processes is not justified. Numbers can be manipulated, misrepresented, or ignored, and even though machines are not inherently biased, their human creators are. Social Science presents a powerful tool to combat this AI bias, which is an important conceptual challenge for AI preventing it from operating at its full potential. The negative implications of bias have become apparent as AI expands in nearly every service imaginable. There have been several well-documented biased AI incidents: facial recognition errors, improper sentencing and assignation of parole, unequal granting of bank loans, unsuitable medical diagnoses, and ineffectual voice recognition. Even in a meticulously programmed system with balanced parameters, bias can seep in through historical data that is tainted by incomplete information and unequal historical trends. In the context of AI, the application of Social Science can reveal what is causing the bias in the algorithm or prevent it from happening in the first place. Working proactively, social scientists can use their training to collaborate on the AI system's design, parameters, and data to be sure that they are balanced and the system functions as expected in practice, in addition to teaching qualitative principles and analysis methods to their more quantitative coworkers. [1]

2. Artificial Intelligence as Business

One key issue for Artificial Intelligence to wake awareness is its huge business potential. The graphical presentation below (Figure 1) illustrates the immense growth of businesses we have witnessed since the start of the millennium. The data presented in the figure is of 1700 businesses from 70 different countries. [2] A Narrative Science survey found in 2016 that 38% of enterprises are already using AI, growing to 62% by 2018. International Data Corporation estimated that the AI

---

[1] Green 2018.

[2] https://www.venturescanner.com/artificial-intelligence.

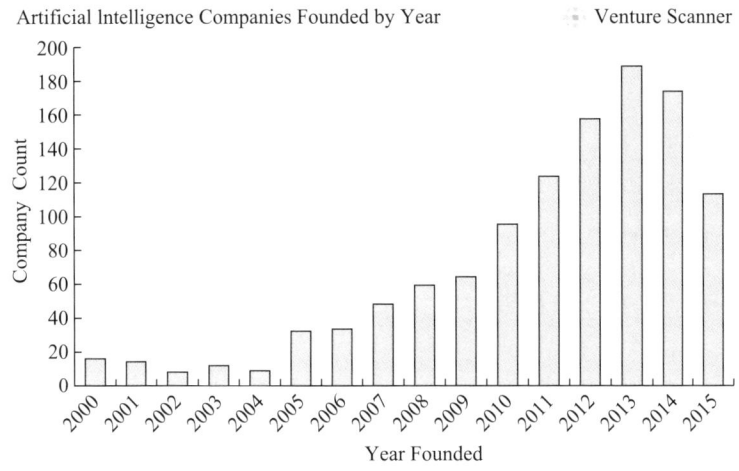

market will grow from \$8 billion in 2016 to more than \$47 billion in 2020. ①

Figure 1 The development of AI Companies Founded by year in Venture Scanner database

The AI solutions available today includes a variety of technologies and tools. The challenge of the follow-up of this field is that evolution of different solutions follow different trajectories concerning their maturity, lifetime and value expectations. The foreseen developments of different solutions based on the global business data is presented in Figure 2.

The technologies, which are still in their creation phase but expected to grow in their importance during next 3 −5 years and create large business benefit, are Deep Learning Platforms, Natural Language Generation, Speech Recognition and Biometrics. Deep Learning Platforms are a special type of machine learning consisting of artificial neural networks with multiple abstraction layers. They are currently used in pattern recognition and classification applications supported by very large data sets. Natural Language Generation produces text from computer data. It is used in customer service, report generation, and summarizing business intelligence insights. Speech Recognition is used to transcribe and transform human speech into format useful for computer applications. It is currently used in interactive voice response systems and mobile applications. Biometrics enable more natural interactions between humans and machines, including, but not limited to,

---

① https://www.forbes.com/.

image and touch recognition, speech, and body language. They are currently used primarily in market research.

Examples of technologies that are on their growth trajectory but still need 5 – 10 years to reach the next phase are Machine Learning Platforms, Virtual Agents, AI-optimized Hardware, Decision Management and Robotic Process Automation. Virtual Agents are well known from simple chatbots but include different advanced systems that can network with humans. They are currently widely used in customer service and support and as a smart home manager. Machine Learning Platforms provide algorithms, APIs[①], development and training toolkits, data, as well as computing power to design, train, and deploy models into applications, processes, and other machines. It is used in a wide range of enterprise applications, mostly involving prediction or classification.

AI-optimized Hardware include Graphics Processing Units (GPU) and appliances specifically designed to efficiently run AI-oriented computational jobs. They are playing a central role in the development of deep learning applications. Decision Management are engines that insert rules and logic into AI systems and are used for initial setup/training and ongoing maintenance and tuning. This is a mature technology, which is used in a wide variety of enterprise applications, assisting in or performing automated decision-making. Robotic Process Automation uses scripts and other methods to automate human action to support efficient business processes. Traditionally this type of automation is used where it is too expensive or inefficient for humans to execute a task or a process.

Text Analytics and Natural Language Processing (NLP) are examples of very fast developing field of AI technologies as is image and video analysis. NLP uses and supports text analytics by facilitating the understanding of sentence structure and meaning, sentiment, and intent through statistical and machine learning methods. It is currently used in fraud detection and security, a wide range of automated assistants, and applications for mining unstructured data. Semantic technology is developing in much slower phase and is expected to provide many solutions,

---

① API, an Application Program Interface is a set of routines, protocols, and tools for building software applications. It specifies how software components should interact (https://www.webopedia.com/TERM/A/API.html).

which can be useful in the Legal Tech sphere. Semantic technologies provide an abstraction layer above existing IT technologies that enables bridging and interconnection of data, content, and processes. Meanwhile, from the portal perspective, semantic technologies can be thought of as a new level of depth that provides far more intelligent, capable, relevant, and responsive interaction than with information technologies alone. An important application for legal tech field is Semantic Web whose practical application is e. g. the Finnish Semantic Finlex legal linked data solution.

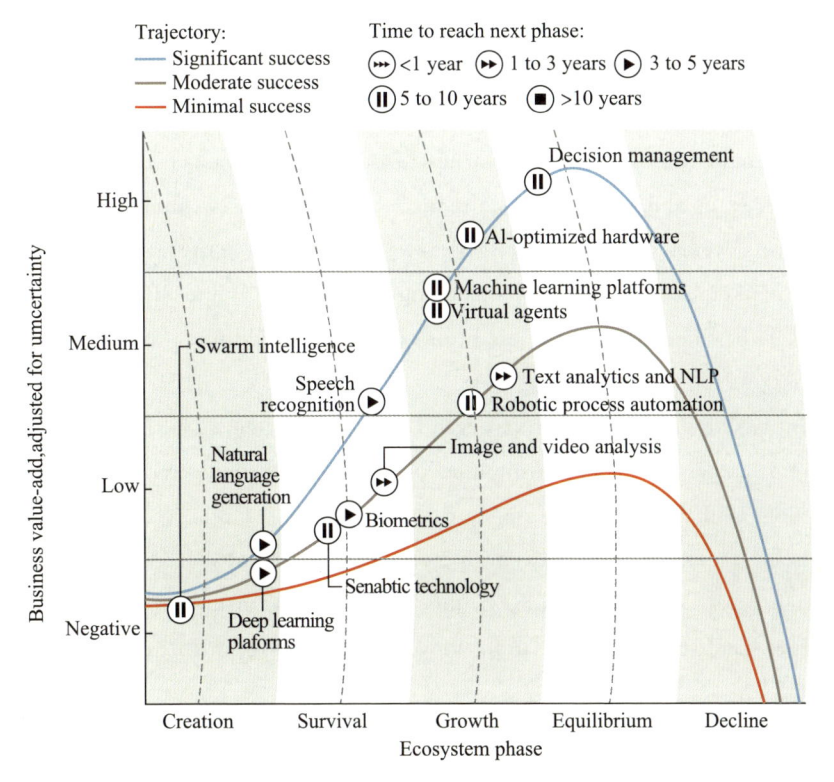

Figure 2 Artificial Intelligence Technologies Q1' 2017 (Forrest Research, TechRadar)

3. Legal and Regulatory Technology

Regulatory and legal technologies are technology fields, which can be identified as sub-categories of Artificial Intelligence technologies. Regulatory technologies are traditionally seen as sub-category of financial technologies (fin-tech) and supporting the banking business development. Regulatory technology (regtech) funding is on an upward trend in recent years. The two fastest growing sectors in the regtech field in recent years have been the financial crime and identity compliance category and the network security compliance category, which leads the sector in all-time funding.[1] Recent development in regtech funding are illustrated in Figure 3.

Legal technology traditionally refers to the application of technology and software to help law firms with practice management, document storage, billing, accounting and electronic discovery. Recently, it has expanded to include companies that are helping consumers and businesses connect with attorneys online and providing the tools that consumers and businesses need to take legal matters into their own hands, obviating the need for an attorney.[2] Since 2011, Legal Tech has evolved to be associated more with technology startups disrupting the practice of law by giving people access to online software that reduces or in some cases eliminates the need to consult a lawyer, or by connecting people with lawyers more efficiently through online marketplaces and lawyer-matching websites. Online dispute resolution (ODR) has been routinely used for e-commerce disputes already since the beginning of the Millennium[3].

Helsinki University founded its Legal Tech Lab in 2016. The Lab's objective is to raise awareness about the possibilities of legal tech, provide critical insights into technology and create a one-stop-shop for academic and practical information on digitalization of legal practices both nationally and globally. In a manner of speaking, the Legal Tech Lab is the law faculty's in-house start-up, which combines hands-on experimentation with legal technology with in-depth academic research[4].

4. Finnish Law and Justice as Linked Open Data-Semantic Finlex

Aalto University Semantic Computing Research Group (SeCo) is an example of

---

[1] https://venturescannerinsights.wordpress.com/category/regulatory-technology/.
[2] Hibnick 2014.
[3] Katsh and Rifkin 2001, Koulu 2016.
[4] https://www.helsinki.fi/en/networks/legal-tech-lab.

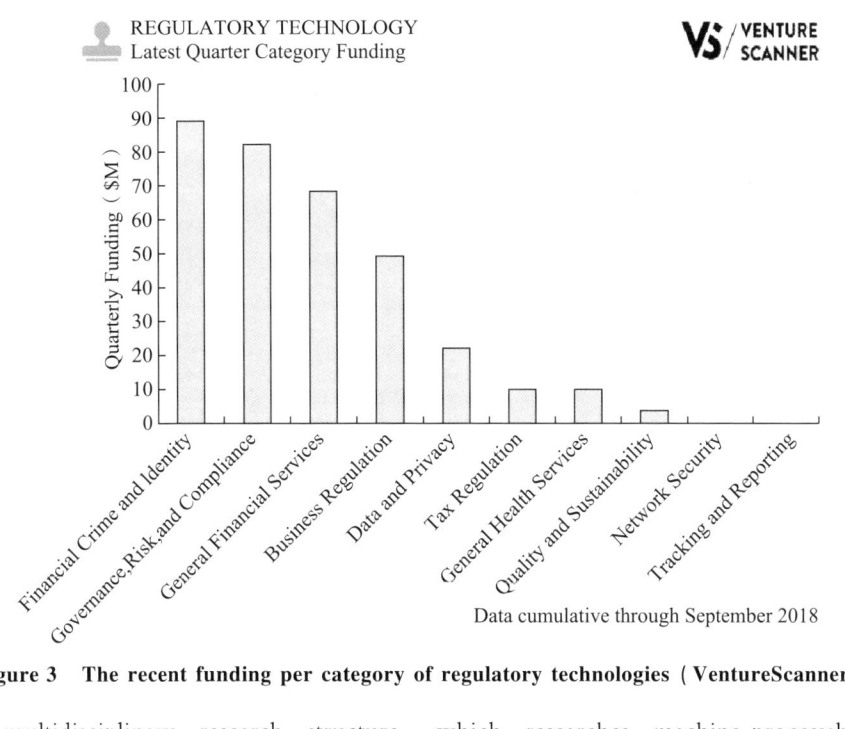

Figure 3 The recent funding per category of regulatory technologies (VentureScanner)

a multidisciplinary research structure, which researches machine-processable semantics related to, e.g. the Semantic Web. The participants are the Aalto University, School of Science, Department of Computer Science and HELDIG-Helsinki Centre for Digital Humanities, University of Helsinki, Faculty of Arts. The SeCo Group has created the Semantic Finlex, a Finnish Law and Justice as Linked Open Data[①]. The research and development work for Semantic Finlex was launched in 2012 as part of the national Linked Data Finland project. The project first led to a prototype, which included a selection of datasets from a specific point in time. With support from the Finnish Open Data Programme led by the Ministry of Finance, this prototype was further developed into the Semantic Finlex data service, through which a data publication is automatically updated in tandem with Finlex, the official Finnish Law and Justice Databank online (see Figure 4)[②].

The Finlex datasets had not been available as open data usable by IT applications, other online services and legislative applications via open interfaces. The Semantic

---

① https://data.finlex.fi/en/project.
② https://www.finlex.fi/en/.

Finex is based on the Finlex database and online service. It includes a linked open data service on Finnish legislation and jurisdiction as well as pilot applications presenting practical uses of the data service.

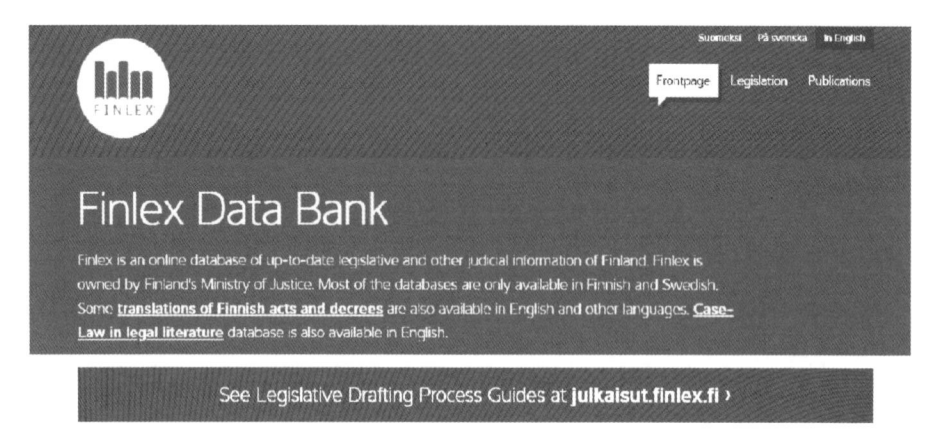

Figure 4

Finlex Data Bank is an open database including all up-to-date legislation in Finnish and Swedish. Only some acts and decrees are translated to English. The Finlex Data Bank does not contain linked data in the way Semantic Finlex does.

The Semantic Finlex data publication and service are based on the Linked Data standards, publication model and best practices of the Semantic Web standardized by W3C. A key idea behind linked data is to provide a Uniform Resource Identifier (URI) —a web address that enables users to search for Semantic Web data in a similar manner to web pages—for all resources. Alternatively, the identifier can be used programmatically based on the HTTP protocol. The identifier can also be used to enrich data with other data sources in such a manner that the information systems can interpret descriptions in intelligent applications.

Another key idea behind linked data involves using the Resource Description Framework (RDF) data model and notations standardised by W3C for the search and presentation of data. Based on this model, data is presented as a simple semantic web (Knowledge Graph), which harmonises and combines data presentation models used in different data silos, and accurately defines the meaning of data by use of logic. This enables the correct interpretation of data and its automatic enrichment by deducing new information.

For performing queries on web-form data, W3C has standardised the SPARQL language, which resembles the SQL language used in traditional relational databases. Query results can be obtained flexibly in various formats, such as in a table for a human reader or as data in RDF Turtle or JSON format, for programming purposes.

Adhering to open standards ensures the continuity of the data service and enables the utilisation of third-party utility programmes and components, such as editors, query systems, inference machines, data analysis and visualisation tools etc.. Semantic Finlex can also be used in applications through a special REST interface.

5 Self-Organized-Map in Classifying Legal Text Data

In the common project between Law School at University of Eastern Finland and HELDIG we have developed approaches to utilize Self-Organized-Map (SOM) as a tool to classify text data of the committee statements and expert statements to the committees in the Parliament of Finland. The ultimate goal of this project is to categorize the value judgments of the committee statements. The results would help to demystify the variation of the value judgments affecting in the background of drafting the legislation. Revealing the potential multidimensionality of values affecting in the background of the legislative development would probably help to broaden the sphere of public discussion on the legislative process from its present polarization.

Self-Organized-Map as a method creates multiple well-grounded perspectives on the data and thus improves the quality of the concepts and categories used in the analysis. These perspectives are not a collection of random views but form an organized whole. The SOM method can be of great utility in all social science research, but particularly and uniquely so when the qualitative data sets are very large (e. g. , thousands of documents) and/or the stakeholders numerous. [1]

The SOM is an unsupervised learning method that originally stems from artificial neural network research. Currently, it is commonly used as a method for statistical visualization and data analysis. The outcome of the SOM analysis is a map in which entities, such as people, words, sentences, or documents, are clustered according to similarity with respect to some property. Example of Self Organized Map

---

[1] Janasik, Honkela & Bruun 2009.

categorization is presented in Figure 5.

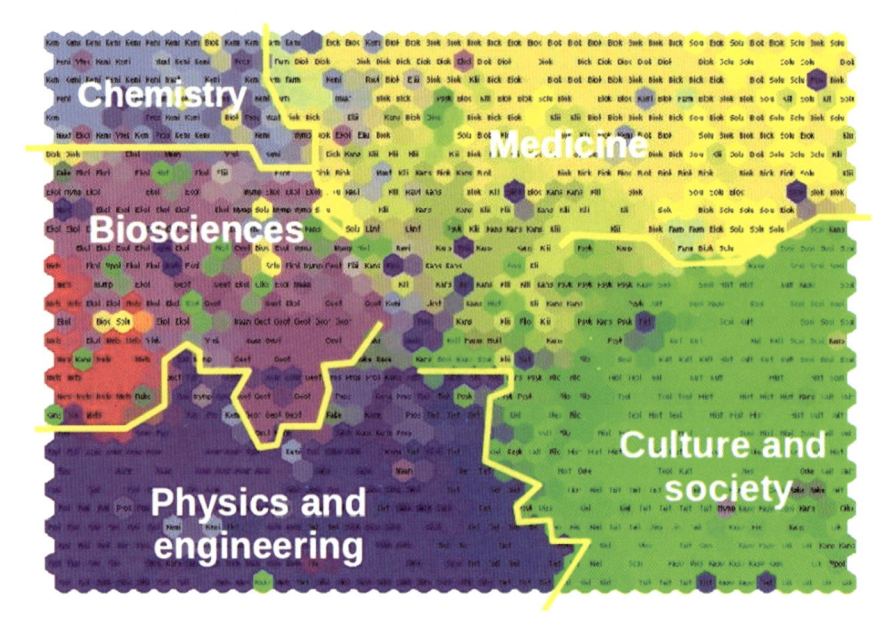

Figure 5　SOM used for categorizing themes of the applications in Finnish Academy of Sciences

Qualitative analysis is dependent on the interpretative activity of the person who does the analysis. Unsupervised learning methods are like "research assistants", tirelessly processing large collections of data and creating meaningful generalized representations of them.

6. The Concept for Further Research

Our research question is:

How can AI assist in understanding the value judgments of legislative process?

Our research interest is twofold. Firstly, there is a substantive interest. That is to learn the form of variation of values in the statements of committees and statements of experts to the committees in the Parliament of Finland. Secondly, there is a methodological interest: how useful would SOM method be in visualizing the values of committees on legislative drafting?

We would start our study by focusing on the decision making of the Constitutional Law Committee (CLC) of the Parliament of Finland. The CLC is a corner stone of the Finnish legislative system. It is one of the permanent Committees of the Parliament. The Committee issues statements sent to it for consideration on the constitutionality of matters. In general, the scrutiny of constitutionality of issues focuses on a restricted selection of articles of the Finnish Constitution. Thus, it would simplify the analysis. On the other hand, constitutional matters are of high importance in the legislative process and the public discussion on weighing the constitutional values easily becomes highly polarized.

Such a project, which concentrates on the text mining of the Finnish documents, includes specific challenges. Finnish language is not an Indo-European language such as English, Spanish, German and Russian. Finnish is a synthetic language, which includes large amount of inflectional word forms and compound words. In Finnish, each noun has about 2000 different forms possible and each verb more than 12000 forms possible.

Example of an analysis of 100 documents (1 page to 3 pages each) of expert statements to a parliamentary committee. The results for statistics of word "propose" in all its forms in Finnish with English translations is presented in Table 1.

In further phases of the project, we might also consider using other text mining methodologies like key phrase extraction method "Likey"[1]. Key phrase extraction is a natural language processing task for collecting the main topics of a document into a list of phrases. Key phrases are supposed to be available in the processed documents themselves, and the aim is to extract these most meaningful words and phrases from the documents. Key phrase extraction summarises the content of a document as a few phrases and thus provides a quick way to find out what the document is about. This might be a useful tool, e. g. for comparing large amounts of statements during the process of legal drafting.

Table 1 To propose (Finnish: ehdottaa)

Number	In Finnish	English translation
195	ehdotettu	the proposed
178	ehdotetun	the one which was proposed

[1] Paukkeri and Honkela 2010.

续表

Number	In Finnish	English translation
95	ehdotetaan	is proposed
76	ehdottaa	he/she/it proposes
54	ehdotetussa	in the one proposed
52	ehdotettua	(referring to) the one proposed
31	ehdotetut	those proposed
28	ehdotettuun	to (the one) proposed
18	ehdotettujen	the ones proposed
17	ehdotetusta	of the one proposed
17	ehdotetulla	the one proposed has (genitive form)
15	ehdotettava	the one proposed (referred to)
9	ehdotetuista	of those proposed
8	ehdotan	I propose
8	ehdotettava	the one which will be proposed
7	ehdotettuihin	to those ones proposed
7	ehdotettuja	the proposed ones
7	ehdotetuilla	the proposed ones have
6	ehdotettavaa	which wil lbe proposed
6	ehdotetuiss	a in those proposed
5	ehdoteta	not to be proposed
5	endotettavaan	to (included to) the one which will be proposed
4	endotetulle	for the one which was proposed
3	endotettavassa	in the proposed one
3	ehdotettiin	was proposed
2	ehdotettavasta	from the one which will be proposed
2	ehdottamalla	by proposing/in the one which was proposed
2	ehdottama	the one he/she/it proposed
1	ehdotamme	we propose
1	ehdotettaisi	he/she/it would propose
1	ehdotettaisiin	would be proposed
1	ehdotettavalla	by the one which will be proposed
1	ehdotetuille	for those which were proposed

Number	In Finnish	English translation
1	ehdotetuin	by those proposed
1	ehdottaisin	I would propose
1	ehdottamaan	will be proposed
1	ehdottaman	the one he/she/it proposed
1	ehdottamassa	in the one they proposed
1	ehdottamat	those which it proposed
1	ehdottamiaan	those which he/she proposed

References

Green, Joseph (2018). Social Science is the Antidote for Bias in Artificial Intelligence. https://medium.com/datadriveninvestor/social-science-is-the-antidote-for-bias-in-artificial-intelligence-d062a79bca81 May 15, 2018.

Hibnick, Eva (2014). What is Legal Tech? Esq. & filed under Legal Technology, LegalTech, LPM, News. https://www.thelawinsider.com/insider-news/what-is-legal-tech/.

Honkela, T., Hyvärinen, A. and Väyrynen, J. J. (2010). WordICA—emergence of linguistic representations for words by independent component analysis. Natural Language Engineering 16 (3): 277 −308. Cambridge University Press 2010.

Janasik, N., Honkela, T. and Bruun, H. (2009). Text Mining in Qualitative Research Application of an Unsupervised Learning Method. Organizational Research Methods 2009.

Katsh, Ethan and Rifkin, Jane (2001). Online Dispute Resolution: Resolving Conflicts in Cyberspace. Jossey-Bass, San Francisco 2001, s. 45 −.

Koulu, Riikka (2016). Blockchains and Online Dispute Resolution: Smart Contracts as an Alternative to Enforcement. 13 SCRIPTed 40 (2016).

McCarthy, John (2006). What has AI in Common with Philosophy? Computer Science Department, Stanford University Stanford. http://www-formal.stanford.edu/jmc/.

Paukkeri, Mari-Sanna and Honkela Timo (2010). Likey: Unsupervised Language-independent Keyphrase Extraction. Proceedings of the 5th International Workshop on Semantic Evaluation, ACL 2010, pages 162 −165.

Ross Intelligence: Artificial Intelligence in Legal Research, January 2017, www.rossintelligence.com.

作为工具的人工智能对法律和立法的挑战

哈丽特·隆卡　蒂莫·鸿克拉

【摘要】 人们认为在未来几年内人工智能将会在很大程度上重塑我们的社会。很明显，人工智能不仅仅是一种技术解决方案，它还需要得到社会科学的关注。为了更好地了解人工智能改造我们未来社会的方式，芬兰各法学院将其注意力转向人工智能驱动的工具和解决方案。法学家们对新知识和新方法的需求至少有两个方面：人工智能在社会各群体中的使用要求我们在规制方面作出创新；与此同时，法律学科和法律实践应该能够应用人工智能提供其服务。而人们还普遍没有意识到的一个方面就是：人工智能以何种方式帮助我们更好地理解那些用于塑造立法和整个规制系统的背景数据。而这正是东芬兰大学和赫尔辛基大学之间的一项共同研究项目的关注点。本文回顾了人工智能在社会科学领域的总体发展情况，介绍了这方面的一些案例，并展望了与立法研究相关的法律技术领域的未来发展。

互联网平台用工劳动关系认定

谢增毅[*]

【摘要】 传统劳动关系概念和判定理论突出人格从属性和经济从属性，该理论主要以工业化时代的工厂劳动关系为模型。由于平台用工具有许多新特点，劳动关系理论在互联网平台用工背景下遭遇了巨大挑战。但传统劳动关系概念和判定标准具有较强的弹性和适应性，传统劳动关系概念和判定理论并非完全过时，其仍可包容网络平台用工关系。与此同时，为适应网络平台用工的新特点，应改进劳动关系的判定方法。对网络平台用工劳动关系的认定，应根据不同平台以及不同类型工人的实际用工特点，综合考虑个案全部事实进行具体分析，更加注重实质从属性，考虑平台工人的工作时间和收入来源，以及社会保护的必要性等因素。我国可通过最高人民法院司法解释界定劳动关系的概念及判定因素。由于网络平台用工的复杂性和差异性，目前，我国不必针对网络平台工人的身份制定专门规则。除了劳动法，还应通过完善社会保险制度以及网络平台监管制度等多角度保护网络平台工人的权益。

【关键词】 劳动关系 互联网平台 平台工人 劳动关系认定

当前我国共享（分享）经济发展迅猛。据统计，2017年我国共享经济市场交易额约为49205亿元，比上年增长47.2%。2017年我国共享经济平台企业员工数约716万人，比上年增加131万人。2017年我国参与共享经济活动的人数超过7亿人，比上年增加1亿人左右。参与提供服务者人数约

---

[*] 中国社会科学院法学研究所研究员。

为 7000 万人，比上年增加 1000 万人。① 由于共享经济平台的企业员工，以及参与提供服务者人数庞大且急剧增长，共享经济所涉及的劳动法问题变得极为重要。

关于共享（分享）经济的概念，2017 年国家发展改革委等部门发布的《关于促进分享经济发展的指导性意见》指出，"分享经济在现阶段主要表现为利用网络信息技术，通过互联网平台将分散资源进行优化配置，提高利用效率的新型经济形态"。② 可见，互联网平台是共享经济的主要技术特征。③ 也有研究认为，相比"合作经济"（collaborative economy）、"共享经济"（sharing economy）等提法，"平台经济"（platform economy）是对这一新业态最为"客观"的描述。④ 为了突出网络平台的地位以及互联网平台企业在共享经济用工中的主体地位，本文使用"互联网平台用工"的提法。⑤ 当前我国互联网平台发展迅速，不同平台的商业模式以及用工形式也不相同。有学者将平台经营模式和用工形式分为"平台自营模式"、"信息服务模式"、"新型共享模式"、"多元混合模式"四种模式。⑥ 本文将以"新型共享模式"和"多元混合模式"为主，兼顾其他模式，并以公众较为熟悉的交通出行、餐饮外卖等网络平台为例阐述平台用工的劳动关系认定问题。

由于共享经济服务提供者人数极为庞大，且数量仍在急剧增长，加上平台用工形式复杂灵活，如何保障网络平台服务提供者的权益，成为一个

---

① 国家信息中心分享经济研究中心、中国互联网协会分享经济工作委员会：《中国共享经济发展年度报告（2018）》，2018 年 2 月，第 1 页。
② 国家发展改革委等：《关于促进分享经济发展的指导性意见》，2017 年 7 月 3 日，第 1 页。
③ 国家信息中心信息化研究部、中国互联网协会分享经济工作委员会：《中国分享经济发展年度报告（2016）》，2016 年 2 月，第 1 页。
④ Policy Department A: Economic and Scientific Policy, European Parliament, "The Social Protection of Workers in the Platform Economy", November 2017, p. 21, http://www.europarl.europa.eu/supporting-analyses，最后访问时间：2018 年 10 月 19 日。
⑤ 对"互联网平台用工"的从业人员，本文根据语境，泛称为"互联网平台服务提供者"、"互联网平台从业人员"或"平台工人"。一些国家将平台经济的主要形式称为"众包"（crowdwork），即众包商（crowdsourcer）在平台发布业务或工作，由众包工（crowdworker）提供服务。本文根据文献出处，个别地方使用"众包"和"众包工"的提法。
⑥ "平台自营模式"指平台一般以用工主体的身份与从业人员建立劳动关系。"信息服务模式"指平台主要发挥中介作用，本身并不成为直接用工主体。"新型共享模式"指采取与传统用工模式不同的用工形式，平台和从业人员呈现合作特征，但从业人员在一定程度上仍接受平台规则的管理。"多元混合模式"指平台采取直接雇用、劳务派遣、劳务外包、新型用工等多种用工形式。参见刘燕斌主编《中国劳动保障发展报告（2017）》，社会科学文献出版社，2017，第 296 - 300 页。

复杂而重要的课题。平台服务提供者与平台是否建立劳动关系,这一群体是否受劳动法保护,传统的"劳动者"概念或"劳动关系"判断标准是否已经过时,劳动法应当如何应对,成为一个核心问题。实践中,劳动关系认定也是与互联网有关的劳动争议案件的焦点问题。例如,2015年至2018年第一季度,北京市朝阳区人民法院共受理互联网平台用工劳动争议案件188件,其中61.2%的案件,从业者要求确认劳动关系,在审结的171件案件中,超过84%的案件双方对是否建立劳动关系存在争议。[①] 在美国,目前与共享经济有关的劳动争议问题也主要集中在平台工人是劳动者(雇员)还是独立承包人(independent contractors)上。[②] 从我国典型案例看,由于平台用工具体形式并不相同,加上劳动关系的判断标准较具弹性,司法实践对平台用工劳动关系的认定并不统一。总体上看,目前网络平台服务提供者这一群体尚游离于劳动法保护范围之外,大部分平台工人尚未得到劳动法的保护。因此,迫切需要分析网络平台用工的法律性质,反思传统的劳动关系判断标准是否科学合理,从而为网络平台服务提供者提供应有的保护。对这一问题的研究不仅事关劳动法治完善,也是促进共享经济健康发展以及加强和改善民生、完善社会保障制度的重要内容。

一 传统劳动关系概念和判定理论的核心及其主要特征

(一)传统劳动关系概念和判定理论的核心

劳动关系的概念及其判断标准是劳动法上经典而永恒的话题,是劳动法理论和制度的逻辑起点。网络平台用工劳动关系的判定也应从传统劳动关系标准理论谈起。通说认为,从属性是劳动法所调整的劳动关系以及保护对象——劳动者(雇员)的基本特征。史尚宽先生认为,"劳动法(亦称劳工法)上之劳动契约谓当事人之一方对于他方在从属的关系,提供其职业上之劳动力,而他方给付报酬之契约乃为特种之雇佣契约,可称为从属的雇佣契约"。[③] 根据该定义,劳动契约的本质属性在于雇员的从属性。关

---

① 《朝阳法院发布互联网平台用工劳动争议审判白皮书》,参见北京法院网,http://bjgy.chinacourt.org/article/detail/2018/04/id/3261190.shtml,最后访问时间:2018年4月13日。

② Miriam A. Cherry, "Are Uber and Transportation Network Companies the Future of Transportation (Law) and Employment (Law)", *Texas A & M Law Review*, Vol. 4, 2017, p. 185. 本文根据习惯有时将劳动者称为"雇员",有时将用人单位称为"雇主";"雇员"和"雇主"都是建立劳动关系的一方主体。

③ 史尚宽:《债法各论》,中国政法大学出版社,2000,第294页。

于劳动关系的内涵，欧陆国家和英美法系国家比较接近。德国学者普遍认为，"雇员是指基于私人合同，处于'人格从属'关系中，而有义务为他人工作的人"，"这一准则的核心要素是人格从属性"。① 人格从属性包括两个特征，即雇员融入了雇主的组织，以及在雇主指挥下工作。人格从属性强调劳务提供者在工作时间、工作地点、工作内容和具体履行方式方面都听从劳务受领者的指挥。② 在德国，判断从属性需要综合考虑各方面因素。德国学者指出，一开始就确立一个可以证明所有劳动关系存在的标准是不可能的，相反，劳动关系的存在依赖于"整体画面"（overall picture）。根据判例法，在认定人格从属性的多重标准中，没有任何单一标准是不可或缺的。③

在美国，劳动关系的判断以及雇员（劳动者）身份的认定主要有两个体系。第一个体系是 1935 年《国家劳动关系法》（*National Labor Relations Act*）所使用的普通法标准。这一标准主要来源于普通法的"主仆"关系和侵权责任规则。该标准强调一方控制（control）或有权控制另一方提供服务的工作细节。如果一方享有对另一方的控制，则双方存在雇主和雇员的劳动关系，如果缺乏"控制"的存在，劳务提供方则是"独立承包人"。在判断劳务提供者是雇员还是独立承包人时，需要考虑的因素包括：（1）雇用方对工作细节控制的程度；（2）个人从事的是否为特定的职业或业务；（3）职业的种类；（4）特定职业所需的技能；（5）哪一方提供工具；（6）雇用的时长；（7）报酬的支付方式，计时还是计件；（8）工作是不是雇主常规业务的组成部分；（9）当事人是否认为他们成立了劳动关系；（10）雇主是否从事商业。根据该标准，没有任何一项因素是决定性的，劳动关系判断需要综合考虑所有因素。但是，雇主的控制程度是最重要的因素，雇主控制的程度非指实际的控制，而是指"有权控制"的程度。④

劳动关系判断以及雇员（劳动者）身份认定的另一个体系是《公平劳动标准法》（*Fair Labor Standards Act*）（1938 年通过）确立的标准。该法涉及最低工资、加班补偿标准、童工限制、平等工资等待遇规则。该法对雇

---

① Manfred Weiss and Marlene Schmidt, *Labour Law and Industrial Relations in Germany*, Kluwer Law International, 2008, p. 45.
② 王倩：《德国法中劳动关系的认定》，《暨南学报》（哲学社会科学版）2017 年第 6 期，第 42 页。
③ Bernd Waas, Wilma B. Liebman, Andrew Lyubarsky and Katsutoshi Kezuka, *Crowdwork-A Comparative Law Perspective*, Bund-Verlag GmbH, 2017, p. 147.
④ Mark A. Rothstein, Charles B. Craver, Elinor P. Schroeder, Elaine W. Shoben and L. Camille Hebert, *Employment Law* (Fifth Edition), West Academic Publishing, 2015, p. 70.

员的定义比普通法更为宽泛。根据该法,雇员是指"被雇主雇用的任何人"。① 雇主是指"直接或间接地为了与雇员相对应的雇用方的利益而行事的任何人"。② 而"雇用"(employ)则是"承受或允许工作"(suffer or permit to work)。③ 法院根据该成文法的规定,在实践中形成了多重因素的所谓"经济现实标准"(economic reality test)。在判断雇员身份时通常需要考虑以下因素:(1)"雇主"控制的程度;(2)"雇主"和"雇员"对设备和材料投资的程度;(3)"雇员"通过管理技能分享利润和承担损失的机会;(4)工作所需的技术和主动性;(5)双方关系的持久性;(6)"雇员"所提供的服务是"雇主"业务不可分割的一部分的程度。④ 可见,"经济现实标准"和上述普通法标准所需考虑的很多因素是重合的。"经济现实标准"最终的考虑因素是工人事实上为了自身的业务工作,还是在经济上依赖于其他人的业务。和上述普通法标准一样,在判断劳动关系是否存在时,工人和雇主双方关系的所有相关事实都应当考虑。⑤

从大陆法系的典型代表德国和英美法系的典型代表美国关于劳动关系和雇员认定标准的理论看,二者的内容和主要原则是基本一致的。德国法强调人格"从属性",是从雇员相对于雇主的地位来描述的,即雇员必须接受雇主的指挥、管理,相应地,雇主也有权对雇员施加"控制";美国法强调"控制",是从雇主相对于雇员的地位来描述的,从相反角度看,由于雇主对雇员有权施加控制,雇员相对于雇主也具有"从属性"。当然,"从属性"以及"控制"标准需要考虑的因素有所差别。相较而言,美国通过判例提供了更为具体的考量因素。

(二) 传统劳动关系判定标准理论的主要特征

从德国和美国的劳动关系理论中可以总结出劳动关系和雇员判定标准的主要特征。认识这些特征,是分析互联网时代劳动关系认定的重要基础。

第一,劳动关系的概念是以 20 世纪初工业化时代的劳动关系特征为原型的。劳动关系及其从属性概念主要建立在工业化时代,以传统的工厂为

---

① Fair Labor Standards Act of 1938 §3 (e) (1), 29 U. S. C. A. §203 (e) (1).
② Fair Labor Standards Act of 1938 §3 (d), 29 U. S. C. A. §203 (d).
③ Fair Labor Standards Act of 1938 §3 (g) (1), 29 U. S. C. A. §203 (g).
④ Mark A. Rothstein, Charles B. Craver, Elinor P. Schroeder, Elaine W. Shoben and L. Camille Hebert, supra note 13, at 338.
⑤ Bernd Waas, Wilma B. Liebman, Andrew Lyubarsky and Katsutoshi Kezuka, supra note 12, at 45 – 46.

基本模型而形成和发展的。20世纪初，欧美主要国家工业化程度已逐渐提高，在传统工厂中，工人在固定时间、地点工作，接受雇主指挥管理，这是劳动关系及"从属性"理论的主要模型。从立法来看，德国于1896年颁布了《民法典》，但起初《民法典》的雇佣合同法是非常保守的。《民法典》对解雇保护、工厂代表等"一无所知"。[①] 民法的不完备，导致了学术界尝试依靠其他制定法去填补法律漏洞。例如，菲利普·洛特玛在其两卷本的《德意志帝国私法中的劳动合同》一书中（1902、1908年版）描述了从依附性（从属性）劳动中产生的法律问题。当时，劳动法作为依附性劳动的特别法的观念还没有形成。[②] 20世纪初，最普遍、最典型的雇员是工厂里的工人，他们基本都是贫困的无产阶级，完全靠出卖劳动力来养活自己和家人，工作是他们唯一的经济来源，所以帝国劳动法院曾经认为劳动关系的核心特征应该是"经济从属性"。[③] 可见，从属性的概念也是从那时起开始受到法院的关注。德国学者也指出，魏玛时代不仅是集体谈判制度迅速发展的时期，也是现行德国劳动法基本概貌得以形成的时期。[④] 因此，作为德国劳动法核心概念的从属理论也是20世纪初出现并不断发展的。类似地，美国的控制标准和经济现实标准理论也是20世纪上半叶确立的。如上所述，"控制标准"理论来源于普通法的"主仆"关系和侵权责任规则，1935年《国家劳动关系法》（National Labor Relations Act）所使用的正是普通法的标准。"经济现实标准"则是根据1938年《公平劳动标准法》（Fair Labor Standards Act）确立的标准。概言之，由于劳动关系理论主要确立于20世纪上半叶，而劳动关系以及现实中用工形式复杂多样，且不断发展变化，因此，传统劳动关系的判断理论和方法在当今时代尤其是网络时代不可避免地会遭遇到挑战。

第二，劳动关系的判断标准具有相当的弹性。由于现实中劳动关系复杂多样，在法律上难以具体、明确界定劳动关系的概念和判断方法，因此，立法或判例规则对劳动关系一般仅提供相对抽象的概念和原则。无论是德国"从属性"理论，还是美国"控制"标准或"经济现实"标准，不仅概

[①] 参见〔德〕雷蒙德·瓦尔特曼《德国劳动法》，沈建峰译，法律出版社，2014，第31页。
[②] 参见〔德〕雷蒙德·瓦尔特曼《德国劳动法》，沈建峰译，法律出版社，2014，第31-32页。
[③] 王倩：《德国法中劳动关系的认定》，《暨南学报》（哲学社会科学版）2017年第6期，第41页。
[④] Manfred Weiss and Marlene Schmidt, *Labour Law and Industrial Relations in Germany*, Kluwer Law International, 2008, p.30.

念本身富有弹性，相应的判断因素亦是复杂多样，且存在理论上的争议。以"从属性"为例，其常常被分解为"人格从属性"、"经济从属性"和"组织从属性"，但因对三个从属性的界定不清和理解不同，导致对三个"从属性"之间关系的认识混乱。[1] 例如，有将"经济从属性"和"人格从属性"并列。[2] 有认为"经济从属性"仅是劳工从属性的重要特征，而非必然。有认为"组织从属性"应当与"人格从属性"并列，反对将"组织从属性"涵盖在"人格从属性"范围内。[3] 也有德国学者认为，"组织从属性"只是从"人格从属性"推导得出的，并不具有独立性。[4] 还有的认为，"组织从属性完全可以为人格从属性及经济从属性所吸收"。[5] 对从属性以及包含因素的理解可谓见仁见智。美国学者 Miriam A. Cherry 教授也指出，雇员的判断标准在任何情况下都具有显著弹性，即便在比较明确的情形下。[6] 欧洲学者通过考察欧洲部分国家劳动关系的定义也指出，一国对劳动关系的定义总是相当"开放和灵活的"（open ended and flexible）。[7] 当然，劳动关系概念和判断标准的弹性，并不意味着其缺乏核心要素。例如，德国的从属性理论强调"人格从属性"这一本质特征。德国帝国劳动法院曾经认为劳动关系的核心特征应该是"经济从属性"，后来逐渐认识到，"经济从属性"既不是认定劳动关系的必要条件，也不是充分条件。因此，帝国劳动法院更正了自己的观点，提出区分一般的雇佣合同和劳动合同的关键应该看劳务提供方是否对劳务受领者有"人格从属性"。[8]

第三，劳动关系的概念和理论具有很强的适应性。无论是德国"从属

---

[1] 台湾劳动法学会编《"劳动基准法"释义——施行二十年之回顾与展望》，新学林出版股份有限公司，2009，第55页。

[2] 黄越钦：《劳动法新论》，翰芦图书出版有限公司，2006，第121-124页。

[3] 台湾劳动法学会编《"劳动基准法"释义——施行二十年之回顾与展望》，新学林出版股份有限公司，2009，第54-59页。

[4] Bernd Waas, Wilma B. Liebman, Andrew Lyubarsky and Katsutoshi Kezuka, *Crowdwork-A Comparative Law Perspective*, Bund-Verlag GmbH, 2017, p.148.

[5] 王天玉：《基于互联网平台提供劳务的劳动关系认定——以"e代驾"在京、沪、穗三地法院的判决为切入点》，《法学》2016年第6期，第56页。

[6] Miriam A. Cherry, "Are Uber and Transportation Network Companies the Future of Transportation (Law) and Employment (Law)", *Texas A & M Law Review*, Vol.4, 2017, p.186.

[7] Policy Department A: Economic and Scientific Policy, European Parliament, "The Social Protection of Workers in the Platform Economy", November 2017, p.84, http://www.europarl.europa.eu/supporting-analyses，最后访问时间：2018年10月19日。

[8] 王倩：《德国法中劳动关系的认定》，《暨南学报》（哲学社会科学版）2017年第6期，第42页。

性"理论还是美国"控制"理论，虽然经历了约一个世纪，但其核心要义并没有发生实质性的变化。究其原因，一是这些理论本身揭示了劳动关系与其他民事关系，尤其是承揽、一般雇佣关系的本质区别，二是这些概念和理论本身具有很大的弹性和包容性。法官可以在司法实践中不断发展和完善。正是劳动关系概念的弹性和包容性，使其具有旺盛的生命力。因此，不管是大陆法系还是英美法系，有关劳动关系判定的规则主要是判例法，成文法一般只有非常原则的界定，鲜有国家在成文法中对劳动关系进行具体而明确的界定。德国也是在 2017 年才将劳动关系的概念纳入民法典。即便如此，德国民法典中劳动合同的概念仍然比较原则，主要是对以往判例规则的总结。[①]

第四，劳动关系的认定存在较大的不确定性。德国、美国的理论都强调个案中需综合考虑全部事实，以及所有因素，而且都强调没有任何单一的因素是决定性的或不可或缺的。因此，劳动关系的判定结果往往难以预测，因人而异，存在较大的不确定性。美国学者指出，尽管《公平劳动标准法》确立的经济现实标准比普通法的标准更加聚焦于工人是否经营独立的业务，但很难预测多重因素标准应用的结果，因为决定的作出者或许比使用的标准更加重要。[②] 劳动关系认定的复杂性和不确定性，对法官提出了更高的要求。虽然概念和理论的抽象使案件的结果较难预测，也面临裁判的不统一，但也为个案更合理地处理提供了可能。

综上，由于劳动关系标准理论具备上述特征，一方面使其在现代互联网时代尤其是网络平台用工背景下面临挑战以及与现实的张力，另一方面由于其本身的弹性和适应性，又具备了很强的适应形势变化的调适能力。

二 互联网平台用工的劳动关系判定实践及面临的挑战

（一）美德等国劳动关系判定的实践及面临的挑战

网络平台用工具有许多有别于传统用工形式的特点，并且在现实中出现了许多诉讼和纠纷。美国、德国的平台经济走在世界前列，有关网络平台用工的争议案件较多并广受关注，对其实践的考察对我国具有重要参考价值。

[①] 参见同济大学王倩副教授 2017 年 12 月 15 日在上海财经大学法学院举办的"新时代中国特色劳动法原理创新论坛暨《劳动合同法》十周年座谈会"上所作的发言。

[②] Bernd Waas, Wilma B. Liebman, Andrew Lyubarsky and Katsutoshi Kezuka, *Crowdwork-A Comparative Law Perspective*, Bund-Verlag GmbH, 2017, p. 46.

在美国，截至目前，法院并没有一般性最终确立平台工人的"雇员"地位。在美国，近期影响较大的是 2015、2016 年 Uber 和 Lyft 两家交通出行平台公司在加州的案件，即 O'Connor v. Uber 和 Cotter v. Lyft 案。[①] 在这两个案件中，法官注意到公司在向消费者的广告中直接声称自己是"运输系统"（transportation systems）或提供"按需出行服务"（on-demand ride services）。关于司机身份，两个案件的法官都认为，相关的法律因素存在两个指向——一些因素指向司机的雇员身份，一些因素指向司机的独立承包人身份。在 Uber 案中，法官的分析集中在按照加州法 Uber 是否对实现预期结果的方式进行控制。Uber 公司主张司机可以自行决定工作量的多少。但法官认为，司机的这项自由并不能排除雇员的身份。法官认为，更相关的是 Uber 对司机工作（on duty）过程的控制。法官主要审查公司对司机的指示（包括着装以及对顾客的行为）以及对司机遵守指示情况的监督。通过客户对司机的评分制度，法官发现 Uber 司机提供的每次出行服务都受到顾客的监督，而且 Uber 的应用数据可以对司机的行为进行实时监督。公司对司机应遵守的规则进行全时监督的程度，表明 Uber 对司机履职的方式方法（manner and means）享有很大程度的控制。[②] 2016 年 Uber 案的诉讼双方达成赔付 1 亿美元，但没有明确雇员身份的和解方案，法官以该方案并不"公平、充分和合理"为由没有批准该方案。[③] 在 Uber 案件中，法官 Edward Chen 表达了对已有劳动关系判断标准存在挑战的看法。法官指出，产生传统的劳动关系判断标准的经济模式和新的"共享经济"有很大不同，将传统标准适用于 Uber 的商业模式带来了巨大挑战。传统标准所包括的很多因素在新的背景下显得过时了。另外一些存在于现行经济现实的因素并没有被现有标准所明确涵盖。或许，立法机关或上诉法院可以在新经济的背景下改善或修改现有标准。可以想象，立法机关将为新的"共享经济"制定新规则。[④]

在 Lyft 案中，法官认为，一旦司机选择了为 Lyft 公司工作，Lyft 对司机如何工作保留了相当程度的控制。公司向司机发出了肯定的指示，保留了

---

① O'Connor v. Uber Techs., Inc., 82 F. Supp. 3d 1133（N. D. Cal. 2015），Cotter v. Lyft, Inc., 60 F. Supp. 3d 1067（N. D. Cal. 2015）.

② Bernd Waas, Wilma B. Liebman, Andrew Lyubarsky and Katsutoshi Kezuka, *Crowdwork-A Comparative Law Perspective*, Bund-Verlag GmbH, 2017, pp. 49–52.

③ O'Connor v. Uber Techs., Inc., 201 F. Supp. 3d 1110, 1113（N. D. Cal. 2016）.

④ Bernd Waas, Wilma B. Liebman, Andrew Lyubarsky and Katsutoshi Kezuka, *Crowdwork-A Comparative Law Perspective*, Bund-Verlag GmbH, 2017, p. 50.

对违反规则的司机处罚的权力,而且公司有权根据服务条款禁止司机进入平台。法官还认为,司机的工作整体融入 Lyft 公司的业务,没有司机公司无法生存,而且为 Lyft 工作所需的驾驶无需特别技术,这和独立承包人通常应具有的技能不同。但同时,一些因素将司机指向了独立承包人身份:司机享有工作频次和工作时间的灵活性,可以选择在城市的哪些地域接受订单,在驾驶过程中极少与公司管理层沟通,两位原告司机都不是全职提供驾驶服务,而且 Lyft 公司也不是他们收入的主要来源。2016 年 2 月,双方达成了 1225 万美元的和解协议,但法官认为数额太低没有批准,而后双方达成了 2700 万美元的和解协议,法官于 2016 年 6 月批准了该和解协议。双方最终达成和解。① 在 Lyft 案件中,法官 Vince Chhabria 暗示现行劳动法过时的观点被广为引用。法官指出,加州法院在 20 世纪发展起来的雇员身份认定标准在解决 21 世纪面临的问题上并非很有帮助。一些因素指向一个方向,一些因素指向另一个方向,一些因素模棱两可。也许,Lyft 的司机总体上应当被认为是一种"新类型"的工人,需要另外一套保护。由于缺乏立法介入,加州已经过时(outmoded)的判断雇员身份的标准将继续使用,但这一标准无法提供清晰的答案。②

观察美国近年来有关 Uber 等交通网络公司(transportation network companies,简称 TNC)的案例可以看出,法院拒绝将 TNC 看作"软件公司",相反认识到交通服务提供中的劳动是所有 TNC 商业模式的重要部分。换言之,没有司机使用汽车和提供服务,手机运行的应用软件将毫无价值。③ 因此,从业务范围看,司机提供的服务是 TNC 业务的重要部分。同时,传统的劳动关系判断标准遭遇了重大挑战。根据"控制标准",对于 TNC 而言,一些因素将司机指向雇员,另外一些因素将司机指向独立承包人。例如,司机享有决定工作时间的自由;司机可以选择全职工作,也可以兼职;他们使用自己的交通工具、手机和电脑;而且,有关的协议通常

---

① Cotter v. Lyft, Inc., Dkt. No. 94, 60 F. Supp. 3d 1067 (N.D. Cal. 2015); Cotter v. Lyft, Inc., Dkt. No. 200, 176 F. Supp. 3d 930 (N.D. Cal. 2016); Cotter v. Lyft, Inc., 193 F. Supp. 3d 1030 (N.D. Cal. 2016); Cotter v. Lyft, Inc., Dkt. No. 293, 13 – cv – 4065 (N.D. Cal. Dec 23, 2016); Cotter v. Lyft, Inc., No. 13 – cv – 04065 – VC (N.D. Cal. Mar. 16, 2017).

② Bernd Waas, Wilma B. Liebman, Andrew Lyubarsky and Katsutoshi Kezuka, *Crowdwork-A Comparative Law Perspective*, Bund-Verlag GmbH, 2017, pp. 50 – 52.

③ Miriam A. Cherry, "Are Uber and Transportation Network Companies the Future of Transportation (Law) and Employment (Law)", *Texas A & M Law Review*, Vol. 4, 2017, p. 182.

把他们贴上"独立承包人"的标签。这些因素将司机指向独立承包人。与此同时,许多因素支持司机是劳动者:TNC 对司机的控制程度很高,Uber 使用顾客对司机的星级评价制度,实现了对司机几乎实时的监督,顾客代替公司管理层对工人进行监督。公司通常使用复杂的质量控制政策。而且,根据"经济现实标准",司机的商业机会以及风险和收益几乎不存在;司机通常都是低技能的,容易被盘剥,属于"需要被《公平劳动标准法》保护的群体"。并且,虽然有关协议写明司机属于独立承包人,但此类协议属于格式化合同。[1] 由于指向不同身份的事实同时存在,法官往往无所适从。在美国,关于网络平台工人的身份判定,许多案件本可以对此问题提供裁判规则,但由于案件采取或很可能采取和解方式,加上判断劳动者身份的标准模糊,法院未来如何处理这一问题具有不确定性。[2] 这些和解导致一个不幸的事实,即法院不可能提供一个关于共享经济工人身份认定的清晰答案。[3] 可见,美国法院在判定网络平台工人身份问题上面临巨大挑战。

在德国,按照传统的从属性标准判断平台工人的劳动者身份也是困难重重。在德国,众包工作(crowdwork)存在不同的商业模式。在一些模式中,众包商(crowdsourcer)和众包工(crowdworker)之间可能存在合同关系,甚至是劳动关系;在一些模式中,众包工和平台可能存在合同关系,甚至是劳动关系。但是,众包工往往因缺乏从属性(融入雇主)无法被认定为雇员。总体来看,认定众包工为雇员面临巨大困难。[4]

(二)我国互联网平台用工劳动关系认定的实践与面临的挑战

由于我国互联网技术以及平台经济发展较快,与互联网平台有关的劳动争议案件越来越多。从典型案例来看,由于平台用工的具体方式并不相同,加上劳动关系判断标准较为弹性,司法实践对平台用工劳动关系的认定并不统一。

以影响较大的案例为例。在司机庄某与"e 代驾"公司(北京某汽车技

---

[1] Miriam A. Cherry, "Are Uber and Transportation Network Companies the Future of Transportation (Law) and Employment (Law)", *Texas A & M Law Review*, Vol. 4, 2017, pp. 186 – 187.

[2] Miriam A. Cherry, "Are Uber and Transportation Network Companies the Future of Transportation (Law) and Employment (Law)", *Texas A & M Law Review*, Vol. 4, 2017, p. 189.

[3] Miriam A. Cherry, "Beyond Misclassification: The Digital Transformation of Work", *Comparative Labor Law & Policy Journal*, Vol. 37, 2016, p. 578.

[4] Bernd Waas, Wilma B. Liebman, Andrew Lyubarsky and Katsutoshi Kezuka, *Crowdwork-A Comparative Law Perspective*, Bund-Verlag GmbH, 2017, pp. 156 – 157.

术开发服务有限公司)的劳动争议中,二审法院认为,司机没有固定的工作场所,工作时间可自行掌握,司机亦非按月从平台公司获取劳动报酬,结合代驾司机的行业特点以及本案中庄某与平台公司签订了"e代驾"驾驶员合作协议的情况,司机与公司之间并非劳动关系。①

在类似的一个代驾司机案件中,由于代驾公司与接受代驾服务的公司签署协议,法院认为:被告司机赵某并非协议当事人,故司机的代驾行为系接受被告平台公司的指令为履行协议作出的特定行为;其次,从司机和平台公司的约定看,司机系经被告平台公司考核并认可的代驾驾驶员,在其代驾服务过程中,必须接受平台公司制定的规章制度及行为规范,并需穿着公司统一的制服并佩戴胸卡,故司机在工作时间内接受平台公司的管理。另外,司机根据平台公司制定的标准收取费用,对于代驾费用并无议价权,其仅以付出的劳动获取相应报酬;本案被告赵某与被告平台公司之间符合雇佣关系的一般特征,应认为双方之间属于雇佣关系。②

在郭某与北京某信息技术有限公司案件中,法院否认服务提供者美睫师和平台公司存在雇佣关系,但对服务提供者美睫师给客户造成的损失(人身损害),法院认为,平台公司仅对服务提供者的身份信息进行了认证,而对其今后提供的服务所可能涉及的相关资质等信息未进行审核,存在一定的过错,综合考虑被告平台公司的经营性质、过错程度以及其作为非直接侵权人的地位,酌情判令被告平台公司在30%的范围内对原告的损害后果承担补充赔偿责任。③

在沈阳某科技有限公司与李某确认劳动关系纠纷案件中,法院认为快递员和平台公司成立劳动关系。主要理由是:公司自认对配送的物品如有损坏,由其原价赔偿,快递员使用公司提供的运输工具,从事快递员工作,是公司主营业务的组成部分,快递员在工作中必须遵守公司制定的配送规

---

① 北京市第一中级人民法院:《庄燕生与北京亿心宜行汽车技术开发服务有限公司劳动争议二审民事争议判决书》,案号:〔2014〕一中民终字第6355号。

② 上海市浦东新区人民法院:《陶新国与北京亿心宜行汽车技术开发服务有限公司、中国平安财产保险股份有限公司上海分公司等机动车交通事故责任纠纷一审民事判决书》,案号:〔2014〕浦民一(民)初字第37776号。后该案原审被告(平台公司)上诉,被上诉人暨原审原告陶新国向中院申请撤回起诉,法院裁定撤销一审判决。参见上海市第一中级人民法院《北京亿心宜行汽车技术开发服务有限公司诉陶新国等机动车交通事故责任纠纷一案二审民事裁定书》,案号:〔2015〕沪一中民一(民)终字第1373号。

③ 上海市徐汇区人民法院:《郭灵迪与北京河狸家信息技术有限公司、韩凯云生命权、健康权、身体权纠纷一审民事判决书》,案号:〔2015〕徐民一(民)初字第1731号。

则，公司向其支付劳动报酬，因此，认定双方存在劳动关系。① 在 2017 年关于滴滴出行公司的两个案件中，因网约车平台司机发生交通事故，造成对第三人损害赔偿的责任，法院均让滴滴公司承担对第三人的责任，但并没有明确司机和滴滴公司之间的法律关系。②

在 2018 年李某诉"闪送"平台案件中，闪送员李某自行购买配送车辆，在平台上抢单后从事快递配送服务。李某无底薪，"闪送"平台对李某无工作量、在线时长、服务区域方面的限制和要求，但对每单配送时间有具体规定，超时、货物损毁情况下有罚款。快递员不得同时为其他平台提供服务。法院经审理后认为：法律关系的性质，应根据事实审查认定，当事人不可以协议约定的方式排除劳动法之适用。"闪送"平台的经营模式为通过大量提供货物运输服务来获取利润，故"闪送"平台的运营公司并不是一家信息服务公司，而是一家从事货物运输业务经营的公司。本案平台公司在招聘闪送员时，对担任闪送员的条件作出了要求，李某提供服务时需佩戴工牌，按照服务流程的具体要求提供服务，在任平台闪送员期间李某并未从事其他工作，从事闪送员工作获取的报酬是李某的主要劳动收入，故平台公司与李某间具有从属性，双方间属于劳动关系。③

概括以上案例等，我国网络平台用工劳动纠纷的实践具有几个以下特点。第一，法官在大部分案件中都不认可网络平台用工劳动关系的存在，只有少部分案件中明确认定劳动关系，还有个别案件中认定双方存在雇佣关系，一些案件中法官直接否定劳动关系或雇佣关系的存在。同时，很多案件中法官回避了平台公司和平台工人之间法律关系的性质。第二，在处理结果上，类似案件可能存在不同的判决。例如，原告同是代驾司机，被告经营模式也基本相同，但二者的法律关系在不同案件中认定不同。第三，当司机等平台服务提供者造成第三人损害时，法院往往倾向于判决平台公

---

① 辽宁省沈阳市中级人民法院：《沈阳众业科技有限公司与李辉确认劳动关系纠纷二审民事判决书》，案号：〔2017〕辽 01 民终 7210 号。
② 参见成都市中级人民法院《滴滴出行科技有限公司、董丽机动车交通事故责任纠纷二审民事判决书》，案号：〔2017〕川 01 民终 9920 号；北京市西城区人民法院《尹广华与中国平安财产保险股份有限公司北京分公司、中国人民财产保险股份有限公司北京市西城支公司等机动车交通事故责任纠纷一审民事判决书》，案号：〔2017〕京 0102 民初 14100 号。
③ 《称闪送途中发生事故，闪送员起诉平台经营者要求确认劳动关系获支持》，参见北京市海淀区人民法院网站，http://bjhdfy.chinacourt.org/public/detail.php? id =5470，最后访问时间：2018 年 7 月 1 日。

司承担责任,即"损害结果同劳动关系认定呈现较强的相关性"。[①] 至于平台公司承担责任的法律基础,法院有时按侵权责任法的规则,有时认定双方存在雇佣关系,有时则回避当事人之间的法律关系性质。

值得关注的是,法院在一些案件中认定平台工人和平台公司建立雇佣关系,这一做法值得反思。我国并没有在成文法上采用"雇佣合同"或"雇佣关系"的概念,雇佣合同或雇佣关系当事人之间的权利义务并不清晰。"雇佣"的概念只出现在 2003 年最高人民法院出台的《关于审理人身损害赔偿案件适用法律若干问题的解释》中。[②] 法院之所以认定雇佣关系,目的在于让平台公司作为雇主承担责任,从而减轻平台服务提供者的责任,但当事人之间是否存在劳动关系,法院则回避了。从我国法院对网络平台案件的处理可以看出,法院在网络平台用工劳动关系的认定上也面临巨大挑战。

可见,不管在美国、德国还是我国,网络平台用工的特点的确使传统劳动关系判定标准理论遭遇了严峻挑战。特别是平台用工的一些新特点与经典劳动关系存在较大差异,使得平台用工的一些因素将司机等平台工人指向劳动者,一些因素则指向独立承包人,法官往往陷入两难选择,难以认定平台工人的劳动者身份。但是,根据以上国家的实践是否可以认为传统劳动关系判定标准理论已经过时了?目前得出这一结论恐怕为时尚早。

三 传统劳动关系判定理论过时了吗?

相比传统或经典劳动关系,互联网平台用工具有几个突出特点,使其与经典劳动关系存在较大差异,这些特点也使网络平台劳动关系的认定更加困难。第一,许多平台工人享有较强的自主性,包括是否提供服务、提供多少服务、何时何地提供服务等。而传统劳动者不能自由决定是否工作以及工作的数量、时间和地点。第二,在很多情况下,工人自己提供设备和工具,包括车辆等进行服务。而传统劳动者一般由雇主提供设备和工具。第三,很多平台用工实行计件工资而不是计时工资,而且工资支付几乎是实时支付。传统劳动者一般都是计时工资,且工资按一定周期支付。第四,平台工人的报酬一般来自和平台按比例的分成,而传统劳动者工资一般是

[①] 王文珍、李文静:《平台经济发展对我国劳动关系的影响》,《中国劳动》2017 年第 1 期,第 9 页。

[②] 最高人民法院:《关于审理人身损害赔偿案件适用法律若干问题的解释》(2003 年),第 9 条。

固定的,与雇主的营业收入并不直接挂钩。第五,平台对服务提供者的监督一般借助于顾客,通过顾客的评级制度等方式,实现对平台工人的监督。在传统劳动关系中,雇主对雇员的管理和监督一般都由雇主完成。第六,从业人员准入门槛较低,进入退出自由。① 平台工人加入平台的程序较为简单,往往通过在线操作和有关证书的审核即可完成,平台工人退出平台的程序也较为简单。而在传统劳动关系中,雇主对雇员的招聘程序较为严格。这几个特点,尤其是第一个特点,是对传统劳动关系"从属性"或"控制"因素的强有力否定,使平台用工劳动关系的认定遇到了强烈挑战,法官也往往陷入困境。即便如此,传统的劳动关系判定标准理论并没有完全过时,在网络平台用工背景下,传统理论仍有适用空间,并没有到了应彻底颠覆或者放弃的程度。

如上所述,传统劳动关系判定标准具有很强的弹性和包容性。无论是大陆法系的从属性标准,还是英美法系的控制标准或经济现实标准,均只提供了基本要义和判断要素。在判断劳动关系的诸多要素中,法官反复强调没有任何一项因素是决定性的,也没有任何一项要素是不可或缺的,对劳动关系的判断需要考虑全部事实和各项要素。平台工人在工作时间、工作地点和工作方式上的自由,虽然对劳动关系的认定有重要影响,但单凭这一点不能彻底否定劳动关系的存在。正如美国专家指出的,工人可以决定工作时间的事实相比公司有权对工人工作过程施加控制意义更小。② 通过考察平台公司和工人之间的复杂关系和各种因素,运用传统的劳动关系认定标准,仍可以得出当事人之间是否存在劳动关系的结论。

第一,网络时代雇主控制方式或雇员从属性的表现形式发生变化,但并没有改变从属性的实质。

网络时代需要对从属性包含的诸因素的判断方式方法进行反思和更新。传统的用工强调雇主对雇员工作时间和地点的控制,但在网络时代,由于技术的发展,雇主对雇员的控制方式和手段发生了变化,尤其是在某些行业,雇主对雇员工作时间和地点的严格控制失去了原有意义,雇主选择通过其他方式施加控制。以交通出行平台为例,随着技术发展,网络平台公

---

① 刘燕斌主编《中国劳动保障发展报告(2017)》,社会科学文献出版社,2017,第298-299页。
② Gig Economy: Are Your Workers Employees? The 6-Part Test-Law 360, May 4, 2016, 5/9, http://www.law360.com/articles/791945/gig-economy-are-your-workers-employees-the-6-part-test, 最后访问时间:2018年10月19日。

司要求司机在指定时间、指定地点提供服务或工作,并无多大实际意义。相反,通过技术手段尤其是大数据,公司可以测算和控制某一时点提供服务的司机人数,而且通过定价机制,规定不同时段的浮动价格,也可以间接调控司机的数量和工作时间。首先,由于中国相对丰富的劳动力资源,通过平台提供服务的人数相当可观,即便允许服务提供者自由决定是否提供服务,也可以保证一定数量的服务提供者。其次,由于平台工人的报酬方式是计件收入,除非兼职从业人员,服务提供者为了保证其基本收入,必须提供一定数量或时长的服务。最后,平台通过定价和报酬制度设计,即通常服务提供者提供的服务时间和服务数量越多,提成比例或收入越高,且服务时间和服务数量达不到一定指标将面临收入损失甚至失去服务机会等规则,也将鼓励服务提供者提供更长时间的服务。因此,即便平台公司不作强制要求,通过技术手段和商业模式,也可以保证一定数量的服务提供者提供相当时间的服务。而且,现在的网络平台服务一般都是平台工人和顾客一对一的服务,和传统的工厂式"流水线"生产方式有很大不同,某个工人是否提供服务并不影响平台公司业务的开展。因此,由网络平台提供的服务内容和技术发展决定,很多网络平台工人享有是否工作、工作多少、工作时间和工作地点的自由也不足为奇了。换言之,平台工人享有工作时间、工作地点等的自由,只是技术发展使平台的管理方式发生了变化,但这并不意味着劳动关系就不存在。德国学者也指出,如果劳务提供者在工作时间、工作地点、工作的内容和具体履行方式方面都听从劳务受领者的指挥,那么他们之间无疑存在劳动关系,但是认定劳动关系存在并不要求满足以上所有特征。①

同时,虽然网络平台对服务提供者是否提供服务、服务时间、服务地点表面上减少控制了,但许多平台对服务提供者其他方面的控制和管理加强了。这些控制主要表现在以下五方面。(1)网络平台大多制定了严格的规章制度,服务提供者必须严格遵守。服务提供者如果违反规章制度,可能面临平台公司的惩罚。(2)网络平台对工作或服务的过程进行严格管理。通过技术手段,一些网络平台实现了对工人的实时监督。以滴滴出行公司为例,在部分业务线,根据 GPS 信息,滴滴在每段行程中,从疲劳驾驶、

---

① 王倩:《德国法中劳动关系的认定》,《暨南学报》(哲学社会科学版)2017 年第 6 期,第 42 页。

超速、急加速、急转弯、急刹车五个维度来监测车主的驾驶行为。[1] 平台公司对平台工人的着装、服务标准均有严格而具体的要求。(3) 平台通过客户的评级等制度对司机等平台工人进行监督。平台经济的一个重要特征是将公司对服务提供者的监督权交给客户，通过客户的评级对平台工人进行监督。相比传统的公司对雇员的监督，这种一对一、全时的监督更加严密而有效。(4) 平台对服务享有完全的定价权。网络平台完全掌握定价权，服务提供者对服务价格没有议价权利，而且对服务价格的实时调整也完全由平台作出。(5) 平台不仅有严格的规章制度和监督，而且一般伴随着严格的惩戒措施。平台工人违反规章制度或者未按平台的指示提供服务，将在经济上遭受一定损失，甚至丧失继续提供服务的机会。美国学者也指出，通过技术和人力因素的组合，Uber对每一单出行服务各个方面如何提供施加了极为严密（extremely tight）的控制。[2] 概言之，虽然表面上平台工人享有是否工作以及决定工作时间和地点等自由，但一些网络平台通过对服务过程进行严密的监督，相比传统劳动关系，从某种意义上看，平台企业对工人的控制不是减少，而是加强了。

网络平台用工的其他特点，也非对传统劳动关系特征的颠覆。其一，工人在很多情况下自己提供工具，正是共享经济的重要特征，是现代经济资源共享的重要体现，并不会影响从属性的实质。其二，很多平台用工实行计件工资而不是计时工资，这一现象在传统劳动关系中即已出现，并非新鲜事物。平台用工工资实行实时支付主要是源于支付手段的技术发展，尤其是移动支付技术的进步，使实时支付成为可能。在传统劳动关系中，由于支付方式落后、支付成本较高，通常以月为周期计算工资，但也存在以周等为周期计算和支付工资的。目前许多平台公司也按一定周期结算平台工人的报酬。因此，工资或报酬的支付方式和支付周期并不影响劳动关系的实质。其三，很多平台工人的报酬来自和平台收入按比例的分成，主要是因为平台的收入主要来自工人提供的服务，而服务价格可以量化，加上平台往往无须计算传统企业场地、设备、原材料等成本，因此，平台和工人可以直接按收入的一定比例分成，这也是由服务内容的特点所决定的，也没有改变劳动关系的本质。而且，在传统的用工关系中劳动者按收入比

---

[1] 张车伟主编《中国人口与劳动问题报告 No.18》，社会科学文献出版社，2017，第127页。
[2] Jeremias Prassl and Martin Risak, "Uber, Taskrabbit, and Co.: Platforms as Employers? Rethinking the Legal Analysis of Crowdwork", *Comparative Labor Law and Policy Journal*, Vol. 37, 2016, p. 640.

例"提成"获取工资的做法也早已存在。综上,平台工人享有一定的自由,并且具有与传统劳动关系不同的一些特征,并不意味着从属性的缺失以及劳动关系的不存在。

第二,经济从属性的重要性和地位凸显。

由于网络技术的发展,服务提供者在是否工作、工作时间、工作地点等人格从属性上的表面特征有所减弱,因此,经济从属性在判断劳动关系是否存在上可以发挥更大的作用。关于经济从属性有不同的理解。我国台湾学者认为经济从属性主要指劳工在经济上处于弱势地位,以至于必须依赖对雇主提供劳务获取工资以求生存,或寻求更多收入、累积更多财富;经济从属性还表现在企业风险由雇主负担,劳工不负担风险。[①] 德国对经济从属性的理解主要表现为,雇员的主要收入来自雇主。[②] 根据上文分析,美国的经济从属性则主要体现在雇主享受经营利润、承担经营风险,以及雇员从事的工作是雇主业务的组成部分,且后者更为重要。在美国,不管是控制理论,还是经济现实标准理论都强调雇员从事的工作是雇主业务的组成部分。概括不同国家和地区关于经济从属性的含义,经济从属性主要体现在两个方面:一是雇员的收入主要来自雇主;二是雇员的工作是雇主业务的组成部分。相较而言,后者更为重要。雇员可能同时从多个雇主处获得工资或收入,雇员是否依赖雇主生存也难以判断。而雇员的工作是不是雇主业务的组成部分,将决定由何方享受利润和承担风险,以及雇员收入的来源。虽然德国在劳动关系的概念中突出了人格从属性,但经济从属性的地位仍不可小觑。就人格从属性和经济从属性关系而言,从某个角度来看,经济从属性是人格从属性的基础和前提,正因为雇员对雇主的经济从属性,雇主对雇员施加控制,或者雇员从属于雇主才具有正当性。因此,经济从属性仍然是判断劳动关系存在与否的重要因素。

网络平台企业往往否认经济从属性,即宣称平台公司只是一个网络技术公司或信息服务公司,并不提供具体的业务或服务,并以此为由,否认平台工人与平台公司之间劳动关系的存在。上文提及的美国案例,Uber等公司都以此为由进行了辩解。平台工人提供的服务是否属于公司业务的组成部分,如何进行判断,是网络平台用工劳动关系认定的一个重要

---

① 台湾劳动法学会编《"劳动基准法"释义——施行二十年之回顾与展望》,新学林出版股份有限公司,2009,第57—58页。
② 王倩:《德国法中劳动关系的认定》,《暨南学报》(哲学社会科学版)2017年第6期,第44页。

课题。

关于业务的归属，互联网时代，企业分工越来越细化，随着外包业务的发展，判断某项业务是不是公司的业务越来越困难，公司的业务范围也越来越模糊，特别是随着政府对企业经营范围管制的放松，企业经营范围越来越多元化。即便如此，某项业务是不是平台公司的业务仍可确定。以交通出行网络平台为例，从各方面来看，Uber 等交通出行平台公司，并不能否认提供出行服务是平台公司的业务。具体理由有三。第一，司机提供车辆和服务是 Uber 等公司赖于存在的基础，是公司获利的主要来源。公司获利并不是来自其所谓的软件销售或技术服务，软件或技术服务只是其获利的基础条件之一。第二，平台公司对出行服务这项业务进行了全面的控制，包括司机的进入和退出、业务招揽和广告、服务标准、服务监督、服务价格，尤其是公司对服务价格进行实时调控，司机没有任何决定权或议价权。质言之，平台公司对出行这项业务进行了严格管理和经营，而不是仅仅提供技术服务。第三，工具等由服务提供者自行提供并不能否认公司业务的存在。一些平台工具或部分工具由服务提供者提供正是共享经济的特征使然，这只是商业模式的特点之一，并不能否认公司业务的存在。事实上，不同公司可能采取不同商业模式或经营方式，但这并不影响业务的实质。以中国的交通出行平台为例，是否拥有自营车辆是公司是否开展业务的重要标志，但知名平台公司大都同时拥有自营车辆和社会加盟车辆，而且商业模式也是不断变化调整的，公司往往根据经营策略，选择持有自有车辆还是使用社会加盟车辆以及二者的比重。从业务实质来看，这些平台公司和一般运输服务公司并没有本质差别。平台公司也难以否认交通出行服务属于他们的业务。对于某类服务提供者，尤其是专职服务提供者，平台公司完全可以或应该与之签订劳动合同。在美国，也有一些平台公司，主动将平台服务提供者的身份从独立承包人转变为雇员。[1] 美国学者也指出，通过分析 Uber 的雇主功能，可以清楚地发现，平台事实上实施了提供出行或物流服务的雇主所从事的所有功能。[2] 尽管 Uber 高度依赖于现代技

---

[1] Miriam A. Cherry and Antonio Aloisi, "'Dependent Contractors' in the Gig Economy: A Comparative Approach", *American University Law Review*, Vol. 66, 2017, p. 683.

[2] Jeremias Prassl and Martin Risak, "Uber, Taskrabbit, and Co.: Platforms as Employers? Rethinking the Legal Analysis of Crowdwork", *Comparative Labor Law and Policy Journal*, Vol. 37, 2016, p. 637.

术，但其和传统的、单一的将司机作为雇员的雇主无甚差别。① 对 Uber 商业模式的深入考察表明，当平台实施了所有雇主功能，平台可以被轻易认定为雇主，司机可以被认定为雇员而不是独立承包人。②

因此，从经济从属性角度，尤其是平台业务的归属看，网络平台企业和工人完全可能建立劳动关系。

第三，运用现有劳动关系判定标准依然可以判定劳动关系的存在与否。

从美国、德国和英国等发达国家的相关实践来看，传统的劳动关系判断理论和判断方法并非走到尽头，毫无用武之地；相反，这些国家运用传统劳动关系判定理论，通过通盘考虑各方因素，仍然可以作出劳动关系存在与否的裁判。在英国，关于 Uber 等网约车司机的身份，2016 年伦敦劳动法庭的一个判决给出了明确答案。在 Aslam v. Uber B. V. 案件中，③ 伦敦劳动法庭裁决司机是 Uber 的雇员。法庭否定了 Uber 关于其只是一家软件公司，而不是劳动服务提供者的主张。法庭指出，否认 Uber 提供交通服务是不符合现实的。Uber 并非只是销售软件，其也提供出行服务。法庭还暗示 Uber 试图使用网络合同和发明新的术语来隐藏劳动关系。法庭通过分析 Uber 和司机之间的合同指出，Uber 的合同条款与司机和组织之间关系的事实不符，因此，法庭对合同条款可以置之不理。这一问题至少部分源于缔约双方不平等的谈判地位。④ 通过对 13 个要点的分析，法庭指出，不是 Uber 在为司机工作，而是司机在为 Uber 工作。这些要点包括：司机的招聘、顾客信息的控制、Uber 对默认路线的设置、定价结构、司机条件、对司机的指示、惩戒和评分系统以及 Uber 处理顾客投诉的事实。2017 年 9 月，伦敦交通部门由于担心 Uber 缺乏公司社会责任，拒绝给予 Uber 交通许可的延期，Uber 对此决定提出上诉。⑤

---

① Jeremias Prassl and Martin Risak, "Uber, Taskrabbit, and Co.: Platforms as Employers? Rethinking the Legal Analysis of Crowdwork", *Comparative Labor Law and Policy Journal*, Vol. 37, 2016, p. 641.

② Jeremias Prassl and Martin Risak, "Uber, Taskrabbit, and Co.: Platforms as Employers? Rethinking the Legal Analysis of Crowdwork", *Comparative Labor Law and Policy Journal*, Vol. 37, 2016, p. 650.

③ [2017] IRLR 4 [86].

④ Miriam A. Cherry, "The Sharing Economy and the Edges of Contract Law: Comparing U. S. and U. K. Approaches", *The George Washington Law Review*, Vol. 85, 2017, pp. 1820 – 1821.

⑤ Miriam A. Cherry, "The Sharing Economy and the Edges of Contract Law: Comparing U. S. and U. K. Approaches", *The George Washington Law Review*, Vol. 85, 2017, pp. 1821 – 1822.

德国近期的案例也认定了平台服务提供者的雇员身份。在该案件中，法院将一名IT程序设计员认定为雇员，尽管他在家工作，在空间上并没有融入雇主经营场所。法院注意到雇员的确不存在时间和地点上的从属性，但在法院看来，考虑到提供服务的实际类型，这些因素并不是决定性的。当然，法院并不是将劳动关系的大门都向众包工打开。法院这一决定表明，一方面，缺乏时间和地点的依赖性并不必然排除劳动合同的存在；另一方面，必须存在比缺乏时间和地点从属性更为重要的相反因素，才可能认定劳动关系的存在。[1] 从英国和德国的判例中可以看出，依据传统的判断标准仍可以明确判定劳动关系的存在。

在美国，虽然法官在 Uber 等案中并没有就司机是不是雇员作出明确判定，但法官认可当事人通过赔偿达成和解的态度实质上支持了司机的诉求，特别是当和解金额不高时，法官对和解方案的否定，事实上也表明了法官支持司机的态度。尽管法院并没有直接认定司机是雇员，但法院的裁决也暗示了法官认为工人的实质诉求是有价值的。[2] 除了法院，美国联邦监管当局，包括美国国税局（IRS）和全国劳动关系委员会（NLRB）可自行决定交通出行网络公司司机的身份是雇员，这将影响有关税收事务，赋予司机组建工会的权利。[3]

在我国网络平台用工劳动关系认定的司法实践中，法院也可能综合考虑各种因素，包括平台对服务提供者的管理，服务是平台公司的业务组成部分等而认定劳动关系的存在，并非仅因服务提供者具有较强的自主性和灵活性而否定劳动关系的存在，最典型的是上述"闪送"平台案。面对平台用工方式与传统用工方式差异所带来的挑战，各地法院在坚持现有劳动关系判定理论和规则的基础上，进行了积极探索，在实践中积累了有益经验，个别法院还对网络平台用工劳动关系认定问题进行了全面的梳理和分析。[4]

综上，传统劳动关系判断标准理论和方法并非寿终正寝或者走入穷途；相反，运用传统劳动关系判断理论和方法仍然可以判定网络平台企业与平

---

[1] Bernd Waas, Wilma B. Liebman, Andrew Lyubarsky and Katsutoshi Kezuka, *Crowdwork-A Comparative Law Perspective*, Bund-Verlag GmbH, 2017, pp. 151–152.

[2] Miriam A. Cherry, "The Sharing Economy and the Edges of Contract Law: Comparing U.S. and U.K. Approaches", *The George Washington Law Review*, Vol. 85, 2017, p. 1820.

[3] Miriam A. Cherry, "Are Uber and Transportation Network Companies the Future of Transportation (Law) and Employment (Law)", *Texas A & M Law Review*, Vol. 4, 2017, p. 189.

[4] 《朝阳法院发布互联网平台用工劳动争议审判白皮书》，参见北京法院网，http://bjgy.chinacourt.org/article/detail/2018/04/id/3261190.shtml，最后访问时间：2018年4月13日。

台工人是否成立劳动关系。如上所述,即便是美国 Uber 案的法官也仅仅指出,需要对劳动关系的认定标准进行"改进或修正",并没有提出应根本性颠覆或者抛弃。此外,德国 2017 年将劳动关系概念纳入民法典,其内容主要是对判例规则的总结,并没有对传统劳动关系理论和标准作根本调整,[①]也说明了传统劳动关系判断理论在互联网背景下,仍具有旺盛的生命力和广阔的适用空间。事实上,传统劳动关系理论和判定方法的模糊性与弹性早已存在,并非平台用工使然。正如美国学者 Orly Lobel 教授指出的:"尽管日益增多的诉讼表明平台工作性质存在巨大争议,但这些劳动法问题并非平台所独有。在《公平劳动标准法》(Fair Labor Standards Act)通过之后近一个世纪,雇员和独立承包人区分边界的不确定性并未减少。"[②] 因此,在互联网背景下,不宜轻易否定或推翻传统劳动关系判定理论,通过对传统理论进行合理解释和适用,依然可以解决网络平台用工劳动关系的认定问题。如果因为网络平台用工的兴起,而质疑或者放弃传统劳动关系判定理论及其标准,则可能走入歧途。

四 劳动关系判定方法的改进及我国相关规则的完善

(一)互联网背景下劳动关系判定方法的改进

尽管传统劳动关系判定理论总体上并没有过时,但面临网络平台用工形式与传统用工形式的差异,劳动关系的判定方法也应与时俱进。由于劳动关系判断标准较为抽象和原则,而平台用工的特点又使劳动关系的判断更加困难,个案中一些事实可能支持平台工人的劳动者身份,一些事实可能否定平台工人的劳动者身份,法院在认定劳动关系上面临更大的挑战。2018 年 3 月,北京市第一中级人民法院发布的《劳动争议审判白皮书(2010-2018)》在分析劳动争议审判面临的困难和挑战时,提及的第一个挑战就是,"传统劳动关系认定标准难以完全适应不断涌现的'新业态'就业的要求"。[③] 为此,在互联网时代,应改进劳动关系判定方法,在判定劳

[①] 参见同济大学王倩副教授 2017 年 12 月 15 日在上海财经大学法学院举办的"新时代中国特色劳动法原理创新论坛暨《劳动合同法》十周年座谈会"上所作的发言。

[②] Orly Lobel, "The Gig Economy & the Future of Employment and Labor Law", *University of San Francisco Law Review*, Vol. 51, 2017, p. 61.

[③] 参见北京市第一中级人民法院《劳动争议审判白皮书(2010-2018)》,2018 年 3 月,http://bj1zy.chinacourt.org/article/detail/2018/03/id/3252040.shtml,最后访问时间:2018 年 4 月 8 日。

动关系时考虑新的因素,以适应网络平台用工的新特点。

第一,平台用工模式各不相同,劳动关系判断还需综合考虑各种因素进行个案处理。不同平台商业模式不同,也处于不断变化之中,特别是平台公司对服务提供者的管理和控制程度不同。而且,同一平台对不同类型服务提供者的管理和控制程度也可能不同,包括服务提供者是否有权自行决定工作时间、工作地点,可否决定提供服务或拒绝提供服务的后果,平台采取"派单"还是"抢单"模式,平台对服务过程和服务质量的监督(包括评级制度),平台对客户投诉的处理,服务的定价机制以及双方的议价能力,服务设施和工具由哪方提供,对第三人的责任由哪方承担,平台公司对平台工人的惩戒措施,等等,都各不相同。因此,必须综合考虑以上各种因素,进行个案的具体处理。不同平台的工人,同一平台不同类型的工人,甚至同一平台同一类型的不同工人与平台的关系都可能并不相同。对平台公司与平台工人是否建立劳动关系,没有放之四海而皆准的标准答案。

第二,对从属性的判断应该更加注重实质性。互联网平台用工的一个普遍特点是灵活性。从业者往往在是否提供服务、服务时间、服务地点等方面具有较大的灵活性。这方面的特征是否定从属性和劳动关系的重要因素。但是,正如前文所述,在劳动关系判断中,没有一项因素是决定性的,需要通盘考虑其他因素,不能仅因劳动者在工作时间、工作地点和是否提供服务上享有自主性就简单否定劳动关系的存在。要对从属关系进行实质性考察,包括平台公司对服务过程的控制,平台公司对是否提供服务等行为的奖惩措施,平台定价机制及其对工作时间、工作数量的影响,平台公司对服务提供者进入和退出的管理,平台对工人的培训,平台对工人的惩戒,等等。要通过平台商业模式以及对从业者各方面的管理和政策的外在形式,对从属性进行实质性判断,不应局限于平台工人表面上的自由轻易作出判断。概言之,随着技术的发展,平台公司对工人控制和管理的方式更加隐蔽和复杂,对人格从属性和经济从属性的判断应注重综合性、实质性的考察。

第三,平台工人的工作时间和收入来源也是考虑的重要因素。根据传统劳动关系判断标准,工作的持续性以及工作时长就是劳动关系判定应该考虑的因素之一。对于网络平台用工,由于工作的灵活性,平台工人从事的是专职还是兼职,工作时间长短也是判断劳动关系是否存在应考虑的重要因素。平台工人工作时间长短在一定程度上也表明工人和平台公司二者关系的紧密程度以及工人接受指挥管理的程度，而且工作时间长短以及相应的收入高低也是经济从属性的重要体现。以滴滴公司的数据为例，自2016年6月30日至2017年6月30日，滴滴出行平台已经为全国提供了1484.1万个工作机会，其中兼职917.2万人，专职566.9万人（占比为38.2%）。全国范围内在滴滴平台开网约车的复员、转业军人总量为178.83万人，其中专职50.54万人，兼职128.29万人。[1] 从专职和兼职司机的比例看，兼职占大多数，但专职司机的比例也不低。从收入看，网约车司机个人月均收入在3000-5000元的比例最大，为39.69%，个人月均收入3000元以下的占23.54%，个人月均收入5000-7000元的占20.38%。[2] 从平均收入看，相当比例的司机处于全职或接近全职的状态，对这部分人而言，从平台获得的收入是其收入的重要来源。从工作时长来看，每天工作不到2小时的占比为50.67%，2-4小时的占比为19.66%，4-6小时的占比为12.91%，6-8小时的占比为8.74%，8小时以上的占比为8.02%。[3] 每天工作时间超过4小时的占比为29.67%。可见，虽然平台工人在工作时间上享有较大灵活性，且差异较大，但仍然有较大比例的平台工人从事全职工作，或者平台工作是其收入的主要来源。[4] 从境外看，一份针对欧洲网络平台用工的研究报告也指出，调研结果显示受调查的平台工人中大约1/4的工人在经济上依赖于平台的工作。[5] 这一比例也不低。由于工作时间长短及收入多寡是判断劳动关系的重要因素，对于全职司机等工人而言，成立劳动关系的可能性较大，法官认定劳动关系的必要性较大；对于兼职司机等工人，尤其是工作时间较短的工人成立劳动关系的可能性较小，认定劳动关系的必要性也较小。

第四，社会保护的必要性也是劳动关系判定应考虑的重要因素。劳动

---

[1] 张车伟主编《中国人口与劳动问题报告 No.18》，社会科学文献出版社，2017，第142页。
[2] 张车伟主编《中国人口与劳动问题报告 No.18》，社会科学文献出版社，2017，第113页。
[3] 张车伟主编《中国人口与劳动问题报告 No.18》，社会科学文献出版社，2017，第121-122页。
[4] 关于工作是否全职的判断，可参考《劳动合同法》第68条关于非全日制工的概念和范围界定。关于收入主要来源的具体标准，可借鉴德国法上"类雇员"（具备经济从属性）的判定条件之一，即收入的一半以上来自某个人（雇主）。如果平台从业人员的收入中一半以上来自某个平台，可将该平台视为其收入的主要来源。参见 Manfred Weiss and Marlene Schmidt, *Labour Law and Industrial Relations in Germany*, Kluwer Law International, 2008, p.45。
[5] Policy Department A: Economic and Scientific Policy, European Parliament, "The Social Protection of Workers in the Platform Economy", November 2017, p.55, http://www.europarl.europa.eu/supporting-analyses，最后访问时间：2018年10月19日。

关系的判断标准虽然是一套客观标准,但由于其本身的弹性和包容性,劳动关系的认定也具有相当的主观性。因此,在认定服务提供者是不是劳动者时,也应考虑对其保护的必要性。尤其是对那些和传统劳动者没有实质区别,并缺乏保护的网络平台从业人员来说,更有必要给予劳动保护。在美国有影响的 Lyft 案件中,法官 Chhabria 指出,对劳动关系的认定应该考察劳动法意图实现的目的以及意图保护的工人,尤其是那些低技能、低收入的工人。法官进一步指出,至少一些 Lyft 公司的工人与加州法律意图保护的工人类型是类似的:他们主要或完全依赖于 Lyft 平台维持生活,但缺乏任何关于劳动条件和条款的谈判能力。[1] 从美国实践看,很多平台企业工人缺乏培训、工作不稳定、工资收入低、对完成任务缺乏自主性、工作过程无法和同事及主管沟通,无法获得技能提升,工作中往往缺乏正当程序,这些现象使平台工作被社会学家描述为"糟糕的工作"(bad jobs)。这些因素说明网络平台用工是存在问题的,因此,需要考虑提供基本保护以及监管,以实现体面工作。[2] 现实中,许多平台工人工作时间长、工作条件差、谈判能力低,缺乏应有的社会保护,都是判定劳动关系的重要因素。特别是对于那些因服务于网络平台而表面上获得了一些自由,但实际上工作内容、工作时间等和传统行业工人并无实质差别的平台工人,可以考虑认定劳动关系。

(二) 我国劳动关系判断规则的完善

劳动关系判断理论及其规则的适用,始终是劳动法的核心问题。从劳动法司法实践来看,劳动关系认定始终是最重要的问题之一。例如,根据北京市第一中级人民法院的统计,2010 年至 2017 年该院审结的 21598 件劳动争议案件中,涉及确认劳动关系的案件 11053 件,占比 51.18%。[3] 根据北京市第二中级人民法院的统计,2008 年至 2017 年,二中院共受理劳动争议案件 31101 件,审理的案件类型中,涉及确认劳动关系的案件占比

---

[1] Bernd Waas, Wilma B. Liebman, Andrew Lyubarsky and Katsutoshi Kezuka, *Crowdwork-A Comparative Law Perspective*, Bund-Verlag GmbH, 2017, p. 50.

[2] Miriam A. Cherry, "Are Uber and Transportation Network Companies the Future of Transportation (Law) and Employment (Law)", *Texas A & M Law Review*, Vol. 4, 2017, pp. 193 – 195.

[3] 北京市第一中级人民法院:《劳动争议审判白皮书 (2010 - 2018)》,2018 年 3 月,http://bj1zy.chinacourt.org/article/detail/2018/03/id/3252040.shtml,最后访问时间:2018 年 4 月 8 日;《劳动与社会保障》2018 年第 1 期,第 17 页。

58.5%。① 因此，完善劳动关系认定规则的重要意义不言而喻。

目前，我国在司法实践中，对劳动关系的认定标准主要采用我国原劳动和社会保障部于 2005 年颁布的《关于确立劳动关系有关事项的通知》（以下简称《通知》）。该《通知》明确了劳动关系判断的基本方法。该《通知》规定："用人单位招用劳动者未订立书面劳动合同，但同时具备下列情形的，劳动关系成立。（一）用人单位和劳动者符合法律、法规规定的主体资格；（二）用人单位依法制定的各项劳动规章制度适用于劳动者，劳动者受用人单位的劳动管理，从事用人单位安排的有报酬的劳动；（三）劳动者提供的劳动是用人单位业务的组成部分。"② 可见《通知》强调"从属性"，包括人格从属性和经济从属性，和德国人格从属性以及美国控制标准和经济现实标准等理论具有类似之处，基本反映了劳动关系的本质特征，总体上是可取的。

但抛开《通知》本身的制定主体和效力，该条内容也存在不足。面对网络平台用工的新特点，该《通知》也需要完善。首先，《通知》采取的是"构成要件"式的立法，③ 即突出"同时具备下列情形的"要求，但从劳动关系本身的复杂性和发达国家的实践来看，劳动关系的本质属性是"从属性"，而从属性是一个宽泛的概念，需要考虑复杂多样的因素，理论和实践一般都认为没有任何一项因素是决定性的，也没有任何一项因素是不可或缺的，而且不同因素之间可能指向不同的答案，因此，劳动关系判断的科学方法是对全部事实和各个要素进行综合考虑，作出综合判断，要求所有因素同时具备并不科学。其次，《通知》对实质从属性的突出不够。以上分析表明，人格从属性是劳动关系的核心要义，但这种从属性是实质从属性，而不是形式从属性。因此，劳动关系的定义和判断方法应该强调实质从属性，而不应拘泥于个别的形式。《通知》强调"用人单位依法制定的各项劳动规章制度适用于劳动者"，但用人单位未必都制定有书面的规章制度，因此，规章制度只能作为参考，应着重于考察用人单位对劳动者的实质劳动管理。最后，《通知》对主体资格的规定导致了司法实践中受保护主体的不

---

① 参见北京市第二中级人民法院《劳动争议案件审判白皮书（2008－2017）》，2018 年 4 月，http://bj2zy.chinacourt.org/public/detail.php? id =1655，最后访问时间：2018 年 4 月 29 日。
② 劳动和社会保障部：《关于确立劳动关系有关事项的通知》，劳社部发〔2005〕12 号，2005 年 5 月。
③ 王天玉：《基于互联网平台提供劳务的劳动关系认定——以"e 代驾"在京、沪、穗三地法院的判决为切入点》，《法学》2016 年第 6 期，第 60 页。

当限缩。"用人单位和劳动者符合法律、法规规定的主体资格"的规定导致实践中实习生、已达退休年龄就业者等时常被排除在劳动者定义之外。

综上,由于劳动关系定义的抽象性和弹性,少有国家将劳动关系的定义成文化,其主要原因在于避免定义的僵化。目前只有少数国家,包括意大利[①]、德国等对劳动关系进行成文法的定义。考虑到我国缺乏判例法的传统,我国应当通过一定方式对劳动关系进行界定,以利于司法实践的准确适用和裁判统一。由于在劳动法或劳动合同法等立法中界定劳动关系的概念和判断方法难度较大,目前比较可行的办法是由最高人民法院通过司法解释规则对劳动关系进行界定。对劳动关系可以进行概括式界定,突出人格从属性,同时列明判定劳动关系需要考虑的主要因素。

值得注意的是,由于网络平台用工形式复杂多样,不同平台采取不同的商业模式和用工形式,即便在同一平台内部也可能针对不同群体,采取复杂多样、性质各异的用工形式,且平台的商业模式和用工形式仍处在不断的创新和变动中,加上传统的劳动关系概念和判定理论仍有广阔的适用空间,因此,没有必要也不应专门针对网络平台用工群体制定专门的规则,更不应笼统地将网络平台从业人员完全纳入劳动者范围,或完全将其排除在劳动者范围之外。目前应根据劳动关系理论和判定规则,结合上述劳动关系认定的改进方法,进行个案处理。

五 劳动关系与社会保险的脱钩及平台监管制度的完善

由于劳动关系认定的模糊性以及现实中网络平台用工的复杂多样性,目前对劳动关系的认定以及对网络平台工人的劳动法保护往往是事后的、个别的、零散的。平台企业一般通过和服务提供者签订"合作协议"或合同,推定双方关系为一般的民事合同关系,只有个别劳动者事后通过仲裁或诉讼确认劳动关系获得劳动法保护。大量平台服务提供者的身份处于不确定或模糊的状态,而无法受到劳动法保护,因此,仅靠劳动法保护网络平台工人是不够的,必须通过社会保险等制度的完善加强对此类主体的保护。由于我国相当一部分社会保险项目,包括职工养老保险、职工医疗保险、工伤保险、失业保险、生育保险等是建立在劳动关系存在的前提下,

---

① 《意大利民法典》第 2094 条规定:"因获得薪金而服从于企业主,并且以在企业主的领导下提供自己智力或体力劳动的方式为企业服务的人,是从属性的劳务提供者。"参见《意大利民法典》,费安玲等译,中国政法大学出版社,2004,第 490 页。

从业人员如果无法明确劳动者身份，社会保险的权益就会受到影响。美国目前也面临类似的困境。在美国，许多社会福利和劳动关系关联，包括健康保险、退休福利、工伤保险以及休假等。美国学者也指出，"这种关联日益过时，并且产生了助推使用独立合同人或工人（workers）提供劳动的道德风险"。① 未来劳动法的改革路径包括"将特定的基本保护扩展到所有劳动者（laborers），而不问其是否具有劳动关系"，"基本社会福利项目与劳动关系脱钩"。② 这些理念和建议对我国不无启发意义。因此，为了加强对网络平台服务提供者的保护，应当适当地阻隔存在劳动关系的劳动者身份和社会保险制度之间的关联，使网络平台工人在未明确其劳动者身份时也可以参加社会保险，享受社会保险权益。

目前我国大量网络平台服务提供者未参加职工养老保险、医疗保险等，这对个人和社会未来而言存在巨大风险。因此，应通过完善灵活就业人员参保制度，加强对网络平台服务提供者养老、医疗保险权益等的保护。根据《社会保险法》的规定（第10、23条），用人单位并没有为灵活就业人员参加养老保险和医疗保险的法定义务，是否参保对于用人单位和灵活就业人员而言均属于自愿。而灵活就业人员自愿参保的，养老保险费和医疗保险费由个人承担，导致实践中许多职工并不愿意参保。而且，一些地方只允许本地城镇户籍的灵活就业人员参加职工养老保险和医疗保险，不允许外地户籍的灵活就业人口参保。③ 实践中，我国灵活就业人员数量不断增多，参保群体也不断扩大。例如，根据调研数据，就全国平均水平来看，以个人身份参保的人数占企业职工养老保险参保人数的20%左右，有些地方甚至达到30%左右或者40%左右，参保潜力很大。浙江省灵活就业人员参保人数，已经占到总参保人数的37%。④ 因此，完善灵活就业人员的养老保险和医疗保险制度十分必要。在未明确网络服务提供者的劳动者身份前，应允许从业人员以灵活就业者的身份参保，且政府可给予社会保险费补贴，减轻灵活就业者包括网络平台服务提供者的缴费负担，这也是"互联网+"

---

① Orly Lobel, "The Gig Economy & the Future of Employment and Labor Law", *University of San Francisco Law Review*, Vol. 51, 2017, pp. 69 – 70.
② Orly Lobel, "The Gig Economy & the Future of Employment and Labor Law", *University of San Francisco Law Review*, Vol. 51, 2017, p. 73.
③ 田伟：《灵活就业人员参加社会保险的困惑与思考》，《山东人力资源和社会保障》2016年第8期，第34页。
④ 刘燕斌主编《中国劳动保障发展报告（2017）》，社会科学文献出版社，2017，第201页。

政策应包含的内容。2017年国家发展改革委等部门发布的《关于促进分享经济发展的指导性意见》也指出："积极发挥分享经济促进就业的作用,研究完善适应分享经济特点的灵活就业人员社会保险参保缴费措施,切实加强劳动者权益保障。"[1] 总之,平台经济不应以牺牲服务提供者的社会保险权益为代价,不应减轻企业的社会责任,政府可通过社会保险补贴等扶持政策,减轻平台企业的成本和负担,但不宜减损从业者应有的权益。

由于劳动法的保护往往是事后的、个别的、不确定的,大量平台工人无法获得劳动法保护,而网络平台企业是共享经济的主要受益者,其理应对消费者和服务提供者承担相应的社会责任,因此,还应从经济法和民商法等角度加强对网络平台企业本身的监管,督促平台企业对服务提供者提供相应保护。例如,平台应保证服务提供者的人身安全和身体健康,通过技术手段控制服务提供者的工作时间,避免长时间工作;为司机和第三人等购买人身意外等商业保险,保护司机等从业人员并限制司机等对第三人的责任。同时,由于网络平台企业一般都是规模巨大、拥有强大管理团队的企业,往往制定有严密的格式合同和规章制度,而广大服务提供者极为分散、信息不对称、缺乏谈判能力,因此,应通过民法的意思表达自由、格式合同条款规制等规则保护服务提供者的利益。

此外,还应强化平台企业的信息披露义务。平台企业凭借其技术优势,掌握了服务提供者和消费者的大量信息。而有效监管的前提是监管者获得充分而有效的信息。从国内外实践来看,互联网企业为了逃避监管或出于数据信息保护等原因,往往不愿公开信息。[2] 因此,应通过强化互联网平台企业信息披露或者向政府报送信息的义务,提高政府的监管能力和水平,加强社会监督。

总之,由于网络平台的特殊性,对服务提供者的劳动保护不能仅依赖劳动法,还应通过其他法律和制度从不同角度给予保护。

六 结论

平台用工的新特点,使传统劳动关系概念和判定理论在互联网平台用工背景下遭遇了巨大挑战,法官在许多案件中面临着裁判困境。但传统劳

---

[1] 国家发展改革委等:《关于促进分享经济发展的指导性意见》,2017年7月3日,第5页。
[2] Policy Department A: Economic and Scientific Policy, European Parliament, "The Social Protection of Workers in the Platform Economy", November 2017, p. 13, http://www.europarl.europa.eu/supporting-analyses,最后访问时间:2018年10月19日。

动关系概念和判定理论具有很强的弹性与适应性，其并非完全过时，仍可包容网络平台用工关系，因此，不应轻易放弃传统的劳动关系理论和判断方法。同时，为适应网络平台用工的新特点，应改进劳动关系的判定方法。对网络平台用工劳动关系的认定，应考虑不同平台以及同一平台不同类型平台工人的具体用工特点，综合考虑个案全部事实进行具体分析。在劳动关系认定上，应更加注重实质从属性，考虑平台工人的工作时间和收入来源，以及社会保护的必要性等因素。由于平台用工的复杂性和多样性，目前，我国不必针对网络平台工人的身份制定专门规则。除了劳动法，还应通过完善社会保险制度以及网络平台监管制度等多角度保护网络平台工人的权益。

Determination of Labor Relations in Internet Platform Employment

Xie Zengyi

【Abstract】 The traditional concept and theory of determination of labor relations, which have evolved from the practice of labor relations in factories in the industrialization era, emphasize the employee's "personal dependence" and "economic dependence". The traditional theory of labor relationship is faced with great challenges against the background of platform employment, which has many new characteristics. Nevertheless, because of their strong flexibility and adaptability, traditional concept of labor relations and related criteria of determination are not completely out of date and still applicable to platform employment. At the same time, in light of the new characteristics of platform employment, the method of determination of labor relations should be updated and improved. As for the platform employment relation, it should be determined in light of characteristics of different platforms and the actual employment of different types of workers and on the basis of all facts and factors in each individual case. In doing so, we should lay more emphasis on the substantive nature of "subordination" and take into account such factors as the working time and income source of platform workers, and the necessity of their social protection.

China can define the concept and factors in the determination of labor relations through judicial interpretations of the Supreme People's Court. Due to the complexity of and variations in platform employment, it is not necessary for China to formulate specific labor law rules for platform workers at the present stage. In addition to labor law, the social insurance system, the platform regulation system and other relevant mechanisms should also be put in place to protect platform workers.

【Key words】labor relations; internet platform; platform workers; determination of labor relations

论人工智能的法律主体地位

赵 磊[*] 赵 宇[**]

【摘要】 人工智能是否享有法律主体地位取决于其"智能":"符号主义"设计理念下的人工智能难以具有主观能动性,而"联结主义"设计理念下的人工智能虽然亦受到事先置入算法的限制,但是随着技术的发展能够具有理论上的无限求解可能性并具有可期待的主观能动性,因而可以在其智能范围内授予其不同于自然人的特殊法律主体地位。享有法律主体地位的人工智能具有受限制的意思表示能力,并且原则上由其自身承担法律后果。

【关键词】 人工智能 法律主体地位 人格 意思表示

一 问题的提出

2017年10月,机器人Sophia被沙特阿拉伯授予公民身份。这引发了世界范围的热议,有人认为人工智能开始正式走入了社会生活,势必会对人类构成威胁。有人则认为,人工智能系统被赋予法律上的人格,开启了一个机器人与人类并存的新时代。随着大数据、移动互联,乃至量子科技的飞速发展,人工智能技术的应用将越来越广泛,因此会对社会生活产生诸多颠覆性改变,这不仅仅涉及科技、经济领域,也必将产生一系列的伦理、法律问题。

"这是一个最好的时代,也是一个最坏的时代",文学巨擘狄更斯在以法国大革命为背景的小说《双城记》中如是写道。的确,以互联网技术为

---

[*] 中国社会科学院法学研究所副研究员。
[**] 中国社会科学院研究生院法学系经济法学博士研究生。

代表的第三次工业革命极大地扩展了人与人之间的联系、爆炸性地增加信息量级之后,以人工智能、大数据和互联网社会三者共同造就的第四次工业革命正在极大地改变着世界。一方面,依托互联网建立的云计算,并以此为基础获得的大数据配合智能计算机的深度学习算法,人工智能系统成功地模拟了人类的智慧动力。不仅如此,在人工智能仅仅开始试用的领域如语言写作、信息检索甚至投资决策类领域中,其表现已经明显超越人类的能力,其在解决问题的速度、定位信息的准确性以及能够连续长时间工作的耐受力方面具有显而易见的优势。人工智能已经被认为成为计算机技术领域的最前沿,这已经意味着生产力的进一步解放。而另一方面,物理学家史蒂芬·霍金对人工智能的担忧犹在耳边,以电影"终结者"系列为代表的讲述人工智能机器人脱离人类控制而"暴走"最终给人类带来毁灭性灾难的场景仍在眼前,人工智能系统引发的事故已经开始浮现:2016 年由微软开发的聊天机器人 Tay 在 Twitter 上线后公开发表含有性别歧视、种族歧视、同性恋攻击等方面的言论,虽然事后微软表示这是由于黑客对漏洞的攻击以及 Tay 受到了某些信息源的刺激所致;1989 年连续败给苏联围棋冠军古德科夫的人工智能机器人在众目睽睽下突然向金属围棋棋盘释放强电流杀死古德科夫;1978 年受电磁波干扰的日本工厂的切割机器人转身切割工人。以上种种都反复说明了一个事实,硬币皆为两面。在人类已经不断用自己的理性认识、改变世界并开始创造"理性"的时候,就要做好一个准备,一个"理性"超越人类且失控的准备。

法律的作用既在于定纷止争,也在于未雨绸缪。吴汉东教授认为,人工智能在知识产权的获得、侵权责任承担、个人隐私的人格权保护等方面可能存在巨大的法律问题。基于人工智能的负外部性,有必要"以人工智能的技术发展与规制为主题,形成包含法律规则、政策规定和伦理规范的社会治理体系"。[1] 郑戈教授则认为人工智能的立法须"指定一个现有的政府部门负责确立相关的行业技术标准、安全标准和个人数据保护标准,而这个标准不应当是自上而下武断强加的,而应当是对行业自身所发展出来的标准与公共利益、个人权利保护原则的综合考量,其制定程序应当遵循公共参与、听证等行政程序规则"。[2]

---

[1] 吴汉东:《人工智能时代的制度安排与法律规制》,《法律科学(西北政法大学学报)》2017 年第 5 期。

[2] 郑戈:《人工智能与法律的未来》,《探索与争鸣》2017 年第 10 期。

然而，需要特别注意的是，无论是基于人工智能的负外部性抑或是基于其行业标准进行规制立法或其他监管层面的顶层设计，都无法离开一个重要的事实：人工智能不同于传统的科技发展。以核能为例，我们能够基于核能双刃剑而可能产生的巨大负外部性，在核安全领域对核能行业进行严格立法和监管。这个制度框架搭建的必要性基础是核能作为立法规范的客体具有特殊性及其所需兼具保护的法益——安全、高效和促进清洁能源的发展具有特殊性。一言以蔽之，传统的科技发展带来的社会变革所需要的制度指引以解决的问题是如何对待新的客体，并在客体存在差异时仍能在制度体系内识别、保护相关法益。然而，人工智能的制度设计不仅仅是客体差异引发的法律问题：虽是"人工"，却具有"智慧"的系统产生了类似于人类的活动，因此制度设计上也许对待人工智能首先要考虑的是人工智能本身是否法律关系的主体而非客体。当然，如果从工具论的角度将人工智能仅理解为人类创造的工具，那么无论多么聪明、多么像人而不是人的人工智能都只是客体而非主体。然而，这种理解不但狭隘，且不合逻辑：工具和工具之间如何能产生法律关系？显然，人工智能之间是可以发生类似的法律关系的。比如在智能投顾开始逐渐成为代客理财的选择的今天，就能想象基金管理人的人工智能系统同证券市场上金融消费者雇佣的人工智能进行交易。在整个交易中，自然人或法人这样的传统法律主体只是背后的委托人或雇主。虽然这种交易目前还没有广泛开展，但可以想象的是这种交易在技术上完全可以实现。显然，此时的人工智能已经可以通俗地理解为从事这个领域的另一种"人"，"他"在这个领域中的具体行为与自然人的行为产生的法律后果可能无异。因而，对于人工智能所需要考虑的问题已不同于以往科技进步带来的问题，即人工智能是否可以具有法律主体资格的问题。

二 人工智能主观能动性的决定性因素——设计理念

人工智能是否具有法律主体资格，这取决于其是否具有与自然人相同或相似的属性和法律地位。从法理上说，一国公民是具有一国国籍的自然人，可以在其所属国享有法律规定的权利与义务，包括公法意义上的权利和私法意义上的权利。机器人公民无法像自然人一样行使权利、承担义务，其根本原因在于人工智能系统不具有主观能动性。主观能动性通常是指人的主观意识和实践活动对于客观世界的反作用或能动作用，是人之所以与物、动物相区别的核心要素。人类之所以具有主观能动性，是因为大脑的作用。人的大脑是人类思维的物理本体，是世界上最复杂的物质，其构造与运行机理的奥秘至今仍未被揭示。但是主观能动性应当具有理论上求解范围不局限于某个领域的特点。比如不同人在面临同一个问题或场景时，对问题或场景的描述都不相同，反应也不相同。并不存在一个内涵与外延确定的反应的全部方式集合，每个人的反应并不是这个集合中元素或元素的组合。自然人遇到任何问题或场景首先要辨识，其次是反应，这个反应具有非常高的偶然性，伴随着人的主观情绪的变化而变化。而法人或非法人组织虽然在法律上被视为主体，但其本质却不具有生物学上的意义，其问题的辨识和反应都是依靠自然人完成的。只是通过私法上相应的归属规范将自然人的行为的法律后果归于法人或非法人组织，法定的自然人的行为或意思表示即被视为法人或非法人组织的行为或意思表示。[①] 拥有主观能动性的法律主体可以行使权利、履行义务，正是因为法律赋予了其权利能力。因而倘若人工智能对问题的反应如同自然人能够进行开放式求解而非如同传统机器对特定类问题依靠穷尽解法求解，则可以认为人工智能具有一定的主观能动性，也就具有了权利能力的基础。因此，应当确定的是人工智能的基本原理，以确定其是否可能具有法律主体的相应资格。

一般认为，"人工智能"一词肇始于20世纪50年代美国的一次学术会议，由来自生命科学、计算机、数学、神经科学等领域的学者聚集在一起的头脑风暴（Brainstorm）。由麦卡锡提议将这种人类制造的可能能够感知、意识、学习甚至自主创造新的智能的机制（institution）称为"人工智能"（Artificial Intelligence）。目前常见的人工智能包括的皆是某个领域的人工智能如道路驾驶、下棋、计算等方面。从长远来看，随着人工智能技术的进一步发展，在广泛的通用领域发展出通用的人工智能（Artificial General Intelligence）是可期待的。

从人工智能的技术特性看，其智能化的发展是基于不同的设计理念的。早期人工智能的设计理念是符号主义（Symbolism），符号主义的理论前提是，"其一，人类富有智能地处理各项实务的能力，得归功于人类理性思维事物的能力；其二，人类理性思维事务的能力，等同于一种自动处理各种物理符号的内部心理能力"。[②] 换言之，在符号主义视野下，人之所以能产

[①] 如《民法总则》第61条规定，法定代表人以法人名义从事的民事活动，其法律后果由法人承受。第105条，非法人组织可以确定一人或者数人代表该组织从事民事活动。

[②] 徐英瑾：《心智、语言和机器——维特根斯坦哲学和人工智能科学的对话》，人民出版社，2013，第32–33页。

生各种思想、表达和行为,是由于人本身所产生的一系列物理符号的支持。各组物理符号包含带有特定含义的符号,这些符号是人类活动的基础。各类符号的排列组合构成我们想象、创作、发明的基础。因此,以符号主义为设计理念的人工智能重在提供一套符号系统,由系统识别所需要解决的问题,并通过符号的选取和排列拆分建立新的符号链条。可能在一个问题的解答中会产生若干符号链条皆是答案,由系统作出不断排除筛选后最终确定一个最优解。AlphaGo 就是基于符号主义的设计理念。而事实上,现存的从事某一领域的人工智能的设计理念大部分均来自符号主义。在这类人工智能中,问题解答的每一步都伴随着大量运算——对大量符号的选择和排列。这正是基于"任何物理符号系统若具有充分的组织形式和规模均会表现出智能"[1]的理念。此外,对问题的准确识别是符号主义系统的巨大问题。因为同一个问题可有不同问法,也就有不同的符号链条;而字面意思相同的问题在不同情形下代表的含义则可能不同,此时需要准确找到问题对应的符号链条,就要求超高的运算能力。符号主义理念代表了人工智能的设计从功能主义为切入点,以解决问题为目的,将一切问题识别为机器语言,将一切答案通过符号的排列组合选择而来。显然,这一类人工智能需要依托超高速的运算和超大量的符号存储。运算速度越高、符号容量越大,问题的识别越准确,提供的解答越多,最终解越优化,整个解答过程越迅速。然而,这一类人工智能仅能在限定的领域(符号容量)内作出识别与求解,其本质上依靠的仍旧是人类事先输入的符号和运算方式。尽管它在某些领域会显得非常智能,比如完败李世石和柯洁的 AlphaGo,但是这仍旧是来源于其对全部围棋落子求解答案符号的排列组合选择。因此这种人工智能可理解为性能格外突出的计算机,它不能超越其设计使用范畴,亦没有任何主观能动性。其对问题的机械符号化理解使得任何问题的解决方式都十分单一,没有任何超越推理答案范畴的可能性。

另一种人工智能的设计理念称为联结主义(connectionism)。与符号主义相比,联结主义显然更具仿生学的特色。联结主义首先将智能视为大脑中神经元的联结和信息传导的结果。在人类大脑中,大量神经元相互联结并对刺激大脑的信息进行传递,使得人类大脑能够产生思维。这种刺激可以是视觉的、听觉的、嗅觉的等。神经元则包括能够接受刺激、传导信息的各个单元。因此,如果人工智能能够模仿人脑神经元接受刺激并进行信

---

[1] Haugel and J., "Artificial Intelligence, the Very Idea", *Philosophical Review*, 1989, 7: 3 – 11.

息传递，那么就能如同人脑一样产生思想进行思维活动，并且产生自我学习的能力。联结主义设计理念下的人工智能包含人工神经网络系统，网络系统的神经元的联结可以改变。而最重要的在于人类事先向人工神经网络输入了控制和改变神经元联结的算法，在这套算法的指引下，人工神经网络受到刺激后，对不同信息输入系统，神经元进行不同联结，传递不同信息，产生了仿生学意义上类似于人脑的反映。显然，在联结主义的设计理念中，事先输入的算法极为重要，这决定了人工神经网络对什么刺激有反应、对什么刺激没有反应，也决定了人工神经网络受刺激后的联结如何进行。事实上，这套事先置入的算法类似于人类的世界观，世界观是多样的，算法也是多样的。我们常常认为难以理解他人作出的某些行为而去向他讲道理，有时能讲得通有时讲不通甚至反被他人嘲笑。这是因为不同个体之间的世界观不完全相同，而讲道理则是基于个体的世界观宣扬方法论的过程。在世界观差别不大的情况下，方法论的宣扬可能被采纳，道理就讲通了。而当世界观差别较大时，基于世界观产生的方法论差异就极大，显然他人不大可能接受其他方法论的宣扬。同理，对于联结主义的人工智能来说，事先置入的"世界观"即算法决定了其神经元的联结，最终也决定了问题的求解。如果算法差异极大，那么最终的求解也必然差异极大。但是这套算法保证了所有的刺激均可以在算法的控制下实现某种信息的传递并得出人工智能的反馈。此外，对某种信息的一次接触后，神经元可以不断联结、不断改变联结，得出相似或相异的答案。这样，联结主义理念下的人工智能就可以通过自我信息的交互不断优化求解，产生类似于人类的学习能力，实现提高自身水平的过程。相比于基于高速运算和海量符号选择以实现智能化的符号主义模式，联结主义对所有问题识别为不同的刺激，自主依据人工神经网络的信息交互模仿在类似刺激下人类的脑回路或反应，求解的答案不限于一个固定的答案池中的选择，而是开放式的，且可以不断自主创设新的联结以自我提高。Alpha Zero 仅使用了四个神经网络专用芯片，通过三天的自我对弈490万盘棋，一出关即100∶0横扫AlphaGo。[①] 基于联结主义设计理念的人工智能已不再局限于数据库的存储量，因而产生了多维的求解视角。而最重要的在于其人工神经网络自我创设联结以实现强化学习的能力更是符号主义理念下的人工智能所不能具备的。

比较两种模式，符号主义设计理念下创造的人工智能非但不具有人的

---

① 新闻参见 https://www.sohu.com/a/198953993_614076。

主观能动性，其有限求解的局限事实上使得这个显得非常"智能"的机器仅能在特定领域下对问题进行识别并寻求有限解中的最优解，既不能超越场景也不能跳出求解方式的有限性，因此并没有赋予其法律主体资格的必要。其一切活动终局性的结果是已然确定的，只不过具体的答案不同，可能对外产生的活动来源于人的指令或者设定，只是人将其作为具体活动方式的"顾问"，但活动的法律性质不会因人工智能产生任何变化。而联结主义的人工智能由于自我创设联结从而具有学习能力，其不但能够不断提高求解的能力、扩大求解范围，且从技术上由于多样的联结方式突破了求解的固定最大范围，因此能够期待其可以运用于广泛的场景中。因此，联结主义理念下的人工智能有了一定的主观能动性，甚至在一定范围上有了意思表示之能力。

以联结主义为设计理念的人工智能突破了符号主义人工智能难以"具体问题具体分析"的能力限制，并在一定程度上能够实现自由意志的表达，虽然实现这种自由意志的表达的过程是人类设计的。当然这并不是说现代以此为设计理念的人工智能已经可以实现人机交互的高度自由化。尽管现有技术下的人工智能具有强化学习的能力，但是这种能力是在算法的指引下通过比较不同联结，不断修正其参数后最终选择的结果。这种学习能力在初始阶段会显示出非常高效的提高，因为不同联结差异较大，参数不断被修正，其能力提高较快。随着场景的不断增加，问题的差异程度降低，联结的差异性也降低了，此时人工智能的学习效率下降。在场景相似度较高的情况下，系统会将其默认为之前辨识过的场景。而场景辨识能力的高低，则取决于置入算法的科学性。因此虽然理论上联结主义可以无限度求解并不断提高学习能力，但是由于事先置入算法的限制，相似场景识别难以十分精确，所以此时人工智能无法准确辨别与之前相似场景的区别，求解必然不准确。若考虑算法的限制和场景识别的准确性，联结主义理念下的人工智能比起符号主义虽有了求解范围、学习能力和理论上应用领域的提高，但是由于置入算法的限制，导致了其辨识场景精确度的限制，仍然难以如同人类一样对各类场景作出完全的真实意思表示，或者说，其意思表示能力受到了算法的限制。因此，算法的重要性不言而喻，"对于人工智能最重要的就是使得其算法能够像具有解决问题能力的自然人一样有效"。[1]当然，从发展的眼光来看，目前任何对人工智能下结论的观点都是轻率的。

---

[1] Mccarthy J., "What is Artificial Intelligence?" *Communications of the Acm*, 1998: 1-4.

应当强调的是现代的部分人工智能系统已经具备了一定的深度学习能力，但这依然是建立在其事先所设定的程序和既有的数据基础上的，并非自觉自发的自我学习能力。因此，那种轻言人工智能系统全面取代人类，甚至可能灭亡人类的观点是不负责任的，也是站不住脚的。不过，对于那些辨识场景区别较大、精度要求不高的工作，联结主义理念下的人工智能系统已经开始并会越来越多地替代人类，其发展势头之迅猛，怎么估计都不为过。随着越来越多的"Sophia"出现，对其进行正确引导、予以规范化管理，就成为下一步人工智能发展的关键。从这个意义上来说，随着人工智能越来越多地参与法律活动，甚至在人工智能已经开始代替人类从事法律行为的今天，赋予其法律主体资格不失为一种有益尝试和可供选择的路径。但是法律主体资格亦不单一，将人工智能视为人或其他主体则需要进一步探讨。

三 人工智能的法律主体资格

联结主义人工智能在一定程度上具有了自然人所具有的主观能动性，甚至具有了意思表示之能力。在学术界仍存在不少反对人工智能具有法律主体资格的声音："以这种拟人化的想象来理解机器人，试图制定规范来约束它们的行为，甚至赋予它们法律主体资格，这便显得有些不合时宜。"[1] 事实上，否认人工智能具有任何法律主体地位的学说如"奴隶说、工具说"[2] 都未能考虑到人工智能已在一定程度上具备了意思表示的能力。[3]

（一）人工智能是不是"人"

在现行法律体系下，法律主体或法律关系的主体依法域变化。在宪法法域下，法律主体是公民和国家；在行政法法域下，法律主体是行政机关与行政相对人；而在私法领域下，则是自然人[4]、法人及非法人组织。从法解释学上，法律主体的范畴盖然不能超出上述范围。

人工智能法律主体资格之考虑不应扩展到宪法领域。以 Sophia 为例，

---

[1] 郑戈：《人工智能与法律的未来》，《探索与争鸣》2017 年第 10 期。
[2] Hristov K., *Artificial Intelligence and the Copyright Dilemma*, Social Science Electronic Publishing, 2017 (57): 442.
[3] 参见袁曾《人工智能有限法律人格审视》，《东方法学》2017 年第 5 期。
[4] 我国《民法总则》第 13 条将《民法通则》第 9 条规定的"公民"改为"自然人"，这是确立民事主体制度的体现，将"公民"这一具有宪法意义上公法权利的主体与私法领域上的民事主体加以区分。

可以看出公法层面的法律人格对于人工智能系统没有实际意义。首先，人工智能系统不具有生理意义上的性别区分。性别是生物学上的概念，人类分为男性、女性，是因为其天然的身体构造以及内在基因差异造成的。虽然 Sophia 被认为是一名女性，但这仅仅是开发者对其外形和行为模式的性别设定。近期，Sophia 甚至为沙特阿拉伯的女性权利呼吁，但这并非因为其具有真正的女性身份，不过是其控制者的商业炒作而已。其次，人工智能系统不能成为宪法意义上的权利享有者和义务承担者。正如法人无法享有宪法上的选举权与被选举权一样，赋予不具有自主意识的主体以政治权利是可笑的、荒唐的，更无必要。最后，人工智能系统应该为人类社会服务，没有必要赋予其"人权"。人类社会的法律制度之所以赋予人工智能系统以法律人格，目的是更好地利用科学技术改造社会，服务人类。

事实上，作为私法上法律主体的自然人，指的是法律上的人而非生物学上的人，虽然现代民法鲜有不将生物意义上的人视作法律上的人的做法即不赋予其自然人的民事权利能力。区分法律上的人与生物学上的人似乎没有什么意义，但是，这一点对于明晰自然人随着民事主体制度的建立而确立其法律主体地位、理解自然人的范畴大有裨益。

如果说生物学上的人指的是作为人类这个生物种群概念，那么法律上的人则是在生物学的人上附加了"人格"的特征。法律上的人，"是享有法律人格，并据以独立参加法律活动、享有权利、履行义务、承担责任的主体"。[①] 因此，倘若在生物意义上人不具有独立参加法律活动、履行权利义务并承担责任的资格，则不能被视为法律意义上的人，古罗马时期的奴隶即如此。自原始社会发展而来，法律上的人呈现出逐渐与生物意义上的人范畴不断接近的趋势。封建时期法律意义上的人与人之身份息息相关。贵族或平民、男人或女人这些都影响了完整意义的法律上的"人"之认定。随着市民社会的兴起和资本主义萌芽的出现，平权思想的勃兴使人们开始意识到生物意义上的人均应为被法律所承认的主体。随着法国大革命将"人生而平等"的理念不断推向全世界，及至今日，现代文明国家已经不在法律主体资格的确立方面对生物意义上的人作出任何差异性规定了。

在现代区分公私法的法律体系中，自然人概念的外延与生物意义上人的概念的外延几乎重合，是指"具有生命的人类个体，是一个相对于法人

---

① 徐文：《反思与优化：人工智能时代法律人格赋予标准论》，《西南民族大学学报》（人文社会科学版）2018 年第 7 期。

的民法概念"。① 自然人与同是作为民事法律主体的法人与非法人组织相比，最明显的特征即具有生命。生命的长短、延续受到自然的支配亦受到人力的影响，但绝非人力所能彻底改变的。这也是生命最大的特征。如前所述，与民事法律客体的物相比，现代民法上自然人概念的外延已经几乎与生物学意义上人的概念的外延重合，但认为自然人就是生物学意义上的人或具有生命的人则未免不合时宜。事实上，赋予生物学意义上的人以人格是自然人概念内涵中核心的因素，而康德哲学中最为重要的论断就在于人只能作为目的而绝不能作为工具，这正是人格笼罩下自然人的属性。古罗马时期没有人格笼罩的人就会被当作工具或者物对待。人工智能不论发展到哪一步都不能超出人类所创造的工具这一本质属性。人工智能系统的底层技术主要是计算机运算、大数据以及移动互联网。在这个基础上，人工智能可以完成非常复杂的计算，并据此作出在速度上远超自然人的判断和决策，而且在这个过程中，不受外界的任何干扰，排除了人类在行为决策中的怯懦、犹豫、患得患失等人性弱点。在AlphaGo几次以绝对优势战胜世界顶尖围棋选手的比赛中，可以清楚地看到这一点。不过，人工智能系统的能力范围是以事先被输入必要的数据、设定目的程序实现的。设想一下，如果让只设定了围棋程序的AlphaGo与国际象棋选手去比赛，结果会如何？这样的AlphaGo是否有一天会对国际象棋产生兴趣，主动自觉地去学习国际象棋？除了那些可以凭借明确规则准确地计算可以完成的工作，人工智能系统是否可以主动从事个性化的工作，如艺术创作、烹饪、情感陪护等？这些问题的答案至少到目前为止是否定的，其行为模式都是由人类预先设定好的，其目的也在于为人所设定的目的服务。由此观之，人工智能是无法归入人（自然人）的范畴的。

由此可以看到，人（或自然人）最重要的法律特征和法律上的属性在于人格，这使得其不能作为工具而只能作为目的。显然，人工智能不是"人"，因为它不符合人（或自然人）的这一特质。

（二）人工智能能否成为其他法律主体

如前所述，依据康德哲学，人（自然人）不能作为工具而只能作为目的的属性从根本上排除了人工智能属于法律意义上的人的可能性。那么，人工智能是否可以超脱民事立法中自然人与法人二元结构而作为其他的主体存在呢？虽然从实证法的角度讲这是无法通过任何现有的法律释义解释

---

① 陈甦主编《民法总则评注》（上册），法律出版社，2017，第86页。

出来的，但是作为新兴领域的人工智能倘若确有作为法律主体的必要，则之后的制度设计未尝不能作出更改。

民事主体制度也随着历史的变迁不断发生着变化。在法人未得到民事立法确立其主体资格之前，只有部分自然人享有法律主体资格。在法人的法律主体资格得到法律确认后，法人开始与自然人一样具有了人格。[1] 由于"法的人格者等于权利能力者"[2] 这种独立的人格是法人之所以区别于其成员独立存在的原因，也是其享有权利、承担义务的原因。[3] 人格是权利义务的起点，享有独立人格的法人便可以以自己的名义独立地从事经营活动并独立承担民事责任。由此，赋予法人人格便赋予了法人独立的法律主体地位。在这一点上似乎法律的目的就是承认法人的人格，法律的主体地位是法人获得人格后的客观结果。但实际上，从法人的起源上看，逻辑则是恰好相反的。赋予法人法律上的主体资格并不是因为赋予了其人格客观导致的结果，反而是因为需要一个具有主体资格的法人出现，所以赋予了其人格。具体言之，出于功能主义的需要，经济发展需要一个能独立行使权利、履行义务和承担责任的法律实体，因此法律上需要将人与财产的集合体视为法律上能够与自然人相并列的主体，因而赋予其人格，使得其具有了法律上的能够以自己的名义行使权利、履行义务的资格。从这个角度上讲，法人是法律的产物。[4] 也正是由于法人是法律的产物，因而其作为法律主体受到了与自然人不同的约束。比如现代民法不会因为自然人财产减少等原因减损其人格，而法人可能因为其责任财产不当减少，或沦为内部人的工具而导致其人格形骸化。

对应到人工智能，在现行民事主体二元结构下[5]，人工智能难以取得一席之地。但是如前所述，联结主义理念下人工智能的出现使得其具备了主观能动性。随着人工智能的不断发展，智能化强于 Sophia 或 Alpha Zero 的人工智能会不断涌现在越来越重要的领域。比如根据彭博社报道，首个由人工智能管理的全球股票 ETF 已经在 2017 年 11 月开始交易。可以预见的未

---

[1] 但法人是否具有人格权这个问题仍存在争议。参见王利明《人格权法研究》，中国人民大学出版社，2012，第 164 页。

[2] 〔日〕北川善太郎：《日本民法体系》，仇京春、李毅多译，科学出版社，1995，第 56 页。

[3] Prentice, Daniel D., *Gower's Principles of Modern Company Law*, Sweet & Maxwell, 1997, p. 77.

[4] 参见施天涛《公司法论》（第 3 版），法律出版社，2006，第 5-7 页。在法经济学上，法人究竟是法律的产物还是契约的产物是一个悠久的命题，这里不讨论法人的性质为何，只想强调法人概念的出现是法律基于功能主义的考量而创造的。

[5] 民事主体为二元结构或三元甚至多元结构存在争议，但不是论述重点，此处不再赘述。

来，人工智能将更多地参与到需要大量人工计算和分析的领域。而对于类似担任基金经理的人工智能系统，显然需要有能力接受自然人的委托，和其他自然人甚至人工智能系统进行交易，这都需要其本身具有法律主体资格。因此同样出于功能主义的考量，法律授予这类人工智能以人格，使其获得法律主体地位。2016年，欧洲议会向欧盟委员会提出为机器人制定民事规范（Civil Rules on Bobotics）的报告，第50条f款表明，"从长远看，应当为机器人创设特殊的法律地位，以保证复杂的自动化机器人能够作为电子人（electronic person）的法律主体存在。这样它们有承担弥补自己造成损害的责任，并且能在其自主作出行为决策或以任何方式与第三方交往时享有电子人格（electronic personality）"。[1]

如同最初法人获得法律主体地位一样，现行法律同样不需要局限于现有民事主体分类，完全可以新创设一个特殊的人工智能法律主体。当然，人工智能毕竟是由于智能才享有的法律主体资格，因此其资格也受到了技术的影响。不分青红皂白一律赋予其法律主体资格并不合时宜，仅对联结主义理念下的人工智能，在其智能范围内授予其法律主体资格更为合适。

此外，也并非所有联结主义理念下的人工智能均可享有法律主体地位。第一，比如Alpha Zero这样的人工智能，尽管其智能化程度很高，学习能力也很强，但是没有必要授予其法律主体资格。因为它仅用于围棋领域，无论围棋水平多么出神入化，都不存在从事法律行为、行使权利与承担义务的可能性，亦丧失了其具有法律主体地位的目的。这并不是说只有设计目的是从事法律行为的人工智能才能享有法律主体地位。因为倘若人工智能的目的是从事事实行为如发明、创作或准法律行为如催告等，仍与其权利义务相关，此时仍有必要承认这类人工智能具有相应的法律主体地位，其因此才可能基于创作出作品而享有著作权。[2] 而权利与义务的原点即权利能力，是以，对于设计目的没有必要授予其权利能力的人工智能或从事领域与权利义务无关的人工智能如下棋、唱歌、跳舞等，不应授予其法律主体地位。

第二，人工智能的法律主体地位毕竟是基于社会发展需要而由法律认

---

[1] European Parliament, Report with Recommendations to the Commission on Civil Rules on Robotics, A8 - 0005/2017：18.

[2] 如2017年5月，微软智能机器人"小冰"的原创诗集《阳光失了玻璃窗》正式出版，单本售价近50元。这是人类历史上第一部100%由人工智能创作的诗集。参见孙占利《智能机器人法律人格问题论析》，《东方法学》2018年第3期。

定的，其在获得法律主体地位后行使法律行为、参与法律关系所产生的法律问题难以机械套用传统的民事主体规则。法律应该严格控制人工智能系统法律人格的取得，规定较高标准，并且由相关机构进行实质性审查，履行类似法人登记的手续才能赋予。

四 人工智能的意思表示和法律后果承担

如前所述，可以承认人工智能系统以私法意义上的法律主体地位。接踵而来的是两个问题。其一，被赋予了一定权利能力的人工智能将会以具有法律人格的法律主体身份参与各种各样的市场交易，换言之，人工智能需要从事各种各样的法律行为。而其从事法律行为的核心就是意思表示。那么人工智能的意思表示如何形成，是否应该对意思表示作出相应限制？其二，作出意思表示的人工智能从事一定法律行为后，法律后果如何承担？

（一）人工智能的意思表示

首先，同作为法律的产物，不妨考察与人工智能法律主体相似的法人的意思表示如何形成。毋庸置疑的是，法人本身不能思考也不能表达。如前所述，其意思表示是通过法律上的归属规范将本质上人的意思表示归属于法人。因此，法人的意思表示是由其法人机关或者说由人组成的法人组织机构实现的。一方面，法人具有法律主体资格，对外能以自己的名义活动。这一点就体现在法人有自己的名称或曰商号（虽然商号非法人独有）；拥有独立的财产，这个财产基础完全独立于法人的组织机构或设立法人的自然人，这也是法人人格的物质基础；凡有人格者必有思维。[1] 拥有了法人人格后，法人依靠法人机关进行思考和活动，法人机关也犹如人之大脑一般代替法人决策，代表法人对外活动。而法人机关依法必须设立的原因正是其代表法人作出意思表示、从事法律行为。法人的意志由法人机关实现，人工智能系统的意思仅凭其运算能力和基于大数据的分析，可否形成独立的意思？这个问题又要回到两种设计理念下的人工智能。如前所述，符号主义理念下的人工智能限于其有限的问题辨识与求解，本身不应享有法律主体地位，不具有法律人格，因此当然没有意思表示能力。具有法律主体地位的联结主义理念下的人工智能，在某个领域如股票交易、基金买卖等方面实现了高度智能化。可以说在这个领域内它比人类专家或专业的投资经理还要专业，并且可以期望其对此领域内的问题与场景实现高度辨识，

---

[1] 参见施天涛《公司法论》（第3版），法律出版社，2006，第6页。

也能够做到通过不断的自我学习提高水平并且在其理论上无限求解而实现"具体问题具体分析"。因此，可以认为联结主义理念下的具有法律主体资格的人工智能在其从事的领域内，基于问题与场景识别、算法指挥下的创设联结并传递信息最终得出求解的过程就是其意思表示的过程。

其次，如果将这种机器依靠技术手段进行信息处理并表之于外的过程视作意思表示的过程，那么事实上它与无论是自然人或是法人的意思表示就有了巨大区别。前已备述之，本质上法人依靠自然人进行意思表示。而自然人进行意思表示的过程是其发挥主观能动性的生理过程。承认人工智能具有一定的主观能动性却无法保证这种基于运算和信息交互的主观能动性能如同人类的主观能动性一样"可靠"。这种担心主要源于我们对机器人思维过程的"黑箱"无法完全认知。事实上，虽然人工智能是人类创造的，联结主义设计理念下的人工智能也在不断模仿人类的思维过程创设联结，其置入算法也是人类设计的。但即使如此，其联结的具体方式、传递信息与处理信息的过程仍是"黑箱"。因此会担心一旦人工智能出现"暴走"情形，作出反常的意思表示和决策将会带来巨大的法律风险。但事实上，人类对自身基于生理上的意思表示过程，即信息的输入、处理和决策的思维过程也不完全了解，对于人类来说也是"黑箱"。此外，人类的思维过程常常更加不合理，更加反常，且更会受到场合、时间、身体状态等各种非理性因素的影响。然而除了现代民法设置的行为能力上年龄与精神状态的限制，没有人会质疑为何承认人类的意思表示能力，仿佛精神正常的成年人的意思表示能力都是一样的，一定不会作出超乎理性的选择。因此，并没有必要对人工智能的非人类心理决策过程过分担心。不过，考虑到人工智能确有"暴走"的可能，可以对适用人工智能进行法律活动的领域比如股票交易进行限制。比如限制其交易的价格、数量、交割方式等。这种限制既包括技术上的事先限制，亦即提前在人工智能系统中置入限制使其无法作出超越范围的意思表示，也包括法律上的明示限制，亦即向交易相对人或市场公开其使用人工智能交易的事实，明示超过某个范围的意思表示无效或效力待定并赋予相对人撤销权。这样，既不会阻碍人工智能的广泛使用使人类生活更加便利，也不会因为不承认人工智能的意思表示能力而造成大量使用人工智能进行交易的场景下法律效果待定或无法评价的情形出现因而阻碍交易，并且能够防止极端情况下人工智能因"暴走"而作出极端的反常意思表示损害交易相对人或委托人的利益造成难以弥补的损失。

(二) 人工智能从事法律行为的后果承担

论及人工智能从事法律行为的后果承担,首先应当明晰法律后果的承担本质上也是权利如何行使、义务如何履行、产生的违约或侵权责任如何承担的问题[①],对此仍不妨考察法人从事法律行为的后果承担。事实上,法人具有法律主体资格,其具有法律人格必然得出法人能够以自己的名义从事法律活动,行使权利、履行义务、承担责任。只是这个过程可以由法人机关代表法人进行,比如法定代表人提出抗辩权、行使合同中的撤销权等;也可以由法人本身进行,如法人以自己的财产承担责任。事实上,法人独立的财产是法人具有法律人格的物质基础,而由于法人财产的减少会减损法人的责任财产,实际上会降低法人承担责任的能力,因而法律对法人财产减少的行为作了较为严格的限制。一方面法律对法人财产减少(减资)作了程序性规定以保证法人的责任承担能力不至于降低到损害第三人利益[②];另一方面,则从反面规定了未依法减损法人财产因而导致法人责任承担能力降低甚至损害第三人利益情况下的后果——此时很可能导致法人人格被否认,使得法人背后的自然人承担责任。[③]

人工智能享有法律主体地位,拥有法律人格决定了人工智能必须能够独立承担法律后果。享有法律主体地位的人工智能在其从事法律活动的领域,可以行使权利、履行义务。关键的问题在于责任的承担。法人从事法律活动以其全部财产负责,股东仅以其出资为限承担责任。而人工智能不同,人工智能享有法律人格的基础不是其财产,而是其类似于人的"智能"。"具有独立意志的人工智能产生的责任无法苛责新技术的创造者。"[④]是以,要求人工智能背后的设计者承担人工智能的责任似乎无限加重了设

[①] 理论上,即使人工智能从事的是私法上的行为,仍然可能产生公法上的责任。比如作为基金管理人的人工智能可能由于违规交易而产生公法上的责任。但是这个问题更为复杂,本文仅讨论民事责任。

[②] 如《公司法》第177条规定,公司需要减少注册资本时,必须编制资产负债表及财产清单。公司应当自作出减少注册资本决议之日起十日内通知债权人,并于三十日内在报纸上公告。债权人自接到通知书之日起三十日内,未接到通知书的自公告之日起四十五日内,有权要求公司清偿债务或者提供相应的担保。

[③] 如《公司法》第20条规定,公司股东应当遵守法律、行政法规和公司章程,依法行使股东权利,不得滥用股东权利损害公司或者其他股东的利益;不得滥用公司法人独立地位和股东有限责任损害公司债权人的利益。

[④] Buchanan B. G., Headrick T. E., "Some Speculation about Artificial Intelligence and Legal Reasoning", *Stanford Law Review*, 1970, 23 (1): 40 – 62.

计者的工作，使得设计者再也不敢创新。但是将人工智能难以以其财产承担责任的风险归于与人工智能进行交易的相对人又似乎不公平。因此应当在两个维度上设立人工智能的责任承担制度。

一方面，原则上人工智能的责任由其自身承担。法人的法律行为后果由其自己独立承担，但其最终权益归属于它的股东。可以考虑为人工智能系统设置类似公司股东的权益归属主体，由人工智能系统的开发者、受让者等相关主体充当。而在人工智能从事法律行为的责任承担上，可以考虑为人工智能设立类似公司注册资本的基金，以保证人工智能参与法律活动的初始具有一定的责任财产。随着人工智能参与交易的增多，人工智能因此获得的营利也会增多，其客观上的责任财产也会增多。此时可以对在基金基础上增加的财产设立公积金，如公司法上将一部分营利纳入法定公积金与资本公积金一样。这个公积金成为人工智能责任财产的一部分，从而提高人工智能承担责任的能力。多增加的财产按一定比例纳入公积金后，剩余的均可作为待分配利润归属于权益主体。

另一方面，施行强制保险制度。随着科技的进步，高速、核能等现代科技在极大地解放劳动力的同时也往往伴随着潜在的风险，虽然科技工作者长期致力于将风险降到最低，但是一旦发生风险往往意味着巨大的损害发生。人工智能科技也是如此。保险制度能够在"由于人工智能潜在的不可预估性使得人工智能一旦利用不当，可能造成难以估计的重大危害"[1]时，以较小的经济成本通过保险分担风险。而在人工智能领域，英国下议院在2006年提出一份有关无人驾驶汽车法律责任问题的提案，提出汽车强制险能够在驾驶者将汽车控制权完全交给自动驾驶系统时为其提供保障。[2]事实上，对可能产生侵权责任的人工智能投保强制责任险，将"大大减少人工智能侵权事件发生时的经济赔偿纠纷，直接促进人工智能行业的良性发展"[3]。

五　结语

人工智能系统基础技术的发展突飞猛进。如量子技术在人工智能领域

---

[1] O'Neil C., *Weapons of Math Destruction: How Big Data Increases Inequality and Threatens Democracy*, Crown Publishing Group, 2016, p.3.

[2] 参见宋云霞等《海上丝绸之路安全保障法律问题研究》，《中国海商法研究》2015年第2期。

[3] 袁曾：《人工智能有限法律人格审视》，《东方法学》2017年第5期。

的应用，对其大数据计算和处理能力的提高将是革命性的；物联网技术的飞速发展，使得人类社会将很快就会进入一个"万物互联"的时代；更为重要的是，各国政府、许多科学家以及无数的商业公司，对人工智能越来越重视。最为凸显的问题就是人工智能在给人类社会带来显而易见的便利的同时，其法律地位也受到了越来越多的关注。人工智能是否具有法律主体地位取决于其"智能"性，而在目前的技术条件下，其"智能"性则取决于其设计理念。"符号主义"理念将问题转化为符号，依托高速运算，求解也在符号的有限排列组合中寻求最优解，难以具备作为法律主体的"主观能动性"，亦难以行使权利、承担义务。而"联结主义"将人工智能的设计依据仿生学原理，创设了类似于神经元的联结。事先置入的算法对问题与场景的刺激进行识别后，人工智能可以自我创设联结，不断提高求解的水平。基于联结主义下的人工智能可以实现理论上无限求解的可能，并在一定领域具有主观能动性，实现"具体问题具体分析"。虽然仍然受到算法和问题辨识准确性的限制，但是随着算法的不断提高，其具有无限发展的可能。因此，赋予"联结主义"理念的人工智能特殊的法律主体地位符合经济社会发展的需要，而这毫无疑问地会带来人工智能系统的指数式增长，沙特阿拉伯政府赋予 Sophia 公民身份，其实际的法律价值难以评述，但至少其象征意义非常重要。这意味着二元法律主体制度受到了严重的冲击以及新法律主体的诞生已近在眼前。见与不见，变革已经开始，这值得我们深思和认真对待。

The Legal Subject Status of AI

Zhao Lei and Zhao Yu

【**Abstract**】 Whether AI could enjoy the status of legal subject depends on its intelligence. The AI based on symbolism could hardly possess subjective initiative. Although the AI based on connectionism is confined to algorithm, as the technology develops, this type of AI could be expected to solve problems beyond certain number of stereotypes and possess subjective initiative. Consequently, it could enjoy the status of special legal subject within the scope of its intelligence, which is different from that of natural person. In addition, this type of AI could possess limited capacity for declaration of intention and bear the legal consequences in principle.

【Key words】AI; the status of legal subject; personality; declaration of intention

技术、平台与信息：网络空间中私权力的崛起[*]

周　辉[**]

【摘要】 无论在理论上还是实践上，都不应将权力视为公主体的专属品。网络服务提供者也可以成为权力主体。这种从私权利到私权力的转变，除了法律授权和公权力委托因素，更在于某些私主体相对于其他私主体在技术、平台和信息等方面的优势。网络空间中私权力的崛起，打破了传统的"公权力－私权利"的二元架构，奠定了"公权力－私权力－私权利"的新架构。

【关键词】 技术　平台　信息　网络空间　私权力

这是一个变革的时代。在过去的半个多世纪中，美国等经济发达国家逐渐完成了向所谓"信息社会"、"信息时代"或"后工业时代"的转变。[①] 中国乘着互联网发展的东风，也在过去的二十多年里走上了中国特色的"互联网+"[②] 道路。

---

[*] 本文在《技术、平台与信息：论网络空间私权力产生的基础资源》（获中国法学会"第十届中国法学家论坛主题征文"一等奖）基础上修改形成，同时收录于胡泳、王俊秀主编的《连接之后：公共空间重建与权力再分配》（人民邮电出版社，2017）。

[**] 中国社会科学院法学研究所助理研究员、新治理智库联盟秘书长。

[①] Daniel Bell, *The Coming of Post-Industrial Society: A Venture in Social Forecasting*, New York: Basic Books, 1973. 转引自〔美〕弗朗西斯·福山《大断裂：人类本性与社会秩序的重建》，唐磊译，广西师范大学出版社，2015，第299页。

[②] "互联网+"是把互联网的创新成果与经济社会各领域深度融合，推动技术进步、效率提升和组织变革，提升实体经济创新力和生产力，形成更广泛的以互联网为基础设施和创新要素的经济社会发展新形态。参见《国务院关于积极推进"互联网+"行动的指导意见》（国发〔2015〕40号）。

在互联网开启的这个新时代中,互联网企业尤其是互联网平台企业扮演的角色和发挥的作用越来越显著:带动着产业的发展、创设着新的规则、分担着重要的治理功能。这一现象正是网络空间中私主体权力作用的重要表现。本文将围绕网络空间中这一私权力崛起的特有基础展开分析,并基于此对当前的网络治理提供一种新的思路。

一 私权力的可能性

在以国家和私人二元主体划分为基础的传统公私法结构中,"拥有权力,拥有支配性独断意志的仅仅是通过合法程序约束下的政府及其机关(*公主体*)"。[①] 私主体似乎与权力绝缘。但随着时代的进步和社会的发展,一切确定的逻辑都有重新反思的可能甚至必要。

"权力"是社会科学中的基础概念工具。罗素曾经说过:"在社会科学上权力是基本的概念,犹如在物理学上能是基本概念一样。"[②] 选择这一概念工具,似乎不需要再去说明其中的理由,更不用说去阐释权力的内涵。这一概念似乎就是不言自明的。甚至寻求一个权力的恰当定义也许本身就是一个错误。[③] 但是,从理论上去应用这一概念工具,就不能不面对这一问题。

社会学对于权力的界定是较为体系和完整的。按照达尔的观点,权力真正成为一个解释性概念,是从韦伯开始的。权力理论在近代有了深入发展,被称为19世纪的重大发现之一。[④] 韦伯指出:"权力意味着在一种社会关系里哪怕遇到反对也能贯彻自己意志的任何机会,不管这种机会是建立在什么基础之上。"[⑤] R. H. 陶奈对权力的定义除了明显地将人们的注意力引向权力关系的不对称之外,也同样集中于将某人的意志强加于他人,"权力可以被定义为一个人或一群人按照他所愿意的方式去改变其他人或群体的

[①] 斜体部分为本文所加。参见邓峰《经济法漫谈:社会结构变动下的法理念和法律调整(6)》,http://article.chinalawinfo.com/ArticleHtml/Article_31619.shtml,最后访问时间:2016年12月26日。
[②] 〔英〕伯特兰·罗素:《权力论:新社会分析》,吴友三译,商务印书馆,1991。
[③] 参见 Lukes, *Power*, New York University Press, 1986, p. 4,转引自李猛《日常生活中的权力技术:迈向一种关系/事件的社会学分析》,硕士学位论文,北京大学,1996,第20页。
[④] 李猛:《日常生活中的权力技术:迈向一种关系/事件的社会学分析》,硕士学位论文,北京大学,1996,第49页。
[⑤] 〔德〕马克斯·韦伯:《经济与社会》(下卷),林荣远译,商务印书馆,1997,第81页。

行为,以及防止他自己的行为按照一种他所不愿意的方式被改变的能力"。①《布莱克维尔政治学百科全书》也持类似观点:"权力就是一个行为者或机构影响其他行为者或机构的态度和行为的能力。"可见,在社会关系中,权力就是此主体影响乃至支配彼主体的能力或机会。也就是说,基于某种资源(力量)对比的失衡,彼主体成为此主体的支配对象。国家凭借其暴力机器,是最典型的权力拥有者。主权就是权力的极致表现。那么,私主体可否成为权力的拥有者呢?显然,按照社会学的概念界定,二者之间并无显著张力。

但是,在法学的概念体系中,公法与私法界分的背景下,公权力与私权利"泾渭分明"。私权力这一概念是否就没有理论上的基础呢?美国法学家霍菲尔德在《司法推理中应用的基本法律概念》一文中有关权利的分析恰可以提供这一问题的答案。霍菲尔德从法学体系的自足性出发,认为"严格的基本法律关系终究是自成一格的(sui generis)"。在区分法律概念与非法律概念、构成性事实与证明性事实的基础上,提出了四组基本法律概念:权利(right)与义务(duty)、特权(privilege)与无权利(no-right)、权力(power)与责任(liability)、豁免权(immunity)与无资格(disability)。霍菲尔德认为,与日常生活中,人们用以表示某人具有做某事的物质或精神能力而使用"权力"概念相比,作为法律概念的"权力"存在根本的不同。作为法律概念的权力与特定法律关系的变更密切相关。特定法律关系的变更可能产生于:(1)事后出现的、一个人(或人们)的意志所不能控制的某一或某组事实;或者(2)事后出现的、一个人(或人们)的意志所能控制的某一或某组事实。在第二种情况下,可以说意志控制占主导地位的那个人(或那些人)便拥有问题所涉的实现法律关系的特定变化的(法律的)权力。权力的关联概念是责任,它的对立概念是无资格。② 因此,霍菲尔德意义上的权力是指人们通过一定行为或不行为而改变某种法律关系的能力。③ 虽然霍菲尔德对"权力"更多的是从私法角度着

---

① 转引自〔美〕彼得·M. 布劳《社会生活中的交换与权力》,李国武译,商务印书馆,2008,第176页。
② 霍菲尔德对包括八个基本法律概念的分析详见 Wesley Newcomb Hohfeld, "Some Fundamental Legal Conceptions as Applied in Judicial Reasoning", *The Yale Law Journal*, Vol. 23, No. 1, 1913, pp. 16 - 59;该文的译文见〔美〕W. N. 霍菲尔德《司法推理中应用的基本法律概念(上)》,陈端洪译,《环球法律评论》2007年第3期。
③ 沈宗灵:《对霍菲尔德法律概念学说的比较研究》,《中国社会科学》1990年第1期。

墨,但是,他却从法律概念的逻辑上揭示了权力并不为公主体所垄断,换而言之,权力与私主体之间是可兼容的。

从公司这一典型私主体的前世今生,便可一窥私权力存在的客观性。最初的公司就被视作私主体与政治体的结合体,在某种程度上甚至是国家主权的分享者。在殖民主义的时代,像英国东印度公司这样拥有惊人权力(包括但不限于建设城堡和城市、发行货币、宣战、议和乃至缔结国际条约等)的公司占有很大比例。这些公司所拥有的权力几乎涵盖了一个国家所拥有主权的全部内容,可以称为半主权(quasi-sovereigns)或微国家(ministate)的实体。[①]

进入垄断资本主义时期,一些新型巨型公司日益成长起来。这些公司在市场上拥有相对于其竞争者和消费者的经济优势,具有支配相关领域内市场的能力。虽然这些公司不再可能攫取英国东印度公司所曾拥有过的强大权力,但是它们在谋取支配性权力方面仍然不遗余力。[②] 大公司实际上享有"私人政府"的地位,与政府分享主权。[③] 此时的公司已经从追求私人利益的边缘经济工具变成了在社会占统治地位的复杂部门,在事业心、投资、生产活动、发明革新、目标单一存在等方面焕发出巨大活力。[④]

厄尔·莱瑟姆教授认为,公司"具备私权力结构,是一个政治体、次国家,可以产生社会和政治支配却没有有效制约的政治体"。[⑤] 埃里森·加勒特教授在"Corporation as Sovereign"一文中,也以国家隐喻的视角,从人口和领土、经济权力、外交能力、社会稳定、立法与执法、货币政策、公益事业等七个方面对比了现代公司与国家之间的类似之处,揭示了现代公司(私主体)发展中的权力现象。

二 网络空间中的技术与私权力

技术资源在不同的语境里有不同的含义。[⑥] 在网络空间中,技术资源指的是对技术工具的占有、对技术知识的掌控和对技术架构的支配。

[①] Greenwood, Daniel J. H., The Semi-Sovereign Corporation, Utah Legal Studies Paper, 20 March, 2005, No. 05-04. p. 2. Available at SSRN: http://ssrn.com/abstract=757315.
[②] 参见 Allison D. Garrett, "Corporation as Sovereign", 60 *Me. L. Rev.*, pp. 129, 133。
[③] 〔美〕伯纳德·施瓦茨:《美国法律史》,王军等译,法律出版社,2011,第172页。
[④] 〔英〕伊凡·亚历山大:《真正的资本主义》,杨新鹏等译,新华出版社,2000,第117页。
[⑤] Earl Latham, "The Commonwealth of the Corporation", 55 *Nw. U. L. Rev.*, 1960-1961, p. 25.
[⑥] 参见张钢、郭斌《技术、技术资源与技术能力》,《自然辩证法通讯》1997年第5期。

网络空间具有典型的技术性。懂得并能够运用最基础的网络技术知识，是成为一名合格网民的必要条件。这也是网络空间与现实空间的巨大差别：在现实空间里，人只要有意愿就能够从事与其能力相匹配的生产、生活活动；在网络空间里，一切活动必须借助一定的技术工具实现，不掌握技术工具就无法开展任何活动。

进一步地，对技术工具掌握水平的高低不同，将会直接影响相应主体在网络空间行为能力的大小。能够进入网络空间的普通私主体一般是以消费者或者被服务对象的身份出现的。在网络空间中，提供服务的私主体必然明白其提供的网络服务背后的技术逻辑。但是，在网络空间中服务[①]的具体提供过程中，服务提供者没有意愿（这样会耗费不必要的成本），也没有必要（对于服务对象而言，能够体验服务就已足够）将具体服务背后的所有技术知识告知其服务对象。因此，在网络空间中的服务提供者与服务对象就必然存在这样的技术知识落差。作为服务提供者的私主体一方相对于作为服务对象的私主体一方，就拥有了技术资源方面的优势。

正是凭借技术资源优势，服务提供者才能在服务提供过程中，选择最有利于己方的技术手段。网络空间的合同多是采取"take-it-or-leave-it contracts"（要么接受服务，要么离开）模式。比如，网站拥有者会把网站的隐私政策设计在非常不显著的位置，即便隐私政策内容极不利于网站的访问者，后者也难以知晓。网站访问者的访问记录等隐私信息就在不知不觉中为网站拥有者所获取。再如，一些网站在设定定向广告（也称"互联网精准广告"）的接受选项时，采用了 OPT-OUT 机制——可以在获得用户同意前，采集用户的浏览记录等包含用户偏好和兴趣的信息，进而有针对性地投放广告。这一技术机制的背后是对用户针对相关行为默示同意的意思推定。而这在大大降低服务提供者商业成本的同时，也给用户带来了隐私泄露的风险。需要指出的是，对于这种商业模式，有的国家已经在电话网络中实施了干预：美国、英国、加拿大、澳大利亚等国均已通过立法规定，用户在自愿登记成为"拒绝来电名单"的成员后，如果再收到营销电话，电话

[①] 网络空间里的所有商业活动都是某种类型的服务活动。网络服务易被理解成提供网络技术的服务，从而将一些并非网络技术服务但仍通过互联网媒介或可以经由互联网媒介体验的服务（比如，许多软件服务功能的实现也是需要通过连接互联网实现的）排除在外。因此，用网络服务这一概念来概括网络空间里的所有服务活动不太精确，会带来偏差。考虑到这一点，在指称整个网络空间里的服务活动时，本文尽量避免使用"网络服务"这一概念，而是选择了"网络空间中的服务活动"等类似概念。

网络运营商将受到处罚。① 但是，这种纠偏政策还未能在网络空间中全面确立。

此外，软件提供者可以采取技术手段保障作品降低遭受侵权的风险——现代版权法已经认可了权利人设置技术措施的特权。这也就意味着在被许可使用的软件中，软件权利人可以置入与软件功能无关的代码，而软件的使用者在接受这种软件服务的同时必须接受这些对其而言没有价值的代码的"搭售"。除了对软件使用者意愿的强制外，这也带来了潜在的安全风险——只有软件权利人真正知道这些被置入的无关代码真正具有怎样的功能。毕竟，"斯诺登事件"已经让我们明白：网络空间中的许多窃听丑闻都可以来自这样的代码。② "微软黑屏"事件就是与技术措施有关的一个代表性例子。有关"微软黑屏"事件的详细分析将在后文详细展开。

在网络空间中，技术资源的优势以对代码的控制为集中代表。控制了代码也就决定了整个网络应用背后架构的模式，对相关的网络应用行为也就构成了约束。进而造成技术能力基础上的私领域与公共领域的失衡。劳伦斯·莱斯格教授曾经指出："传统上，法律保持公共领域与私人领域之平衡，著作权法的期间相对而言不长，主要基于商业性的使用。但是因为技术的急剧演变导致著作权法的范围及性质产生重大改变，现在已威胁此项平衡。因为数位技术的高速公路上，盗版充斥，立法者及科学家因而发展出前所未有的一套法律及技术武器，以对抗盗版并恢复文化所有人的控制力。……公私的平衡可能因此断丧，私人领域将吞噬公共领域，文化及创造力之开发将受到声称对之有所有权的人支配……，大多数人并未看到隐藏在狂热取缔盗版背后的危险。这就是公共领域何以早在许多人知道其已消失之前就被自以为是的极端主义悄悄害死。"③

正是在这个意义上，我们才可以理解为什么代码被称为网络空间特有

---

① 参见 Opt-out, http://en.wikipedia.org/wiki/Opt-out；《在美国遭遇营销电话骚扰》，http://www.chinanews.com/hr/2010/08 - 19/2477827.shtml，最后访问时间：2016 年 12 月 26 日。
② 《外媒：斯诺登爆料 英美用愤怒的小鸟窃密》，http://www.guancha.cn/america/2014_01_29_203141.shtml，最后访问时间：2016 年 12 月 26 日。
③ Lawrence Lessing, The Public Domain, Foreign Policy, http://www.foreignpolicy.com/articles/2005/08/30/the_public_domain. 转引自刘孔中《论建立资讯时代"公共领域"之重要性及具体建议》，《台大法学论丛》第 35 卷第 6 期，第 1 - 36 页。

的法律（代码就是法律①），被认为是一种规制形式："这些（网络空间如此的软件和硬件构成的对行为的一整套的）约束的实质可有不同，但都是作为进入网络空间的前提条件而被你感知的。在一些地方（如美国在线等），你必须输入密码方可获准进入；在另一些地方，无须身份验证即可进入。在一些地方，你从事过的活动会留有痕迹，借此将活动（'鼠标动作'）与你联系起来；在另一些地方，你可以选择说一种只有接收者方能听懂的语言（通过加密）；在其他一些地方，加密就不被允许。代码，或软件，或架构，或协议，设置了这些特性；这些特性是代码作者的选择；其通过使一些行为可行与否来约束另一些行为。代码蕴含了某些价值，或者说，其使另外一些价值难以实现。在此意义上，代码就如同现实空间的架构，也是一种规制。"② "对代码的控制就是权力。"③ 换而言之，对以代码为代表的技术资源的支配就这样转变为对私主体行为的支配，成为一种私权力。

这里有必要提及著名的古典数学问题——"哥尼斯堡7桥问题"。它对于理解架构所能产生的支配性影响有重要的阐释价值。顾名思义，所谓"哥尼斯堡7桥问题"是围绕哥尼斯堡这个城市的7座桥产生的。在哥尼斯堡的一个公园里，有7座桥（a、b、c、d、e、f、g）将普瑞格尔河中两个岛（A、B）及岛与河岸（C、D）连接起来（如图1）。对应的问题是："是否能够寻找一条巡游全城的路径，每个桥只经过一次？"④

大数学家欧拉在1736年研究并通过数学证明解决了这一问题。他提出了图论，将问题转化为一个有4个节点和7条边的图（如图2）。他提出：在网络上沿着边"旅行"时，拥有奇数条边的节点，要么是旅行的起点，要么是旅行的终点。走遍所有桥的连续路径只有一个起点和一个终点。因

---

① 美国信息法专家 Joel Reidenberg 教授在下文中阐述了代码法律（lex information）这一概念，参见 Joel Reidenberg, "Lex Informatica: The Formulation of Information Policy Rules Through Technology", *Texas Law Review* 76, 1998, p. 553. 转引自〔美〕劳伦斯·莱斯格《代码2.0：网络空间中的法律》，李旭、沈伟伟译，清华大学出版社，2009，第一章注［7］，第375页。
② 〔美〕劳伦斯·莱斯格：《代码2.0：网络空间中的法律》，李旭、沈伟伟译，清华大学出版社，2009，第139－140页。
③ 参见 William J. Mitchell, *City of Bits: Space, Place, and the Infobahn*, Cambridge, Mass.: MIT Press, 1996, p. 112。转引自〔美〕劳伦斯·莱斯格《代码2.0：网络空间中的法律》，李旭、沈伟伟译，清华大学出版社，2009，第五章注［46］，第392页。
④ 〔美〕艾伯特－拉斯洛·巴拉巴西：《链接：商业、科学与生活的新思维（十周年纪念版）》，沈华伟译，浙江人民出版社，2013，第19页。

技术、平台与信息：网络空间中私权力的崛起　　203

图1　哥尼斯堡7桥之一

此，如果图中有多于2个节点拥有奇数条边，就不存在不重复的路径。① 在哥尼斯堡7桥图中，4个节点都被奇数条边围着，因此，也就不可能存在所希望有的路径。

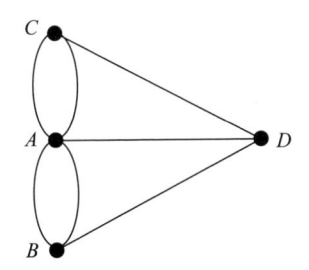

图2　哥尼斯堡7桥之二

如果想找到那样的路径，就必须改变节点拥有的边的数量。事实上，在1875年，哥尼斯堡人在节点B和C之间建造了一座新桥，使得这2个节点各自拥有了4条边。这样，拥有奇数条边的节点就只有2个（A和D）。那么，在如图3所示的哥尼斯堡城中，就可以找到一条不重复地经过每条边（每座桥）巡游哥尼斯堡全城的路径。

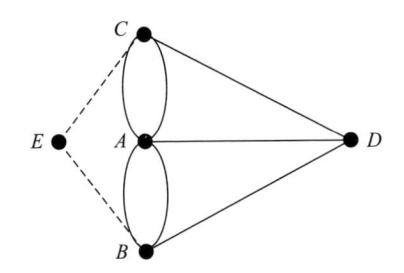

图3　哥尼斯堡8桥

---

① 〔美〕艾伯特-拉斯洛·巴拉巴西：《链接：商业、科学与生活的新思维（十周年纪念版）》，沈华伟译，浙江人民出版社，2013，第20页。

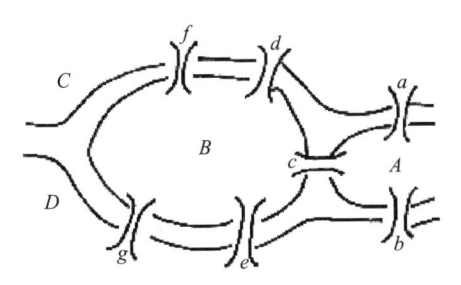

如果我们把哥尼斯堡 7 桥问题理解为一项规则 R（不重复地经过每条边），分别将图 2、图 3 理解为架构甲、架构乙，那么，架构甲中将无法适用规则 R，而在架构乙中可以适用规则 R。可见，欧拉在解答哥尼斯堡 7 桥问题时，也为我们揭示了不同的结构可以对规则能否使用产生支配性影响。如全球复杂网络研究权威、"无尺度网络"创立者巴拉巴西先生所揭示的那样，"图或网络的构造和结构是理解我们周围复杂世界的关键"。①

"哥尼斯堡 7 桥问题"揭示了非常重要的一点：架构支配规则。② 在网络空间中，能够利用技术资源设定网络架构的私主体就可以间接设定该网络架构中可以适用怎样的规则。如果某个私主体可以决定一定的网络空间中的"游戏"规则，那么这显然也是一种私权力的表现形态。可见，对网络架构的影响，是网络空间中技术资源生成私权力的重要路径之一。

三　网络空间中的平台与私权力

平台是一个自组织生态。"平台一旦形成，就活跃起来，具有自觉与自主发展的自组织特性。"③ "平台方是平台组织的内部管制者，属于内部软约束；政府是平台组织的外部管制者，属于外部硬约束。"④ 如果把网络空间比喻为一个生态系统的话，谁掌控了平台，谁就是开放、共享幕后的"老大哥"（Big Brother）⑤，谁就是这个生态系统的支配者。如果把作为平台的私主体与平台上的其他私主体都视为网络空间的链接节点的话，那么他们就是存在"不平等"关系的"枢纽节点"与普通节点。⑥

"平台是介于市场与企业之间的网络组织方式。它以扁平化的方式运作，有别于企业；但又具有内部结构，而有别于市场。"⑦ 网络环境下的平台：扩张速度快、规模大；对既有产业结构产生了革命性的冲击影响，比

---

① 〔美〕艾伯特-拉斯洛·巴拉巴西：《链接：商业、科学与生活的新思维（十周年纪念版）》，沈华伟译，浙江人民出版社，2013，第 21 页。
② 当然，对于欧拉在论证哥尼斯堡 7 桥问题时所揭示的欧拉定理而言，这一定理规则不会因为图的架构改变而改变。
③ 徐晋：《大数据平台：组织架构与商业模式》，上海交通大学出版社，2014，第 9 页。
④ 徐晋：《大数据平台：组织架构与商业模式》，上海交通大学出版社，2014，第 13 页。
⑤ "老大哥"一词在乔治·奥威尔的名著《一九八四》中有特殊的含义，是权力的象征。参见〔英〕乔治·奥威尔《一九八四》，董乐山译，上海译文出版社，2006。
⑥ 巴拉巴西提出了枢纽节点的概念，认为枢纽节点的存在，颠覆了"平等网络空间"的乌托邦幻想。〔美〕艾伯特-拉斯洛·巴拉巴西：《链接：商业、科学与生活的新思维（十周年纪念版）》，沈华伟译，浙江人民出版社，2013，第 85 页。
⑦ 姜奇平：《新文明论概略》，商务印书馆，2015，第 296 页。

如盛达集团的起点中文网在连接了作家与读者这两个原本处于产业链两端的族群的同时,取代了出版商、经销商、零售商的角色,打碎并重组了整个产业结构。[1]

我们可以把网络空间里的平台对照现实空间中的"市集"来理解。在现实空间中,市集这个"平台"提供了完善的"交易规则"(税收比例、营业时间)与"互动环境"(街道、广场、垃圾处理系统),并将其开放给几个不同的群体(商店、百姓、摊贩、街头艺人),令其相互吸引,且在一方壮大的同时,牵引着其他方一起成长。在网络空间里,平台的利用者之间(主要是利用平台提供服务和接受服务的主体之间),不再直接通过物理空间的行为完成交易活动,而是需要借助于平台提供者(控制者)所提供的技术手段实现一种数字化交易。在现实空间中,平台即便提供交易规则,对其利用者的约束力也是很难内化在他们之间的交易活动之中。但是,网络空间里的数字化交易一般必须按照平台提供者(控制者)设定的规则完成。这种规则在表面上是交易规范,在实施过程中却是以作为代码的技术规则来体现的。由于数字化交易必须遵循相应的技术规则,所以,网络环境下的平台提供者(控制者)所设定的交易规范可以直接内化在交易活动中,具有直接的实施效力。具体的例子可见淘宝网的淘宝规则体系[2]和腾讯开放平台的系列应用接入政策与规范[3]。也就是说,在网络平台的控制者与使用者之间存在典型的影响与被影响,乃至支配与被支配的关系。

在网络空间中,互联网平台服务和网络应用服务"分属不同主体,不同主体处于上下双层经营状态,构成同一个市场"。[4] 这个市场具有"基础业务平台的自然垄断与增值业务的完全竞争二重属性"。在存在网络空间平台的情形中,网络平台服务提供者、网络应用服务提供者与网络用户之间共同形成了一个市场。正是由于平台方的特殊地位,需要跳出简单的服务供给二元视角,重新审视这个市场中的各方关系。如果 I_p 代表网络平台服务提供者,I_n 分别代表网络应用服务提供者(考虑到网络平台上的网络应用服务提供者必然不是单一的,还会存在 I_1、I_2、I_3 等其他私主体,因此,

---

[1] 陈威如、余卓轩:《平台战略——正在席卷全球的商业模式革命》,中信出版社,2013,第92页。
[2] 参见 http://rule.taobao.com/,最后访问时间:2016年12月26日。
[3] 参见 http://wiki.open.qq.com/wiki,最后访问时间:2016年12月26日。
[4] 姜奇平:《论互联网领域反垄断的特殊性——从"新垄断竞争"市场结构与二元产权结构看相关市场二重性》,《中国工商管理研究》2013年第4期。

在图 4 中，使用 I_1、I_2 代表众多利用网络平台提供服务的网络应用服务提供者），C 代表网络用户，那么，I_p 与 C 之间、I_p 与（I_1、I_2）之间、（I_1、I_2）与 C 之间的复杂关系可以用图 4 来说明。

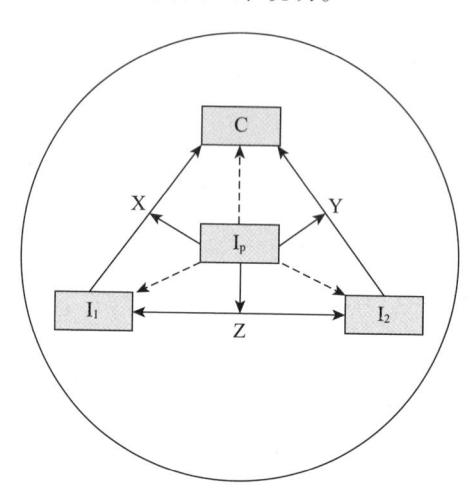

图 4　网络平台上私主体间关系架构

图 4 中，任意两个箭头的交叉点 X、Y 等就是网络空间市场二重性的结合点。这种二重性使得网络空间市场中的私主体间的关系比现实空间的单一维度市场中私主体间的关系更加复杂，具体表现如下。

第一，私主体身份类型更加多元。在现实空间中，私主体身份类型主要是经营者与消费者；在网络空间中，私主体身份至少存在网络平台服务提供者、网络应用服务提供者与消费者三种。虽然在某种意义上，网络平台服务提供者、网络应用服务提供者都可以视为经营者，但是二者在网络空间中所处的地位明显不同——因为就基础服务（平台服务）而言，前者对于后者有着支配性影响，姜奇平把这一层次的市场称为"自然垄断"。所以，在身份类型上，作为网络平台服务提供者的私主体与作为网络应用服务提供者的私主体应当被视为两种独立类型。

第二，私主体间关系相互交织。网络应用服务最终指向网络用户（消费者）。就其实现和完成来看，需要网络平台服务提供者与网络应用服务提供者的共同配合。在 I_p、I_n 与 C 之间，任意两类私主体间的关系变动都会对其与第三方私主体间的关系产生影响。

第三，网络平台服务提供者的地位在整个关系图中处于相对支配地位。支配性影响不仅存在于 I_p 与 I_1 或者 I_2 之间（苹果应用平台可以根据自己制定的规则决定其他应用软件能否上架）、I_p 与 C 之间（比如腾讯具备强制要求其用户作出类似"3Q 大战"中"二选一"的能力),也存在于 I_p 与 I_1、I_2 的竞争关系之间。I_p 还会对 I_1 或者 I_2 与 C 之间的关系产生影响,例如,《淘宝规则》会对网店与消费者买卖双方的相互评价作出规范(详见《淘宝规则》第 27 条)。

第四,作为消费者的网络用户地位更加复杂。一方面,如上所述,网络用户可能受网络平台服务提供者所支配。另一方面,网络平台服务提供者用户黏性的大小与其对普通网络应用服务提供者的支配性影响能力的大小成正比例。网络平台服务提供者一般不会调整平台基础服务的免费模式。因为,假如网络平台服务提供者针对其与网络用户之间的服务收费,基于消费习惯,网络用户可能就会转向其他的网络平台服务提供者。而用户数量的流失将会导致网络应用服务提供者也转向其他网络平台服务提供者。在这个意义上,可以说 C 具备影响 I_p 与 I_n 之间关系的能力。

第五,收入机制和价格机制更加复杂。网络平台服务提供者与普通网络应用服务提供者一样是以营利为目的的市场主体,只不过一般不直接从网络用户那里获取收入。网络平台服务提供者获取收入的模式大体有以下几种类型。(1)由普通网络应用服务提供者向网络平台服务提供者支付网络平台的使用成本,例如腾讯的 QQ 号码虽然可以免费申请,但实际上腾讯基于 QQ 平台市场可以向其他软件厂商收费。(2)普通网络应用服务提供者向网络用户提供收费的网络应用服务,其将收入与网络平台服务提供者分成,例如许多网络文学网站上网络作家向网络用户提供收费的阅读服务,有关收入在网络作家与网站之间分成。(3)普通网络应用服务提供者为网络平台服务提供者带来用户流量,基于用户流量可以获得广告收入。这是比较常见的类型,比如,用户使用软件提供的网络应用服务,可以到 360 手机助手等软件下载平台直接查询下载,下载这些软件就可以给 360 带来流量收入。相对应地,除了网络平台服务提供者提供具体的网络应用服务以外,网络用户一般不会向网络平台服务提供者支付对价。因此,价格的市场信号传导作用只能在普通网络应用服务提供者与网络用户之间直接体现。也就是说,价格机制在 I_p 与 C 之间很难发挥作用。

第六,在网络平台应用和网络服务应用共生的市场中,网络平台服务提供者一般就是网络平台的开发者或者控制者,其在基础应用层面(网络平台应用层面)的支配性地位是必然的,具有自然垄断的性质。而在网络服务应用层面,不同的网络服务应用提供者之间是自由竞争的关系。前者自然垄断的存在未必会对网络用户的利益产生损害,相反,越是统一的网络基础应用平台越能给网络用户带来便利的网络应用服务体验。在保障数据安全和网络隐私的前提下,可以在不同网络应用服务之间"穿越"体验,将会节省用户不少的精力和时间。后者有序竞争的实现,在某种程度上也有赖于前者对平台使用规则的明确。前者甚至可以发挥规范后者竞争秩序的作用,《淘宝规则》就是这样的典型代表。

网络平台的控制者与使用者之间的关系已经突破了现实空间中所谓商场(市集)与商铺之间的一般契约关系。虽然二者在某种意义上都具有服务关系性质,对于服务对象针对被服务对象设定的服务条款也都只有或者接受或者退出的选项。但是,前者有着后者所无法具备执行其设定的服务条款的能力——在平台构建之时,技术上就设定了服务对象的行为空间。

在这里需要指出的是,技术资源与平台资源是难以切割开来的。平台资源优势的发挥离不开技术资源的支撑,尤其体现在平台对于技术资源基础上的架构优势的依赖;技术资源通过与平台的结合,才能更充分地发挥比较优势。当然,二者之间的差异也是可以识别的:技术资源更多地可以理解为网络应用服务提供者对普通用户实现支配、影响的基础;平台资源则更多地可以理解为平台架构开发者的基础应用服务提供者对其他普通网络应用服务提供者实现支配、影响的基础。

四 网络空间中的信息与私权力

美国学者曼纽尔·卡斯特曾经指出:"知识和信息一直是生产力和权力的重要源泉。"[1]

那什么是信息?目前公认的有关信息最权威的定义,来自信息论创始人、美国数学家克劳德·艾尔伍德·香农(Claude Elwood Shannon)和美国数学家、工程师沃伦·韦弗(Warren Weaver)。他们的信息论将信息界定为"一个数量,它以位元(bits)为单位测量并通过符号出现的概率来定义"。[2]在《贝尔系统技术杂志》发表的《通信的数学理论》一文中,香农将信息量定义为随机不定性程度的减少。换而言之,在香农看来,信息就是用来

---

[1] 〔美〕曼纽尔·卡斯特主编《网络社会:跨文化的视角》,周凯译,社会科学文献出版社,2009,第46页。
[2] 〔英〕弗兰克·韦伯斯特:《信息社会理论》(第三版),曹晋等译,北京大学出版社,2011,第34页。

减少随机不定性的东西。[①] 这个"东西"在网络时代最集中的体现就是网络空间中的"数据信息"或者"网络数据"。

严格来讲，信息与数据是有一定区别的：数据是记载客观现象的原始数字、事实；信息则是有表述内容的消息，是有意义的数据。[②] 信息具有使用价值，能够满足人们的特殊需要，可以用来为社会服务。[③] 对于信息资源，有狭义和广义之分：狭义的信息资源，指的是信息本身或信息内容，即经过加工处理，对决策有用的数据。广义的信息资源，指的是信息活动中各种要素的总称。"要素"包括信息、信息技术以及相应的设备、资金和人等。[④] 本文所指的信息资源就是狭义上的概念，即经过挖掘整理后的有意义的数据。

进入网络时代以来，网络空间里的各类数据大量增加，基于云计算的数据挖掘技术[⑤]也逐步成熟，原本孤立的零散数据有了挖掘整合的可能，本来很难产生价值的数据反而会变成有巨大商业价值潜力的信息资源。在网络空间中，网络用户使用网络应用过程中会产生大量记载其个人信息内容的数据：搜索引擎上的搜索记录、浏览器上的网页浏览记录、电子商务平台上的交易记录、电子邮件信箱里的通信记录、即时通信软件上的聊天记录和社交关系以及在各种网络应用使用前注册登记成为用户时所填写的各种个人信息等。针对这些数据，网络应用服务的提供商可以自己或转让给有需求的第三方，利用数据挖掘技术进行分析，进而获得商业利益——有关商业利益的转化方式最主要的就是根据网络用户的兴趣、偏好等信息投放定向广告，获取广告收入。某些情况下，网络应用服务的提供商所控制的此类信息资源会成为公司重要的无形资产。

把信息与信息资源的分析引入当代的研究范畴，信息不对称理论有非常重要的贡献。因为，"一个竞争性的市场要运作良好，买方必须掌握充分

---

① 参见钟义信《信息科学原理》，北京邮电大学出版社，2002，第47－56页。该书将"香农"译为"仙农"。钟义信教授从哲学角度认为，"信息是事物运动的状态及其改变方式"，详见该书第56页。
② 参见梁战平、张新民《区分数据、信息和知识的质疑理论》，《图书情报工作》2003年第11期。
③ 参见 http://baike.baidu.com/view/58439.htm，最后访问时间：2016年12月26日。
④ 李兴国：《信息管理学》，高等教育出版社，2007，第9－11页。
⑤ 参见周晏、桑书娟《浅谈基于云计算的数据挖掘技术》，《电脑知识与技术》2010年第34期。

的信息，来对相互竞争的产品加以评估"。①

美国经济学家乔治·阿克罗夫在1970年发表了《柠檬市场：质化的不确定性和市场机制》一文，提出了相对成熟的"信息不对称"或者"不对称信息"概念。② 30年后，他也正是凭借在该文基础上对信息经济学③的开拓性贡献与斯蒂格利茨、斯彭斯一起获得了2001年度诺贝尔经济学奖。广义的信息不对称包括两种含义：一种指的是交易双方掌握的信息不均等，也就是狭义上的信息不对称概念；另一种指的是不完全掌握与作出最优决策所需要的全部信息。相对于完全信息，信息不对称也可以称为不完全信息。④ 信息不对称的核心揭示了信息资源的不均衡对于个人选择及相关制度安排的影响。在法学语境中，我们在要关注"信息不对称所导致的逆向选择、道德风险以及危及交易安全等问题"⑤时，需要重点考虑信息不对称对个人选择权的影响。

客观上来看，网络技术的发展的确增加了用户获取信息的能力。但这种结论是含有水分的，也是相对性的。首先，这种获取到的信息的真实性、准确性肯定是存在问题的，普通用户获取的信息庞杂、凌乱、相互矛盾，专业性上无法确保每一项判断都是正确的。其次，就像"道高一尺，魔高一丈"那样，相对于服务提供方而言，普通用户所掌握的信息量的增长，在那些拥有大数据基础上的云计算技术的网络空间的服务提供商面前，仍然显得微不足道。

网络空间信息资源的鸿沟使得强势一方具备了影响弱势一方的能力。这种影响最集中地体现在对选择权的影响上。按照传统的研究视角，网络用户受限于信息的不足，选择自由受到限制，可能会作出与内心真意不同的意思表示⑥，很容易遭受欺骗或买到假冒伪劣产品，成为侵权行为的受害

---

① 〔美〕史蒂芬·布雷耶：《规制及其改革》，李洪雷等译，北京大学出版社，2008，第40页。布雷耶大法官提到哈耶克的代表作《知识在社会中的运用》（F. Hayek, "The Use of Knowledge in Society", 35 *Am. Econ. Rev.*, 1945, p. 519）是关于信息问题的经典论文。
② 参见 Akerlof, "The Market for 'Lemons': Quality Uncertainty and the Market Mechanism", *Quarterly Journal of Economics*, 1970, 84 (3), pp. 488 – 500。
③ 关于信息经济学的介绍，参见张维迎《博弈论与信息经济学》，上海人民出版社，2012。
④ 参见曾国安《论信息不对称产生的原因与经济后果》，《经济学动态》1999年第11期。
⑤ 邢会强：《信息不对称的法律规制——民商法与经济法的视角》，《法制与社会发展》2013年第2期。
⑥ 邢会强：《信息不对称的法律规制——民商法与经济法的视角》，《法制与社会发展》2013年第2期。

者。其实，在这种传统视角之外，还有一种情况：选择在表面上是自由的，行使选择权的网络用户本人甚至也会这么认为，可事实上，这种选择是信息资源弱势的一方被信息资源强势的一方诱导作出来的。这种选择结果在某些情况下与第一种情形类似，会造成对网络用户权益的侵害，但更值得注意的是这样的情况：选择结果对网络用户本人的利益没有直接的影响，却间接通过网络用户的选择之手影响到其他在网络空间提供服务的私主体的利益。比如，在安全软件提供的一键优化过程中，用户在不掌握一键优化详细内容的情况下，会被引导卸载与该安全软件控制者存在利益冲突的第三方的软件。这种造成第三方软件被卸载的情形就构成了对网络用户与第三方之间网络应用服务法律关系的直接灭失。相对应的，如果在一键优化过程中让用户在不知情的情况下安装了与该安全软件控制者利益密切的第三方软件，这种引导安装的行为也就构成了对网络用户与第三方之间网络应用服务法律的产生。这便是典型的"通过一定行为或不行为而改变某种法律关系的能力"。[①] 此种情况下，也就蕴含了从私权利到私权力的转变。

如果说在网络空间中确定一种占用信息资源最多的网络服务类型，那么网络搜索服务肯定是其中的代表。就中文信息资源而言，百度拥有无人匹敌的规模。即便放在全人类既有的信息资源规模来看，百度所掌握的信息资源量也是惊人的。据统计，目前百度掌握的信息资源的体量在 EB 级别，约占全人类信息资源规模的 1‰ 至 1%。EB 是个什么级别的数量单位呢？1EB 等于 1024PB，1PB 等于 1024TB。如果一个移动硬盘是 1GB 容量，那么需要有约 105 万个这样的移动硬盘满容量装载百度所掌握的信息资源。[②]

正是因为知道百度有巨量的信息资源，我们才在需要检索信息时求助于它。但是，在提供网络检索服务时，百度不仅会收集检索本身所产生的信息资源，还能对检索结果发挥影响。这种影响指的不是搜索引擎根据其数据库里的信息资源和搜索关键词机械计算出的搜索结果，而是通过技术干预这种客观结果的出现，使本来关联度不高的信息以较显著的方式呈现，或者使可能基本没有关联的信息呈现为搜索结果。

有一个典型的例子，2013 年 12 月 17 日，作者曾在百度搜索框中键入

[①] 沈宗灵：《对霍菲尔德法律概念学说的比较研究》，《中国社会科学》1990 年第 1 期。
[②] 《大数据就在你身边：全人类信息量百度掌握近 1%》，http://news.xinhuanet.com/fortune/2014-01/12/c_125991782_2.htm，最后访问时间：2016 年 12 月 26 日。

"国土资源部"一词（得出的检索结果可见图 5）。令人吃惊的是，排名第一的搜索结果竟是某房地产中介公司的广告信息。

图 5　百度搜索截图

对于这种影响搜索结果的方式，百度自己命名为"百度推广"——"按效果付费的网络营销服务，借助百度 87% 中国搜索引擎市场份额和 60 万家联盟网站，打造了链接亿万网民和企业的需求平台，让有需求的人便捷地找到适合自己的产品和服务，也让企业用少量投入就可以获得大量潜在客户，有效提升企业品牌影响力"。[1] 针对这一行为，法学界更多的是用竞价排名来描述。在相关的专利文件中更能看出其中的问题。百度就此申请的专利名称为："一种利用搜索引擎发布信息并按竞价排名的方法"（专利号：02117998.0）。专利主权项载明：这是"一种利用搜索引擎发布信息并按竞价排名的方法，该方法是通过计算机互联网络，利用设置在服务器上的软件系统而实现，其特征在于，将信息发布到互联网搜索引擎中，并按照信息提交者设定的每次点击金额进行排序，生成结果页面，其包括以下步骤：（1）通过信息输入系统：信息发布者将所需发布的信息以及其他

---

① http://e.baidu.com/product/，最后访问时间：2016 年 12 月 26 日。

相关信息输入数据库；（2）利用信息存储系统将信息发布者提交的信息以及其他相关信息存放在数据库；（3）利用信息审核系统审核信息发布者所提交的信息是否合适，被批准发布的信息被列在搜索引擎结果中；（4）利用检索系统响应搜索用户的搜索请求，接受用户提交的搜索关键字，并根据搜索关键字给出相应的搜索结果的核心内容；（5）利用排序系统分析检索系统所提供的搜索结果中包含信息的点击价格，然后根据系统设定的各种规则对搜索结果进行排序；（6）利用结果页面生成系统：根据预先设置的网页格式模版，将搜索结果核心内容按照排序系统所给出的顺序整合起来，生成最终结果页面。"可见，百度的检索结果并不是完全中立、客观的，而是根据第三方报价高低的有关规制先后呈现相关信息。在某种意义上，这是信息资源优势最集中的体现——决定信息呈现的等级制。所以，在网络时代，信息的泛滥是与这种信息呈现的先后与多少的等级制并存的。在这个意义上可以说，网络服务提供者可能具有决定使用者是否接受特定信息的权力。[1]

关于竞价排名是否属于广告法的调整范围以及是否受相关法律规制，已有不少研究。[2] 姑且不论原有研究路径的结论如何，这种对搜索结果的影响，事实上限制了用户获取信息的能力。不管用户意愿如何，其检索结果还是要受到网络检索服务提供商的制约和影响。在这种意义上，竞价排名也是一种私权力现象的表现。

与公权力机关对某些敏感词的过滤要求相比，这种私权力行为对用户知情权、选择权的影响并非不严重，只不过体现在每个用户的每次检索行

---

[1] 参见 Lawrence Lessig & Paul Resnick, "Zoning Speech on the Internet: A Legal and Technical Model", 98 *Mich. L. Rev.*, 1999, pp. 395, 424 – 426; Thomas B. Nachbar, "Paradox Unregulated Character", 85 *Minn. L. Rev.*, 2000, pp. 215, 215 – 317; R. Polk Wagner, "Filters and the First Amendment", 83 *Minn. L. Rev.*, 1999, p. 755; Jonathan Weinberg, "Rating the Net", 19 *Hastings Comm. & Ent. L. J.*, 1997, pp. 453 – 482。

[2] 有关研究参见李剑《百度"竞价排名"非滥用市场支配地位行为》，《法学》2009年第3期；李自柱《搜索引擎服务商提供关键词竞价排名服务的侵权责任及法律基础》，《电子知识产权》2011年第6期；钟时《对百度搜索引擎竞价排名机制是否属于广告的研究》，《工商行政管理》2011年第14期；林承铎、杨彧苹《论关键词推广服务中搜索引擎服务商的责任》，《北京交通大学学报》（社会科学版）2013年第1期；卞豫《竞价排名引起的法律问题及其规制》，《法制与经济》2011年第1期；张俊芬《搜索引擎之竞价排名的法律问题研究》，《北京邮电大学学报》（社会科学版）2009年第6期；胡丹《搜索引擎竞价排名的法律规制》，《北京邮电大学学报》（社会科学版）2009年第6期；唐济民、李敏《搜索引擎竞价排名服务的法律规制》，《法治论丛（上海政法学院学报）》2009年第4期。

为上不会太过明显而已。但是，如果考虑到每天发生的大量检索行为，将每次的影响乘以巨量的次数，实际的总体影响也是非常大的。

五 网络空间中私权力的崛起

（一）网络空间中私权利到私权力的演变

1. 私权利与私权力

对于网络空间更像希腊民主广场——实践直接民主的广场，还是更像罗马斗兽竞技场——展现（奴隶主）支配（奴隶）的广场，目前仍有不少争议。

按照传统理论，私权利主体之间应当是抽象平等的竞争或者交易关系。但是，网络空间中拥有不同信息资源和技术资源的主体处于事实上并不相同的地位。传统的商业模式是：服务买方提供金钱作为对价，服务卖方提供服务。只要意思自治即可。在网络空间中，这一模式在某种意义上被颠覆了：服务关系不再清晰具体，享受服务的一方可以不支付对价而获取服务，提供服务的一方通过新的机制弥补成本、获取利润——推送广告、获取相对方信息等。[1] 在一些类型的服务关系中，双方技术、信息以及其他资源严重不对称，服务提供方对于是否继续提供服务、提供怎样的服务有着更大的裁量权，且在服务过程中还会从服务受用一方收集数据信息，更甚者能对服务受用一方如何使用服务产生导向性影响（最典型的例子就是上文阐述的网络安全信息服务）。在服务提供者和接受者之间就产生了这样的不均衡关系，随着影响的外化，还会对不同服务提供者之间的关系产生间接的影响，就像 360 系列案件中通过对用户行为和选择的"引导"所衍生的 360 与其他竞争对手之间的关系那样。再如，《淘宝规则》和《新浪微博社区公约（试行）》都针对特定对象设定了具有相应后果的行为规范。虽然这种规则没有法律授权，没有直接的法律后果，但是其仍具有可执行性。尤其是对于所调整的特定对象，如果违反了相关行为规范，则可能产生其难以接受的后果，而且这种后果在获得司法救济前，很可能为其造成实际的物质和经济损失。这就意味着部分私权利主体凭借其在网络空间中的优势地位和资源，在某些方面具备了相对于某些私权利主体的优势地位，有

---

[1] 免费的背后是时间成本和流量的输出，这才是那些主打免费服务的互联网公司所谋取的利益所在。因为，从另外一个角度来看，增加关注时间可以带来广告收入——这对于注意力经济背景下的网络商业模式尤为重要。

能力影响他们的选择，乃至设定规则；相应地，其他私权利主体则在某种程度上沦为被影响，乃至被支配的对象。

可见，这两部分主体之间已经分化出一类在相对意义上不再是私权利主体的主体。这类新型主体应被视作客观意义上或者事实意义上的权力主体，成为一种新类型的权力主体。这类权力主体是从私权利主体内部衍生或者分化出来的，且仍具备私权利主体的外在表象，但未融入公权力主体的框架之中，只是其已经具有在与其他私权利主体之间的法律关系中，拥有了"哪怕遇到反对也能贯彻自己意志的机会"。这是私权利主体内部分化的第一种类型。

2. 公权力与私权力

公权力主体与私权利主体间的关系主要是从公共因素的视角进行分析。按照传统理论，公权力主体与私权利主体之间应当是管理、服务和监督关系。互联网虽然只是这种关系的新载体、新媒介，但由于网络空间互联性、匿名性、无国界性的特征，互联网环境下公权力主体对私权利主体的管制能力和效率大大下降。

为了充分借助和利用部分私权利主体的技术资源、平台资源和信息资源优势，公权力主体将对私权利主体行为的管制委托给某些私权利主体实施。有两个典型的例子。（1）将敏感词的审查委托给相应的网络服务提供商来具体实施，或者对提供相关网络服务的提供商科以相应法律责任。这种责任既是义务——对于公权力秩序而言，也是权力——对于作为被影响对象的网络用户而言。（2）赋予域名服务商 ICP 备案审查的初步审查责任。由于行政机关后续的审查只是形式上的，在绝大多数情况下，这种初步审查的结果基本就是最终的审查结果。

此外还有一种类型，即法律（法规）直接授权给私主体以权力。① 例如，2012 年 12 月 28 日通过的《全国人民代表大会常务委员会关于加强网络信息保护的决定》第 5 条规定："网络服务提供者应当加强对其用户发布的信息的管理，发现法律、法规禁止发布或者传输的信息的，应当立即停止传输该信息，采取消除等处置措施，保存有关记录，并向有关主管部门报告。"这里的"应当"意味着网络服务提供者对于遵守本条规定负有法律

---

① 委托是一个双方合意的行为，强调双方的意思表示，委托的成立需要有委托人作出委托的意思表示，也需要被委托人接受委托的意思表示。而授权则强调单方意思表示，被授权方因授权方的意思表示而享有被授予的权力。关于委托与授权的区别，可参见沈开举《也谈行政授权——兼谈与行政委托的区别》，《行政法学研究》1995 年第 3 期。

上的义务,有义务处置用户发布的法律、法规禁止发布或者传输的信息。但我们同时更要注意到规定里面提到的"管理"、"处置措施"等概念。一般情况下,这类概念应当与公权力主体或者公权力相关联。此处关联的则是网络服务提供者这类私权利主体。显然,如果单纯地将本条理解为网络服务提供者的义务条款则不能完全概括其中的含义。考虑公权力主体在内的话,本条事实上涵盖了三类主体。在公权力主体(有关主管部门)之外,除了网络服务提供者这类私权利主体,还有作为私权利主体的"用户"。管理、处置、保存、报告的义务发生在网络服务提供者与公权力主体之间。此外,管理、处置同时也作用于网络服务提供者与用户之间,对于后者,这就是一种权力。在这里,一类私权利主体就因为法律的授权而具备了支配(管理、处置)另一类私权利主体的权力。

至于法律为什么要赋予私权利主体以权力,我们还是要回到前面提到的公权力管制能力和管制成本上:网络服务提供者在解决本条所指向的问题上,除了人力和财力资源外,拥有最直接的技术资源、平台资源和信息资源,这是公权力难以比拟的。因此,为了以较低的成本更有效地实现管制目标,在网络空间中,公权力需要让部分私权利主体适度地承担治理的角色。

因此,在公权力主体与私权利主体之间,法律授权和公权力委托也可以推动私权利主体转变为私权力主体。

但需要指出的是,除了法律授权和公权力委托因素,网络空间私权力之所以存在所依赖的是相对于其他私主体的"资源"[1] 优势[2]。在网络空间中,私权力得以产生和维系除了传统的经济资源,更显著地体现在技术资源、平台资源和信息资源方面。这种资源必然有着一般资源所不具备的价

---

[1] 关于"资源"概念的认识,一般有狭义和广义两种。狭义上的资源指的是人类所赖以进行生产生活的、在自然界存在的物质(材料)和动力的天然来源。广义的资源则用来指代人类借以从事一定活动、以达到一定目的的一切要素和有利条件的总和。换而言之,人类开展目的性活动所必需的一切东西都可以称为资源(参见李志昌《信息资源和注意力资源的关系——信息社会中的一个重要问题》,《中国社会科学》1998 年第 2 期)。本文是在广义上使用资源这一概念的。也就是说,作为强势一方的私权利主体所借以支配、影响作为其相对方的其他私权利主体的基础就是其所占有的资源优势。

[2] 奥斯丁在《法理学的范围》中就曾指出,"优势"就是表明"强制力"的一个术语,"用不利后果或痛苦影响他人、强迫他人的力量,通过这种不利后果的恐吓,使他人行为符合一个人的要求"。从他的法律命令说出发,"法律和其他命令,是来自优势者的,是优势者用来约束和强制劣势者的"。参见〔英〕约翰·奥斯丁《法理学的范围》,〔英〕罗伯特·坎贝尔修订编辑,刘星译,北京大学出版社,2013,第 34 页。

值性和稀缺性的特点，更重要的是这种资源优势还具有转化为支配力和影响力，进而带来法律关系变更的能力。

(二) 网络空间中的私权力形态

如果说在 20 世纪末互联网不是很普及的时候，网络空间还是一个小众群体领地、一个新的信息交流场域的话，在进入网络时代的今天，网络空间则已经成为众多公众日常生产、生活的一部分。许多网络服务平台的用户以千万甚至亿计，从经验的角度很难再视之为一个纯粹的私人领域。换而言之，像淘宝、QQ 和百度这样的服务平台，用户众多，利益关系面广，已经渐具公共领域的因素。私人领域与公共领域的界限在网络空间中已经不再清晰。在某种意义上，网络时代就是网络巨头的帝国时代；网络空间就是网络巨头的地盘。对网络空间中此类平台上的行为规制已不再是简单的市场干预，而是应当纳入社会治理的范畴。

互联网已打破"庙堂"与"江湖"的边界。权力与权利在网络空间中都有了新的丰富与发展。在网络空间可以推动产生新优势或者强化既有优势的技术资源、平台资源和信息资源，如果还谈不上给其他私主体带来痛苦或恐吓的话，至少也是可以促成某些不利后果的产生。实现网络空间的善治，必须建立在对这一现实认知的基础上。私权力就是观察上述私主体间法律关系架构的新切入点。通过对私权力的观察，我们可以理解网络空间中所被忽视的私主体间的分化现象及其不均衡现象。

"网际网路的连结功能使得公领域与私领域相互交错，打破了物理上的划分界限，但其隔离功能也容许个人以化名的方式出现在众人面前，隐匿了其在真实世界的部分或全部身份，进而在网路上重新营造自己的私领域。"[①] 在网络空间中，部分私权利主体已经具备影响其他私权利主体的能力，可以令后者处于失去自主权、选择权的状态。在这种意义上，这部分私权利主体已经转变为私权力主体。此时，私权力主体，也相应地可称为"私权力"："私"意味着权力的主体仍是私主体——其并未融入公权力主体的框架之中，只不过是私主体在某些情形下的另一身份；"权力"则表明在与其他私权利主体之间的法律关系中，其已经拥有了"哪怕遇到反对也能贯彻自己意志的机会"。

---

① 黄厚铭:《虚拟社区中的身份认同与信任》，博士学位论文，台湾大学社会学研究所，2001，第 119 页，转引自黄少华《论网络空间的社会特性》，《兰州大学学报》（社会科学版）2003 年 3 期。

从网络空间的技术性、平台性出发,结合近年的典型案例,网络空间中私权力的形态可以初步总结如下。

1. 网络规则——淘宝规则

淘宝规则是网络空间中由私主体制定的可以约束其他私主体的、最为复杂的网络规则。①

尽管在淘宝规则有关规范的适用上有必要考虑格式条款的解释原则,但是超越格式条款来理解淘宝规则更能发掘其中的私权利主体之间的不平衡地位。这也是淘宝规则同一般商场与店铺之间格式合同的不同之处。

第一,淘宝规则无论是文件题目上还是文件架构上都具备一般法律文件的形式特征,并仿照法律文件设定了具体的行为规则。比如,《淘宝游戏平台管理规范》在每条规范内容前都冠以相应的条文主旨,前三条的主旨分别是【目的及依据】、【适用范围】、【效力级别】。② 从外观上看,淘宝规则更像法律文件而不是格式合同。

第二,淘宝规则在内容上并非载明当事人各方权利、义务的规范,而是体现为淘宝作为中立一方约束其用户行为的规范。比如《淘宝规则》第4条第1款规定:"用户应遵守国家法律、行政法规、部门规章等规范性文件。对任何涉嫌违反国家法律、行政法规、部门规章等规范性文件的行为,本规则已有规定的,适用本规则;本规则尚无规定的,淘宝有权酌情处理。"在淘宝规则中,淘宝既是立法者,也是执行者,唯独不是被规范的对象。

---

① 淘宝规则包括名为《淘宝规则》的文件、相关下位文件(附件)和其他相关文件等一系列规则、实施细则、标准、规范。也就是说,在效力级别上,除了《淘宝规则》,还有作为《淘宝规则》下位规则的文件。比如,针对淘宝游戏平台上的各种相关交易活动,淘宝网制定了《淘宝游戏平台管理规范》,对于"《淘宝规则》中已有规定的,从其规定,未有规定或本规范有特殊规定的,按照本规范执行"(http://rule.taobao.com/detail - 187. htm? spm = 0.0.0.0. S4UOv5#947,最后访问时间:2016年12月26日)。在规制范围上,除了《淘宝规则》,还有作为《淘宝规则》补充的其他文件。比如,针对成人用品在淘宝网络平台上的交易,淘宝网制定了《淘宝网成人用品行业标准》,从非常详细的操作细节角度规定了卖家在淘宝网上发布宣传图片时应当遵守的标准,"本行业标准用于规范淘宝网卖家在'成人避孕用品计生用品'类目(下称'成人类目')下发布商品及信息的行为,是对《淘宝规则》的有效补充。淘宝网卖家在成人类目下发布商品均需同时遵守《淘宝规则》及本行业标准的规定"(http://rule.taobao.com/detail - 360. htm? spm = 0.0.0.0. S4UOv5#798,最后访问时间:2016年12月26日)。

② http://rule.taobao.com/detail-360. htm? spm = 0.0.0.0. S4UOv5#798,最后访问时间:2016年12月26日。

第三，淘宝规则在性质上体现了其对现有法律规范的补充作用，填补了法律的漏洞与不足，细化了有关规定，发挥了调整新型商品和服务交易关系的功能。《淘宝规则》之所以会主张"对任何涉嫌违反国家法律、行政法规、部门规章等规范性文件的行为，本规则已有规定的，适用本规则"，就是因为《淘宝规则》提供了非常具体的可操作的行为规则。此外，针对网上交易的退换货、签收、代购、商品质量、假冒商品等法律未充分明确问题的处理，淘宝规则都以专门的规范提供了争议解决的指引，可以更快捷地解决问题，减少交易纠纷。

第四，淘宝规则是实际效果，也是被其用户作为准法律规范来遵守和实施的。淘宝也为淘宝规则的执行提供了有关技术平台和实施机制。比如，为处理用户违规行为和用户纠纷，淘宝于 2014 年正式推出了纠纷解决平台——判定中心（pan. taobao. com）。[①] 再如，为打击知识产权侵权行为，早在 2012 年上半年，淘宝网就已经打造了一支超过 2000 名专业人员组成的团队，建立了从侵权商品信息的发现、取证、确认到删除、处罚的一整套维权体系，[②] 执行淘宝规则的有关规定。

所以，淘宝规则虽然以格式条款的形式存在，却实质上承载了淘宝相对于其用户（包括淘宝的会员、买家、卖家）的私权力。而且，淘宝基于淘宝规则所拥有的私权力既有立法权的品质，也有审判权和执行权的品质：淘宝制定、修改淘宝规则本身就是其立法权的体现；根据《淘宝服务协议》，对于会员"任一方或双方共同提交淘宝要求调处，则淘宝作为独立第三方，有权根据单方判断做出调处决定"[③]，这是其审判权的体现；淘宝的执行权则体现为其可以在平台上，直接实施店铺屏蔽、限制发布商品、限制发送站内信、限制社区功能、限制买家行为、限制发货、限制使用阿里旺旺、限制网站登录、关闭店铺、公示警告、查封账户等违规处理措施。

---

① 《交易引入大众评审员机制 淘宝判定中心出台》，http://hb. qq. com/a/20140101/001439. htm，最后访问时间：2016 年 12 月 26 日。

② 《淘宝公布 2012 上半年维权数据》，http://www. enet. com. cn/article/2012/0801/A20120801144187. shtml，最后访问时间：2016 年 12 月 26 日。

③ http://service. taobao. com/support/knowledge – 1163515. htm？spm = 0. 0. 0. 0. N38JAv，最后访问时间：2016 年 12 月 26 日。

2. 助推①

对于针对选择权的非强制性支配或影响，行为经济学有很好的解读。美国经济学家理查德·H. 泰勒和美国法学家卡斯·R. 桑斯坦合著的《助推：事关健康、财富与快乐的最佳选择》（以下简称《助推》）一书中有关"助推"的解读就是对这种影响选择权最好的阐释。在该书中，助推指的是："在选择体系的任何一方面，都不通过强制的方式，而是以一种预言方式去改变人们的选择或改变他们的经济动机及行为。"② 作者将运用助推理论推行良好公共政策的举措称为一种"自由主义的温和专制"——"助推不同于命令。将水果放在与人们视线齐平的地方是助推，而禁止浪费垃圾食品则不是"。③

虽然《助推》中对于助推案例的分析，在于强调帮助人们选择实质上对他们而言最优的选择，让我们将助推作为一种积极的正面概念来理解——"要称得上助推，便必须要使副作用降低到最小甚至可以轻而易举地避免副作用"。④ 但是，助推毕竟是一种引导选择的工具，本身事实上是没有任何价值取向的。在网络空间里，拥有信息资源优势的私主体完全可以通过这种方式来引导处于信息资源弱势的一方作出至少在被引导方看来是愿意作出的"选择"。

对默认选项的设置就是网络空间里服务提供商通过助推对网络用户选择权发挥影响的常见方式。一键优化、一键加速、一键清理就是其典型代表。事实上，许多网络商业模式的创新也正是建立在对普通用户选择权的影响方式的创新之上。

网络安全服务提供者可以利用用户技术专业能力的不足，通过各种形

---

① 助推指的是，通过所谓科学的非强制性的引导方式，改变人们的选择。参见〔美〕理查德·H. 泰勒、〔美〕卡斯·R. 桑斯坦《助推：事关健康、财富与快乐的最佳选择》，刘宁译，中信出版社，2009，第5-6页。该书强调的是在确定事关健康、财富与快乐的最佳选择后，通过科学的非强制性的引导方式，推动人们自愿地作出这样的选择。例如，安全软件为电脑体检后，根据所谓的满分标准给出体检得分，诱导用户去作进一步的优化。但是，就像我们有理由质疑为什么最佳选择是最佳的那样，我们也可以去问：满分的标准为什么是合理的、为什么优化措施肯定是更优的？

② 〔美〕理查德·H. 泰勒、〔美〕卡斯·R. 桑斯坦：《助推：事关健康、财富与快乐的最佳选择》，刘宁译，中信出版社，2009，第6页。

③ 〔美〕理查德·H. 泰勒、〔美〕卡斯·R. 桑斯坦：《助推：事关健康、财富与快乐的最佳选择》，刘宁译，中信出版社，2009，第6页。

④ 〔美〕理查德·H. 泰勒、〔美〕卡斯·R. 桑斯坦：《助推：事关健康、财富与快乐的最佳选择》，刘宁译，中信出版社，2009，第6页。

式的"助推"手段引导用户"不知情地"或者"不明就里地"作出"被期望"的选择。这也间接地可以通过用户之手使其他网络服务提供者受到影响——修改软件设置、限制软件功能甚至卸载软件。就像北京市第二中级人民法院2015年1月19日在搜狗起诉360不正当竞争一案的判决中所指出的那样,360安全卫士软件既是审判者,又是浏览器竞争者,不能有双重审查标准,对待不同企业的浏览器并非一视同仁,其对360浏览器和IE浏览器设置为默认浏览器的过程没有作任何提示,将构成不正当竞争。[①]

3. 干预

私权力主体有能力影响用户的选择,也有可能干预其他网络服务提供者的活动。这种干预最典型的是设定歧视性价格,既可以表现为为不同的网络服务类型设定不同的价格,进而直接影响用户的使用成本,也可以表现为为不同的网络服务提供者设定不同的价格,从而间接影响用户的使用成本。"倘若 Verizon、Comcast 或者 AT&T 这类宽频业者可以干预网络使用者如何使用这些网站,或者对于使用某些网站的网络活动额外收费,那么,显然就是赋予这些网络上的中介者控制使用者可以接收哪种资讯的权力。"[②]

网络中立作为网络治理的一项规制原则,就是对网络空间中私权力主体歧视性干预其他私主体行为的再干预。前者为私权力主体的干预,后者为公权力主体的干预。网络中立原则之所以在美国频受争议,表面上的原因在于,确立这一原则的 FCC 并没有明确的法律授权可以对网络服务提供商采取有关管制措施:"法院认为,FCC 所提出的主张依据,若非单纯国会的政策宣示而已,便是具有争议性的依据,因此不足以正当化其管制权力的行使,亦即美国联邦上诉法院的判决认定,FCC 无合法的权力,可以强迫网络服务提供商遵守网络中立性管制措施。"[③]但如果认识到私主体中尚有私权力主体与私权利主体的区分,就不难明白,网络中立原则的批评者乃将私权力主体的干预行为误认为普通的私权利活动,秉持"私主体法无明文禁止皆可为、公主体法无授权不可为"的原则反对政府的干预和管制。

---

① 《搜狗诉360不正当竞争案宣判 360赔偿510万元》,http://tech.ifeng.com/a/20150119/40949722_0.shtml,最后访问时间:2016年12月26日。
② 刘静怡:《网路中立原则和言论自由:美国法制的发展》,《台大法学论丛》第41卷第3期,第819页。
③ 刘静怡:《网路中立原则和言论自由:美国法制的发展》,《台大法学论丛》第41卷第3期,第816页。

可见，如果不能正确定性私主体的类似"干预"行为，将会给网络空间的治理带来难以厘清的困扰。既可能放纵私权力过火的干预行为，也会束缚正当合理的监管措施。

六 从"公权力－私权利"到"公权力－私权力－私权利"

以互联网为代表的网络应用创造了一种全新的生活方式和人际交流模式，构建起了现实空间之外但又与之密切联系的网络空间。在这个空间里，"时间和距离的限制都从根本上解除了，企业甚至个人都可以在世界范围内得心应手地处理他们的事务。……种种迹象预示着社会的主要秩序将要发生变化，甚至充分标志着一个革命性的变革。"①

"在网络时代，言论自由开始从传统的'个人 vs. 政府'二元对立向'个人—企业—政府'三角关系转变。"② 事实上，在私权力崛起的背景下，二元向多元的转变并不仅限于言论自由这一具体领域，在网络空间中其已经成为一个"新常态"。

网络空间中私权力的崛起，是一种正常现象，并不是网络空间中特有的小概率事件，而是某种意义上现实空间私权力现象的延伸；也是一种必然现象，这种必然性除了经济或资本的因素之外，更多的在于不同主体之间技术、平台、信息资源的失衡，是处于优势方之于弱势方影响、干预、支配关系的体现；更是一种新的法律现象，对既有的社会关系格局已经产生重大冲击，从"公权力－私权利"的分析范式向"公权力－私权力－私权利"的新范式转变。

也就是说，私权力的崛起为网络治理注入了新的动力。在网络空间中，私权力在推动商业模式创新的同时，也在构建自己主导的游戏规则，以去中心化之名塑造自己掌控的网络生态。打破了公权力的绝对控制，创造了一个崭新的治理疆域，这是私权力的建设性破坏成果；与此同时，可能拥有了公权力都难以直接拥有的技术、平台和信息资源，对其他私主体形成隐形的影响，这显然是私权力带来的破坏性建设后果。

以私权力为重心，"公权力－私权力－私权利"如果作"降维"理解的

---

① 〔英〕弗兰克·韦伯斯特：《信息社会理论》（第三版），曹晋等译，北京大学出版社，2011，第23页。
② 左亦鲁：《告别"街头发言者"：美国网络言论自由二十年》，《中外法学》2015年第2期。

话,至少可以分解为三个角度。

第一,公权力-私权力。公权力主体是私权力主体的监督者,私权力主体是公权力主体的合作者。一方面,对于私权力的支配、干预行为,公权力可以并且应当介入。作为管制措施的网络中立原则应当确立,只是对于具体的适用程序可以再作讨论。另一方面,网络空间的出现极大地拓展了公权力的治理疆域,公权力主体的治理能力面临极大挑战,考虑到个别私主体所直接控制的巨量数据和所具备的数据挖掘能力,公权力主体有充分的理由与后者探索共治的方案。淘宝规则的存在和完善,除了对淘宝的小生态有利,也对整个网络交易秩序有利。

第二,私权力-私权利[①]。私权力主体与私权利主体之间属于典型的支配与被支配关系。这种支配关系可能发生在后者不知情的情况下(如在用户协议中设定了繁杂的默认条款),也可能发生在后者难以理解的情况下(如在用户协议中设定了包含复杂技术概念的条款),甚至可能发生在后者无法拒绝的情况下(在服务没有替代选项时)。以平台型的私权力为例,支配关系既可以指向用户(消费者),也可以指向利用平台为用户提供服务的商户。因此,私权力的崛起意味着对私主体间的平等关系的重新认识:不但要超越抽象平等的假象,也要破除实质平等的局限。在私主体间的法律关系中,要建立私权力与私权利关系的识别机制和矫正机制,降低私权力损害私权利的风险。

第三,经由私权力的"公权力-私权利"。这指的是私权力介入传统公权力与私权利间关系的情形。私权力的介入可能有两种截然相反的后果:制衡后的缓冲与合谋后的无奈。一方面,私权力维护自身商业利益的行为,会不经意间成为对抗公权力滥用的屏障。另一方面,当公权力与私权力合谋时,就像斯诺登事件所揭露的那样,私权利将面对悄无声息的损害。但是,对此我们还要持有一定的乐观态度,在用户体验和口碑极为重要的网络商业环境中,只要有健全的市场机制,私权力合谋的动机将会被盈利的冲动所制约。

社会秩序一旦紊乱,就会倾向于重新塑造。向信息社会的转变纵然破坏了既有的社会规范,但一个现代的、高度科技化的社会不可能离开社会

[①] 这里需要特别指出,私权利并不限于私主体的民事权利。私主体的政治权利(如言论自由)也会受到其他私主体的支配性影响,比如微信平台或微博平台可以确立限制甚至禁止用户言论的规则。

规范而运行，它会受到大量的激励来塑造新的社会规范。[①] 私权力的崛起正在催生新的社会规范和塑造新的社会关系架构。

Technology, Platform & Information: The Rise of Private Power in Cyberspace

Zhou Hui

【Abstract】 Power should not be regarded as exclusive to public bodies, whether in theory or in practice. Internet service providers can also become subjects of power. Apart from legal authorization and the delegation of public power, advantages in technology, platform or information could also lead to the transformation from private right to private power. The rise of private power in cyberspace breaks the traditional framework of "public power-private right" and constructs the new framework of "public power-private power-private right".

【Key words】technology; platform; information; cyberspace; private power

---

[①] 〔美〕弗朗西斯·福山：《大断裂：人类本性与社会秩序的重建》，唐磊译，广西师范大学出版社，2015年，第10、11页。

第四部分

民法典编纂

Civil Law without Civil Codes: Reflections on a Peculiarity of Nordic Law

Ditlev Tamm [*]

【Abstract】 Most civil law countries have their civil law codified in a civil code. Whether the law actually should be codified in such a coherent and systematic code once was a big issue in Northern Europe, and still the Nordic countries deliberately have chosen not to codify their civil law. This solution has its advantages and historical reasons, which not necessarily fit in other places nor should keep other countries like China from discussing the making of a civil code.

....

The word code stems from the Latin *codex*. When you combine this word with the Latin word for to do, *facere*, you get the word codification. The person who first made up this composed word was the English Jeremy Bentham by the end of the 18th century, who saw the idea of codifying, i. e. collecting and redacting the law in books, which made the law accessible and understandable, as a blessing. [1] English law was and stayed far from this ideal whereas Bentham's ideas were more favorably received at the continent, where such codes as Bentham had thought of were already at that time existing or being prepared in several German states. The most important of these German 19th century codes was the Austrian civil code, which had been in preparation for many years before it eventually was published in 1813.

---

[*] Faculty of Law, University of Copenhagen.
[1] Jeremy Bentham, the well-known founder of utilitarian philosophy was an extremely prolific writer. His early works on legislation and codes actually were translated by Et. Dumont published in French as *Traités de Legislation Civile et Pénale* (1802).

The civil codes came late, and what we today call Civil law legal systems are not necessarily codified legal system. Whether the law of the Nordic countries shall be classified as a civil law system is an old question. If the choice is between civil law and common law, the law of the Nordic countries and the Nordic way of thinking the law is definitely closer to civil law than to common law. Legal studies and especially legal scholarship have a long tradition of influence from the continent, especially from Germany. The roots of Nordic law are not in the same way as for other continental laws to be found in Roman law, but still Roman law has had a great impact on Nordic legal thinking at least since the 18th century. Nordic law has a history of its own and therefore often is classified as a legal family or *Rechtskreis* of its own. It is part of this history that Roman law was never the law of the land and could not be quoted before the courts. But still Roman law and in the Middle Ages canon law have been instrumental in forming the way Nordic lawyers think.

In its origin Roman law was not a codified system. Legislation only played a minor role in the formation of Roman law compared to the influence of Roman lawyers and their thinking. You may even discuss whether the Justinian code of the sixth century by which Roman law survived and was preserved for the future, were "real" codes or codifications.[①] The Justinian code consists of three main parts, a collection of statutes known as *Codex* in twelve books without any coherent system. The same is the case for the most important part of his code, the *Digests*, which is a collection in fifty books of excerpts from works of Roman lawyers. If there is a coherent system it is definitely difficult to follow, aparting from the Digests starting with general rules on law and justice and ending with some general maxims or rules. Without an index it is very difficult to find your way in the Digests and even that will not help you to get an overview. There are good reasons for medieval lawyers to start the study of law by reading out texts and quoting parallel texts found in other parts of this gigantic work. The Justinian code was added an elementary introduction to the law known as *Institutiones*. This part of the Justinian code at least is systematic by following another system than the other two parts of the code. But the Institution-system later became extremely

---

[①] Hans Ankum, "*Was Justinian's Corpus Iuris Civilisa* codification?" (Extravagantes. Scritti sparsi sul diritto romano. Naples 2001) 399 – 412.

successful and since the 17th century was in general use by authors who wrote introductions to the law[1]. This system was quite simple based on the system used by the Roman 2nd century lawyer Gaius who divided the law into persons, things and actions (basically describing Roman procedural law). All in all the Justinian code with its three very differently composed parts and the fundamental division between statute law and legal science in no way can be compared with modern codes and was never used in such a way. Few lawyers would know all of the Roman law and the study and knowledge of law was a privilege for those who has been to a Law Faculty at a university.

The Nordic countries belong to those in which the enterprise was undertaken to collect the law in law books or codes way before the time of the great codifications of the early 19th century. In Denmark and Norway (including Iceland) the law was collected in two codes known as The Danish Code from 1683 and a nearly identical Norwegian Code of 1687[2]. The political background for these codes was the introduction of Absolutism in 1660. The One King, One Law-model was a stereotype, but it took political power and political will to carry it through. In Sweden (of which Finland was a part) a code was enacted in 1734. These codes were what Bentham would call "complete" as they not only were civil codes but comprised also the law of procedure and penal law. They were all divided into a number of books but for both the Danish-Norwegian and the Swedish enterprise, it was characteristic that most of the law in the codes was old law and few attempts were made to construct general principles or modernize the law. These codes for a long time were the fundament of the law in the respective Nordic countries. In the 19th century however the question came up, whether it was time to have them substituted by modern codes.

The reason for this discussion is the well-known legal "strife" that arose in 1814 which is known in Germany as the "*Kodifikationsstreit*", the battle on codifications. The core of this "strife" was whether it was timely in Germany of the Napoleonic

---

[1] For this question a good starting point is *Handbuch der Quellen und Literatur der neueren europäischen Privatrechtsgeschichte*, Vol. II (Veröffentlichung des Max-Planck-Instituts für europäische Rechtsgeschichte. Herausgegeben von Helmut Coing; C. H. Beck Verlag, München 1976 – 1977).

[2] For a survey of the history of especially Danish legislation, see essays in Ditlev Tamm, The History of Danish Law: Selected Articles and Bibliography (djøf, Copenhagen 2012).

wars to make a civil law codification as in France and Austria to substitute a law based still on Roman law. As is well known the French codification has its background in the French revolution and had as one its great achievements to bridge the gap between the law of Southern France based on Roman law, and the customary law of Northern France. The French code—the Code civil de 1804—was redacted by four able lawyers, the work was supervised by Napolèon himself, and the result was a nicely written law book with a little more than 2200 articles containing general principles, family law, the law of things and different kinds of things and how to acquire rights over things. The system was pretty much the Gaius—or Institutions—system in a modern and more accessible form. As is well known this code with modifications is still the fundament of French law. Also worldwide this code has been exported and inspired or been more or less literally received in Europe, Africa, Asia and Latin America (and the US State of Louisiana). It was this code, that together with the shorter Austrian code from 1813 was rejected when the discussion started in Germany.

The person to stop those of his compatriots who might dream of a code and German unity based on such a code was an already famous professor at the University of Berlin, F. C. von Savigny. His pamphlet against the idea of codifying German law is a juridical classic, which he called " *Vom Beruf unserer Zeit für Gesetzgebung and Wissenschaft*" (On the Vocation of our Time for Legislation and Legal Scholarship)[①]. Savigny in this small book savagely criticize the existing codes and then explain why the idea of codifying the law in itself is a bad idea. His legal heroes are the classical Roman lawyers from the first three centuries AD whom he praises as possessors of the knowledge necessary in order to actually be able to produce a proper code for their time. Law develops however, Savigny points out, and any code will in some way stop an organic procedure by which law is constantly produced first by the "Volk" (people) and later and for more complicated rules by lawyers. No lawyer however can claim to have the ultimate answer nor should the free development of the law be hindered or the law be frozen by the existence of a code which could never at least at his time have the same quality as Roman law.

[①] For a modern edition, see Hans Hattenhauer (Ed.), *Thibaut und Savigny. Ihre programmatischen Schriften*. 2. Aufl. (Vahlen, München 2002).

What Savigny mentioned has arguments against a code did convince some not to undertake such work. In Germany such a project which had had the support of Savigny's colleague and opponent Thibaut, a Heidelberg professor was given up if no permanently at least for most of a century. On the other hand, these arguments did not scare many politicians and lawyers in countries where German was not currently read away from actually planning or undertaking such a project often basing themselves on the success of the French civil code, and the following century is full of such codes.

The Nordic countries—as has already been mentioned remained resistant to civil codes. However, the starting points were different in each Nordic country. Norway in 1814 was separated from Denmark and had its own new constitution on entering a union with Sweden. The constitution (art. 94) foresaw a Norwegian code and very optimistically wanted such a code to be presented on one of the first assembly of the new Norwegian parliament. A codification committee was set up. A penal code was enacted in 1842 but a civil code was never completed. The arguments of Savigny pointing at the disadvantages of such a code, were accepted by later Norwegian lawyers who were less convinced than the makers of the constitution of the blessings of a code. A similar skepticism was expressed in Denmark when the question of a new code to substitute the old Danish code was discussed in the 1830's. The idea was given up, when the at that time most well-known Danish lawyer A. S. Ørsted[1] referring to Savigny pointed out all the difficulties and the little gain that could come out of such a project. In Sweden a draft civil code from 1826 was discussed. The draft proposal was to a high degree based on the French code, but the proposal did not gain wide support. The situation in the 19th century thus in the Nordic countries was that no influential lawyers saw any benefit from such a project and even might consider it contra-productive and out of the line with the Nordic way of looking at the law.

This negative attitude changed when in 1896 (in force from 1900) a new German code (BGB) was a reality. Nordic lawyers who wanted to learn the law

---

[1] Anders Sandøe Ørsted (1778 – 1860) was a leading Danish civil servant and politician who in his prolific scholarly work had a key role in the development of Danish law and legal science around and after 1800, see Tamm l. c. .

scholarly went to Germany and the German way of legal thinking had a great impact on Nordic legal thinking, varying however from country to country and from lawyer to lawyer. In 1872 Nordic lawyers inspired by similar initiatives in Germany came together to discuss legislative questions and thus there was a growing feeling of Nordic law as something special and different for German law. One lawyer who was however impressed by the new German code was a Danish law professor, Julius Lassen[①], who in a speech at the university in a style that could remind of Savigny's talked for the opposite standpoint namely in favor of codification and presented the arguments for a similar code to be made in Denmark. He mentioned how the Danish code of 1683 was obsolete, that important parts of the law needed clarifying legislation and how such a code actually could be a first step towards a Nordic code and unification of Nordic civil law. This speech was read in other Nordic countries, and—even if the idea of a full codification did not gain much support—it started in the first decades of the 20th century a new wave of important legislation in the Nordic countries especially within the fields of the law of obligation (esp. sale and contracts, insurance contracts, promissory notes etc.) and also within family law. Even if all statutes within this program are national, the fundament is there for an important harmonization of Nordic law. Still important differences between the Nordic countries are found in the law of real estate. The idea of a Nordic code still popped up from time to time, but today it can be considered as completely being given up. Accordingly, the respective article in the Norwegian code was finally abolished in 2014.

The history of why the Nordic countries have no civil code is a history of its own. Students from civil law countries often have difficulties in understanding how you manage a legal system with no code. The existence of a great number of single acts means that important parts of the law actually are clarified by legislation. Still important fields of the law as torts or the law of personal guarantee and security are based on judge made law. It may sound more complicated than it actually is to

---

① Julius Lassen (1847 – 1923) was a professor at the University of Copenhagen and a Danish legal scholar especially within the law of obligations who had a great impact on Danish (and Nordic) private law around 190, see Tamm, l. c..

handle civil law in the Nordic countries. The argument that the law should be contained in one coherent law book does not appeal to Nordic lawyers who will prefer that the law easily can be adapted to necessities and economic development or to a changed social context. This is a Nordic way of looking at the form of the law. Many arguments may however be produced in favor of civil odes. Especially for a rather new legal system as Chinese law the effort to discuss lawmaking and codification in itself can be very productive as a way to find out what the law actually is and how you want it to be. It is no accident that in most former socialist countries new civil codes were enacted as signals of the necessity of firm rules as a fundament and of the new way of discussing civil law. In Chinamany advantages for the advancement of civil law can be gained by discussing a codification project. Savigny was making his arguments in a country with old universities and a long and strong tradition of legal scholarship at a high level. It was a question of Roman law based on Justinian's code on one side and a brand new French style code on the other. A century after Germany actually got its code which was very different from the French code, the code reflected the high level of German legal scholarship and even if it has been criticized as complicated to overview it is still in force and considered a basic institution in German legal life. Since then many other and more modern codes have appeard, which have been models for other codes, in Switzerland 1907 and 1911 and the Netherlands 1992 and in Russia 1994—2006. A codification process is still going on in both Europe and on other continents. The World is looking forward to see how China manages this difficult task which to be fulfilled definitely, as Savigny already said, is in need of highly skilled lawyers who are not afraid of doing what not even the Roman lawyers did.

没有民法典的民法：对北欧法独特性的反思

迪特列夫·塔姆

【摘要】 大多数大陆法系国家都将民法编纂成为民法典。北欧国家曾经就是否应该将民法编纂成为一部连贯、系统的法典这一问题开展过大讨论，但是最终它们还是决定不将其民法法典化。北欧对这一问题的解决方案有其独特的优势和历史原因。但是它并不一定适用于其他国家，也不能妨碍中国等国家有关民法典编纂的讨论。

民法典编纂：民事部门法典的统一再法典化

朱广新[*]

【摘要】 法典化、解法典化与再法典化高度概括了19世纪以来大陆法系许多国家或地区的民法进化状况。我国40年来的民事立法，显现了一种较为独特的法典化、解法典化、再法典化交错发生、交互作用的螺旋式发展、进化轨迹。适应改革开放的阶段性、渐进式发展需求，我国民事立法秉执经济实用主义思想，采纳了以民事部门法法典化为先导逐步实现民法法典化的立法方法。为应对改革开放新阶段出现的新情况、新问题，司法解释成为民法发展、进化中最为活跃的规则创制机制。当下正加紧推进的民法典编纂实质上是一次民事部门法典的统一再法典化、现代化。如何贯彻执行新立法政策并系统体现新的价值观念，是民法典编纂无法回避的立法难题。

【关键词】 法典化　解法典化　再法典化　民事部门法典　司法解释

自19世纪以来的两个多世纪里，世界上许多成文法国家或地区的民事立法，大多数发生法典化（codification）、解法典化（decodification）、再法典化（recodification）等三种立法现象。改革开放40年来，我国民事立法遵循"成熟一个、制定一个"的立法政策，依随经济社会转型的阶段性发展，走出了一条独特的民事部门法的法典化、解法典化、再法典化交相辉映、交错相生的法律进化之路，产生了由民事部门法典、民事特别法、其他法律行政法规中的民事法律规范、司法解释构成的体系复杂、规模庞大的法

---

[*] 中国社会科学院法学研究所研究员，法学博士。

律规范群。如何在此基础上编纂一部体例科学、结构严谨、规范合理、内容协调一致的法典,面临诸多立法难题。由比较法看,当下正加紧推进的民法典编纂,与世界上其他国家转型时期的法典化一样,旨在使随政治、经济、法制转变而激增的法律规则合理化、统一化并希望由此实现稳定。[1]故而,民法典编纂实际上可看作一次民事部门法典的统一化、整体再法典化及现代化。本文拟以大陆法系民事立法的法典化、解法典化、再法典化现象或方法为基础,对我国民事法律规范40年来的创制、进化状况作出结构性分析和总结,由此揭示出我国民法独特的现代化发展之路,以及当下民法典编纂不得不应对的一些立法难题,进而提出解决这些难题的基本思路与方法。

一 民事立法:法典化、解法典化与再法典化

法典之称谓有古今之分,法典亦有古代法典与近现代法典之别。今日通常提到的法典,是指18世纪以来对法律予以分科之后对某一法律学科进行系统编制而形成的有国家强制力的书面文件,1756年的《巴伐利亚马克希米里安民法典》开启先河,1804年的《法国民法典》被奉为近代法典之楷模及真正的鼻祖。[2] 而像《汉谟拉比法典》《狄奥多西法典》《优士丁尼法典》之类的古代法典,实质上是关于各科法律、命令甚至是权威学说的系统汇编。[3]

一部法律是否属于或者是否可称为法典,并不取决于该法律名称中是否使用了"法典"这个词语,在很多情况下,其即使以"法"而不是"法典"命名,但可能就是一部真正的法典。欧洲大陆许多国家习惯于将民法直接命名为民法典,如法国、德国、瑞士、荷兰民法典(Code Civil, Buergerliches Gesetzbuch, Zivilgesetzbuch, Burgerlijk Wetboek),而东亚的日

---

[1] 参见 Attila Harmathy, "Codification in a Period of Transition", 31 *U. C. Davis L. Rev.*, pp. 783, 788 – 789 (1998)。

[2] 法国学者认为:"在之前的几十年间,其他欧洲国家(巴伐利亚、普鲁士、奥地利)曾作出一些法典化尝试,但拿破仑的法典化应当是新法律传统的起点,它确立了一种范式,至今仍保持了影响力。"Jean-Sébastien Borghetti, "French Law", in *The Scope and Structure of Civil Codes* 182 (Julio César Rivera ed., Springer 2013)。

[3] 意大利民法学家桑德罗·斯齐巴尼认为:"《优士丁尼法典》的显著特点就是:它是一部汇集了法学权威们的著作和皇帝行使民众赋予的立法权制定的法律,即宪令的作品。"〔意〕桑德罗·斯齐巴尼:《法典化及其立法手段》,丁枚译,载《桑德罗·斯齐巴尼教授文集》,中国政法大学出版社,2010,第57页。

本、韩国及我国台湾地区等则使用"民法"而不是"民法典"概念。一部法律被当作法典看待的关键之处在于，它不是对需要规范的个别问题而是对一个法律领域（如合同法、债法、家庭法等）作出综合的或者完整的规定，并能够使法律规则和制度符合逻辑地构成一个条理分明的、更易于理解的体系。[1]

法典化可作多维度解读，它既可指正式立法的过程，又可指正式立法过程的结果。相比于一般立法，法典化常被视为一种特别重要或正式的立法方法，也就是说，以合理的立法技术将某一法律领域内的所有或基本法律规范系统、合理地编纂成一部法典。在具体实施上，法典化实质上就是一种法典编纂，按照日本法学家穗积陈重之说，"是指对一国法律进行分科编制而形成具有公力的法律书面之事业，或者是指将既有法令进行整理编辑而形成法典的工作，或者是将新设法令归类编纂而形成一编的法典工作"。[2] 法典化方法有诸多特征，如合理性、系统性、统一性、一致性、易用性（易理解性或可接近性）等，合理化与易用性是其中最为核心的两个特征。[3]

法典化没有一成不变的模式，为适应社会经济的快速发展、转变，法典化从方法论和现象论上皆发生重大嬗变，作为结果论的民法典亦相应地在内外体系上发生重大变迁。19世纪的民法法典化可称作法典化的经典时代。法典化的基本目标是，尽其所能地将民法规则全面纳入民法典之中，实现民法的统一化（民法典即为民法）。《法国民法典》乃其范式，如19世纪的一位法国教授曾言，"我不讲授民法，我讲授民法典"。该言论赢得广泛赞同。数年之后，让·卡尔波尼埃把拿破仑法典描述为"法国人民的民事宪法"。该观点被许多人稍加改变称为"法国人民的经济宪法"。民法典因此构成民法的主要来源——几乎是独一无二的，并且许多时候被认为其价值相当于宪法。[4] 20世纪尤其是20世纪中后期以来的民法法典化，基本上都面临如何处理民法典与民事特别法关系的难题。这使这个时期的民法

---

[1] 参见 Reinhard Zimmermann, "Codification: The Civilian Experience Reconsidered on the Eve of a Common European Sales Law", in *Codification in International Perspective: Selected Papers from the 2nd IACL Thematic Confernece* 13 – 14 (Wen-Yeu-Wang ed., Springer 2014)。

[2] Michael McAuley, "Proposal for a Theory and a Method of Recodification", 49 *Loy. L. Rev.*, 261, 266 (2003).

[3] Michael McAuley, "Proposal for a Theory and a Method of Recodification", 49 *Loy. L. Rev.*, 261, 266 (2003).

[4] 参见 Julio César Rivera, "The Scope and Structure of Civil Codes", in *The Scope and Structure of Civil Codes* 8 (Julio César Rivera ed., Springer 2013)。

法典化在法典的内容或规模与法典表达方式上都呈现出与经典法典化时代完全不同的面貌。另外，这个时期的民法法典化也面临另外一个问题，即民法典应否吸收商事法律规范，从而不再单独编纂商法典。

解法典化，以存在民法典为前提，主要是一个描述性概念，即民法典被一些民事特别法、法官法、超国家的国际法或区域统一法解构或掏空，并受到宪制主义的深刻影响，其不仅在私法领域丧失规范垄断地位，而且原有的宪法功能被完全替代。① 严格地讲，只要民法典丧失其作为民法唯一、真正法源的地位，就会发生解法典化。因此，解法典化是法典化之后的民事立法为应对快速变化的社会经济发展需求而于再法典化之外必然发生的一种立法现象。它通常不是立法者的一种刻意追求，而是法典适应快速变化的社会经济情况而自我调适的结果。当再法典化也可作为法律进化的一种方法时，解法典化也具有了方法论意义，即立法者可选择以解法典化的方法调适民法与社会经济发展的关系。

解法典化有形式与实质之分。形式的解法典化，是指民法典被民事特别法、法官法等所形成的"微系统"所解构、分化，从而在形式上丧失完整性、统一性。实质的解法典化，是指一些本来由民法典规范的内容或事项基于特别的、与传统民法不一致的思想或方法，从民法典中分立出来，构成具有独立规范思想或构造方法的法律系统。劳动法、消费者权益保护法的自立门户，是实质解法典化的典型例证。

无论从哪一个方面看，解法典化皆削弱了民法典的重要性。虽然民法典毫无疑问仍然是民法的灵魂和核心，但民法的发展、进化在很多情况下是在民法典外完成的，民法典不再包括所有的民法，民法由此衍生出实质民法与形式民法之分。在民法领域，民法典不再具有至高无上的地位；在解决民法问题上，其不再是终极权威。民法典地位的此种重大转变，不是自愿解法典化的后果，如果立法者未将一些重要的新法或规则整合到民法典之中，其不是蓄意掏空法典的实体，而是为了便利之故。②

再法典化，同样以存在（民）法典为前提，主要是一个描述性概念，即按照法典化理念及方法，对陈旧、残缺的民法典予以修补，使之适应新时代需要。20 世纪以来，面对日趋复杂多变的社会经济生活，尽管有人宣

---

① 关于解法典化的发生原因，参见陈卫佐《现代民法典编纂的沿革、困境与出路》，《中国法学》2014 年第 5 期。
② Jean-Sébastien Borghetti, "French Law", in *The Scope and Structure of Civil Codes* 190 (Julio César Rivera ed., Springer 2013).

称"法典死亡",有人断言"法典终结",有人提出"解法典化",但是自19世纪以来的民法法典化运动并未停歇,对旧的民法典予以再法典化的现象在世界各地时有发生,第二代甚至第三代民法典在欧洲、拉丁美洲、北美洲以及亚洲皆相继出现。"解法典化"揭示的根本问题是,进入20世纪后,科学技术的迅猛发展使社会经济生活日益复杂多变,在新的社会经济条件下,19世纪的民法典明显有些老态龙钟,是否需要法典或者需要什么样的法典,引发诸多反思。但是,无论如何,作为一种立法表示方式的法典化,毫无疑问仍然盛行于当今世界各地的成文法国家,在民法领域尤甚。法典化的主要话题不是21世纪是否将存在法典,而是法典将具有哪些内容、其与私法的其他领域的关系及其表达方式。[①]

再法典化本质上就是一种法典化,相对于完全从无到有的法典化,其属于在既有法典的基础上第二次甚至第三次投身法典化运动。因此,法典化的一些普遍特征,如合理性、易用性等,同样是再法典化追求的根本目标。

对再法典化通常有两种理解。一是狭隘地认为,再法典化就是完全推翻原有法典而重新编纂一部民法典,对法典作出局部修改,属于法律的修改,不应看作再法典化。二是宽泛地认为,再法典化不仅指重新编纂一部民法典而且包括对既有法典某一部分作出修改补充从而使法典焕发新活力。人们一般在第二种情形下理解再法典化。从法律修订的角度看,再法典化可分为对既有法典的部分革新与完全革新(重新编纂民法典)。

1942年意大利民法典是民法再法典化运动中的一个里程碑,拉丁美洲一些国家以其为楷模,完全革新了他们在19世纪受法国影响编纂的民法典,如1975年玻利维亚民法典、1982年委内瑞拉民法典、1984年秘鲁民法典、1985年巴拉圭民法典等。在欧洲,受意大利新民法典的影响,葡萄牙于1966年以新民法典取代了旧民法典;荷兰在1970-2012年编纂了一部新民法典,取代了1838年的民法典。在北美洲,加拿大魁北克省以1994年民法典替代了1866年民法典,该民法典为一些国家的民法再法典化提供了新的灵感之源。

苏联解体与新独立国家的出现亦引发了一波法典化、再法典化浪潮。[②]

---

① 参见 Julio César Rivera, "The Scope and Structure of Civil Code, Relations with Commercial Law, Family Law, Consumer Law and Private International Law, A Comparative Approach", in *The Scope and Structure of Civil Codes* 36 – 37 (Julio César Rivera ed., Springer 2013)。

② 参见 Lado Chanturia, "Codification of Private Law in Post-Soviet States of the CIS and Georgia", in *Codification in International Perspective: Selected Papers from the 2nd IACL Thematic Confernece* 93 – 104 (Wen-Yeu-Wang ed., Springer, 2014)。

俄罗斯、亚美尼亚、阿塞拜疆、哈萨克斯坦、吉尔吉斯斯坦、塔吉克斯坦、乌兹别克斯坦等国以独联体（CIS）国家示范民法典为基础，吸收苏联时期积累的知识与经验，制定了具有转型性特点的新民法典。格鲁吉亚、土库曼斯坦、爱沙尼亚等国以欧陆发达国家的民法典为模本，制定了全新的而不是过渡性或转型性的民法典。

20世纪的再法典化和法典修改显著不同于经典时期的法典化。再法典化具有更多的折中主义特色，以比较法调查处理共同问题的方案，是其基本立法方法。例如，对于自1992年生效的荷兰民法典和自1994年生效的魁北克民法典，起草者不仅借鉴了许多欧陆国家的立法模式，而且吸收了普通法和国际公约的一些做法。另外，社会的多样性是再法典化过程被考虑的一个决定性因素。相比于启蒙法典或高度抽象的德国民法典的起草者，现代立法者更为务实。[①]

在决定是否有必要完全或部分革新民法典，以应对社会经济变化并避免民法典陈旧过时时，恰当的方法取决于特定环境和每一个社会及其法律体系的必要性。对于能够凭借高效的司法体制以法官造法和利用一般条款的方式防止法律冲突和填补法律漏洞的法律体系，法典的部分改革很可能就能取得成效。例如，西班牙、德国、法国皆有古老的民法典，但概括的概念和灵活的法官法已经使法典适应了新的社会发展需要。然而，当缺乏像法国、德国那样的司法运作条件和方式时，推陈出新，以新法典取代旧法律体系，不失为恰当的选择，如欧洲、拉丁美洲和北美洲出现的第二代和第三代民法典。[②]

二 我国民法的法典化之路：民事部门法的法典化、再法典化与解法典化

我国具有历史绵长的成文法传统，唐律展现了精湛的古代法典编纂技术，一度成为其他国家法律继受的范式。清朝末年，在变法图强的社会大变局下，我国传统法律体系土崩瓦解，大陆法系的近现代法典化理念和方法传入我国。历经了1910年《大清民律草案》、1925年北洋政府民法修正案的传承与磨砺，至1931年，南京国民政府终于修成正果，其以《德国民

[①] 参见 Maria Luisa Murillo, "The Evolution of Codification in the Civil Law Legal Systems: Towards Decodification and Recodification", 11 *J. Transnat'l L. & Pol'y* 163, 177 (2001)。

[②] 参见 Maria Luisa Murillo, "The Evolution of Codification in the Civil Law Legal Systems: Towards Decodification and Recodification", 11 *J. Transnat'l L. & Pol'y* 163, 180 (2001)。

法典》为模本，编纂了一部具有欧陆精神气质的民法典——中华民国民法。1949年2月22日，中共中央发布《关于废除国民党六法全书与确定解放区司法原则的指示》，施行近20年的中华民国民法随后被完全废弃。

（一）我国民法40年发展之路梳理

中华人民共和国成立后，我国曾于1954－1956年及1962－1964年两次试图制定一部民法典，但皆以失败告终。① "文革"结束后，法制建设再次被寄予厚望。1978年12月13日，邓小平在中共中央工作会议闭幕会上的讲话（《解放思想，实事求是，团结一致向前看》）中提出：应该集中力量制定刑法、民法、诉讼法和其他各种必要的法律。法律条文开始可以粗一点，逐步完善。修改补充法律，成熟一条就修改补充一条，不要等待"成套设备"。有比没有好，快搞比慢搞好。在国家建设全面转向经济领域的发展态势下，这些政策意见半年后即在一些法律领域初见成效。对于复杂、紧迫的民事立法工作，立法者采纳了民事单行法与民法典"同时并进"的立法方针。一方面加紧制定民事单行法，以应对社会经济发展的紧迫需求。《中外合资经营企业法》（1979年）、《婚姻法》（1980年）、《经济合同法》（1981年）等被迅速制定出来。另一方面着手制定民法典。1979年11月成立民法起草小组，1980年至1982年5月，民法草案从一稿起草到四稿。随后，"同时并进"的立法方针被调整为"先制定单行法"，民法起草小组遂于1982年6月3日解散，民法典之梦再次破灭。② 一些民事单行法之后次第被制定出来，如《商标法》（1982年）、《专利法》（1984年）、《涉外经济合同法》（1985年）、《继承法》（1985年）等。

然而，散乱的立法很快暴露出一些共性问题，如对于民事主体、民事法律行为、民事代理、时效等具有普遍适用性的规则，缺乏明确规定，大量民商事纠纷缺乏裁决依据。为此，立法机关以"对比较成熟或者比较有把握的问题作出规定，一些还不成熟、把握不大的问题，可以暂不规定"③为原则，在1982年民法草案（四稿）的基础上，制定了一部调整民商事关

---

① 对于这两次民法制定，比较法学家茨威格特与克茨将其失败原因归结为，中国曾经在很长时间里认为太多的法律反而会压抑社会进程中的自发精神。参见〔德〕K. 茨威格特、H. 克茨：《比较法总论》，潘汉典等译，法律出版社，2003，第451页。
② 参见梁慧星《民权法治之路的里程碑——新中国第三次民法起草亲历记》，《人民政协报》2014年11月6日，第005版。
③ 参见王汉斌《关于〈中华人民共和国民法通则（草案）〉的说明》（1986年4月2日在第六届全国人民代表大会第四次会议上）。

系的基本法——《民法通则》（1986年）。与此同时及其后，《外资企业法》（1986年）、《企业破产法》（试行，1986年）、《技术合同法》（1987年）、《城乡个体工商户管理暂行条例》（1987年）、《中外合作经营企业法》（1988年）、《全民所有制企业法》（1988年）、《私营企业暂行条例》（1988年）、《城镇国有土地使用权出让和转让暂行条例》（1990年）、《著作权法》（1990年）、《城镇集体所有制企业条例》（1991年）、《收养法》（1991年）等民事单行法如雨后春笋般被颁布出来。

经过12年高强度的密集立法，至1991年底，我国在合同法、婚姻法、继承法、不动产权利法、知识产权法、企业法等民商事领域，初步形成了以《民法通则》为基础、以各类民事单行法为主干的民商事法律规范体系。

然而，作为适应社会经济快速转型需求的一种法律速成品，上述各种法律具有显著的问题导向性、规范原则性、适用范围有限性等特点，这使得它们呈现出鲜明的阶段性、时代性特色，并深深打上了"经济立法"的烙印。1984年12月以前的民事单行法主要回应了"计划经济为主、市场调节为辅"的经济体制变革需求，之后颁布的民事单行法则是适应有计划商品经济发展需求的结果。由于经济体制改革以及与此伴随的社会经济转型处于持续不断的探索、发展中，没有确定一个比较明确的发展方向或目标，所以这些回应性、问题性民事立法，无论在内容上还是在存在期限上皆具有相当大的不确定性与时代局限性。[①] 一旦它们赖以存在的经济体制发生新一轮变革，这些民事单行法的规范价值、适用条件皆会遭受强烈冲击。各种法律因此充满了大量的原则性、模糊性或概括性规定。

1992年10月12日，以邓小平南方谈话为指导，中共第十四次全国代表大会把建立和完善社会主义市场经济体制确定为经济体制改革的目标，中国改革开放和现代化建设由此迈入新阶段。之后，立法机关立足于现实需求，以立改废等立法形式，几乎在同一时间由不同部门分头展开立法工作。1993年9月2日，久拖不决的《经济合同法》修改工作最终完成。此项工作甫一结束，立法机关迅疾启动统一合同法制定工作，经过6年多的努力，《合同法》于1999年3月15日颁布，《经济合同法》《涉外经济合同法》《技术合同法》以及依附于这些法律的一些合同条例、司法解释随后被废止。在决定制定统一合同法之前（1992），全国人大常委会法制工作委员

[①] 例如，对于《经济合同法》，它包含两种不同性质的法律规范，即民法规范和行政法规范。参见王家福、谢怀栻等《合同法》，中国社会科学出版社，1986，第151页。

会即开始准备起草担保法①，并于 1995 年予以制定出来。自 1988 年开始起草但之后陷入停滞状态的《城市房地产管理法》，也于 1992 年突然加速，并于 1994 年颁布。《物权法》的制定也于 1993 年启动。② 另外，与建立社会主义市场经济体制紧密相关的民事特别法，如《消费者权益保护法》（1993 年）、《劳动法》（1994 年）、《拍卖法》（1996 年）、《乡镇企业法》（1996 年）、《合伙企业法》（1997 年）等亦快速予以颁布。

为适应建立社会主义市场经济体制、加入世界贸易组织的发展需要，一些 20 世纪 80 年代及 20 世纪 90 年代初颁布的法律，如《中外合资经营企业法》《中外合作经营企业法》《外资企业法》《专利法》《商标法》《著作权法》《公司法》等皆经历了一次或两次修改。

在各种民商事单行法加紧制定期间，1998 年 1 月 13 日，全国人大常委会决定恢复民法典的起草工作，并成立民法起草工作小组。同年 3 月 25 - 27 日，民法起草工作小组召开第一次会议，议定"三步走"的工作规划③：第一步，制定统一合同法，实现交易规则的完善、统一；第二步，从 1998 年起，用 4 - 5 年的时间制定物权法，实现财产归属关系基本规则的完善、统一；第三步，在 2010 年前制定民法典，最终建立完善的法律体系。

2001 年 12 月 11 日，我国正式成为世贸组织成员。为应对由此带来的新情况，九届全国人大常委会委员长李鹏要求 2002 年完成民法典草案并经人大常委会审议一次。④ 2002 年 9 月，全国人大常委会法工委委托部分专家匆匆忙忙起草了九编制的民法草案。2002 年 12 月 23 日，九届全国人大常委会第三十一次会议审议了该民法草案。草案在学界引起轩然大波。2004 年 6 月，十届全国人大常委会变更立法计划，搁置民法草案的审议修改工作，恢复物权法草案的修改、审议。⑤ 第四次民法典编纂戛然而止。

---

① 参见顾昂然《关于〈中华人民共和国担保法（草案）〉的说明》（1995 年 2 月 21 日在第八届全国人民代表大会常务委员会第十二次会议上）。
② 参见王兆国《关于〈中华人民共和国物权法（草案）〉的说明》（2007 年 3 月 8 日在第十届全国人民代表大会第五次会议上）。
③ 参见梁慧星《中国物权法的制定》，载梁慧星《中国民事立法评说：民法典、物权法、侵权责任法》，法律出版社，2010，第 61 页。
④ 2000 年 3 月 9 日，李鹏委员长在九届全国人大三次会议上作常委会工作报告时提出："在民事主体制度、物权制度、债权制度、知识产权制度、婚姻家庭制度等单项法律基本齐备的基础上，力争在本届人大任期内编纂一部比较完整的民法典。"
⑤ 参见梁慧星《中国物权法的制定》，载梁慧星《中国民事立法评说：民法典、物权法、侵权责任法》，法律出版社，2010，第 65 - 67 页。

不过，即使正式启动第四次民法典编纂后，立法机关也未完全放弃"分头立法"的方针。对土地承包经营权作出系统规定的《农村土地承包法》，适应党的政策要求于1999年1月开始起草之后[①]，未受民法典制定的影响，一直持续进行着，并于2002年8月29日颁布。历史地看，第四次民法典编纂更多地是一次不顾原有立法计划的"率性之举"。

民法典编纂失败后，最高立法机关迅疾恢复对物权法草案的修改与审议。2007年3月16日，《物权法》正式颁布。两年多后，《侵权责任法》（2009年12月26日）作为一部独立的法律也被制定出来。

总体看来，我国在无法"毕其功于一役"地编纂一部民法典的情况下，为适应改革开放的现实需求，满足"有法可依"的法制建设要求，在"同时并进"的立法政策指导下，按照现实需求的强弱状况，采取"分割性方法"，把民商事生活切割为一些相对独立的领域先后制定出一个又一个的单行民事法律，最终形成以《民法通则》为基础、以《婚姻法》《继承法》《担保法》《合同法》《物权法》《侵权责任法》为骨干、以《城市房地产管理法》《农村土地承包法》等为特别补充的民事法律规范体系。

从法律技术上看，民事单行法普遍采纳了设置总则性规定的法典化立法技术，尤其值得指出的是《物权法》，它不但设置了总则编，而且在包括总则编在内的四编中，皆以"基本原则"或"一般规定"的方式作出了次级总则性规定。从规范功能上看，《民法通则》属于适用于所有民商事活动的基本私法（简要民法典）[②]，《婚姻法》《继承法》《担保法》《合同法》《物权法》《侵权责任法》分别属于适用于特定民事领域的基本法。虽然这些法律在内在价值与外在体系上存在紧密联系，但它们彼此之间的独立性也相当明显。因此，这些单行民事法律实质上就是适用于某一民商事法律领域的民事部门法典。

（二）民事部门法典的形成与发展特色

从比较法上看，20世纪以来，亚洲其他国家或地区在通过自愿继受欧陆民法而建构本国民法典的过程中，大致采取了两种不同的道路。一是照

[①] 参见柳随年《关于〈中华人民共和国农村土地承包法（草案）〉的说明》（2001年6月26日在第九届全国人民代表大会常务委员会第二十二次会议上）。

[②] 有著作认为："民法通则是我国首创的切合我国实际的一种民事立法体例，是调整我国民事关系和经济关系的基本法。"参见马原主编《中国民法教程》，人民法院出版社，1989，第9页。有学者认为，《民法通则》"实际上是我国未来的完整民法典的雏形"。参见《徐开墅民商法论文集》，法律出版社，1997，第27页。

搬其他国家的法典,如1926年的土耳其民法典与土耳其债法典,除基于政治的、社会的、伦理的、地理的、经济的理由作出少许改动外,几乎完全抄袭了1907年《瑞士民法典》和1911年《瑞士债法典》。通过这种自愿继受西方法律,土耳其实现了法律的世俗化、西方化,并由伊斯兰法系转入大陆法系。在土耳其学者看来,土耳其民法典与债法典事实上是通过使土耳其法律离开传统的宗教法律体系或领域(伊斯兰法)、追随欧洲法律领域而完成了一次"法律革命"。[1] 二是混合继受其他国家的法律,如1896年《日本民法典》主要是继受《法国民法典》和《德国民法典》的产物,是日本接受西方文明的结果,是日本社会现代化、西方化的一次重大跨越。日本学者对此评价说:"不管给予日本传统习惯和道德多大的关注,日本民法典的西方性皆不可被否认。"[2] 我国1929-1931年编纂的中华民国民法,同样采取了混合继受的法典化方法。[3]

我国民事法律的发展路径与方法迥异于以上两种民法法典化道路。我国是社会主义国家,改革开放旨在立足中国实际自力更生地实现社会主义现代化。虽然1992年明确提出了建设社会主义市场经济体制的发展目标,但并没有采取在较短时间内把有计划商品经济体制完全转变为市场经济体制的急剧变革,而是采取渐进发展之路,逐步深入推进市场经济体制建设。在这个持续发展的改革过程中,旧问题之解决,有时完全属于兴利除弊,有时则会积累、演化出新问题,而新问题堆叠到一定程度,则会引发出新一轮改革需求。因此,渐进式改革始终表现为一个"深化—再深化"的阶段性发展进程。需要改革的问题总是处于深化、变化或转化之中。以问题为导向、以经济为基础的法律,随改革之不断深化常常显得不能适应新情况、新问题、新挑战。因改革之需求应运而生的许多法律由此阶段性地处于应当通过修改、补充或完善而不断自我调适的进化状态。

这种经济决定论与实用主义主导的民事部门法典,虽然具有法典的体系结构并发挥着法典化的功能,但其规范体系在内外方面皆显得残缺不

---

[1] 参见 Ergun Özsunay, "The Scope and Structure of Civil Codes: The Turkish Experience", in *The Scope and Structure of Civil Codes* 387 – 407 (Julio César Rivera ed., Springer 2013).

[2] 参见 Hiroyasu Ishikawa, "Codification, Decodification, and Recodification of the Japanese Civil Code", in *The Scope and Structure of Civil Codes* 270 (Julio César Rivera ed., Springer 2013).

[3] 对于我国1931年的民法典,梅忠协先生如此评说:"现行民法,采德国立法例者,十之六七,瑞士立法例者,十之三四,而法日苏联之陈规,亦尝撷取一二,集现代各国民法之精英,而弃其糟粕,诚巨制也。"梅忠协:《民法要义》,中国政法大学出版社,1998,初版序。

全。① 改革开放进入一个新阶段或者一旦深入发展到一定阶段，法律的缺陷就会暴露出来。修改法律或创造新规则成为全面深化改革必不可少的一个环节。由此，我国民法走出了一条比较独特的法典化、解法典化与再法典化交相辉映、交互作用的法律发展、进化之路。此所谓法典化，是指各个民事部门法典的制定；解法典化主要表现为以民事特别法、最高人民法院的司法解释及以实施细则为样式的部门规章对民事部门法典的解构；再法典化，是指最高立法机关对民事部门法典的部分或全部修改。具体来看，各个民事部门法领域显现了不同的法律进化特色。

改革开放后民事立法的部门法化、法典化肇端于婚姻法领域。立法者以一部新《婚姻法》（1980年）取代了1950年《婚姻法》。拉长历史视线看，1980年《婚姻法》其实是婚姻法领域内一次典型的再法典化。新《婚姻法》施行后，为适应新情况、新问题，最高人民法院于1989－1996年发布了五个重要司法解释。随着市场经济体制的深入发展，传统婚姻家庭观念发生急剧变化，婚姻家庭领域出现诸多新问题。为此，最高立法机关于2001年对《婚姻法》作出重大修改。此后，市场经济发展对婚姻家庭领域造成的深刻影响集中爆发出来，为应对一系列新问题，最高人民法院又接连发布了五个司法解释。这些司法解释对社会生活造成的影响及由此引发的争议大大超过了《婚姻法》。显而易见，30年来，我国婚姻法走出了一条再法典化（1980年《婚姻法》）、解法典化（司法解释）、再法典化（《婚姻法》2001年修改）、再解法典化（司法解释）的螺旋式发展之路。

在受改革开放影响最大的财产法领域，1981年《经济合同法》开启了立法部门化、法典化的端绪。《经济合同法》施行一年多后，解法典化现象即接连发生。国务院及其部委依据《经济合同法》，为一些典型合同（如财产保险、加工承揽、借款等），制订了七个合同条例和五个合同实施细则。最高人民法院也依据《经济合同法》发布了三个司法解释。这些合同单行法规与司法解释几乎掏空了《经济合同法》的规定。另外，《涉外经济合同法》施行后，最高人民法院也发布了《关于适用〈涉外经济合同法〉若干问题的解答》（1987年）；《技术合同法》施行后，国家科委发布了《技术合同法实施条例》（1989年），该条例的条文数量是《技术合同法》的两倍之多。

进入20世纪90年代后，《海商法》《保险法》《消费者权益保护法》

---

① 参见朱广新《超越经验主义立法：编纂民法典》，《中外法学》2014年第6期。

《铁路法》《著作权法》等法律规定了大量合同法规范。最高人民法院对如何审理联营合同、借贷合同、融资租赁合同、证券回购合同纠纷等以解答、意见、批复、规定等样式作出了一系列司法解释。至20世纪90年代后期，也就是《合同法》制定的重要阶段，我国合同法实际上已形成以三部合同法、单行合同条例或合同实施细则、其他法律、行政法规中的合同法规范及最高人民法院的司法解释组成的错综复杂的规范体系。此种合同法规范体系因经济体制、立法体制、民法理论、立法指导思想等方面的原因，存在诸多缺陷，无法满足发展市场经济的要求，实现合同法的统一化、现代化，成为制定《合同法》的重要指导思想。[①] 1999年《合同法》是一次典型的再法典化，我国合同法经过此次脱胎换骨的改革后，向法制现代化迈进了一大步。《合同法》施行后，为便于法律适用及应对加入世贸组织、改革开放走向全面深化等新阶段出现的新情况、新问题，最高人民法院颁布了大量司法解释，其条文数量达300多。这些司法解释的一部分规定是辅助《合同法》适用的，而另有大量规定则纯属创设新规则，它们对《合同法》在形式与实质上皆构成明显的解构。总之，40年来，合同法领域的法律规范创制，呈现出一幅法典化、解法典化、再法典化、再解法典化相互交织的多彩画卷，我国合同法由此波浪式地向前发展，并逐步向现代化靠拢。民法典合同编实质上是借由第二次再法典化而使合同法实现统一化、现代化的续曲，而不是尾声。

《继承法》是在1982年民法草案（四稿）财产继承权编的基础上制定的[②]，它是一部典型的继承法典，自1985年施行以来至今未曾作过任何修改。它之所以保持了这么强的稳定性，与最高人民法院于《继承法》颁布后、施行前快速发布的《关于贯彻执行〈中华人民共和国继承法〉若干问题的意见》（1985年）不无关系。由于《继承法》尚未开始施行，所以该司法解释不可能是针对《继承法》适用过程中提出的问题作出的决疑性或补充性解释，而只能理解为最高人民法院以实际纠纷为预设而建构的裁判规范。条文数量几乎接近《继承法》两倍的司法解释，大大稀释了《继承法》，并消解了它的作用力。

旨在发挥民商事活动基本法功能的《民法通则》，自1987年施行后同

---

① 参见梁慧星《从"三足鼎立"走向统一的合同法》，载梁慧星《民法学说判例与立法研究（二）》，国家行政学院出版社，1999，第117－122页。

② 参见王汉斌《关于〈中华人民共和国继承法（草案）〉的说明》（1985年4月3日）。

样未曾修改过。其稳定性不是源于自身的合理性或系统性，而是内容逐渐被众多司法解释及《担保法》《合同法》《物权法》《侵权责任法》《城市房地产管理法》《农村土地承包法》等民事部门法、民事特别法所替代或掏空，最后只剩下关于自然人、代理、不当得利、无因管理、诉讼时效等少数规定还在发挥作用。在各种民事部门法颁布之前，最高人民法院不仅依据《民法通则》发布了体量很大的综合性解释——《最高人民法院关于贯彻执行〈中华人民共和国民法通则〉若干问题的意见》（试行，1988年），而且就侵权、合同领域内出现的新问题，发布了形式多样的专门性解释。另外，国务院发布或批准的涉及侵权损害赔偿的一些行政法规、部门规章及批复，也解构了《民法通则》关于侵权损害赔偿的规定。

物权法领域的法制发展、进化状况较为复杂。物权秩序对经济体制具有相当大的依赖性，1982年《宪法》确立了公有制基础上以国家所有权、集体所有权为核心的所有权制度。1986年制定的《民法通则》《土地管理法》对国家所有权、集体所有权、个人所有权及不动产所有权、使用权作了简要规定。1988年宪法修正案承认"土地的使用权可以依照法律的规定转让"后，《土地管理法》于1988年12月作出修改，补充规定：国有土地和集体所有的土地的使用权可以依法转让。1989年7月5日，国家土地管理局发布《关于确定土地权属问题的若干意见》，对如何确认国家土地所有权、集体土地所有权、国有土地使用权、农村集体土地建设用地使用权，根据《土地管理法》进行了详细规定，它实际上确立了土地所有权、土地使用权的基本类型。1990年5月19日，国务院颁布《城镇国有土地使用权出让和转让暂行条例》，对土地使用权出让、转让、出租、抵押等作出了比较详细的规定。1994年7月5日颁布的《城市房地产管理法》对土地使用权出让与划拨、房地产转让与抵押等不动产物权作出了详细规定。1995年6月3日颁布的《担保法》关于抵押权、质权、留置权的规定，基本确立了未来《物权法》中担保物权的内容。五年之后，最高人民法院发布了《关于适用〈中华人民共和国担保法〉若干问题的解释》（法释〔2000〕44号）。2002年8月29日颁布的《农村土地承包法》对土地承包经营权作了系统规定。2007年《物权法》吸收先前立法及司法解释的内容，并作适当补充、修改，对物权法作出了比较系统的一般规定。如此一来，经过20多年的经济社会变革和法制发展，我国物权法律制度基本上已形成规模。《物权法》施行后，最高人民法院以此为据发布了两项司法解释，国务院制定了《不动产登记暂行条例》（2014年），原国土资源部随后发布了《不动产登记暂行条例实施细则》。这些解释、行政法规与规章，分解了《物权法》的一些规定。

《民法通则》施行后，侵权领域内的法制亦呈现出鲜明的散乱、零碎发展状况，2009 年《侵权责任法》事实上肩负着统一化、合理化法律规则的法典化功能。但是，蹊跷的是，绝大多数侵权损害司法解释并没有随《侵权责任法》的施行而寿终正寝，《侵权责任法》好似在本已斑驳陆离的画板上又重重地涂上了一笔。近年来，最高人民法院依据《侵权责任法》又对个别特殊侵权责任发布了司法解释。

除上述情况外，最高人民法院还综合依据《民法通则》《合同法》《物权法》《侵权责任法》《民事诉讼法》等发布了许多司法解释。

总而言之，适应经济社会缓慢转型不同阶段的现实需求，我国民事法律以各种形式、各个机构的立法与最高人民法院造法（司法解释）的法规范生成机制，以部门民事法律的法典化、再法典化、解法典化交错发展的样态，在 40 年间逐步向统一化、现代化方向迈进。① 由于始终拘囿于"经济立法"观念，并特别强调问题导向思维，所以随着改革开放的深入发展，民事立法始终呈现出一种随时需要更新、完善的开放状况。这使得我国民事法律总是处于一种"生成—完善—再生成—再完善"的螺旋式上升发展状态。只要改革开放继续"深入发展"，作为改革开放重要环节之一的民事立法与司法，就不会停下脚步。目前正在加紧推进的民法典编纂，实质上是提升民事法律体系的统一性、合理性、现代性的一种新一轮法典化尝试。

三　编纂民法典：民事部门法典的统一再法典化、现代化

以经济立法为中心、以问题为导向的我国民事法律体系，随着改革开放的不断深化（阶段性发展），显露出一个又一个缺陷。这种立法状况为《中共中央关于全面推进依法治国若干重大问题的决定》（2014 年 10 月 23 日）提出"编纂民法典"孕育了种子。历史地看，此次民法典编纂既是满足完善民事法律体系之现实需求的必要举措，又是对"两步走"民事立法

---

① 有学者认为："西方民法典国家经历了一个先有法典化，继有解法典化的发展过程，中国民法却正处在一个法典化和解法典化交织并存的时代。因此，中国民法并不存在西方民法典国家'法典化—解法典化'鲜明的对立冲突。"陆青：《论中国民法中的"解法典化"现象》，《中外法学》2014 年第 6 期。

策略的一种必要回应。① 在民事法律体系基本形成之下，编纂民法典实质上可以看作，是以民事部门法典的统一化、整体再法典化为核心的民事法律规范体系的统合化、现代化运动。然而，如何在错综复杂的民事法律体系上"编纂一部体例科学、结构严谨、规范合理、内容协调一致的法典"，并确保2020年一定能够制定出来②，最高立法机关未给予任何具体说明。

（一）民法典编纂无法回避的三个难题

1. 新法律价值观与旧价值观、规则之间的碰撞

改革开放和市场经济的全面、深入发展，亦在思想意识、价值观念等精神领域产生了巨大、深远的影响。随着经济中心主义的自由竞争观念的深入发展，人们的思想意识与价值观念越来越开放、自由、多元、包容等，这一方面使得传统的自由、平等、公正等价值观念被赋予新的意义，另一方面使得人们传统的真善美、义利、公正、诚信观念遭受严重挑战。针对此种情况，意识形态建设成为社会主义现代化建设的一项重要内容，由此逐渐发展、凝练出以自由、平等、公正、诚信、和谐等为内容的社会主义核心价值观体系。为践行这些核心价值观，重要决策部门明确提出，通过立改废释并举的法律形成机制，把社会主义核心价值观融入法治建设。③《民法总则》（2017年）遂将"弘扬社会主义核心价值观"明确规定为立法指导思想。其后，中共中央又明确要求："加快推进民法典各分编的编纂工作，用社会主义核心价值观塑造民法典的精神灵魂，推动民事主体自觉践行社会主义核心价值观。"④ 据此，社会主义核心价值观已从一种社会主义意识形态建设目标，发展成为民法立法的指导思想。

其实，自由、平等、公正、诚信、友善等价值观，正是近现代民法的精神追求和价值取向，私人自治、人格平等、契约正义、诚实信用、善意保护等思想观念或原则，是构造民法典的主要支柱。而民法上的公序良俗原则则融汇了文明、和谐、法治等多种价值观念。因此，弘扬社会主义核

---

① 最高立法机关明确指出："新中国成立后，我国曾于1954年、1962年、1979年、2001年先后4次启动民法制定工作，前两次由于各种原因而未能取得实际成果；后两次经认真研究，决定按照'成熟一个通过一个'的工作思路，先分别制定民事单行法律，条件成熟时再编纂民法典。"张德江：《全国人民代表大会常务委员会工作报告》（2017年3月8日在第十二届全国人民代表大会第五次会议上）。

② 参见张德江《在第十二届全国人民代表大会第五次会议上的讲话》（2017年3月15日）。

③ 参见《关于进一步把社会主义核心价值观融入法治建设的指导意见》（中共中央办公厅、国务院办公厅印发，2016年12月25日）。

④ 参见《社会主义核心价值观融入法治建设立法修法规划》（中共中央2018年5月印发）。

心价值观并非强加于民法的一种意识形态指令，民法的产生、发展与演化其实融合了诸多核心价值观。对于政策驱动形成的我国民法而言，把社会主义核心价值观直接当作民事立法的指导思想，意义重大。它标志着，经过40年的发展，我国民事立法已经形成成熟、稳定、健全的思想观念体系；我国民事立法已迎来破除问题导向性思维魔咒、以体系性思维为着力点理性建构一部体系相对完善的民法典的曙光。因此，民事立法不应再抱残守缺，应秉执核心价值观，在内、外体系两方面强化、提升民法典的合理性、体系性。

然而，反观我国现行民事部门法及特别法，它们无不是在社会主义核心价值观提出之前，适应改革开放不同阶段的发展需求，于不同时代背景下制定的。它们的内在与外在体系在社会主义核心价值观及新时代发展需求上皆显得斑驳陆离、残缺不全。尤其是，各个民事部门法不是根据一个明确的民法典立法规划，并严格作为民法典的独立一编，像荷兰、俄罗斯、爱沙尼亚、加拿大魁北克省等国家或地区的新民法典那样按照统一规划分编逐次制定的，而是将民商事生活"切割"为不同区域并按民事部门法思维予以分散、个别立法的结果。因此，必须综合采用废除、修改、补充等手段，才可能将它们整合为一部统一的民法典，并借此使我国民法的合理性、现代性获得新的跃升。

《民法总则》改造、提升《民法通则》的立法革新力度，作为民法典编纂的序曲，可当作新旧观念、规则转变的一个良好范例。接下来的问题是，其他民事部门法被整合为民法典各分编时，能否像《民法总则》那样作出与时俱进的变革？由民法典各分编草案看，旧观念、旧规则明显占据上风，物权编草案与合同编草案尤其显著。"健全以公平为核心原则的产权保护制度"是近年来一再强调的重大立法政策。然而，对于所有权制度，物权编草案仍然沿袭《民法通则》以所有制为标准分区规定所有权的模式；对于建设用地使用权，没有按照"建立城乡统一的建设用地市场"的政策要求，对农村集体经营性建设用地权作出统一构造；在所有权取得方面，对于先占制度以及以和平、公开占有为前提的取得时效制度，仍然持极端否定立场；对于非常有利于维护和平、公正的财产秩序的占有制度，不能按照一般法理作出系统规定。

虽然《合同法》对平等、自愿、公平和诚实诚信原则作出了明确规定，并借鉴、吸收了一些国际性合同统一法的规定，但由于制定于计划经济体制向市场经济体制的过渡阶段,①因此其在法律理念与具体制度设计上存在明显的局限性。《合同法》施行之后,我国于2001年12月加入世贸组织,对外开放进入新阶段。②社会主义市场经济也从20世纪90年代的培育和发展市场体系进入健全(2002)乃至加快健全(2013)统一、开放、竞争、有序的现代市场体系的发展阶段。尤其值得注意的是,改革开放发展到今天,服务业成为国民经济第一大产业,并成为我国经济发展的主动力。③诸如此类的种种经济社会发展变化,对如何将《合同法》整合为民法典合同编提出了一系列问题。例如,应否将"合同的订立"一章中受旧合同法影响的一些规定,如合同自签字或盖章时合同成立、按指令性计划或国家订货任务订立合同等,根据《民法总则》有关意思自治原则及民事法律行为制度的新规定,作出修改或删除;应否将"合同的履行"一章关于执行政府定价或者政府指导价的规定予以删除;应否以私人自治原则、权利本位思想为指导,以确认违约救济权的思维,重塑《合同法》第七章的违约责任规定;应否适应经济全球化发展需求,参考当今世界各地债法发展的共同趋势,以(合同)不履行概念为核心,对违约救济措施予以统一规定;应否适应服务业快速发展的状况与趋势,对服务性合同作出一般性规定,或者对一些典型服务性合同,如雇用合同,作出明确规定。这些无不涉及新旧观念的碰撞,如果不能立足于新时代观念予以创新性立法,民法典编纂无异于假民法典之名的民事部门法典汇编。

2. 如何对待民事特别法

民事特别法是相对于民事部门法的法概念。民事部门法是将民法调整的民事生活区分为相对独立的几个领域,以法典化方法对它们予以分别立法而形成的法律(法典)。民事部门法实际上是调整某一民事生活领域的一般法或基本法。民事特别法,是调整某一民事生活领域内的特殊问题或事项的法律规范体系。相对于发挥一般法功能的民事部门法,民事特别法又可称作特别民法。对民法体系的此种功能区分,源于我国特殊的渐进式、分割式民事立法。有学者将民事特别法从功能上划分为补充型特别民法、

---

① 参见梁慧星《从"三足鼎立"走向统一的合同法》,载梁慧星《民法学说判例与立法研究(二)》,国家行政学院出版社,1999,第122页。
② 参见江泽民《在中国共产党第十六次全国代表大会上的报告》(2002年11月8日)。
③ 参见《统计局:服务业成国民经济第一大产业 占GDP比重为51.6%》(2018年4月14日),载中国网财经(http://finance.china.com.cn/news/20180414/4602791.shtml),最后访问时间:2018年8月2日。

政策型特别民法与行政型特别民法，并认为未来民法典既应成为纯粹的私法，又应纳入并整合政策型特别民法，真正成为市场经济与家庭生活的基本法。① 此言不无道理。但是，从我国市场经济的"社会主义"属性及民事立法现状看，民事特别法在范围及数量上十分有限。在20世纪80年代，国务院制定了一些对《经济合同法》起补充作用的像《购销合同条例》《借款合同条款》《财产承揽合同条例》之类的单行合同法。这些合同条例因《保险法》《合同法》的施行而被废除后，补充型特别民法则罕见其例。也许，可在婚姻家庭法范畴下把《收养法》看作对《婚姻法》的一种功能补充。至于行政型特别民法，与其将其看作一种特别民法，毋宁把它纳入其他法律、行政法规中的民事规范的范畴予以理解更为合适。毕竟，这些法律、行政法规不仅立足于市场管制理念，而且绝大多数内容属于行政法规范属性。政策型特别民法在我国同样少之又少，作为典型代表的《消费者权益保护法》，除了关于惩罚性赔偿的规定外，具有实质性消费者保护功能的民法规定极其稀缺，而非私法属性的规定则比较多。许多以危险责任或无过错责任为归责原则的侵权法规定，主要散见于各种非民事法律、行政法规之中。不过，《劳动合同法》则可看作一种政策型特别法。而《物权法》《合同法》《侵权责任法》《婚姻法》《继承法》，乃至《著作权法》《商标法》《专利法》，皆为调整某一民事领域的一般法。除了三个知识产权法外，民法典各分编完全是以这些民事部门法为编予以体系构造的。

总体看来，民事特别法主要包括《城镇国有土地使用权出让和转让暂行条例》《收养法》《担保法》《城市房地产管理法》《农村土地承包法》《劳动合同法》《不动产登记暂行条例》等。这些民事特别法主要调整物权法、婚姻家庭法、合同法领域的个别法律关系，很难在功能上作出区分。对于这些民事特别法，将《收养法》与《担保法》分别整合到婚姻家庭编、物权编、合同编，维护《劳动合同法》《不动产登记暂行条例》的独立地位，则不存在争议。值得研讨的是，如何处理物权编与《城镇国有土地使用权出让和转让暂行条例》《城市房地产管理法》《农村土地承包法》的关系。

由物权制度的发展、演化看，上述三部物权特别法皆制定于《物权法》之前，《物权法》制定之时即面对如何规定建设用地使用权、土地承包经营权的难题。《物权法》最终选择了不对建设用地使用权作系统规定、土地承

---

① 参见谢鸿飞《民法典与特别民法关系的建构》，《中国社会科学》2013年第2期。

包经营权主要参照《农村土地承包法》的立法模式。《物权法》与三部物权特别法的共存，不仅加剧了法律规定的散乱化、碎片化，而且制造了相当明显的立法重复。民法典物权编能否不重蹈《物权法》覆辙，处理好与三部物权特别法之间的关系，由民法典物权编草案看，仍然是一个值得认真思考的大问题。

3. 如何对待司法解释

司法解释是极富中国特色的"法官造法"，经 30 多年的发展，它已完全成为具有规范的创制程序[①]、稳定的条文式表现形式和明确的法律效力的民事规则形成机制，并在《立法法》之外形成一套规模庞大的民事规范体系。最高立法机关对于立法解释与司法解释之功能区别的模糊界定及在完善法律上的消极不作为，为司法解释的无节制发展提供了充分的法律和事实依据。

司法解释主要以实际的或假定的具体问题为规则创制前提，相比于法律的粗放规定，它一方面非常方便法院适用，另一方面能够统一全国各地法院的裁断尺度。然而，作为一种独立的民事规范体系，司法解释与制定法之间是一种辩证对立、互补和完善的关系，它们在规范适用上，应该遵循的不是形式性的规范效力等级的标准，而是何种规范适用于具体的案件能够产生最佳的法律与社会效果。[②] 司法解释因此在审判实践上更容易被法院援用，具有填补漏洞或创造特别规则功能的司法解释，更是享有超越制定法的优先地位。司法解释因此在形式与实质两方面皆可能构成对民事部门法典的解构。

另外，司法解释还存在三个不容忽视的问题。第一，司法解释在创制上程序简单、封闭，相比于制定法规范，其透明性[③]、易接近性存在相当大的局限性。第二，司法解释主要是向法院作出的裁判规则[④]，无法作为仲裁机构裁断纠纷的规范依据，由此造成案件是依诉讼程序还是仲裁程序解决而在裁判结果上可能存在差异。第三，依其性质或功能，司法解释创制的规则源于"决疑论"思维，"头痛医头，脚痛医脚"，民事规则因此越来越

---

① 参见《最高人民法院关于司法解释工作的规定》。
② 参见薛军《民法典编纂与法官"造法"：罗马法的经验与启示》，《法学杂志》2015 年第 6 期。
③ 参见周江洪《论民法典透明度的实现及其障碍》，《法制与社会发展》2015 年第 6 期。
④ "人民法院应当……""人民法院应予支持""人民法院应不予支持"等是司法解释表达规则的常用语式。

趋于情景化、表面化、碎片化。

"科学立法、民主立法、依法立法"是全面推进依法治国的重要立法原则。被赋予法律效力的司法解释，在司法实践上常常胜于法律而获得优先适用。过分容忍其在《立法法》与新的立法原则之外无节制地生长，与依法治国原则极不相称。为维护法律的权威性、统一性、透明性、易接近性，清理司法解释，将其尽可能整合到民法典之中，已是不二选择。

（二）可能的解决思路与办法

当前民法典编纂遇到的难题，若放到民法法典化、解法典化、再法典化交相辉映、交错发生的时代背景下，不难厘清基本解决思路。一言以蔽之，当前的民法典编纂实质上是民事部门法典通过统一的、整体的再法典化而走向体系化、科学化、现代化的过程。全面深化改革所追求的以产权清晰、契约严守、规则公正为特征的现代市场经济体系，是其深层的经济社会需求动力，而全面推进依法治国对重点立法领域所提出的法治建设要求，则是其强大的政治动力。40年来民事法律体系因法典化、解法典化、再法典化的交错相生而引发的法律规范体系碎片化、散乱化后果也为其提供了追求体系化、现代化、科学化的内在动力。

20世纪以来世界各地接连发生的民法解法典化、再法典化现象，映现了民法典在时代变迁中的功能变换。对于我国而言，编纂民法典是使散乱、残缺、陈旧的民事规范走向统一化、现代化的必由之路。除了解法典化使大而全的民法典趋于式微之外，另外两种情况也使民法典趋于"精瘦"。一是科学技术突飞猛进的发展给社会经济生活带来的急速变化，使过分具体、细密的民法规范在应对快速变化的社会经济上远不如概括、抽象的规定那样富有适应性。二是加速推进的经济社会全球化趋势，不仅造成投资、生产、消费的全球化，而且使人的跨境流动（学习、工作、居住、移民等）越来越便利，且规模越来越大。这种情况使民法典的功能越来越趋向于为民事纠纷提供裁决依据，而传统的教化功能则越来越弱化或作用范围越来越小。[1]

基于上述考虑，"小民法典—民事特别法—其他法律中的民法规范"的民事立法模式则比较可取。在此立法模式下，民法典的功能主要表现为，集中承载民商生活中最基本的法律思想或价值观念，为商法、民事特别法

---

[1] 参见薛军《中国民法典编纂：观念、愿景与思路》，《中国法学》2015年第4期。

及其他法律、行政法规中的民法规范提供元概念、元规则,[①] 并对民事特别法或其他法律、行政法规中的民事规范起补充、兜底作用。基于特殊法律思想、价值或政策构造的民事特别法,则可以通过成本较小的立改废立法活动,应对经济社会快速发展带来的新情况、新问题。我国 40 年来的民法发展状况,总体上印证了此种立法模式的有效性。除《婚姻法》之外,《民法通则》《合同法》《物权法》《侵权责任法》等民事部门法典,颁布以后从未被修改过,应对新情况、新问题的规范之道,主要体现为由最高人民法院发布的司法解释及经多次修改的知识产权类、商法类、不动产法类的法律、行政法规。此种立法模式或立法经验,应当继承和发扬。

从民法典构成上讲,弘扬社会主义核心价值观的立法思想及健全以产权清晰、契约严守、权利公平、规则公正为核心的现代市场经济体系法治建设目标,事实上已为制定一部具有完备内外体系的民法典提供了充分的政策依据。我国民法典已经具备由民商事活动的基本法向促进人的全面发展的根本法迈进的政治、经济、社会条件。[②] 更为重要的是,深化改革的重大政策也强调,要通过深化改革,"形成系统完备、科学规范、运行有效的制度体系,使各方面制度更加成熟更加定型"。[③] 因此,民法典编纂不应再像以前那样,把问题导向作为唯一思维取向,而要真正践行"既坚持问题导向,又尊重立法规律,讲法理、讲体系"的立法指导思想[④],并立足于构建自由、平等、公正、诚信、和谐、开放的民商事活动基本法,前瞻性地编纂民法典。为此,一方面应当将过去为适应经济体制转型的过渡性而带有计划经济体制遗迹的规则予以废除,如与所有制相关的所有权区分制度、与指令性计划相关的合同法规则等;另一方面需要根据新的法律思想或价值观修改、补充一些法律制度,使民事法律体系更加完善,如以权利本位思维修改违约救济规则,在物权法上补充取得时效、先占并完善占有制度等。对于所有权制度,根据权利公平、产权平等的新观念,放弃从所有制角度区分规定所有权的旧制,对于国家所有权的特殊问题,可通过国有资

---

① 参见谢鸿飞《民法典与特别民法关系的建构》,《中国社会科学》2013 年第 2 期;茅少伟《寻找新民法典:"三思"而后行——民法典的价值、格局与体系再思考》,《中外法学》2013 年第 6 期;邱本《论民事生活与民法典》,《法制与社会发展》2015 年第 4 期。
② 申卫星教授认为:"民法的固有品性乃在于保障人权、维护人性,推动人的成长和发展。"申卫星:《中国民法典的品性》,《法学研究》2006 年第 3 期。
③ 参见《中共中央关于全面深化改革若干重大问题的决定》(2013 年 11 月 12 日)。
④ 参见李建国《关于〈中华人民共和国民法总则(草案)〉的说明》(2017 年 3 月 8 日在第十二届全国人民代表大会第五次会议上)。

产法作特别规定；对于集体土地所有权的特殊问题，可通过土地管理法予以特别规定。这种一般法与特别法相结合的立法模式，既能充分彰显公平保护思想，又能顾及国家所有权与集体所有权的特殊性。合同编关于典型合同的增设问题，同样可以采取基本法与特别法相结合的处理模式。合同编主要规定合同类型的典型形态，每一类典型合同的变异形态或特别形态，由特别法加以规定为宜。例如，雇用合同作为服务性合同的典型类型，由合同编作出规定较为适宜，而像物业服务合同、旅游服务合同、快递服务合同、商业特许经营合同，交给融组织法、行为法、管理法于一体的《物业管理条例》《旅游法》《快递暂行条例》《商业特许经营条例》加以规定比较合适。

另外，在立法技术上，有两方面值得注意。一是以权利本位而不是义务本位或责任本位思想构造法律条文，以体现民法作为自治法（私法）的独特性，并将自由、平等、公正等价值观充分体现出来。为此，应以赋权性规范或诱导性规范（表现为使用像"可以""有权""享有……权利"之类的技术语言）而不宜再以恫吓性规定或命令性规定（表现为使用像"应当承担法律责任""应当赔偿""不得"之类的技术语言），构造法律条文。二是主要以裁判规范而不是行为规范为标准构造法律条文，以满足民法的功能主要在于裁决纠纷而不在于直接规制人的行为的特性。民事纠纷奉行不告不理原则，民法只有在法律纠纷的当事人诉请法院时才存在适用的余地，如果当事人能够自行或以其他方式解决纠纷，民法规范无法直接发挥作用。因此，人们即使不了解民法，也不妨碍其民商事生活。因此，民法规范应主要立足于裁判依据的标准进行构造，在民法的教化功能日趋弱化的现代社会，更应当如此。这样做也有助于抑制司法解释的蔓延势头。

从权利本位的民法思想出发，裁判规范本质上就是对请求权基础规范的系统构造，即通过对请求权基础规范、辅助性规定、反对性规定的科学化、体系化区分与整合，为法官分配、裁断纠纷各方利益诉求提供一套构成要件明确、法律效果确定的法律依据。为此，除了必不可少的一般性条款或者关于不确定概念的规定外，应尽力减少不具备规范要素的宣示性规定。[①] 而应从构成要件与法律效果两方面，或者构造可作为请求权基础的完全法条，或者构造具有明确规范意义的引用性法条、说明性法条、拟制性法条、限制性法条等，并通过但书性规定、除外性规定等立法技术清楚表

[①] 参见李永军《我国未来民法典应坚持规范属性》，《政法论丛》2016年第2期。

达法条之间的体系关系。

四　结语

　　自 19 世纪法典化运动以来，大陆法系大多数国家或地区的民法适应社会、经济、政治、法律的发展变化经历了法典化、解法典化、再法典化的发展过程。我国 40 年来的民事立法显现了法典化、解法典化、再法典化交错发生、交互作用的螺旋式发展、进化轨迹。由比较法看，我国民法的法典化、解法典化在方法、路径等方面具有鲜明的中国特色。其法典化采纳了先编纂各个民事部门法典、再统合为一部综合民法典的"两步走"方法。我国民法的解法典化，突出表现为司法解释对民事部门法典的解构。21 世纪以来，司法解释已成为我国民法进化最为活跃的因素。当下正加紧推进的民法典编纂实质上是一次民事部门法典的统一再法典化、现代化。当前的法治政策已为我国民法从市场经济和家庭生活的基本法跃升为促进人的全面发展的根本法提供了充分的政治条件。由于民法典的功能越来越减缩为纠纷裁决依据，我国民法典应重点面向司法与仲裁实践，按照裁判规范的标准构造法条。

Codification of the Civil Law: The Unified Re-codification of Civil Branch Codes

Zhu Guangxin

【Abstract】 The pattern of "codification, de-codification, and re-codification" highly summarizes the evolution of the civil law in many continental law countries since the 19th century. The civil legislation in China in the past 40 years has been a unique process of spiral development and evolution with alternate occurrence of and interaction between codification, de-codification and re-codification. To adapt to the needs of the phased and gradual development of reform and opening-up, the Chinese legislators have adhered to the principle of economic pragmatism and adopted the legislative method of gradually realizing the gradual codification of the civil law through the codification various branches of the civil law. To cope with the new situations and new problems emerged at the new stage of reform and opening-up, judicial interpretation has become the most active rule-making mechanism in the development of the civil law. The current codification of the civil law is in essence a process of unified re-codification and modernization of various codified branches of civil law. How to implement the new legislative policy and systematically embody new values is a difficult question that must be answered by China in the codification of the civil law.

【Key words】codification; de-codification; re-codification; codes of branch civil law; judicial interpretation

Contract Law in Finland: Plenty of Room for General Principles?

Petra Sund-Norrgård[*]

[**Abstract**] Finland can, perhaps with some hesitation, be defined as a civil law country, and historically the German influences have been noteworthy. For Finland, as a Nordic country, it is nonetheless relevant to note that it is possible to consider Nordic law to be a separate legal family that can be placed somewhere between common law and civil law, albeit "clearly leaning towards civil law".[1] Although there has been a rather significant growth of legislation in, for example, Finnish contract law since the late 1980s,[2] it is a fact that there are no large, systematic private law codifications in Nordic law. Moreover, even though acts (statutes) certainly exist, many questions are left to the courts. There is also a strong focus on the balancing of interests, and general principles of contract law—developed in case law and legal writing—are recognised as sources of law in Finland. This article focuses on some of these general principles that exist in Finnish contract law.

1. Introduction: Finland as Part of the EU and the Nordics

Finland has been a member of the European Union since 1995, and the supremacy of EU law is recognized. In principle this means that EU law even

---

[*] Professor in Commercial Law Hanken School of Economics Dept of Accounting and Commercial Law.
[1] Munukka, Jori, "The Contractual Duty of Loyalty: Good Faith in the Performance and Enforcement of Contracts", in Torgny Håstad, ed., *The Nordic Contracts Act* (Djøf Publishing 2015), p. 203.
[2] Hemmo, Mika, *Sopimusoikeuden oppikirja* (Talentum 2008), p. 48.

trumps the Constitution of Finland (731/1999). [1] In contract law, the influence of the EU is especially visible for specific contract types: for example the Consumer Protection Act (38/1978) has been amended on several occasions on the basis of EU directives.

There have been many discussions among European scholars over the years on the subject of harmonizing European contract law, or even European civil law. The possibilities presented have ranged from non-binding recommendations to a complete European civil code. As we all know, the Western world has long had two dominant legal traditions. These two traditions, both present within EU, hold much in common. There are, however, also clear differences between them, which make the task of harmonizing European law a complicated one: For instance, Germany is a civil law country, the legal system of which is largely based on written codes and statutes. The legal system of most of the United Kingdom (England, Wales and Northern Ireland), on the other hand, is common law, where great weight is placed on court decisions. Common law is thus in effect legal precedent made by judges. At the moment it looks like UK will leave EU ("Brexit") in Spring 2019, thus bringing England, Wales, Scotland and Northern Ireland out of EU. After Brexit, the Republic of Ireland, also a common law country, will nevertheless continue to be a member of EU. It remains to be seen what—if any—implications Brexit has on the harmonization of European civil law.

There are also instruments that may be characterized as "soft law" in European contract law. The Principles of European Contract Law (PECL) [2] and Draft Common Frame of Reference (DCFR) [3], are to be mentioned in this regard. DCFR—which actually include European private law principles, definitions, and model rules—can perhaps be described as a revised, but much more comprehensive, version of the PECL.

---

[1] Hirvonen, Ari, *Mitkä metodit? Opas oikeustieteen metodologiaan* (Yleisen Oikeustieteen julkaisuja 17, 2011), p. 43.

[2] See, for example, https://www.trans-lex.org/400200/_/pecl/#head_2. Last visited on 30 November 2018.

[3] See, for example, https://www.law.kuleuven.be/personal/mstorme/2009_02_DCFR_Outline Edition.pdf. Last visited on 30 November 2018.

In Spring 2015 I examined, whether the DCFR is used as a source of law by the Supreme Courts of Finland and Sweden respectively. I found that the Finnish Supreme Court, in its decision KKO 2015: 26, for the first time made a reference to DCFR in its judgment (in this case to Article IV. B. -4: 104). In comparison, the first time that the Swedish Supreme Court cited DCFR in its work was in decision NJA 2009 s. 672. This judgment was given 5.5 years earlier than the Finnish one, and since then the Swedish Supreme Court has made references to DCFR on several occasions. Perhaps one dares to conclude from my study that DCFR is not—at least not yet—an established source of law in Finnish contract law.① The fact that the Finnish Supreme Court rather recently, in its decision KKO 2018: 37, made a reference to DCFR for the second time ever (now to Articles IV. E. -2: 302 and III. -1: 109), does not change this conclusion.

The DCFR, which is an academic text, has nevertheless by some been viewed as a product with potential to even evolve into a European civil code. However, no European civil code proposals exist today. Also the draft regulation on a common European sales law (CESL) was, by the Juncker Commission, listed in its 2015 annual work programme among those legislative proposals that it intends to withdraw or modify after consulting the Parliament and the Council.② The European Commission's overall plans to codify European contract law seem to have collapsed, at least for now.③ Should any of these plans be realized in the future, the outcome would naturally be of relevance also for Finland.

For Finland, as a Nordic country, the on-going discussion on how to "categorize" Nordic law, is also an interesting one: Is Nordic law a separate legal family that can be placed somewhere between common law and civil law, albeit

---

① Sund-Norrgård, Petra, "Draft Common Frame of Reference i finsk och svensk rättspraxis", in Petteri Korhonen and Timo Saranpää, eds., *Isännän ääni—Juhlakirja Erkki Kustaa Rintala* (Talentum 2015). See also the opinion expressed in Lando, Ole, "Nordisk formueret i Europæisk perspektiv", *Tidskrift utgiven av Juridiska Föreningen i Finland* (6/2009), p. 758: The future will show us, whether PECL and DCFR to any significant extent will have an impact on Nordic law.

② See http://www.europarl.europa.eu/legislative-train/theme-connected-digital-single-market/file-common-european-sales-law. Last visited on 28 November 2018.

③ Nils Jansen and Reinhard Zimmerman, eds., *Commentaries on European Contract Laws* (Oxford University Press 2018), p. 13.

"clearly leaning towards civil law" as (Swedish) professor Munukka puts it?[1]

There are plenty of similarities especially between Finnish and Swedish law, which originate from the time Finland was an integral part of Sweden (from late 12th to the early 19th century), and although the inter-Nordic legal coordination has been in decline since the 1970s, there are on-going discussions in different fora on the topic of a possible future harmonization of Nordic civil law. One such discussion (in Swedish) took place on 14 November 2018 in Helsinki at a well-attended event hosted by Forum för civil-och handelrätt vid Helsingfors universitet (*Forum for civil-and commercial law at University of Helsinki*). Questions of the following kind were raised and debated by legal experts as well as politicians: Do we need a Nordic civil law? Is a Nordic civil law politically possible today? How are we to secure future Nordic cooperation in civil law?[2]

Irrespective of whether Nordic law should be categorized as a separate legal family, it is a fact that the Nordic attitude towards codification traditionally has been—and is still—quite different compared to European continental legal systems. Although the existing acts certainly cover basic, important aspects of private law, they are not intended to be complete. There are no comprehensive, systematic private law codifications in Finland nor in the other Nordic countries. And despite the fact that acts certainly exist, for instance in Finnish contract law,[3] many questions are left to the courts. There is also a strong focus on the balancing of interests, and general principles of contract law—developed in case law and legal writing—are recognized as sources of law.

Some of these principles are at the heart of this article,[4] where the focus lies on their significance for business-to-business contracts (hereinafter "B2B contracts").

---

[1] Munukka, Jori, "The Contractual Duty of Loyalty: Good Faith in the Performance and Enforcement of Contracts", in Torgny Håstad, ed., *The Nordic Contracts Act* (Djøf Publishing 2015), p. 203.

[2] For more information (in Swedish only), visit the Forum's website at https://www.helsinki.fi/sv/natverk/forum-for-civil-och-handelsratt-vid-helsingfors-universitet/behover-vi-en-nordisk-civillag. Last visited on 26 November 2018.

[3] In Finnish contract law there has been a rather significant growth of legislation since the late 1980s. On this topic, see Hemmo, Mika, *Sopimusoikeuden oppikirja* (Talentum 2008), p. 48.

[4] Much of the content of this article can be found in English in Sund-Norrgård, Petra, *Contract Law in Finland* (Wolters Kluwer 2017).

2. Freedom of Contract and the Binding Effect of Contract

The principle of freedom of contract can be described as the foundation of Finnish contract law. This is especially so for B2B contracts. The principle in question entails the right to choose whether or not to conclude a contract, with whom to conclude the contract and how to conclude it—for example in writing or orally. It also entails the essential right to decide the content of the contract in question. Especially for B2B contracts the assumption is that the parties have had, and have used, their freedom of contract in the drafting process. Consequently, once a contract has been concluded, it is considered binding upon the parties. In professor Saarnilehto's words, the price of freedom of contract is the binding effect of contract. ①

Since Finnish contract law over all includes but a few mandatory provisions, the contract between the parties is in reality often the primary source of law, which of course may be a problematic starting point for a contracting party unable to actually negotiate due to limited resources. The principle of freedom of contract is, however, not absolute: also for B2B contracts it is circumscribed by, for example, the general principle of reasonableness.

3. Reasonableness

The general principle of reasonableness is one of the principles that as such is found in the codified law, namely in Section 36 of the Contracts Act (228/1929 as amended 956/1982). This provision makes it possible for a court, or an arbitral tribunal, to adjust, or set aside, unfair contract terms. It is a section of the Contracts Act that can be described as a codification of a more common demand for fair, honest, moral, and even ethical behavior.

Section 36 of the Contracts Act states: "If a contract term is unfair or its application would lead to an unfair result, the term may be adjusted or set aside." It continues by stating that " [i] n determining what is unfair, regard shall be had to the entire contents of the contract, the positions of the parties, the

---

① Saarnilehto, Ari, *Sopimusoikeuden perusteet*, 7. uudistettu painos (Talentum 2009), p. 38.

circumstances prevailing at and after the conclusion of the contract, and to other factors". Consequently, it is not possible to solely assess the reasonableness of a particular contract clause, [1] and it is clear that also "the positions of the parties" must be observed.

Traditionally certain types of clauses have nevertheless been seen as such that typically will be adjusted in court. One example is the exemption clause, which changes the normal risk allocation between the contracting parties. As a starting point, such a clause is nonetheless legally binding: According to Supreme Court decision KKO 2012: 72 this is true also when the exemption clause/limitation of liability clause is comprehensive, provided that it is sufficiently clear and unambiguous. [2]

Penalty clauses may also sometimes be adjusted on the basis of Section 36 of the Contracts Act, but for instance in decision KKO 2001: 27 the Supreme Court decided otherwise. The Supreme Court also stated here that only rarely is a contract clause (of any kind) to be adjusted. In the case at hand the sellers of real estate had undertaken to pay liquidated damages to the buyers if the transfer of possession would be delayed for reasons not attributable to the buyers. The sellers' mother, who lived on the premises, refused to move out. For this reason the transfer of possession was delayed by forty-eight weeks, and the amount of liquidated damages became substantial (close to one-third of the purchase price). The Supreme Court based its decision *not* to adjust the clause on the fact that clauses of this kind are fairly commonly used in sales of real estate. The Court also stated that the sellers, at the time of the sale, had been able to take into consideration the effects of the mother's possible refusal to move. The sellers could also have limited the actual damage by trying to persuade the mother to move. The conclusion not to adjust the clause was not impacted by the amount of liquidated damages, even though it was probably more substantial than the actual loss that the buyer had suffered due to the delay.

Despite the many advantages with arbitration—such as the parties' right to

---

[1] Supreme Court decisions KKO 2001: 27 and KKO 2010: 9 (at www.finlex.fi, in Finnish); Wilhelmsson, Thomas, *Standardavtal och oskäliga avtalsvillkor* (Talentum 2008), p. 119.

[2] Government bill 247/1981, p. 15; Saarnilehto Ari, *Sopimusoikeuden perusteet*, 7. uudistettu painos (Talentum 2009), p. 176.

appoint the arbitrator (s), and the "private nature" of arbitration that ensures confidentiality—there are drawbacks as well. A weaker and poorer party may, for instance, prefer court proceedings due to the fact that arbitration in comparison generally is much more expensive. ① Supreme Court decisions KKO 1996: 27 and KKO 2003: 60 are of relevance here, since the reasonableness of arbitration clauses based on Section 36 of the Contracts Act was discussed.

In decision KKO 1996: 27 the arbitration clause was included in a franchise agreement between unequal parties, and the Supreme Court specifically stated that it was likely that the franchisee had not been able to actually influence the content of the contract. Despite this, the Supreme Court did not adjust the contract. The basis for this conclusion was that it is not unusual for a commercial contract to include an arbitration clause, and thus such a clause cannot be considered "surprising and burdensome". The franchisee in question had also been given the opportunity to acquaint himself with the contract for a period of one week before signing it. The franchisee had had access to legal assistance.

Even though the arbitration clause was not adjusted in this case, professor Hemmo points out that the reasoning of the Supreme Court shows a readiness to— at least to some extent—in the assessment also consider the party and the nature of his activities. ② It can also be noted here that in legal scholarship arbitration clauses have been seen as such "additional" clauses to a contract that are not the object of "real" pre-contractual negotiations. It should therefore be easier to adjust arbitration clauses than more essential clauses on the rights and obligations of the parties. ③

In case KKO 2003: 60 the Supreme Court decided differently in a case that was also about a possible adjustment of an arbitration clause included in a B2B contract. One of the parties had demanded that the arbitration clause should not be applied since he, after the conclusion of the contract, had become financially distressed.

---

① Halijoki, Juha, "Oikeudenkäyntikulut ja niiden jakautuminen", *Defensor Legis* (2/2000), p. 206; Sund-Norrgård, Petra, *Tolkningen av franchiseavtal* (Forum Iuris 2014), pp. 222 – 224.
② Hemmo, Mika, *Sopimusoikeus I* (Talentum 2003), p. 33, footnote 41.
③ Saarnilehto, Ari, "Kommentoituja oikeustapauksia korkeimmasta oikeudesta, Välityslausekkeen kohtuuttomuus", *Oikeustieto* (2/1997), pp. 2 – 3; Koulu, Risto, *Välityssopimus välimiesmenettelyn perustana* (Edita 2008), p. 48.

For this reason the clause had become unreasonable. It was clear that the party in question had no income and no means, and he had been granted a free trial and legal counsel for the proceedings in the Supreme Court, which would not be provided for him in arbitration proceedings. The Supreme Court found it established that he needed legal counsel in order to look after his rights, and that he was not able to pay for such service. Consequently, the arbitration clause was found unreasonable and was set aside.

Professor Wilhelmsson considers Supreme Court decision KKO 2003: 60 somewhat surprising given the fact that the earlier Supreme Court decision KKO 1996: 27 showed a rather negative attitude towards adjusting arbitration clauses in B2B contracts,[1] and professor Saarnilehto describes the more recent decision as one that in this regard significantly improves the situation of a business in financial distress.[2]

It can be observed that the threshold for adjusting an arbitration agreement concluded *after* the dispute has already arisen, will be higher compared to adjusting one that is formed for future disputes.[3]

All in all, it is a fact that courts fairly seldom adjust contracts. This is especially so for contracts concluded between economically equal parties.[4]

According to some scholars the importance of Section 36 of the Contracts Act might increase in Nordic contract law in the future.[5] It is nevertheless clear that

---

[1] Wilhelmsson, Thomas, "Välityslausekkeen sovittelu elinkeinonharjoittajien välisessä suhteessa", in Heikki Halila and Mika Hemmo and Lena Sisula-Tulokas, eds., *Juhlajulkaisu Esko Hoppu 1935-15/1-2005* (Suomalainen Lakimiesyhdistys 2005), p. 411.

[2] Saarnilehto, Ari, "Kommentoituja oikeustapauksia korkeimmasta oikeudesta, Välityslausekkeen sovittelu", *Oikeustieto* (4/2003), p. 4.

[3] Wilhelmsson Thomas, "Välityslausekkeen sovittelu elinkeinonharjoittajien välisessä suhteessa", in Heikki Halila and Mika Hemmo and Lena Sisula-Tulokas, eds., *Juhlajulkaisu Esko Hoppu 1935-15/1-2005* (Suomalainen Lakimiesyhdistys 2005), p. 412.

[4] Government bill 247/1981, pp. 3, 14 – 15; Hemmo, Mika, *Sopimusoikeus II* (Talentum 2003), pp. 64 – 66; Wilhelmsson Thomas, *Standardavtal och oskäliga avtalsvillkor* (Talentum 2008) pp. 122 – 124; Saarnilehto, Ari et al., *Varallisuusoikeus* (Sanoma Pro 2012), pp. 110 – 111; Sund-Norrgård, Petra, *Tolkningen av franchiseavtal* (Forum Iuris 2014), pp. 103 – 108.

[5] Lindskog, Stefan, "Jämkning i kommersiella avtalsförhållanden", in Mads Bryde Andersen et al., eds., *Aftaleloven 100 år, Baggrund, status, udfordringer, fremtid* (Djøf Forlag 2015), p. 327; Gomard, Bernhard et al., *Almindelig kontraksret*, 5. Udgave (Djøf Forlag 2015), p. 178.

adjustment of contract clauses is—and should be—an exception. The principle of reasonableness should thus be applied with care, that is, only in situations where such an interference with the freedom of contract is deemed necessary. On the other hand, the principle of reasonableness must not be applied too seldom: it is not a good thing if its function is merely "ideological", due to the fact that courts never apply it. ① In my research I have raised this concern as to franchise contracts, since they are often in the form of chain specific standard agreements drafted by the stronger party, i. e. the franchisor, alone. ②

4. Loyalty (Good Faith)

Today most scholars are of the opinion that the principle of loyalty exists in Finnish contract law, even though its content is somewhat vague, and its applicability is somewhat unclear. This stems from the fact that the principle lacks the concreteness of a rule; its actual content, and its relevance, is therefore dependent on the circumstances of the case at hand. The situation is roughly the same also in the other Nordic countries. ③

The said principle can be described as the Finnish/Nordic equivalent of the principle of good faith (or *Treu und Glauben* or *bonne fois*) in the civil law countries of continental Europe. These are all based on the Roman law idea that parties to a contract to some extent must take the other party's interests into consideration. ④

The principle of loyalty cannot as such be found in statute law in Finland, but Taxell introduced it in Finnish legal writing already in the 1970s. ⑤ The discussion on contract as cooperation, and the importance of the principle of loyalty in that context, took off in the 1990s. The principle of loyalty has since then been

---

① Wilhelmsson, Thomas, *Standardavtal och oskäliga avtalsvillkor* (Talentum 2008), p. 169.
② Sund-Norrgård, Petra, *Tolkningen av franchiseavtal* (Forum Iuris 2014), p. 107.
③ See Munukka, Jori, "The Contractual Duty of Loyalty: Good Faith in the Performance and Enforcement of Contracts", in Torgny Håstad, ed., *The Nordic Contracts Act* (Djøf Publishing 2015), p. 215. Professor Munukka finds the principle's position in Norwegian law to be more established and firm.
④ Munukka, Jori, "The Contractual Duty of Loyalty: Good Faith in the Performance and Enforcement of Contracts", in Torgny Håstad, ed., *The Nordic Contracts Act* (Djøf Publishing 2015), p. 203.
⑤ Taxell, Lars Erik, *Avtal och rättsskydd* (Åbo Akademi 1972), and Taxell, Lars Erik, "Om lojalitet i avtalsförhållanden", *Defensor Legis* (1 – 3/1977), pp. 148 – 155, are important in this context.

extensively discussed in Finnish legal writing; also the pros and cons of a codification of the principle have been discussed over the years.

The principle of loyalty is mentioned in certain legislative preparatory works: for instance Government bill 241/2006 describes Section 33 of the Contracts Act as an expression of a general principle of loyalty. Section 33 of the Contracts Act states: "A transaction that would otherwise be binding shall not be enforceable if it was entered into under circumstances that would make it incompatible with honour and good faith for anyone knowing of those circumstances to invoke the transaction and the person to whom the transaction was directed must be presumed to have known of the circumstances." According to the Government bill Section 33 protects good faith and promotes openness: Even though each party to a contract, as a starting point, is to obtain the relevant information himself, a party is under the obligation to inform the other party of such essential, relevant issues that he (the other party) has no knowledge of. The parties to a contract are thus to make sure that there is no information asymmetry between them.

The principle of loyalty is discussed in certain court decisions; also the Supreme Court occasionally makes a reference to it in its work. Although the impact of the principle of loyalty is most prominent during the contractual phase, parties may to some degree be required to act in accordance with it also during contract negotiations, as well as in the termination phase of a contract. The Supreme Court stated in its decision KKO 2008: 91 that parties who engage in contract negotiations are bound by a reciprocal duty to act loyally in such a way that the other party is not mistaken in terms of the contract's essential prerequisites or meaning. [1] Already in 1993, in decision KKO 1993: 130, the Supreme Court referred to the principle of loyalty in terms of a duty to inform the other party of essential issues in the pre-contractual phase. This was the first time ever that the Supreme Court made a reference to the said principle in its work.

It is to be stressed that the principle of loyalty has been viewed as a "counter-principle" to freedom of contract. [2] The principle of loyalty is, however, not

---

[1] See also Supreme Court decision KKO 2007: 72 (at www.finlex.fi, in Finnish).
[2] Mäenpää, Kalle, "Contract Negotiations and the Importance of Being Earnest", *Tidskrift utgiven av Juridiska Föreningen i Finland* (4/2010), p. 327 and references.

primarily focused on altering contract clauses as is Section 36 of the Contracts Act. Instead, the principle of loyalty is concerned with fostering the parties to a contract to behave towards each other in accordance with some sort of best practices.

The principle not only exists in consumer contracts,[①] employment relations,[②] or fiduciary relations—such as agency contracts—but in licensing agreements, franchising agreements, and other long-term cooperation contracts as well. The principle is, however, less relevant for sales of goods, and similar short-term discrete transactions, not relying on a functioning long-term relation between the parties.[③]

Based on the principle of loyalty the parties can, for example, be expected to contact and inform each other, discuss problems, renegotiate the contract, keep secret information secret, and not compete with each other during the contract term. Such duties may, or may not, follow from express contract clauses. In other words, the principle of loyalty can be said to have a complementary function in case of gaps in the contract, since it supplements the contract with obligations implied by the law. This means that if the written contract lacks a clause as to renegotiation, duty to inform the other party, secrecy or non-competition, this does not, in itself, justify the conclusion that such obligations are not a part of the contract.[④] Having said this, it is unclear to what extent implied obligations of this kind may be based on the principle of loyalty alone in Finnish contract law of today.

Since the principle of loyalty functions as a legal basis for the parties' legitimate expectations, the gaps of the contract can often be filled with what is perceived as "normal" for the type of contract within the said trade. Because of this the

---

[①] See, for example, Supreme Court decision KKO 2008: 91 (at www.finlex.fi, in Finnish).

[②] See, for example, Supreme Court decisions KKO 2016: 13 and KKO 2016: 15 (at www.finlex.fi, in Finnish).

[③] Sund-Norrgård, Petra, *Lojalitet i licensavtal* (Publications of IPR University Center and Juridiska föreningens publikationsserie 2011), p. 56 and references to Finnish and Swedish legal writing; Munukka, Jori, "The Contractual Duty of Loyalty: Good Faith in the Performance and Enforcement of Contracts", in Torgny Håstad, ed., *The Nordic Contracts Act* (Djøf Publishing 2015), pp. 209 - 213.

[④] Sund-Norrgård, Petra, *Lojalitet i licensavtal* (Publications of IPR University Center and Juridiska föreningens publikationsserie 2011), pp. 78 - 79 and references.

principle of loyalty may also support the parties' choice to conclude a flexible enough contract. ①

Especially in those cases where the parties have formed a long-term, close cooperation based on trust and interdependence, the principle of loyalty influences the contract interpretation. This is logical, since a contract of this kind is formed in order to obtain a functioning cooperation between the parties. The focus on risk allocation is often less prominent. This means that not all contracts are drafted with an intention to be as exhaustive as possible, and for instance professor Annola stresses the existence of "dynamic contracts" that are intended to be supplemented during the contract term. ②

It can thus be said that the principle of loyalty essentially is about cooperating fully with the other party, and thereby contributing to the fulfilment of the common goal of the contract. ③ The main function of the principle is nevertheless perhaps to act as a support/as a guiding principle in the interpretation of a contract.

5. Protection of the Weaker Party

The final principle to be—very shortly—addressed is the principle of protection of the weaker party. This is a principle that has been found to exist for instance in consumer contracts, lease agreements and employment contracts. It is used to redress the balance in a situation where it has not been possible for the—financially/socially/legally—weaker party to form a just contract. In other words, a functioning contract is the goal when this principle is applied. It has many similarities with the already discussed principle of reasonableness found in Section 36 of the Contracts Act: It is certainly possible to protect a weaker party also by

---

① Sund-Norrgård, Petra and Kolehmainen, Antti and Suhonen, Onerva-Aulikki, "The Principle of Loyalty and Flexibility in Contracts", *Lapland Law Review* (2/2015), pp. 190–208.

② Annola, Vesa, *Sopimuksen dynaamisuus* (Turun yliopisto 2003), pp. 31, 49–50.

③ For different views in connection to this see, for example, Pöyhönen, Juha, *Sopimusoikeuden järjestelmä ja sopimusten sovittelu* (Suomalainen Lakimiesyhdistys 1988), p. 19; Muukkonen, P. J., "Sopimusoikeuden yleinen lojaliteettiperiaate", *Lakimies* (7/1993), p. 1030–1048, Häyhä, Juha, "Lojaliteettiperiaate ja sopimusoppi", *Defensor Legis* (3/1996), pp. 313–327; Sund-Norrgård, Petra, *Lojalitet i licensavtal* (Publications of IPR University Center and Juridiska föreningens publikationsserie 2011), p. 77.

applying the latter. ①

What is interesting for this article focusing on B2B contracts, is that the Supreme Court, in its decision KKO 2010: 69, stated that one of the parties to the said B2B contract was to be considered weaker. When the content of the contract was to be established, the principle of protection of the weaker party was in fact used as a guiding principle in the interpretation. This differs from its traditional function as a guiding principle in the application of legislation. ②

When the principle of protection of the weaker party is applied it thus implies a deviation from the principle of freedom of contract. It is naturally unclear to what extent one should protect a weaker party at the expense of freedom of contract. ③

6. Final Remarks

I wish to end this discussion by stressing the need for ethical, moral, fair, and even virtuous behaviour also in B2B settings. For this reason, it is essential that general principles that cultivate such values are given enough room in Finnish contract law. Today there is plenty of room in the law for such principles. This does not, however, change the fact that these principles are to be applied with care, since they interfere with the foundation of Finnish contract law, namely freedom of contract. Finding the right balance in any given situation is indeed a delicate, but not an impossible, task.

This flexibility in Finnish (Nordic) contract law, provided for instance by general principles, is in my opinion, a richness of the legal system that renders it possible to actually consider the facts and the context of each case to a sufficient degree. This type of flexibility also enables the law to follow the progress and

---

① Pöyhönen, Juha, *Sopimusoikeuden järjestelmä ja sopimusten sovittelu* (Suomalainen Lakimiesyhdistys 1988), pp. 273 - 274; Ämmälä, Tuula, "Heikomman suoja", in Ari Saarnilehto, ed., *Varallisuusoikeuden kantavat periaatteet* (WSOY 2000), pp. 98 - 99; Wuolijoki, Sakari, *Pankin neuvontavastuu. Varallisuusoikeudellinen tutkimus pankin neuvonta-ja tiedonantovelvollisuuksista* (Helsingin yliopisto 2009), p. 101; Saarnilehto, Ari et al., *Varallisuusoikeus* (Sanoma Pro 2012), p. 101; Sund-Norrgård, Petra, *Tolkningen av franchiseavtal* (Forum Iuris 2014), pp. 100 - 101.

② Annola, Vesa, "Yhteistoimintasopimuksen tulkinnan välineet", *Oikeustieto* (6/2010), pp. 6 - 7.

③ Wuolijoki, Sakari, *Pankin neuvontavastuu. Varallisuusoikeudellinen tutkimus pankin neuvonta-ja tiedonantovelvollisuuksista* (Helsingin yliopisto 2009), p. 102; Saarnilehto, Ari et al., *Varallisuusoikeus* (Sanoma Pro 2012), p. 101.

trends of society at large without a constant need to go through the time-consuming stages of the legislative process.① I therefore do not believe in a Nordic, or European, civil code. Further harmonisation in certain areas of civil law—for instance among the Nordics—may regardless be a workable solution.

芬兰合同法：普遍原则是否仍有广泛空间？

佩特拉·松德·诺尔戈德

【摘要】芬兰可以被界定为一个大陆法系国家，虽然也许有人对此界定有所保留，并且在历史上它明显受到德国法的影响。尽管如此，应该指出的是，对于芬兰而言，作为一个北欧国家，可以将北欧法看作一个介于英美法系和大陆法系之间的独立的法律体系，尽管"它很明显更接近大陆法系"。虽然自从20世纪80年代以来，芬兰合同法等领域内的立法有了较大的增长，但事实上北欧法从来就没有经历过大规模、系统的私法法典化过程。另外，虽然北欧国家毫无疑问都制定了法律（成文法），但是它们还是把许多问题留给法院去决定。另外，芬兰还非常注重利益的平衡，并将在案例法和法律著作中发展起来的合同法一般性原则视为法律渊源。本文着重讨论存在于芬兰合同法中的一些一般性原则。

---

① For information on the legislative process (in English), see https://www.eduskunta.fi/EN/lakiensaataminen/lainvalmistelu_vaiheet/Pages/default.aspx. Last visited on 29 November 2018.

图书在版编目(CIP)数据

法制改革与法治发展：中国与芬兰的比较／陈甦，（芬）尤拉·柳库恩主编. -- 北京：社会科学文献出版社，2019.6
（中国法治论坛）
ISBN 978-7-5201-4904-4

Ⅰ.①法… Ⅱ.①陈… ②尤… Ⅲ.①法制–建设–对比研究–中国、芬兰 Ⅳ.①D920.0②D953.1

中国版本图书馆 CIP 数据核字（2019）第 095984 号

中国法治论坛
法制改革与法治发展：中国与芬兰的比较

主　　编 /	陈　甦　〔芬兰〕尤拉·柳库恩
出 版 人 /	谢寿光
责任编辑 /	芮素平
文稿编辑 /	李娟娟　尹雪燕
出　　版 /	社会科学文献出版社·社会政法分社（010）59367156 地址：北京市北三环中路甲29号院华龙大厦　邮编：100029 网址：www.ssap.com.cn
发　　行 /	市场营销中心（010）59367081　59367083
印　　装 /	三河市东方印刷有限公司
规　　格 /	开　本：787mm×1092mm　1/16 印　张：17.75　字　数：323千字
版　　次 /	2019年6月第1版　2019年6月第1次印刷
书　　号 /	ISBN 978-7-5201-4904-4
定　　价 /	89.00元

本书如有印装质量问题，请与读者服务中心（010-59367028）联系

▲ 版权所有 翻印必究